# Daidalos at Work

A Phenomenological Approach to the Study of Minoan Architecture

# Daidalos at Work

## A Phenomenological Approach to the Study of Minoan Architecture

Clairy Palyvou

*Published by*
INSTAP Academic Press
Philadelphia, Pennsylvania
2018

**Design and Production**
INSTAP Academic Press, Philadelphia, PA, USA

Library of Congress Cataloging-in-Publication Data

Names: Palyvou, Klairē, author.
Title: Daidalos at work : a phenomenological approach to the study of Minoan architecture / by Clairy Palyvou.
Description: Philadelphia, Pennsylvania : INSTAP Academic Press, 2018. | Includes bibliographical references and index.
Identifiers: LCCN 2017050310 (print) | LCCN 2018012595 (ebook) | ISBN 9781623034269 (e-book) | ISBN 9781931534949 (paperback : alk. paper)
Subjects: LCSH: Architecture, Minoan. | Architecture--Historiography.
Classification: LCC NA267 (ebook) | LCC NA267 .P375 2018 (print) | DDC 722/.61--dc23
LC record available at https://lccn.loc.gov/2017050310

*Front cover: photo by Marinos Papadantonakis of the loggia above the Throne Room in the Palace of Minos at Knossos in 2012.*

*Frontispiece: aerial photo of the Palace of Phaistos by Gordon Gahan, National Geographic Creative.*

You yourself are the entrance. The doors open
effortlessly to the eye and let you in.
Others have been here before you, and left shadows behind
that fit you: head, hand, body
and hesitating foot. Only the voice urges onward,
from echo to echo and is already in the center
with its fleeting arguments. The body
stands dolefully at the beginning: too many tracks
trace away from it through the sand,
and none is decipherable.
*Close your eyes and go!*

Excerpt from "In the Labyrinth"
Michael Krüger (1982)

# Table of Contents

# List of Figures

# List of Abbreviations

| | |
|---|---|
| cm | centimeter(s) |
| diam. | diameter |
| EM | Early Minoan |
| EN | Early Neolithic |
| esp. | especially |
| FN | Final Neolithic |
| ht. | height |
| ha | hectare(s) |
| INSTAP SCEC | Instiitute for Aegean Prehistory Study Center for East Crete |
| km | kilometer(s) |
| LM | Late Minoan |
| m | meter(s) |
| mm | millimeter(s) |
| MM | Middle Minoan |
| pers. comm. | personal communication |
| SPAB | Society for the Protection of Ancient Buildings |
| w. | width |

# Preface and Acknowledgments

*When the exit no longer concerns you, you have reached the goal. (Krüger 1982)*

Architects of all times could not have found a better archetypal figure than the mythical Daidalos working in Crete for the legendary Minos. All that is related to the works of Daidalos and Minos, and all that has been exposed through archaeological excavations of Bronze Age sites on Crete, draw up the picture of a fascinating, brave new world (Figs. 1, 2). This was a world of affluence and innovation, a unique moment in the early history of architecture, created literally out of the blue sea of the Aegean. In a bizarre way, that moment seems to echo another brave new era much closer to our times, so much so that one is tempted to see the shadows of Le Corbusier and Frank Lloyd Wright in the mythical body of Daidalos.

Daidalos makes his first appearance as "an architect at work"[1] in Homer (*Il.*18.590–594), drawing on the ground a circle, the most perfect of all geometrical shapes—for some, the archetypal form of the house. With this circle he cuts and bounds a piece of land, transforming it into a locus, a place wherein Ariadne can perform her dance.[2] By the movement of her body, Ariadne bestowed on architecture the third dimension of space: the vertical. Through the making of the archetypal circle—a manifestation of the act of separation—Daidalos instigated the τέχνη (*techne*; craft/art) of architecture, only to lift it to the utmost heights of ingenuity and sophistication by creating another archetypal

Fig. 1. Theseus fighting the Minotaur, as depicted on an Attic black-figure vase. After Michailidou 1981, fig. 5.

form, the labyrinth, for some the symbol of life itself and for others of the horrors of the way, the step into the forbidden, where the walls serve only to delineate the motion that carries the true meaning (Miller 1982). The labyrinth, as a paradigm of order, stands for the primordial idea of architecture and a metaphor of human existence (Pérez-Gómez 1985, 51).

Daidalos's tasks, the myth informs us, were multifold: time and again he was challenged to solve the most intricate and absurd problems set by authorities, social demands, religious beliefs, or personal drives. His ultimate task, in other words, was to shape the physical world so as to suit a way of life set by a specific society; in this, the ethical function of architecture is acknowledged. It took indeed two legendary figures for the miracle to happen in Crete in the second millennium B.C.: a king Minos, representing the commissioner, the client, or the patron, and an ingenious Daidalos, representing the architect, for Daidalos did not act on his own behalf, and he did not create magnificent edifices for their own accord. He was following orders and satisfying desires, some explicit, others implicit, and some even lustful. The history of architecture could indeed be written as the history of the relationships between patrons and architects.

Of the materials (υλικά; *ylika*) that nature provides, wood (ύλη; *yle*) was the first to attract Daidalos's interest. More than the materials, however, it was his way of working—cutting and joining—that defined his metier (Karvouni 1999, 106). He was a *te-ko-to-ne* (τέκτων [*tekton*], mason), a *to-ko-do-mo*, and a *na-u-do-mo* (shipbuilder), and, if there were such a word, he would have been known as an aircraft builder as well. The name Daidalos means "cunning worker" or "skillful one;" he is architect, civil engineer, surveyor, and mechanical engineer all in one, and, of course, he is above all the inventor who combines physical observation and mental inquiry with craftsmanship. He is also a fugitive and a traveler, and therefore a carrier of ideas and technical knowledge ready to be engrafted at his next destination, be it Athens, Egypt, Crete, Sicily, or Ugarit, under different personifications such as Hephaistos, Kothar, or Ilish (Morris 1992, 73–100).[3]

The myth, as a store of experiences and mental themes, will always interfere with our perception of the past: it lurks in the shadows of the ruins of the Palace of Minos at Knossos and in the nebulous images of its missing parts. It also lingers in the perpetual quest for the true Ithaca or the intangible Atlantis. For myths look ahead, into the future, and not into the past that generated them, constantly seeking responses and new interpretations (Pallasmaa 2005a, 132, 187). From myth to reality the distance is one that cannot be bridged, for they do not represent opposite sides of the same land; they belong to different worlds that mirror each other through the broken looking glass that separates the world of ideas from the factitious world of sticks and stones. They both partake,

Fig. 2. Map of the island of Crete showing major Minoan sites. Map C. Palyvou.

however, in our efforts to understand the realities of the past as much as in our endeavors to unravel the myths of the art of architecture.

This rather free reference to the myth of Daidalos was meant as an introduction to both the goals and the context of what follows. This is primarily a book on architecture, and as such it seeks to bring forward the deeper forces that guide the work of all the sons and all the daughters of Daidalos. Architecture is the protagonist, whereas the prehistoric time of this architecture is as important as any other historical time. This book is firmly based on the realities of a long-silenced world available to us today through the agency of archaeology. In that sense, it addresses archaeologists, architectural historians, and architects alike, in the hope that it will prove useful to those interested in understanding the Minoan world through its architecture as much as those interested in exploring architecture through the Minoan paradigm. This dual goal emanates from my deep belief in the timeless and universal values of architecture. As a teacher of (history of) architecture, the challenge has been to bring history into the studios where future architecture is formulated, to engage history in the discourse on current architectural ethos and practices, and to show that an analytical and critical approach to the past is a potent tool for advancing architectural awareness and educating future architects. I am equally confident that such an approach will return its benefits back to history, for it will provide new tools of thought and methods of interpretation of the relics of the past.

Having set the scope of this book, it is only fair to add what is not included in its goals: the reader will not find a descriptive account of Minoan buildings and sites nor a list of the major architectural achievements in chronological order. This is due not only to the enormous amount of relevant information that has been accumulated to date, but also to an altogether different interest in the subject, as described above. Time, however, is crucial: “We have a mental need to grasp that we are rooted in the continuity of time, and in the man-made world it is the task of architecture to facilitate this experience” (Pallasmaa 2005b, 32). Time-related issues, therefore, such as permanence and change or tradition and innovation, will concern us.

The structure of the book follows, more or less, the long-valued Vitruvian triad of *firmitas*, *utilitas*, and *venustas*, interpreted in the 17th century by Sir Henry Wotton as firmness, *commodité*, and delight and in the 20th century by the Modern Movement of architecture as structure, function, and form (Kostof 1985, 13).[4] It aims at nothing less than the totality of architecture, from its "intentions" to its "ethical function[s]," to borrow from the titles of two seminal books by Christian Norberg-Schulz (1997) and Karsten Harries (2000), respectively, which guided my path and sharpened my vision, if not my pen; a vision that comes from the "eyes of the skin," to add the work of Juhani Pallasmaa (2005b), whose sensibility helped soften the edges of reason and scientific positivism.

The methodology draws on the field of phenomenology, discussed in Chapter 1, while Gestalt theory lingers in the background, albeit tempered by Pallasmaa's warning that architectural elements are not mere visual units but encounters that interact with memory (Pallasmaa 2005b, 63). Each topic is explored in two subsequent stages: having raised a question, it is first discussed within a broader theoretical context and then follows an analysis of the Minoan paradigm. Questions addressed are of the type: What is the meaning of entrance as an act of crossing a boundary and how is this expressed in the Minoan world? Why did the Minoans—and only them—come up with the idea of the pier-and-door partition as a mutable barrier? Why are there so many staircases in a compound? What is a light-well as opposed to a court? Totalizing and homogenizing assumptions of Minoan architecture are generally avoided, taking into consideration the problems that arise when dealing with such broad and diverse material. Yet the aura of a distinct style seems to emerge throughout, a style that through a strange whim of history seems to have foreshadowed the works of the early years of the 20th century A.D. This is the main topic of the Chapter 11.

The material used in this book derives primarily from the available publications, but also from my personal, long acquaintance with the prehistoric monuments and sites of Crete (Fig. 2). It corresponds to approximately 200 buildings ranging from huts to palaces and spans the Neolithic to the Neopalatial eras, a time period that covers more than 1,500 years. The emphasis, however, is on the so-called golden era of the Late Bronze Age, approximately 200 years of affluence and creativity for which we are best informed.

A book is written in silence and solitude, yet under the constant immaterial presence of all those who toil in the field. To the people who have undertaken the difficult goal of unwinding the clew of the Minoan world, I am deeply indebted: colleagues of all disciplines, archaeologists, architects, conservators, and many more, with whom I have often joined forces in the archaeological cause, be it in the dig, the laboratory, or the library. My gratitude extends equally to colleagues and scholars who strive to reveal the deeper essence of architecture, a precious legacy for generations to come to which this book will hopefully add a small contribution. Iris Tzachili, Nanno Marinatos, and George Rethemiotakis are three colleagues and friends whom I wish to mention separately, for their constant support and valuable advice throughout the writing of this book. Jan Driessen and Martin Schmid, both highly experienced in the intricacies of Minoan architecture, reviewed the manuscript and offered valuable advice. Their comments and suggestions were very productive and helped me concretize crucial points of this book.

I am also thankful to Nektarios Karadimas for assisting in the collection of the bibliographic material, and I am deeply indebted to Kostas Athanasiou, Niki Apostolou, and Zacharias Mavroeidis for their valuable help with the digital drawings of this publication, as well as to Douglas Faulmann, Archaeological Illustrator at the Institute for Aegean Prehistory Study Center for East Crete (INSTAP SCEC), for his advice in adjusting these drawings to the INSTAP Academic Press standards, under the vigilant supervision of Susan Ferrence, Director of Publications. Scientific work, research, and writing can hardly take place without some very real material support, such as the research grant offered unsparingly by INSTAP, for which I am indebted to Malcolm Wiener and Phillip Betancourt.

Family support is rather taken for granted, yet, it is always worth acknowledging. I must therefore thank my children, Martha and Zacharias, for their patience when they were little, while waiting for their mother to finish drawing one rock after the other (not exactly the "rockstar" of a mother they may have had in mind). Fully grown up today, they encourage and help me in a very real way by offering their valuable advice as outsiders to the field of archaeology.

Last but not least, I am thankful to my students in the School of Architecture at the Aristotle University of Thessaloniki for the hard time they give me in trying to persuade them of the usefulness of history; an effort that pays back when each year I see a new group of students leaving the classroom with a fresh mind toward the works of the past and a stronger belief in its value for the future. It also pays back when I think of the subtle, unconscious ways history will find its way in their own work in the years to come, even if they will probably remain unaware of this, since "the history that is most useful for the architect is the history he has forgotten" (Moholy-Nagy et al. 1967, 196).

## Endnotes

1 This quotation is in reference to John Coulton's book *Ancient Greek Architects at Work: Problems of Structure and Design* (Coulton 1977). *Daidalos at Work* is, in a sense, a prelude to ancient Greek architects at work. For a meticulous discussion on the many attributes of Daidalos, his relation to royal power, and the ambivalent meaning of *techné* as art and architecture, see Frontisi-Ducroux 1975.

2 Warren excavated three circular platforms at Knossos and identified them as ritual dancing floors (Warren 1984a, with references to circular ritual dances in art).

3 In a well-known Ugaritic epic, the gods Ba'al and 'Anat ask for Kothar-wa-Hasis to be brought from Kptr (generally identified with Crete) to erect a splendid house/palace. Whatever the identity of Kothar and his relations to Daidalos or Hephaistos, the allusion to a highly appreciated Cretan craftsmanship is straightforward. Interestingly, Kothar is also related to Ilish, the carpenter god. That the "house of Baal" would require the services of a builder who is also an excellent carpenter is of special significance in light of the importance of timber in the building technology of Ugarit and the Aegean Bronze Age civilizations (Palyvou 2007).

4 As Lefas points out, Vitruvius does not simply say that buildings must be firm, useful, and beautiful. He addresses durability, convenience, and beauty as the three poles of reference for every technical activity, paralleled with the fundamental principles of *ordinatione*, *dispositione*, *eurythmia*, *symmetria*, *decore*, *eurythmy*, and *distributione* (Lefas 1997, 57 n. 1.108).

# Introduction

## Architecture and Archaeology: Tasks and Tools

*[Buildings] are instruments and museums of time. They enable us to see and understand the passing of history, and to participate in time cycles that surpass individual life. (Pallasmaa 2005b, 52)*

Architecture and archaeology are two very different disciplines, each with its own tasks and tools and each with its own innate ambiguities and unresolved problems. They converge, however, in their quest for human ethos—the way people dwell on this earth. Time is important in both disciplines: they share the same starting point in the present and depart from there to the future and to the past, respectively, only to find that they are circling around the eternal present (Fig. 3).

The task of architecture, as Sigfried Giedion defined it long ago, is to serve and interpret as best as possible a way of life valid for a period (Giedion 1967, xxxiii). Archaeology, on the other hand, in seeking to understand human behavior and cultural change in the past, goes the opposite way: it starts with the material remains of the past—architecture being the most conspicuous—and it seeks to decipher them in order to arrive at the way of life they once served (Trigger 1989, 370–371). Archaeologists, in other words, are venturing to reverse the process of planning, designing, building, and using that resulted in the ruins revealed through excavations so as to arrive at the parameters

Fig. 3. Architecture and archaeology circling around the eternal present. Drawing C. Palyvou.

that dictated their genesis and transformations. This is no easy task for two main reasons. The first is the capacity of architecture to absorb time and change, a gift to archaeology, as much as a curse. It is a gift because "architecture enables us to perceive and understand the dialectics of permanence and change, to settle ourselves in the world, and to place ourselves in the continuum of culture and time" (Pallasmaa 2005b, 71); and it is a curse because it results in an inextricable skein of successive planning-designing-constructing-using cycles, each corresponding to a different period of time and a different way of life, a phenomenon commonly referred to as the palimpsest. The second difficulty, inherent in any attempt to decode a work of architecture, past or present, derives from the nebulous nature of the design process itself. This is a serious drawback in any archaeological interpretation that is rarely acknowledged. Architects, however, are painfully aware of the fact that there is no easy way to conceptualize the complexity of a design process, as there is no easy way to teach it.

One naturally wonders if it is so difficult to describe and explain the design process in its genesis, how is one expected to unfold the design process of a work of architecture that was created more than 3,500 years ago and has survived to our time in ruins through numerous modifications and destructions. Yet, this is precisely what we are doing when seeking to reach out to the numerous parameters and intentions that guided the design (and redesign) of Minoan buildings now lying in ruins.

In this respect, the task of archaeologists has much in common with that of architectural critics, for they too work backward in quest of initial intentions. According to Manfredo Tafuri, there may even be a tautology here, for history can only be critical (1986). On the other hand, the starting point for critics is what archaeologists are missing: the response of the people who actually use or have used the work of architecture in question. Prehistorians dealing with silent worlds and haunted spaces are at a great disadvantage. The inescapable absence of peoples' voices—in vivo or in writing—through which to glimpse how architectural space was perceived and experienced within the context of their way of life is a serious deficiency, for their testimony is the only true evidence of how a work of architecture fulfills its function (on the meaning of function, see this vol., Ch. 9).

Notwithstanding the above shortcomings, we embark on this compelling and promising intellectual journey as best prepared as possible. Asking the right kinds of questions, in the light of what the available data can offer, is laying a proper beginning to this journey. It is also essential for choosing the right tools of thought: methodologies, theoretical models, and conceptual frameworks may be borrowed, combined, constructed, or reinvented, and they are unavoidably influenced by shifting philosophies and worldviews (Bintliff 1984, 38). Yet, this is more a fact than a problem; after all, it is not so much about finding answers but seeking different ways to ask the same questions. These different ways will hopefully reveal the multiple meanings of architecture and enrich our understanding of how people interact with their environment.

## A Phenomenological Approach

*First of all, things speak to us. That speech is silenced only by the reduction of things to mere objects, a reduction presupposed by science. (Harries 1993, 53)*

In seeking theoretical and methodological tools, one cannot but point out the deficiencies of architecture in comparison to archaeology. As an applied science that flirts with art, architecture was rather delayed in producing its own theoretical framework that would explain intentions and meaning in the production and consumption of built space; indeed, it relied too long on art for this.[1] The very concept of space—initially used in mathematics and science—appeared in the context of architecture only in the late 19th century. Giedion's seminal book *Space, Time and Architecture: The Growth of a New Tradition*, first published in 1941,[2] was to mark the beginning of a new perception of architecture, with time and space as its protagonists.

Broadly speaking, there are two predominant lines of thought: the analytical or scientific and the holistic or phenomenological. The analytical is based on the potentials of the human mind for abstract thinking, such as mathematical or statistical analyses, on the assumption that they can help detect clusters, attributes, compositional patterning, and syntax that will lead eventually to conceptual understanding of meaning. Space Syntax is a typical example of a tool of this sort (Hillier and Hanson 1984). Other exponents of this trend, working mostly within the fields of structuralism and semiotics, are Geoffrey Broadbent, Juan Pablo Bonta, Umberto Eco, Donald Preziosi, and Alan Colquhoun (Agrest and Gandelsonas, 1996, 110–111; Barthes 1997a, 166–167).

The holistic or phenomenological school, on the other hand, urges a return to the archetypal ontological essence of things, as opposed to mental constructions, on the assumption that things speak to us. Martin Heidegger, Giedion, Christian Norberg-Schulz, Hans-Georg Gadamer, Tadao Ando, Vittorio Gregotti, and Henri Lefebvre represent, among others, this line of thought (Norberg-Schulz 1996, 412–413; Leach 1997b). Norberg-Schulz, in particular, was the scholar who introduced phenomenology to architecture, maintaining that the environment is experienced as meaningful and that the "spirit of the place" (genius loci) is equally important as the "spirit of the age" (1980, 10–11).

The rift between the two approaches has taken serious dimensions at times. The analytical school claims objectivity, implying pejoratively that the individualized assessments of the phenomenological school cannot be considered objective knowledge. They reject any mysterious, expressive values deriving from the nature of things alone, and they place more value in the expressiveness arising from the dialectic between significative forms and codes of interpretations (Eco 1997, 189). Another line of dissent comes from Postprocessual thinkers who emphasize variance across time and space, as well as class, gender, age, and so forth, as opposed to phenomenologists who work on the presumption of the universality of the human body and its response to natural stimuli. The exponents of the phenomenological approach answer back that architectural space is not the product of mathematical and logarithmic structures nor the invention of people who react to space as if they have no means of verbal communication, and that things are silenced only when they become mere objects for scientific observation.

Analytical methodologies in architecture may indeed give the impression of a mental exercise—a kind of *architectura ex machina* (Tafuri 1980, 173)—which risks losing sight of values that cannot be measured, such as the power of ποίησις (*poiesis*; making) inherent in architecture. Heidegger writes, "dwelling can be unpoetic only because it is in essence poetic" and adds that "our unpoetic dwelling, its incapacity to take the measure, derives from a curious excess of frantic measuring and calculating" (Heidegger 1997b, 118). Analytical thinking relies very much on the quantitative aspect of the data; yet counting thresholds on a plan, for example, without taking into account their liminal nature and the potentials of the door in announcing a barrier, is a strong understatement of what the door contributes to architecture.[3]

Analytical thinking also relies on the accuracy of the data; a door must be a door and not an unidentified gap in the wall. The realities of the archaeological records, however, seldom allow for such confident assumptions. The ambiguity of the evidence cannot be treated as such: the tool cannot deal with uncertainty. This can be fatal for the process of interpretation, for it invites false data to creep into the system and contaminate it, jeopardizing the whole line of thought. Notwithstanding the above skepticism, analytical thinking has its benefits, especially as a means to organize and handle information in a systematic manner. Interestingly, it is gaining ground in the study of prehistoric architecture.[4] One of the probable reasons (and at the same time a cause of concern) why analytical tools appeal to the prehistoric archaeologists is that they are seemingly easy to apply to the two-dimensional world of most prehistoric sites.

At the other end of the spectrum, phenomenology is problematic in its very definition as, according to Heidegger (1967, xiv), "the process of letting things manifest themselves" (quoted in Relph 1985, 15 n. 2). The holistic approach, adverted by phenomenology, offers a depth model for understanding human existence, commensurate to psychoanalysis or structuralism, hence phenomenology "claims to have recourse to a deeper symbolic level; it seeks to go beyond the codifying capacity of semiology to reveal a richer understanding of the world" (Leach 1997b, 84). These claims, however, also reveal its weak point, for there can be nothing to legitimize them. As Neil Leach points out, phenomenology lacks normative foundations and is in effect a highly individualized interpretive venture based on a self-referential system (1997b, 84).

Despite its epistemological fragility, phenomenology is very popular among architectural circles, especially in schools of architecture. It is indeed very difficult, if not impossible, to teach architectural composition through structuralism and semiotics. Phenomenology, on the other hand, provides just the means for healing the rifts between art and science, seeing and understanding, knowledge and action, and designing and building (Seamon 1993, 1). Moreover, as Leach points out, "in an age of virtual reality the very corporeality of the body cannot be ignored when addressing the experience of space" (Leach 1997b, 84). This line of thought has found prolific grounds also in archaeology, as a way to address sensory aspects of past human experience that cannot easily be approached through traditional archaeological methods (Tilley 1994, 7–34). It was first applied in the study of archaeological landscapes, mostly to Neolithic ritual sites of northwest Europe, focusing on issues of visibility and monumentality, but it is spreading rapidly in other areas as well, including the Aegean Bronze Age.

My inclination toward phenomenology as a conceptual framework for studying the architecture of the prehistoric Aegean has become rather apparent by now. That said, however, I should add emphatically that theories are not cults: one person's theory is not another person's heresy. Choosing one theoretical tool does not necessarily mean renouncing the other. On the contrary, one should try to find ways to benefit from all tools available, as several scholars have suggested. After all, no single analytical method suffices for the study of the past. What's more, there are no strict lines of separation between them, as one might think. Even the most zealous exponents of the two schools described above have yielded to the other side at some point: Norberg-Schulz, a devout phenomenologist, is at times analytical in dealing with the elements of place, Bill Hillier is interested in genotypes (Kotsiopoulos 1985, 221–222), and David Seamon, an environment-behavior researcher and prolific writer on phenomenology, explains at length his interest in Hillier's Space Syntax, aware that this may sound bizarre to some (Seamon 1994). I would agree, therefore, with John Bintliff's urge "to bridge that gap between what the data permit us to infer as strict scientists, and what we would like to be able to pronounce on as historians or 'social analysts'" by making the best out of both schools of thought (1984, 34).

On a final note, it should be stressed that methodologies for understanding human perception of space are potent tools for shaping the future as much as for decoding the past. In accepting Hillier's analytical method as valid for any period of time in history, Eugenia Yiannouli points out that in architecture more recent is not necessarily more unambiguous and "the older is not necessarily the more alien" (Yiannouli 1992, 43).[5] I could not agree more, and I would add that precisely because of the ubiquitous and timeless nature of architecture, architects of all times have looked back to the works of the past to learn and understand their deeper meanings and formative powers (even when renouncing their corresponding ideologies), just as archaeologists look into the present for ways to capture human responses to the built environment.[6]

## Managing Absence and Image Making in Archaeology

*[T]here is no objective past, constant over time, but only a continual refraction of the absent in the memory of the present. (Forster 1982, 15)*

The question arising in the context of prehistoric studies is: Can one discuss in phenomenological terms the architecture of a long-silenced people that has survived to our days partially and in ruins? Can phenomenology be applied to the semi-phenomenal, to that which is only partially accessible to our senses, especially vision, as the Greek word phenomenon literally means, either because it has not survived or because it lies hidden beyond the limits of the excavation trench? In other words, are imagination and extrapolation legitimate tools of phenomenological thinking in archaeology?

Juhani Pallasmaa states emphatically that "our faculty of imagination is the foundation of our very mental existence and of our way of dealing with stimuli and information" (Pallasmaa 2005a, 129). Imagination is the ability to think in terms of images of things not present. It draws on the memory of things seen and experienced in the past. Perception, memory, and imagination are thus in constant interaction—just as in Italo Calvino's *Invisible Cities* (1972), all the cities one has visited are precincts in the metropolis of the mind, "forever enrich[ing] the urban geography of the world" (Pallasmaa 2005b, 67–68; see also Pallasmaa 1996, 447).

Our way into the past is no different: "ruins offered gateways to ancestral worlds" (Castro 2007, xii). Like visiting a foreign country, these can only be crossed with the aid of memory and imagination.[7] At a first level, experiential and cognitive memory will help us fill in the missing parts of a building with walls, floors, and ceilings, whereas extrapolation and inference will help add the specifics of the architecture in question, borrowing from other buildings of the same "style." If confident (or innocent) enough, one might even invent forms "in style" to fill in the picture, as Eugène Viollet-le-Duc did in the 19th century when restoring Gothic monuments according to a generic "Gothic style," and, to some extent, what Arthur Evans did at Knossos through his reconstitutions, discussed in Chapter 11 (Fig. 4). The danger, of course, is that invented forms may creep in the authentic architectural vocabulary.

A crucial note of concern is that we cannot always define with certainty what is missing and what was never there (Fig. 5). In fact, when dealing with the absent, archaeologists often respond with a kind of *horror vacui* attitude: they are more inclined to think in terms of things missing rather than not existing. Relevant to this discussion is Gestalt theory.[8] Robert Wenger, an art educator, artist, and archaeologist, sees many parallels between visual art, archaeological studies, and Gestalt theory, for they all base their inquiries on visual perception. He describes the archaeologist at work as follows: "Faced with such visual complexity, the excavator begins a search for the most stable and least disturbed arrangements within the archaeological whole. The challenge is to re-establish the ancient order by noting the similarity, continuity, proximity and degree of closure in the visual elements that remain" (Wenger 1997, 39). Gestalt principles are indeed inherent in every interpretive approach of the architecture of the past, even if guised under an archaeological terminology, such as "density" and "concentration" instead of "proximity."

Fig. 4. West Wing of the Palace of Knossos during excavation (top) and after Evans's reconstitution work (bottom). Images © Ashmolean Museum, University of Oxford.

Following Wenger's line of thought, other Gestalt principles applied in the visual perception of material data, such as emergence, reification, multistability, and invariance, could also be projected to archaeology. But the Gestalt principle most relevant to the current discussion is that of closure—that is, the urge to fill in gaps and discontinuities through inference and interpolation in order to complete a figure, and doing so to increase its regularity. According to Gestalt theory, the impulse for closure in the process of perceiving the world comes naturally as the need to move toward the most stable and complete forms with definite boundaries, an accomplishment that brings relaxation and ease. This applies well to archaeology: the quest for closure is a strong urge for the excavator and the archaeologist, and it is pursued through contemplation of what lies beyond the excavated trench as much as what is no longer there.

Fig. 5. Stone fence on a Cycladic island, intact (top) and in ruins (bottom). Konstantinidis 1975, figs. 26, 27.

Fig. 6. Reconstructed Piano Nobile of the Palace of Knossos and surrounding landscape, from the west. Photo C. Palyvou.

Another problem we need to address in dealing with the absent is our addiction to the phenomenology of the ruin. Standing in the middle of the Central Court of a Minoan Palace, or walking on the reconstructed Piano Nobile of the Palace of Knossos, our perception of the surrounding buildings and the landscape beyond is way off the reality it once presented (Fig. 6). We roam through areas restricted in the past and have access everywhere since we embody King Minos, the priestess, the visitor, and the servant all in one; we move through door-less openings that were once closed to sight and access; we follow random paths where there was once a strict hierarchy and meaning of movement; and we see where most paths lead to, whereas most of them were hardly visible as paths to begin with. We experience the site, in other words, the way we read a two-dimensional plan: as an abstract maze of walls and voids. The reality, of course, was very different, but no matter how well this fact is embedded in the cognitive sphere of our minds, our constant exposure to ruins still affects our sensory perception of architectural space, because it has acquired the power of experiential memory. Site management—access routes, viewpoints, and so forth—can also interfere with our perception of the ruins and our effort to imagine the original totality. To give an example, Evans's decision to enclose a specific part of the excavated area at Knossos within a green belt of tall trees has obstructed our understanding of the close interaction between the Palace and the surrounding town (Fig. 7). In fact, it promotes the image of the Palace, while downgrading that of the town, and it conveys an aura of landscape architecture rather than that of an urban environment.

The process of image making, therefore, has to rely on abstraction as much as on addition: there is need for constant cleansing of our perception from images that may have crept in from our customary exposure to Minoan ruins. We should also acknowledge the limitations of our data: we may analyze at length the access to the Palace of Knossos

a b c

Fig. 7. Theatral Area at Knossos: (a) from the northwest as found in 1923 (Evans 1921–1935, II.2, fig. 363); (b) today, after Evans's interventions, from the northwest (courtesy M. Papadantonakis); (c) from the west, isolated by a green zone and now alluding to landscape architecture (Davaras 1986, fig. 43; © Hellenic Ministry of Culture and Sports–Archaeological Receipts Fund).

through the Corridor of Procession, but we will never have a full and proper understanding of this path since we cannot tell if the corridor was amply lit with windows that offered a great view to the surrounding landscape, stretching as far out as the sacred mass of Mt. Juktas, or if it was an enclosed, dark space, making procession a self-conscious, introverted act. It is in the twilight between knowledge and imagination that we are confounded to linger.

Fig. 8. Our perception of Minoan architecture is highly influenced by stereotypical images of Knossos, such as this widely published watercolor of the Central Court by Piet de Jong. Courtesy Archaeological Museum of Herakleion, Hellenic Ministry of Culture and Sports–Archaeological Receipts Fund.

At the end of the journey, the assumed totality arrived at through our studies needs to be represented and communicated. There are two ways to do this: verbal (oral or written) and iconic (pictorial). The quantity and quality of information conveyed by the different modalities of representation varies greatly, and so does the corresponding impact on our perception of the past. Naturally, the most powerful effects are generated when filling in the gaps literally through restorations and reconstitutions that add involuntary masses to the ruins, like those performed by Evans at Knossos: their full-scale size and material substance results in an experience analogous to that of the original parts (even when restoration work complies with the norms that demand clear distinction between the authentic and the new; knowing does not necessarily affect perception).

Iconic representations aim at some sort of virtual reality. The means are: sketches, architectural drawings (e.g., plans, elevations, sections), isometric or perspective black and white drawings, color paintings, models, and nowadays digital three-dimensional visualizations (Fig. 8). The images thus produced form powerful stereotypes strongly embedded in our perception of the Minoan past—the closer to virtual reality the stronger the impact. These images tend to constitute an autonomous body of iconic data, perpetually reproduced in the publications, which sometimes outshine the actual finds; they become a kind of paper museum, so to speak, raised to the status of original documents.[9] Factual drama is another means of representing the past. It goes one big step further in that the represented realities are now inhabited by humans acting assumed roles and therefore reacting emotionally and spiritually to one another and to their environment.[10] Despite the strong liveliness of the end product, the familiarity with the art of cinema allows the viewer to keep a proper distance—Minoans speaking English, for example, is a convention that will always keep us alert.

Verbal communication, on the other hand, relies on imagination. The advantage of imagination is that it allows for pictures to emerge in our minds that need not be absolutely precise or consistent throughout:

they can be crispy clear in one area and quite blurred or fuzzy in another, depending on the accuracy of our information. We can also zoom in and out at will, without necessarily scaling every detail proportionally. Imagination can create strong impressions of places no matter how weak the details. We can all identify with Pallasmaa when he describes how he cannot remember the windows of his childhood room but he can remember very well how it felt looking out of them (Pallasmaa 1996, 451).

This is probably why visual representations generate more objections and debates than verbal descriptions; materialized reconstructions usually fail to satisfy or even disillusion us. In the early years of Minoan archaeology, David Hogarth complained that, "Restorations like the Throne Room are not a question of methods, but of the gratifying of a desire to reconstruct tangibly what must otherwise only be imagined" (letter to Evans, reproduced in Cottrell 1961, 137; see also Bintliff 1984, 35). This is true for most graphic reconstructions as well: drawings, even the most sketchy, do not allow for the free roaming through space that imagination thrives on. They have to be precise; a facade, for example, has to include a specific number and type of windows, thus producing not an idea of what was once a totality but an involuntary personal version of it. Suffice it to compare different images (graphic representations) of the Palace of Knossos to realize how concrete the picture they convey is and therefore how they betray both reality and imagination (see Klynne 1998; see also response in Driessen 1999).

Imagination is an image-making process that works with the eyes shut, just as we close our eyes when dreaming, listening to music, or caressing the beloved, so as to "dim the sharpness of vision and invite . . . tactile fantasy" to use Pallasmaa's beautiful wording once again (Pallasmaa 2005b, 46). The process, however, has two serious deficits: it is elusive and temporal, and it is also personal and non-communicative. Imagined pictures and emotional reactions cannot be easily conveyed or shared; they cannot even be recalled in the same way as they were first produced in our minds.

## Endnotes

1 Kruft (1994) and Trigger (1989) wrote two excellent books on the historiography of theoretical thinking in architecture and archaeology, respectively. During the second half of the 20th century, both architecture and archaeology started borrowing heavily from other disciplines, especially from the human sciences; this fusion of ideas and methodologies is stronger today than at any other time.

2 Giedion showed that architecture, past and present, could be approached in terms other than classification, styles, and periodization. He promoted the concept of space articulation as a potent tool for understanding the communicative role

of architecture. The book has been reprinted several times; Harvard University Press published the latest (fifth) revised and enlarged edition in 2008.

3 For a heated debate on the potentials and the shortcomings of analytical thinking, see Leach's comments on Hillier's Space Syntax (Leach 1978), as well as Hillier's response (Hillier et al. 1978). "Hillier et al. write as if the only space that is occupied by buildings is at ground floor level" (Leach 1978, 397). Leach also points out that though Hillier's method is able to devise syntactic rules that would generate certain space-use patterns, "the same rules would also generate meaningless space-use patterns and there are many empirical space-use patterns for which the syntaxes so far devised would not account" (Leach 1978, 400). The debate, far from being resolved, has taken other directions as well: Osman and Suliman (1994), for example, contest biased ways of western thinking, such as the predilection for calculating the shortest path.

4 Preziosi (1983) was a pioneer in this field, followed by his pupil Hitchcock (Hitchcock and Preziosi 1997). See also Yiannouli 1992; Thaler 2002; Fisher 2009; Athanasiou 2011; Letesson 2013; Fisher gives a comprehensive account of the growing interest in Space Syntax in the context of the architectural studies of past civilizations but also of the concerns and criticism regarding its limitations (Fisher 2009, 442), hence his preference for an integrative approach combining analytical methods with environmental psychology.

5 Interestingly, though Yiannouli is using analytical tools and Space Syntax, she concludes her dissertation with the following sentence:

> "[I]f phenomenology elicits understanding through the contemplation of the object, then space seems to have been then as much as it is now a symbolic form or meaning re-enacted but embodied in the construction of building. The oscillation between creation and its spatial expression is a 'wonder' that is, as always, with us" (1992, 183).

6 See n. 5, above.

7 *The Past is a Foreign Country* is the title of a very influential book (Lowenthal 1985).

8 For a concise annotation on Gestalt theory in architecture and references to bibliography, see Roth 2007, 67–71.

9 The "paper museum" alludes to the Roman patron and collector, Cassiano Dal Pozzo, and his famous *Museo Cartaceo* of the early 17th century, a collection of more than 7,000 watercolors, drawings, and prints that aimed at creating a visual database of all human knowledge (Campbell 2004).

10 Atkinson (2011) discusses model-making in analogy to real building (the case study is Myrtos Phournou Koriphi). Regardless of how effective such comparison can be, it is interesting that the very topic of the paper is the process of constructing a model.

# 1

# Minoan Architecture in the Turmoil of the 20th Century

## The Pioneers

Minoan archaeology is an offspring of the 20th century, with Evans in the double role of the midwife and the godfather, giving birth to and naming to the Aegean prehistoric studies. Evans worked in the early years of the century, at a time of turmoil, subversion, and overwhelming developments, not only in Europe but the whole world. This was a period of transition, pregnant with new ideas and new material possibilities for mankind, which affected greatly all fields of thought and practice, not least those of architecture and archaeology.

In the field of architecture, this was a time of definite break with the past. A new ideology, boiling for some time, was crystalized into a movement that redefined the meaning of the modern in juxtaposition with the stereotypes that had remained anchored in the Greco-Roman past. The classical ideal, or any existing ideal for that matter, was rejected as a tool for the creation of new (modern) architecture, and the Vitruvian conditions of architecture, *firmitas*, *utilitas*, and *venustas*, were reordered and renamed. Function (*utilitas*), understood basically as use (but including structure as well), replaced commodity (*firmitas*) and took the lead, whereas *venustas* (beauty, ornament), now described as form, was degraded to a subordinate role. "Form follows function" became the dogma of the new movement and the International Style in

Fig. 9. Arthur Evans, Theodore Fyfe, and Duncan Mackenzie at Knossos in 1901. Image © Ashmolean Museum, University of Oxford.

the 1920s, around the same time Evans was writing his voluminous report on the Palace of Knossos.

Evans had a classical education and a background that probably did not favor the new Modern Movement. Nevertheless, the bold, innovative, and extravagant character of Minoan architecture, especially in its highest palatial expression, caught his eye and his pen immediately. As an archaeologist, however, his main concerns were of a different kind: excavating at Knossos was a difficult task for more than one reason. In the first place, he had to conduct an excavation of many layers of debris and to understand and date a preclassical culture for which he had no parallels to guide him. Secondly, his duty was to preserve the material evidence of a multistory building compound constructed of rubble stones, mudbricks, and disintegrated wood; yet another task for which he had none of the ethical and technical advice available today. As he sensibly stressed, the conditions were very different from the "mighty stone buildings of Egypt, or the massive brick structures of Mesopotamia or those of Classical Greek and Roman sites" (Evans 1927, 258). In this light, his reconstitutions, notorious though they may have become in the face of our ethics today, were a systematic and earnest effort to preserve what he rightly thought was valuable information (for Evans's interpretive approach to the ruins of Knossos, see Zois 1996; Papadopoulos 1997; Kienzle 1998; Warren 2000).

His approach to the world he was bringing to light was of a holistic nature, and his totalizing narrations unavoidably contain much that needs to be revised or to be left unanswered. In a way, the same applies for the so-called ruins he produced through his reconstitutions, for the message they seem to convey is not so much that of the limited knowledge of what was once the Minoan totality but of a partial picture of this reality. Evans of course was not alone in his endeavors; he sought help from architectural professionals (Fig. 9). In this he was once more a pioneer, for he was one of the first excavators to have a trained architect always on site,[1] hardly the case with many digs even today. It was through the architects who worked at Knossos by his side (Theodore Fyfe, Christian Doll, de Jong, and Francis Newton)—or rather under his heavy shadow—that the Modern Movement found its way into the reconstitutions of the ruins, as a touch of Art Deco (see this vol., Ch. 11). These architects have hardly published anything in writing concerning their work at Knossos or their thoughts in regard to Minoan architecture. It is basically through the drawings they left behind that we may appreciate their contribution to Minoan archaeology—drawings, however, that were meant primarily to guide technically demanding reconstitution work at Knossos (Fig. 10; Palyvou 2003).

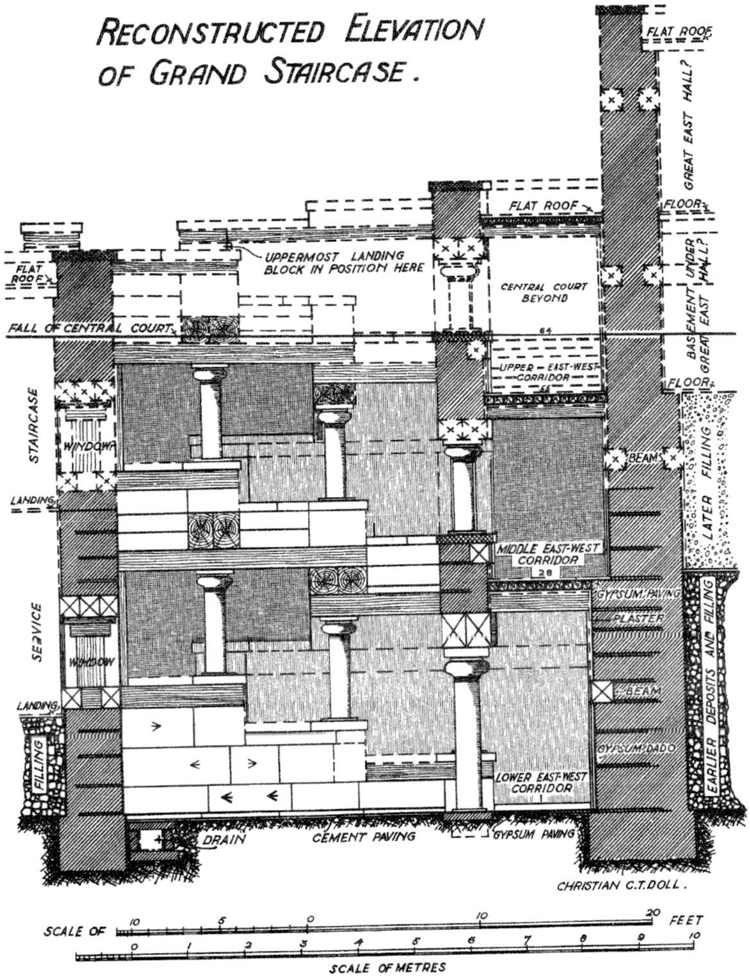


Fig. 10. Section through the light-well of the Domestic Quarters at Knossos, looking toward the Grand Staircase, by Christian Doll. Evans 1921–1935, I, fig. 247.

Following the discovery of Knossos, Crete became the scene of intensive archaeological research, with excavations taking place all over the island. Evans was very interested in architecture, as evident in the five volumes of *The Palace of Minos*—and so were the excavators of most Minoan sites around Crete—but J. Walther Graham was the first to deal with Minoan architecture in its own right. Writing in the 1960s, he focused mostly on the large building compounds that had already been labelled Palaces by their excavators. In his book *The Palaces of Crete* (Graham 1972), and in his numerous articles, he has presented what is still to this day a comprehensive account of the architecture of Crete in the Late Bronze Age. Most of his observations on the character and the aesthetic values of Minoan architecture remain relevant, more or less, to this day. A decade later, Joseph Shaw was the next scholar to present an overall account of Minoan architecture from the point of view of materials and building techniques. His book, *Minoan Materials and Techniques*, written in 1971 and recently republished in a slightly revised form (Shaw 2009), is a systematic compilation of data regarding the building technology of Minoan Crete and its evolution through time. It is an invaluable textbook for those working in the field.

In more recent years, there has been an impressive shift of interest toward the study of architecture, especially evident in the publications of major sites that now include extensive reports on architecture written by architects who participated in the excavations, such as Martin Schmid (Malia), W. Wilson Cummer (House A, Kea), John McEnroe (Mochlos and Pseira), Shaw (Kommos), and the present author

(Akrotiri, Thera). On the same account, the bibliography on Aegean architecture is steadily enriched through the works of Donald Preziosi, Jan Driessen, Ilse Schoep, Vasso Fotou, Anna Michailidou, Eugenia Yiannouli, and others. The influx of ideological frameworks and methodological tools imported from other disciplines, such as phenomenology, Marxism, feminism, linguistics, semiotics, structuralism, and deconstructionism, is evident in many of these works. Preziosi introduced semiotics to the field of Aegean prehistory through his book *Minoan Architectural Design. Semiotics of the Built Environment: An Introduction to Architectonic Analysis* (1983). Despite its insights, the book has had a rather low impact on Aegean studies, perhaps because of its analytical approach that may have discouraged some readers (for a review, see McEnroe 1984). Analytical methodologies, nevertheless, have found more followers since then, starting with Preziosi's pupil Louise Hitchcock, and continuing with several exponents of the new generation, such as Michael C. Nelson, Quentin Letteson, Ulrich Thaler, Eleftheria Paliou, and Kostas Athanasiou, all of whom are interested in experimenting with new theoretical tools. It is also encouraging to welcome to the field of Aegean prehistory exponents of other disciplines, such as Eleftheria Tsakanika-Theochari, a civil engineer who studied the Minoan building technology from the point of view of her discipline, in quest of structural systems, bringing fresh insight to the understanding of this magnificent and challenging architecture.

In sum, a considerable amount of scholarly work regarding the architecture of the Minoans has accumulated during a period of over 100 years of research and study. In the early writings, Evans and his fellow pioneer archaeologists strived to present a complete historic framework for Crete, spanning from the very beginning to the end of the Bronze Age. For their toil we shall be eternally grateful, for it provided the primal canvas upon which all who follow add or deduct information, construct or deconstruct theories, and accept or reject assumptions. Theirs was a hands-on approach, aiming predominantly at putting order to the original material they were unearthing. Their interpretations, though seemingly lacking the clarity of the methodological approaches we profess today, were reasonable, and many still stand true today to a large degree.

## On Words, Names, and Terms: "Must a Name Mean Something?"

*"Must a name mean something?" Alice asked doubtfully. [. . .]*
*"When I use a word," Humpty Dumpty said, in rather a scornful tone, "it means just what I choose it to mean—neither more nor less."*

*"The question is," said Alice, "whether you can make words mean so many different things."*
*"The question is," said Humpty Dumpty, "which is to be master—that's all."*
*Lewis Carroll,* Through the Looking Glass *(1917, 93, 99)*

Prehistoric Aegean archaeology was nourished in the late 19th century within a climate of romanticism that favored traveling in time, space, and imagination. Heinrich Schliemann, Wilhelm Dörpfeld, and other pioneer scholars sought truths and realities in mythology and Homer, as many still do today while searching for Ithaca, Menelaion, or Atlantis. Their sources provided names of renowned places, great people, and outstanding events, names that lured with their quasi-historical pretense and fascinating narratives.[2] But even if one was to accept Homer's nomenclature as corresponding to the Aegean Bronze Age, there was still much that had not been said or had to be clarified. For Evans, this was a challenge he had to face from the very beginning of his work at Knossos.

Today, many believe that the wording Evans chose to describe the hitherto unknown civilization of Crete was too personal and biased. Hence, Evans's vocabulary became a topic of debate and dubiety in its own right. As a consequence, new designations are being devised for the same things (a trend that found many followers from the 1990s onward). These ought to be as neutral as possible, and should refer solely to form avoiding any shades that might imply function: for example, "megastructure" or "court-compound" (Preziosi 1983, 78; Driessen 2002, 1) instead of "Palace" (see Day and Relaki 2002). The result, however, is extreme abstraction and reduced significative effectiveness. Form or size are inadequate designations to describe a work of architecture of the complexity and aura of what we all understand today as a Minoan Palace, even if we do not interpret its function in the same way. Of course, if we were to adopt unanimously a new name to replace what Evans called a Palace, it would only be a matter of time for this to become a name as good as any. The question is, which is to be master? The new name would eventually build up a history of its own, yet always in juxtaposition to the initial name, Palace, it replaced. But would that really affect the meaning of things and our understanding of their essence? Would it "truly help to liberate Aegean prehistory from lingering culture-historical and essentialist attitudes and paradigms?" (Karadimas and Momigliano 2004, 243). Names will always be autonomous and independent of the reality they represent.[3] That names cannot convey meaning is also reflected in the way the multi-lingual international family of Aegean prehistorians gets lost in translation. For example, Evans used the word Villa almost as self-explanatory, but when translated into French, Italian, German, or Greek the word becomes a term that carries very different meaning (an English villa is not the same as a Greek έπαυλη).

The distinction between words, names, and terms is often not taken into account in prehistoric studies. To clarify: a word can stand on its own with literal or practical meaning, as in a frame hanging on the wall of a classroom, showing the word bird next to its picture, whereas a name is a word or set of words by which a living being or thing is known, addressed, or referred to. Names draw meaning from the things they stand for; they do not render meaning to the thing, they simply mirror it. A term, finally, is a word with a specific definition, collectively acknowledged and often of a technical nature. In the context of architecture, for example, the light-well and the court are terms clearly defined in the textbooks, and it is essential that they are used properly and exclusively for what they stand for (in Minoan architecture there are actually few true light-wells, as we shall see, and the West Court of the Palaces is anything but a court). The proper use of architectural terminology is fundamental for communicative purposes but also for appreciating the rich and subtle nuances of architectural forms.

In the context of this book, to avoid complicating things even further, I decided to refrain from proposing or using new names as much as possible. This is not to say that name-giving is not important or that I find existing names satisfactory; quite the contrary, precisely because words can get in the way of thinking, there is ample discussion on the meaning and the context of the nomenclature commonly used today in Aegean studies. The reason for avoiding new designations, however, is that the old ones carry narratives that have a long story to tell and hence a strong communicative value. The Minoan Palace stands for a debate that began with Evans in 1900, and it embodies all the speculations and trends of the formative period of Aegean prehistory. The same holds for the Villa, the West Court, and the Theatral Area among several other terms in this book. To differentiate their value as names—and not words or terms—they are capitalized in this volume. Another reason for avoiding new names is that in many cases it is not the choice of name that is problematic but the innate difficulties of defining a distinct group that corresponds to a given name (esp. evident in the case of the Palace). It is the fluidity of the architectural continuum that is mostly responsible for the lack of consensus in name-giving. The question is, to quote Alice, whether you can find a word to "mean so many different things" (Carroll 1917, 99).

To illustrate the ambiguities words carry with them, and their changing meanings through time, let us look into the two words that correspond to the protagonists of this book: the noun architecture and the adjective Minoan. Self-evident though the word architecture may seem, it is still in need of clarification because not all agree as to what should be considered a work of architecture and what should not; does a path or a fence, for example, count as architecture? Giedion's (1967, xxxiii) definition of the task of architecture as the interpretation of a way of life valid for a period, discussed in the Introduction, answers to a certain degree the question, for it surely implies much more than the way of life in the

Palaces or the houses: the building of a fence, the creation of a path, or the construction of a retaining wall, a road, a bridge, a threshing floor, a dam, or a well, are peoples' interventions on the environment intended to serve their way of life. All these works require formulating the tasks, programming, and designing as much as technical knowledge and dexterity—in other words, they require all that makes architecture.

Not all theoreticians and historians of architecture endorse this definition: there are many who adhere, one way or another, to the earlier division between making architecture and building. Hillier, for one, in seeking a definition of architecture, states, "if the word is to serve a useful purpose we must be able to distinguish architecture from building. . . . The essence of our definition must say what architecture adds to building" (1996, 3). His line of thought is based on the understanding of architecture as a process as much as an end product, with emphasis on the social parameter. Letesson, discussing Hillier, concludes that there is no clear-cut limit between building and architecture and suggests two preconditions for architecture to be effective: (a) analytical knowledge in action; and (b) invention at the level of the genotype (Letesson 2010). The discussion becomes even more complicated when tradition versus innovation, as well as vernacular versus polite, are included.

This debate goes back to the writings of John Ruskin and the heated discussions of his time regarding the definition of the architectural monument. In the introduction of his *Seven Lamps of Architecture*, Ruskin states that, "It is very necessary, in the outset of all inquiry, to distinguish carefully between Architecture and Building" (1849, 7), the former seen as high art that transcends the practicalities of the simple act of building. Nikolaus Pevsner's famous distinction between a bicycle shed and a cathedral representing a building and a work of architecture, respectively, encapsulated forcefully this distinction (1948, xix). Spiro Kostof was among the first to castigate this approach as an aristocratic attitude equating the history of architecture with a history of monuments: a complete view of the manmade environment should include both monumental and vernacular architecture, Kostof and others argued (Kostof 1985, 13–15; Roth 2007, 5).

Minoan archaeology was born within such an aristocratic milieu, as reflected in the spectacular recovery of a legendary Palace and Europe's earliest so-called throne. Evans, followed by Graham, focused basically on palatial and elite architecture, though this was soon to change, starting with Harriet Boyd Hawes who dug a Minoan town at Gournia only a few years later. Following the quest for a pluralist approach to history, scholars gradually endorsed all aspects of the human-made environment and sought to understand all that shaped and gave meaning to the landscape: a dam on the small island of Pseira, fish traps near Ierapetra, and roads and bridges belonging to a network of land communication systems have added valuable information regarding the management of the land and its resources and have contributed to the formation of

Fig. 11. Cultivation terraces on Syros. Lavvas and Philippidis, eds., 1983–1991, II, fig. 225; courtesy Melissa Publishing House.

a more complete picture of the architecture of the time.

Landscape and rural architecture is of a simple and unpretentious nature and often leaves few traces behind. Moreover, it is repetitive and timeless, and one can hardly distinguish chronologically its multiple layers and origins. The rhythmical terraces that transform an arid land into rich pockets for cultivation must have been typical of the Aegean landscape ever since humans chose to live there (Fig. 11; Rackham and Moody 1992, 129). Despite their seemingly simple logic and appearance, such structures involve many of the basic principles of the art of building—retaining walls that will resist the pressure of accumulated soil, effective drainage, access systems, and so forth—including knowledge of the properties of the building materials, such as wood, stone, and clay. They also involve planning and designing, that is, setting out requirements and goals, checking for options and restrictions, and preparing an action plan. This, I believe, suffices to make us stop in awe at the sight of a threshing floor or a retaining wall and leave neither outside the definition of architecture.

In regard to the adjective that assigns time and place to the architecture we are dealing with, Evans's use of the adjective Minoan—following others before him (Karadimas and Momigliano 2004)—was effective in that it not only alludes directly to a specific time and place but it also reflects the ambiguity of a past lingering between myth and reality. It has been criticized, nevertheless, for predisposing those using it in favor of kingship and cultural homogeneity (both of which need not have been the case). According to Colin Renfrew, the adjective Minoan should pertain to the prehistoric inhabitants of Crete, and it should not imply any necessary "collective awareness or corporate identity on their part" (1996, 2).[4] In other words, the designation Minoan should be understood primarily as a geographical and chronological determination. Nevertheless, the material culture of the Palatial period revealed through excavations all over Crete reflects a significant degree of homogeneity, despite the varying biographies of individual sites.[5]

## The Impossible Typology of a Continuum

Typology is a process of classification of artifacts according to their characteristics. It is a common tool in archaeology that nevertheless risks entrapping things in categories that can hardly carry their variability.

It has been pointed out that Minoan architecture is very resistant to categorizations and strictly defined typologies. Sometimes it seems indeed easier to define what all Minoan buildings have in common, rather than explain what makes one building a house and a slightly different one a Villa. McEnroe's venture to provide a typology of Minoan houses, by comparing a number of buildings along concrete criteria, ultimately did more to emphasize the architectural continuum of Minoan architecture and reveal the problems involved when attempting to break it down (1982, 10).[6] A continuum is by definition a scheme where there can be only two ends at a time, no matter how you break it down; it is therefore a fluid situation and its importance lies in the fact that none of the middle parts can gather together to form a separate, intermediate pole. McEnroe's tripartite categorization of Minoan houses is precisely that: it has two ends, well defined (types 1 and 3), whereas the in between type 2 is rather elusive.

The two ends of the Minoan architectural continuum may be conceptualized as the two foci of an ellipse: one represents the house (the physical, the private, and the profane) and the other the Palace (the spiritual, the public, and the sacred).[7] Like two strong magnets, the poles of the ellipse enact centrifugal and centripetal forces defining the exact position of the in-between situations and keeping the ellipse in equilibrium. Each one of the two poles releases a series of offspring: thus, the simple house gradually evolves into its more sophisticated relative, the Villa, whereas the Palace gradually dissolves into its lesser relatives, called indiscriminately palatial building, central building (Kommos, Hagia Triada, Archanes, Petras), or local central building (Makrygialos, Vathypetro, Pyrgos; Driessen 1989–1990, 5). The shades of gradations are infinite, and this is what gives each Minoan building its dual character of belonging to a nebulous archetype while at the same time retaining its strong individuality. This was also the challenge in writing this book: to explore Minoan architecture in all its fluidity and diversity and at the same time to track down those properties or principles of design that produce the ambience immediately recognized as Minoan.

The diversity of Minoan architecture is not exhausted in lesser Palaces and richer houses: in a sophisticated society as the Minoan, collective activities and public services were complex and demanding as to their spatial needs, thus giving birth to a variety of distinct architectural forms designed for special purposes. These buildings represent satellites of the ellipse described above, offshoots of the Palace/public end of the continuum. They constitute an important addition to the corpus of Minoan buildings: Hagia Photia, Zominthos, the Caravanserai, and Kommos, to name but a few, are buildings produced to cope with specific functions, even if their precise use often escapes us (see McEnroe 2010). Their existence, nevertheless, is of great significance, for they give proof to a high level of social complexity and hierarchy and mirror an advanced level of architectonic thinking.

## Relative Time, Absolute Chronologies

At the end of the day, the dismal remains of a past lifetime that have been meticulously collected from the dig will be of little value if they cannot be represented in time and space. The former is primarily the task of the archaeologist and the latter of the architect. Both are in need of systems of reference—dates and datums—and both use two such systems, one relative and the other absolute. The relative system is a convenient ad hoc solution of a temporary nature that defines zero (as time or space coordinates) arbitrarily, whereas the absolute is a universal system aiming at an all-inclusive account of world history.

Absolute time is what relates our existence to a remote past and punctuates all that has passed in between. Its quest therefore is of primal, almost existential importance, and it is no wonder that it often results in unrest and frustration. The so-called time anxiety syndrome, as I dubbed it, is especially acute in prehistoric studies (Palyvou 2007, 43), for like some kind of elective amnesia, the data we collect from our excavations is fragmented and scattered in place and time. To cure the syndrome scholars resorted to the indisputable verdict that only scientific positivism can provide, and the curators in the field soon found a name for themselves: archaeometers. Archaeometry is indeed based on the assumption that the past is measurable. Its methods bring to the nebulous world of prehistoric archaeology a breath of certitude that is much needed, but also the risk of being overassertive in that all that can be counted is what counts. Gaps and serious discrepancies between the two systems, the relative and the absolute, are naturally not acceptable. An example of this case is the still unresolved clash we have been witnessing for some time now in the Aegean studies caused by the new dating of the eruption of the Theran volcano proposed by archaeometry that places the event 135 years earlier than hitherto assumed by Evans based on material associations between Egypt and the Aegean.[8]

If absolute time is the gift archaeometry is striving to offer history, relative time is a heuristic tool that the archaeologists invented in order to deal with the situation in the meantime. It is a system for organizing things along a conventional "before and after" and a resilient "in between" lingering in the midst that will allow for the narrative to take place. This tripartite scheme is ingrained with the Darwinian concept of birth, maturity, and decline, and it therefore carries a latent system of values as well. Moreover, it is extremely intricate, a nightmare for the students of Aegean prehistory, and inaccessible jargon to the non-initiate.

Archaeologists working with the Bronze Age today use two different systems of time reference: the most popular is the timetable Evans provided based on associations with literate Egypt. This timetable is being constantly refined and tuned for each region separately, in juxtaposition to the archaeometric finds that claim to provide indisputable absolute chronologies, disengaged from any archaeological bias. The second system of time reference is the one proposed by Nikolaos Platon in the late 1960s based on a sequence of marking events, such as extensive rebuilding operations following major disasters (see list below; Platon 1968). It is a relative, nonnumerical system that can stand on its own, regardless of the exact time and duration of the event, but it has the disadvantage that it can only refer to places that share impact from the same event.[9]

Conventional chronologies for the prehistoric Aegean are as follows:[10]

Neolithic (ca. 7000–3000 B.C.)

Prepalatial (ca. 3000–1900 B.C.)

Protopalatial (ca. 1900–1750 B.C.)

Neopalatial (ca. 1750–1490 B.C.)

Middle Minoan (MM) III (ca. 1750–1700 B.C.)

Late Minoan (LM) IA (ca. 1700–1580 B.C.)

Late Minoan (LM) IB (ca. 1580–1490 B.C.)

Final Palatial (ca. 1490–1360 B.C.)

Postpalatial (ca. 1360–1200 B.C.)

Time counts differently for archaeology and architecture. Archaeology has been traditionally concerned with the long duration of time corresponding to chronologies and periodizations. Aegean and Near Eastern studies have even been accused of chronocentricism; in other words, for prioritizing chronology at the expense of exploring other, more interesting lines of enquiry (Croucher 2005, 611). Today, scholars have shifted from Evans's linear, totalizing narratives to individual competing stories; this is especially important when dealing with architecture, for most buildings (and sites) have their own biographies that need to be read independently before any synthesis or comparison is attempted. Furthermore, as the study of the past is shifting toward unravelling the ordinary patterns of everyday living, scholars are increasingly forced to confront the short-term time scales of lived reality (Foxhall 2000). Part of the ordinary patterns of everyday living are house building, maintaining, remodeling, expanding, or demolishing. Changes may occur to the form, the structure, or the use (or all three) of a building for far too many reasons, some of which concern the specific household alone, whereas others are of a more general nature reflecting the adventures of a community or the spirit of the age. Changes may happen time and again upon the same initial fabric, over a long span of time, for buildings outlive both their architects and their initial commissioners and users. Architecture testifies the passing of history and reflects time cycles that surpass individual life (Pallasmaa 2005b, 52). The question of time in architecture, therefore, is one of fluidity, adaptivity, capacity, and tolerance, expressed through binaries such as permanence and change, tradition and innovation, and depression and affluence.

A relevant question is, what was time for the Minoans? In the absence of their own testimony, our only evidence comes from their art. Iris Tzachili, studying the wall paintings of the saffron gatherers from Akrotiri, Thera, points out that "time in works of art, and therefore as a concept, is never abstract: it is concrete and indicated through a variety of activities and tangible manifestations" (2005, 113). Some activities are successive and repetitive, punctuating cycles of life, death, and regeneration. They correspond to circular time that is often associated to cosmological concepts. There is, however, also evidence of things happening in succession, one after another, which indicates that there was some kind of perception of the linear sequence of past, present, and future. The latter is crucial to the concepts of monumentality, symbolism, and identity, discussed in the relevant chapters.

## Endnotes

1 Brown refers to the architects as "somewhat of a novelty" (Brown 1989, 30). The Germans had set the example: the excavations at Olympia, which began in 1875, had a field team led by one art historian, one archaeologist, and two architects, Friedrich Adler and Wilhelm Dörpfeld.

2 See Darque's strong objections to giving names to places based on Homer where no evidence from Linear B tablets exists (2003).

3 Tzachili (2011, 17–23) distinguishes four categories of names and terms and discusses how they interfere hermeneutically with our perception of Minoan art: (1) terms borrowed from contemporary artistic trends (e.g., naturalism); (2) terms laden with sentimental or symbolic values (e.g., joyful); (3) words used to describe things (e.g., Palace); and (4) adverbs and other words implying interrelations between things and people as users or beholders (e.g., up/down, in front).

4 McNeal observed that the term Minoan, as Evans and others used it, denoted Childe's three types of archaeological terminology all in one—the geographical, the chronological, and the cultural—and he saw a certain logic in such usage since Minoan culture was, or at least was thought to be, one entity from beginning to end (Childe 1964, 365; McNeal 1975, 395 n. 37).

5 Cunningham, discussing divergence and variation as strategy in the Minoan world, observes that similarities in the material culture are related to social reproduction (ideologies), whereas variation is manifested in social production; homogeneity, in other words, is attested in the elite manifestations "by virtue of membership and participation in an island-wide group" (2007b, 106).

6 Tzedakis and Chrysoulaki (1987, 115) disagree with such a typology. Hitchcock and Preziosi (1997, 57–59) criticize "reductivist and essentialist observations," as they call them. See also McEnroe 2010, 105, n. 40 for his own reevaluation of his typology.

7 The idea of the ellipse is based on Harries who writes that, "Architectural theory has turned not around one but two paradigms: An ellipse that has one focus in the house, tied to the family more than the individual; the other in the church or the temple" (1993, 56).

8 For an overview of the new (high) and old (low) chronologies, see Rehak and Younger 1998, 97–100; Warren 2010; Manning 2014.

9 Platon's time system is closer to the "kairological" concept of time (as opposed to the chronological), which was popular in pre-industrial societies up until the mid-19th century A.D. (McEnroe 2010, 5–6). Chronological and kairological concepts of time correspond to the two Greek words for time: χρόνος and καιρός. Χρόνος is absolute quantifiable time, whereas καιρός is qualitative time of opportunity, chance and mischance.

10 After McEnroe 2010, table 1.1.

# 2

# Land Matters

## The Accident of Location

In discussing mobility, Karsten Harries complains that place is no longer destiny, for today technology carries the liberation from "the accident of location into the world" (2000, 172–173). Nevertheless, land, place, and site still matter, and the relevant discourse is rich and fascinating, especially when involving multidisciplinary approaches, as in the book *Site Matters: Design Concepts, Histories, and Strategies* that inspired the title of this chapter (Burns and Kahn, eds., 2005).

Environmental issues related to the accident of location have always been top in the list of parameters that affect people's choices in architecture, as trenchantly stated in the Vitruvian treatise on architecture. Deterministic interpretations of this interaction, however, have been questioned, and it is generally accepted that people's aspirations go far beyond the practical need to control the physical conditions of his environment, and that social or spiritual aspects might sometimes take the lead, even if environmental factors demand otherwise (Rapoport 1969). As Bruce Trigger points out, on the other hand, this line of thought, valid though it may be, should not be overrated, as some Postprocessual thinkers have done. His stand is that even though ecological determinism may not explain all aspects of human behavior, there is still much to be said in regard to ecological constraints on such behavior. By affirming cultural particularities, he continues, some scholars seem to overlook or even deny cross-cultural uniformities and hence lose sight "of a significant aspect of the ontological reality of what they are studying" (Trigger 1990, 119).

The oscillation between environmental and cultural determinism is also reflected in what John Cherry has called "a 'Great Divide' of another sort," referring to the differences between the Processual school of thought and the postmodern archaeologies of landscape (Cherry 2003, 158). The former employs scientific and quantitative methodologies to read the interrelationship between nature and human occupation, whereas the latter regards sites as systems and settings that represent the dynamics of human perception of landscape, both physically and spiritually (Cherry 2003, 158–159). Cherry rightly concludes that bringing the two broad approaches into closer dialogue will be for the benefit of scholarship.

In an effort to keep the equilibrium balanced, we shall refer here first to the physical qualities of the Cretan landscape and then elaborate on the potential spiritual and symbolic qualities of this landscape. The data in the first instance is factitious, whereas the reasoning regarding the latter is based on the assumption that there are indeed timeless cross-cultural uniformities in human responses to their surroundings, as Trigger suggests.

Before we proceed, let us consider briefly why and in what way land characteristics matter in architecture. The dialogue between the built and the natural environment starts with the path providing access to the site. Next, the land must be prepared to receive the edifice: this involves molding and shaping the soil, inflating or contracting its volumes, and bending, folding, or stretching its surface to conform to the manmade geometry it is about to admit. Then, the foundation trenches are dug, scarring the land irrevocably. Even if there comes a time when nothing is left of the building itself, the imprints of its presence will always be there in the trenches of its foundation. As the building rises above ground the intercourse between manmade space and nature also mounts up. Thereafter, they engage in a constant interplay of shapes, volumes, colors, textures, shades, and much more in their interchangeable roles of figure and background.

This close interaction between the built and the un-built is seldom given proper attention in the archaeological record, especially in their iconic representations (perhaps because architecture is perceived primarily through its masses rather than its voids). In the majority of publications today, buildings are represented in a vacuum, in black and white line drawings floating within a blank background. Very rarely is there any information regarding the undulation, the texture, the colors, and the peculiarities of the ground that has received the edifice. Such inadequately informed drawings become thereafter the basis for scholarly thinking, often without ever having experienced the way this architecture—even if in ruins—reflects in the landscape. This deficiency is best described through its opposite: the revelation, admiration, and awe expressed after having had the experience of the land. Listen, for example, to Oliver Rackham and Jennifer Moody—two scholars whose work on the Cretan landscape is seminal—talk about Crete: "A land of hollow boulders and hollow cliffs, of mountains cracked across like pebbles, of bizarre plants known nowhere else, of tremendous birds, haunted by the ghosts of surrealist beasts; nothing is quite what it seems" (Rackham and Moody 1996, xi). If nothing is quite what it seems, there is next to nothing for what has not been seen at all. One should never lose sight of the fact that human activities occur in a system of settings that includes the whole cultural landscape, manmade and natural.

The natural environment of Crete has been the stage of numerous scientific studies and research projects in recent years, and elaborate methodologies are applied to this end. Environmental data, such as pollen findings, are now used along with archaeological data to reconstruct landscapes of the past. What these studies are showing is that though deterministic views have been challenged because of overemphasizing or monopolizing the effects of the natural environment on cultural developments, there is still much to be said regarding the influence of climatic and environmental factors, such as sea level fluctuations and increased tectonism, in the changing organization of culture on Crete. Knowledge regarding the specifics of the natural environment of Crete and its physical resources in the Bronze Age is much richer today than it was in Evans's time (for an historiography of landscape research on Crete, see Gkiasta 2008). Benefiting from this accumulated knowledge, we may move on to discuss some further issues regarding the natural environment of Crete, from the stand point of this book.

## The Genius Loci and the Poetics of the Natural Environment

*If you deconstruct Greece,*
*you will in the end see an olive tree, a grapevine, and a boat remain.*
*Odysseus Elytis, "The Little Mariner" (1998, 72)*

The Aegean is considered a highly regionalized landscape, both climatically and environmentally, a trait that is reflected in its cultural expression as well. Lewis Mumford has captured eloquently this particularity by comparing the Aegean world with the Near East in terms of their lands and products: "In Crete and Greece we pass from a barley and beer culture to a wine and olive culture" (Mumford 1966, 142). To these he later adds the sea and the mountain as opposed to the river and the desert/valley.

Within the broader region Crete holds a special place: it is the largest island in the Aegean (250 km long and 12–58 km wide) and the fifth largest in the Mediterranean. Its size and diversity attribute a mainland rather than an insular character that is reflected, among others, in the choice of settlement patterns: major towns have always looked inland, whereas ports and harbors were places of dispatch rather than centers of attraction. Habitation and land appropriation were also influenced by the diversity of the coastline: to the south there is a massive wall of mountains cutting off the hinterland from the Libyan Sea, except for a few passages, narrow valleys, and gorges, such as Ierapetra to the east and the Omalos gorge to the west. The northern coast was always preferred for habitation, for it is friendlier, with rich coastal plains and deep bays that offer excellent harboring (for a concise overview, see Warren 2008, 15–18).

Crete is famous for her densely covered mountains. Like the pleats of a drop curtain extending from one end of the island to the other, they gather together into high peaks and awesome masses of stone alternating with furrows and gentle hillsides. Mountain ranges divide the island into distinct regions, while in between there are plateaus and fertile valleys, the largest one being that of Mesara to the south with 40,485 ha of cultivable land. Numerous caves—more than a thousand—carved into these mountains have offered shelter and refuge at all times, while fresh water runs abundant in springs, lakes, and rivers.

The traditional Mediterranean triad of olive, grain, and wine appeared early on Crete (Warren 2003). Olive culture was practiced already in the Late Neolithic, 1,000 years earlier than on the Greek mainland, and it may be responsible for triggering rapid cultural developments in the Early Bronze Age. Systematic production of wine, on the other hand, began during the Protopalatial period and became preeminent during the Neopalatial period, a time when oil production was also established (Rehak and Younger 1998, 102 n. 38). To the richness of the land one should add its particular fauna and very large variety of endemic plants. Above all, however, it is the temperate climate and the clarity of the air that makes the living easy and allows for the blessings of the land to be appreciated and enjoyed.

These qualities of the land of Crete, as experts tell us, have remained more or less unchanged since the Mesolithic period, except perhaps that the climate was moister until the Early Bronze Age and therefore more favorable for cultivation. Hence, much of what we see and experience today when visiting Crete, in terms of its land and climate, is more or less the same as in the Bronze Age. This facilitates and legitimizes the attempt to discuss its landscape from a phenomenological point of view; fully aware of course, that those opposed to the methodologies of phenomenology, on the basis that there are no timeless and universal human reactions toward the natural objects that surround us, will probably renounce such an endeavor as being subjective. To such an objection I would join voices once more with Harries: "[T]o hold that there is nothing that transcends human beings and speaks to them, that reality itself is mute and meaningless, means nihilism" (Harries 2000, 133). The book of nature is there for us to read as long as we keep our eyes of perception cleansed.

Fig. 12. Plain of Mochlos, from the southeast. Courtesy I. Swindale.

One of the first chapters of this book of nature for Crete could be entitled Unity in Multiplicity. Variety is indeed a strong element of the topography of the island: valleys and ravines, high mountains and soft hillsides, bays and promontories, and sandy beaches and cliffs cuddle together in constant interchange (Fig. 12). With them are interchanged forms, outlines, textures, and colors. Strong though the contrasts may be, this interchange has a certain fast rhythm that is soon captured as a characteristic trait of the landscape: what the eye and the other senses perceive at any point in time or space is pregnant with a rich variety of elements, materials, shapes, and odors. It is only in the vastness of the sea that the eye might rest, though even there the moods of Poseidon may alter the picture at any moment. Constant change and rhythm end up eventually as the unifying elements par excellence of the landscape; nothing remains the same for more than an hour's walk, and nothing is quite what it seems.

People moving on this land have to cope with its variety and adjust to quick change by activating all their senses. This, in other words, is a landscape that promotes adaptive mechanisms and flexibility. And is it not the same with its wet borders, some inhospitable and awesome and others friendly and embracing? Unlike drifting with the current of the river, seafaring asks for a bold and daring nature and a vigilant eye. Moving down from the mountain to the valley and from there to the seaside, within only a short period of time everything is in constant transformation: what the eyes can see (forms, volumes, and colors); what the hands and the feet may touch (rocks, soft soil, and warm sand); the odors enjoyed through the scents of the herbs and the mountain bushes, and the tastes savored from the fruits of the valleys and the salty air of the sea; and finally what caresses the ears, from the silence and the serenity of the mountain to the roaming sounds of the sea.

What is important is that quick though the change may be it is seldom too abrupt. Between the highest mountain peak and the level of the sea there are all possible gradations: from the nearest hillside to the farthest mountain one can distinguish all the rich shades of blue, green, and gray that guide the gaze to the far end of the horizon, emphasizing the effects of depth and perspective (Fig. 13). This variety has a further advantage: within one's field of view there are crowded numerous landmarks

Fig. 13. A rich range of shades guide the gaze to the far end of the horizon. Photo C. Palyvou.

and reference points that can help organize and memorize one's ephemeral presence there. Mountain tops and gorges, rocks that stimulate the imagination with their shapes and colors, and bays and stepped terraces that take you down to the sea all huddle in harmony within the range of vision.

A natural corollary of the variety and polymorphism of the landscape is its capacity to absorb manmade intrusions. There is one precondition: that they adhere to the basic rule of human scale. Human scale is a characteristic of the natural environment of Greece that has been praised by many intellectuals, writers, poets, architects, and artists (Giannopoulos, Pikionis, Michelis, Elytis, Henry Miller, and Le Corbusier, to name but a few). It alludes to the ability to perceive and evaluate forms, sizes, and dimensions of distant objects by reference to the human body and its parts. A landscape consisting of elements that can be easily distinguished and conceived by comparison to the human body is thought to be in accordance with human scale and therefore familiar and friendly, whereas the opposite is awesome and intimidating.

Such reading of the landscape is possible thanks to the clarity of the air that allows for a single bush to be identified from a great distance. This clarity goes hand in hand with the unique qualities of the soft light that creates an infinite array of subtle nuances and allows for all details to be pronounced. Thus, even the smallest and seemingly insignificant element attains its unique identity while retaining its relationship to the whole. There is indeed nothing vast or limitless in the natural environment, since even the largest can be analyzed into smaller components. Vincent Scully writes, "Because of the ordered variety, clarity and scale in the landscape, the human being is neither engulfed nor adrift in Greece" (1962, 9). Tasos Tanoulas adds, "even the sea is calculable through the deep bays and the islands that cluster around the shores of the mainland and, like stepping stones, permit the calculation of the distance to the land at the other end of the sea" (1991, 159). This aura of familiarity is further enhanced by the mild climate that makes outdoor living not only possible but desirable (Fig. 14).

Fig. 14. The mild climate of the Aegean promotes outdoor living. Konstantinidis 1975, fig. 2.

The harmonious coexistence of the part and the whole under the unifying power of light, the unity in multiplicity, and the human scale are indeed the very essence of many Greek landscapes, and the Cretan in particular. At the risk of sounding over simplistic, I would say that the harmonious coexistence of the part and the whole is even detected in the character of the people (today of course), in the way they are overwhelmingly open and sociable and at the same time deeply individualistic. One may also add that the above traits have affected to some extent peoples' choices of vernacular architecture. This is apparent in Minoan architecture as well: in the architectural continuum of soft gradations from big to small, high to low, in and out, light and dark, and so on; in the manner in which the distinct parts of the Palace integrate and blend into the larger entity that is the town while retaining their individuality; and in the multiple choices of movement through memorable paths. Human scale prevails in all aspects of Aegean architecture; vast is unknown and all parts of an edifice can be calculated in analogy to the human body. Minoan architecture is about open forms, loose outlines, gradated volumes, irregularity, and variety that have nothing to do with the picturesque, haphazard, or agglomerative. It is the outcome of the poetic forces of the landscape and its genius loci, and of the peoples' response to the vocation of the place (Norberg-Schulz 1980, 23), both of which remain to be explored through the pages of this book.

## A Nature Inhabited by Gods, Artists, and Geometers

That nature is inhabited by gods is as cross-cultural and timeless a belief as any. In the Minoan world, proof for this comes from the exclusive use of certain natural elements, such as peaks and caves, as religious settings; it also derives from the special role nature plays in the art of the era.

Nature is not a neutral commodity, and its qualitative differentiations inspire and stir our senses accordingly (Eliade 1961, 20; Edlund 1987, 33–36). Certain landscapes comprise elements that invoke powerful emotions and symbolic correlations: high places, summits of hills, and mountain peaks stir our senses as much as our spirit and so do their counterparts: clefts, caves, chasms, and gorges. It is in such settings that holiness resides to be revealed to humans through dreams, visions, or ecstatic experience.

For a holy place to become sacred, however—that is, for the personal revelation to be communicated and communalized, and for the ephemeral to acquire permanence—a sign is required, something that will mark the place for all to know and care (Fig. 15). This is the role of architecture: it provides strong visual means that express and eternalize the genius of the place. To quote Heidegger's perhaps most famous phrase in reference to the Greek temple, "By means of the temple, the god is present in the temple. This

Fig. 15. Baetyl and enclosure wall in the Eileithyia Cave. Betancourt et al. 2000, fig. 5.

presence of the god is in itself the extension and delimitation of the precinct as a holy precinct" (Heidegger 1997a, 119).

Temples, as a distinct architectural category of religious architecture, did not exist in the Minoan world, except for a few architecturally undifferentiated so-called shrines, as at Gournia and Malia (Hood 1971, 133–136; McEnroe 2010, 65–66). Theirs was primarily an open-air cult (Lebessi and Muhly 1990): the enclosure wall, the baetyl, the platform, and the procession road were for the Minoans the architectural signs of sanctity (Fig. 16). This is religious architecture in its genesis, born from the outside, from nature herself. It is architecture aiming primarily at appropriating the land. The third dimension, the vertical, is provided by nature by the prominent mountains of Crete and the cosmic axes they provide.

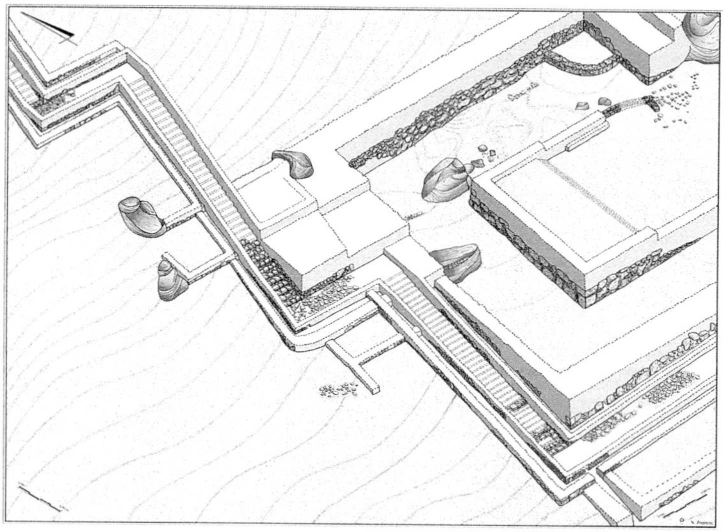

Fig. 16. Plan showing the enclosure wall, platform, and procession road of Kato Syme. Zareifis 2007, table 180.

Peaks and caves, two archetypal forms par excellence in nature, coexist as sacred places in the Minoan world and supplement each other. They represent, respectively, the qualities of the convex and the concave, the conspicuous and the hidden, the explicit and the implicit, light and darkness, and outside and inside. These complementary traits are unmistakable from the phenomenological point of view and bring out the liminal nature of Cretan ritual sites.

Sacred peaks and cosmic mountains are to be found in most ancient civilizations and also in many living cultures today.[1] Peak sanctuaries are among the few undisputable places of worship in the Minoan world and a strong manifestation of the importance of mountains in Minoan religion, as many scholars have shown them to be. Most peak sanctuaries stand out conspicuously within their broader region, even though not always literally on a peak. The apical sanctuary of Kato Syme is a fine example (Fig. 17): sublime though the mountainous environment may be, and conspicuous the presence of fresh water in the nearby spring, it is the impressive architectural appropriation of the site through enclosure walls, procession paths, and raised platforms that assigns to this isolated mountain pocket its high significance as a place where communication with the holy is enacted (Lebessi and Muhly 1990, 332–334).

The absence of any architectural sign on a mountain peak, on the other hand, only signifies that this peak has not been marked out as sacrosanct, but it may still be holy to the minds of the people (for a discussion on religion and environment, see Herva 2006). Religious meaning may be assigned to such conceptualized landscapes in other ways; for example, through ritual ascent or prohibition of access.[2]

Fig. 17. General view of the sanctuary of Kato Syme., looking southeast Zareifis 2007, pl. 14α.

Caves carved out from the masses of these mountains are the flip side of the same cosmic presence. Ellen Adams sees a pattern of hierarchy in their distribution within a region: Mt. Juktas, for example, is the only peak sanctuary at the center of a region of sacred caves. Could this be intentional so as to emphasize the supremacy of Mt. Juktas and its dominance over the area, she rightly asks (Adams 2004, 32)?

For a place to stand out in nature as sacred it needs to be distinguished from mundane habitation. As Ingrid Edlund points out, "It is, in fact, the tension between the settlements and nature, between city and country, that gives the clue to the most basic concepts of the meaning of sanctity in nature" (Edlund 1987, 30). The Juktas massif has almost no sign of human occupation other than the peak sanctuary and the temple at Anemospilia. This underlines and enhances its sanctity (Sakellarakis and Sapouna-Sakellaraki 1997, 68; Adams 2004).

Architects were not the only ones to serve the sanctity of a place in the Minoan world. On a much larger scale, it seems that geometers were also involved (architects and geometers are, of course, only conventionally referred to here as representing varying modes of involvement in the art of building). Lately, scholars have been exploring visibility issues between built and un-built elements, and have literally drawn their results from the lines of visual connections they assume to have existed between points of interest, both natural and manmade; lines that are understood as intentional and meaningful.[3] This approach is not new: it was put forth by Scully in his seminal work *The Earth, the Temple, and the Gods* (1962). In this book he deals mainly with the settings of classical Greece but also includes a brief reference to Minoan sites, pointing out the visual connection between a peak sanctuary and the Central Court of a Palace. Scully's position is that tension between special terrestrial and celestial points of focus defined placement and orientation of temples and sacred places in general (Scully 1962, 44). Evans, Graham, Shaw, Preziosi, and others have also discussed the orientation patterns of palatial compounds, attributing their standardization to cosmological parameters.[4] Lucy Goodison and Joseph Alexander MacGillivray have further affirmed the cosmological dimension by relating the design of tholos tombs and Palaces to the movement of the sun or the stars, while Marinatos adds to the picture a Solar Goddess (Goodison 2004, 342–346; MacGillivray 2004, 331, 337; Marinatos 2010).[5]

Mt. Juktas illustrates the above trenchantly: the focal point of the peak sanctuary is a deep chasm on the rock that acts as a receptacle; a magnet, drawing heavenly forces into the earth where chthonic deities reside. The presence of a cosmic axis is almost tactile. By directing the Central Court toward the peak sanctuary, the cosmic axis is appropriated by the Palace. Combined with the orientation of the Court toward the cardinal points (north, south, east, and west), the result is an absolute system of reference that links the mundane power of this world to the cosmic domain of the universe (Figs. 18, 19).

Cosmological issues go hand in hand with geometry, measurements, and calculations. There is indeed a point to be made here: in an architecture of proximity and variation, as is the Minoan, there is one element that stands out for its accurate measurements and standard orientation, and this is the Central Court of the Palace. There must be a reason for this. It is tempting to recall here Alexandre Koyré's argument that in the world of the *à-peu-près* people understood absolute order and precise measurement as belonging exclusively to the celestial sphere (1948; see this vol., Ch. 6); the precision of the Central Court—the political and religious hub of the Minoan world—may indeed reflect the precision of the celestial world and the corresponding cosmological order.

Nature, finally, is also inhabited by artists; especially so in the case of the Minoans (Fig. 20). Artists, as the eyes and the brush of a society, have represented nature in all possible media and all possible scales and context (Fig. 21): from cartographic renderings of sacred groves and mystified natural landscapes, to the individual rock or flower (see Tzachili 2011). In the absence of written evidence, art comes as a blessing and a pitfall at the same time, a book of images we must consult mindfully. Minoan art is indeed so imbued with nature that one might easily get carried away to over- (or mis-)interpretations. We need not reiterate here what scholars have read into the art of the Minoans—this is far too big a topic—or to what extent and in what way iconic landscapes are ideational landscapes. Suffice it to say that if nature in Bronze Age Crete was inhabited by gods, then artists seem to have tagged behind them everywhere, capturing their intangible presence on vases, seals, rings, and wall paintings. Art offers a unique opportunity to get a glimpse of how the specific society understood humanity's presence on earth and its interaction with nature. Yet such transparency should not be overrated, for "Nature is as wild as man's emotions will permit, and the peace of grazing animals and quiet shady groves reflect the poet's own state of mind" (Edlund 1987, 35).

Fig. 18. Aerial photo of the Palace of Knossos with Mt. Juktas on the horizon, facing south. Photo Gordon Gahan, National Geographic Creative.

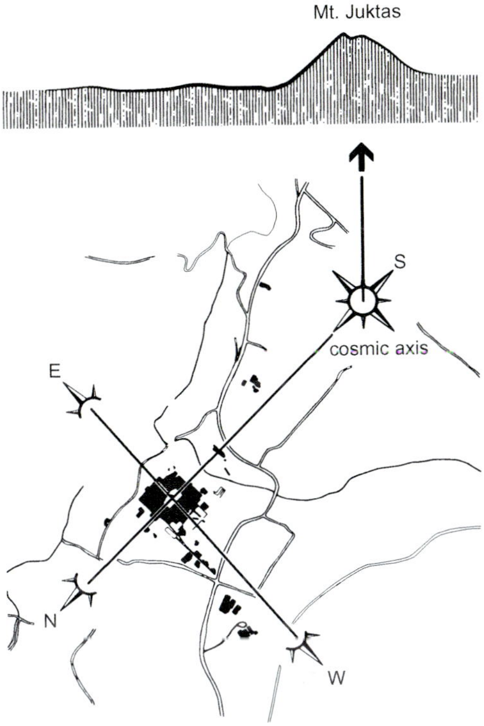


Fig. 19. The orientation of the Central Court of the Palace provides the primary cardinal directions (north, south, east, and west), whereas the peak sanctuary provides the vertical third dimension, the cosmic axis. Drawing C. Palyvou.

Fig. 20. Wall painting from the House of the Frescoes, Knossos. Courtesy Archaeological Museum of Herakleion, Hellenic Ministry of Culture and Sports–Archaeological Receipts Fund.

Fig. 21. Protopalatial krater with flowers in relief from Phaistos. Ht. 45.0 cm. Courtesy Archaeological Museum of Herakleion, Hellenic Ministry of Culture and Sports–Archaeological Receipts Fund.

## Endnotes

1 Marinatos (2010, 107–113) discusses at length the significance of sacred mountains as gates to the netherworld in Near Eastern cosmology, and she redefines the symbolic function of the Minoan Horns of Consecration as referring to sacred mountain peaks. She also points out, rightly, that the chasm on the peak sanctuary of Mt. Juktas creates an axis uniting the heavens with the world below.

2 Sacred mountains exist in almost all civilizations of all times. The most common attitude toward a sacred mountain is ritual ascent. There are, however, also cases where prohibition of access is believed to be the proper way to acknowledge sanctity, as with Mt. Kailash, one of the tallest peaks in the Himalayas.

3 For references and a critical approach that devalues the importance of visibility and landscape location in peak sanctuary cult, see Doxtater 2009; see also Briault 2007, 135–137.

4 Shaw 1973; Preziosi 1983, 501–509. For an interpretation of the north–south orientation of the Central Courts of the Palaces based on the need to provide more spaces looking east, see Palyvou 2002, 170.

5 MacGillivray (2004, 331, 337) suggests that the peak sanctuaries were astral observatories and argues that reliable orientation and timekeeping were essential to the Aegean sailors. Goodison (2004, 342–346) sees dawn alignments and east orientations as definite elements in the design of certain Minoan buildings. On a similar line of thought, it has been suggested that the tripartite shrine at Sklavokampos is possibly aligned deliberately along the spring and autumn equinoxes (Driessen and Sakellarakis 1997, 72). On ritual orientation worldwide, see Rapoport 1969, 51.

# 3 

# The Circle and the Square

*Form does not follow function. Form does not arise out of its own accord. It is the great decision of man to make a building as a cube, a pyramid, or sphere. (Hollein and Pichler 1963, 14)*

In architecture, what matters are the choices people make in shaping their world: "[T]he greater the number of possibilities, the greater the choice—but there is never any inevitability, because man can live in many kinds of structures" (Rapoport 1969, 59). These are choices based on polyparametric evaluations weighed against several alternative options. One way to approach the multivariant decision-making process, therefore, is to juxtapose basic binary options: Why and when people choose the circle, for example, instead of the square? Why adopt centrality as a design principle and not linearity? Why is zoning preferable to accretion? Why horizontality and not verticality? Why maximal instead of minimal circulatory options? These are some of the questions we shall investigate in the following pages, in the hope that they might reveal some of the prime underlying intentions—what Norberg-Schulz (1997) calls the core of architecture—which formulated the Minoan built environment.

Gestalt psychology affirms that the mind tends to simplify the visual environment in order to understand it by reducing forms to the simplest and most regular shapes, for these are easier to perceive. On the

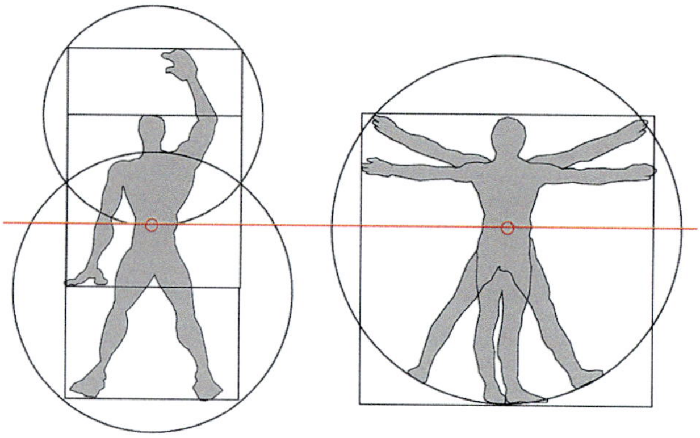

Fig. 22. Human body encapsulated in circles and squares: *Modular Man* (left) and Vitruvian man (right). Left: after Le Corbusier 1954, fig. 100; right: after Leonardo da Vinci.

same account, regular shapes are preferred in creating the built environment. The circle and the square are two regular shapes par excellence (the latter as one of the infinite polygons that can be inscribed in the circle). They both encapsulate the human body in action and are present in the very beginnings of architecture (Fig. 22).

In the Age of Enlightenment, in the context of the nascent anthropology and the interest in the primitive, the question of form in incipient settlement was raised to a major topic of debate. To this day, architectural historians remain passionately engaged in an intellectual tug-of-war over the primacy of house form: What came first, the circle or the square? Is there an evolutionary line of transition from one to the other? And is there some meaning in these choices?

In this discourse, the circle and the square have been correlated to the cave and the forest, respectively. Most scholars, starting with Vitruvius, accept both as essential to the genesis of the paradigmatic house, but just as many acknowledge a certain precedence of one form over the other (Harries 2000, 114–115). Marc-Antoine Laugier (1755, 11–12), one of the exponents of the rationalist philosophy of the Enlightment, is well known for his treatise on the prevalence of the forest concept and hence the rectilinear form (quoted in Harries 2000, 112). In the long run, however, it seems that the cave and the circle prevailed. Norberg-Schulz, for one, acknowledges the circle as the primal spatial element, on the basis that the vertical-horizontal binary of the rectilinear forms corresponds to a more advanced ordering principle (1997, 125). This assumption was corroborated by anthropological research, especially through Kent Flannery's work, which affirmed the relationship between pit-house architecture and incipient settlement worldwide (Flannery 2002).[1] The debate, however, is far from being resolved and is still quite heated at times, as is evident in Flannery's strong response "Will the Real Model Please Stand Up?" to Saidel's "Round House or Square?" where he expresses his disappointment for having been largely misinterpreted (Flannery 1993; Saidel 1993).[2]

Coming to our own case study and the primal choices that shaped the architecture of Minoan Crete, we may note that rectilinear forms triumphed over curvilinear from the very beginning, and with them the post-and-beam structural system. This is not to say that the circle was excluded from architectural practice, but it is very questionable if it ever played a primal role in domestic architecture. It was used conspicuously, on the other hand, in funerary architecture, and it is this choice that we shall examine below.

The primordial round or elliptic hut made of perishable materials such as wood and reeds and sometimes of stone, is a common feature of many human landscapes, and it was presumably present in Crete as well in prehistory as it is still today. Sporadic traces of such structures of an early date (Final Neolithic [FN]–Early Minoan [EM]) have been found at Phaistos, Petras, and other sites (Di Tonto 2011, 16 n. 6, 17 n. 7). These huts, however, had no impact on the architectural history of the island; rectilinear stone houses have always been the norm.[3]

Fig. 23. Elevated circular platform at Knossos, from the northwest. Warren 1984a, pl. 31:c.

Circular structures of non-funerary function are very limited in Crete (Fig. 23). Most conspicuous are the circular elevated platforms, which are believed to have served dancing performances alluding to Ariadne's dance (Warren 1984a; see also Cadogan 2006, 452–454). Such dancing floors also appear in the form of clay models (Fig. 24). There is also a small number of cylindrical subterranean pits of varying sizes, interpreted as water reservoirs, cisterns, swimming pools, silos, or potholes for planting trees (Figs. 25–27), to which we may add the so-called Hypogaeum at Knossos, of an early date (EM III or MM IA). It is cut in the soft rock and is approached via a spiral stairway. It is impressive in size (8.32 m in diameter, 15 m deep), and it has been interpreted as store pit, guardhouse, or cistern (Wilson 1994).

Fig. 24. Male figurines set on a circular platform with low parapet and Horns of Consecration from the Kamilari tholos tomb. Ht. 17.5; diam. base 14.3 cm. Courtesy Archaeological Museum of Herakleion, Hellenic Ministry of Culture and Sports–Archaeological Receipts Fund.

Round structures built above ground are to be found at the Palace of Malia. They are arranged in two rows of four units each, all of the same diameter (ca. 4 m). Only the lower part of the stone walls survive, with no indication of doors, while five of them had a central pillar. The form of their superstructure is unknown, but it is commonly assumed that they were domed (in which case the pillar is an oddity) and that they served as silos or granaries (Fig. 28). It is important to emphasize that this is a unique case of circular structures of a non-funerary function, and, if indeed domed, they are an early and rare example of this sort in Crete.[4]

For a culture that has no obvious tradition in circular buildings it comes as a surprise to find that they were nevertheless represented in art (Figs. 29, 30). In the case of two-dimensional media, such as seals, there are some doubts as to if a circular building is indeed depicted (McEnroe 2007, 7). The three-dimensional

Fig. 25. Circular pit or kouloura at Knossos. Evans 1921–1935, II, fig. 382.

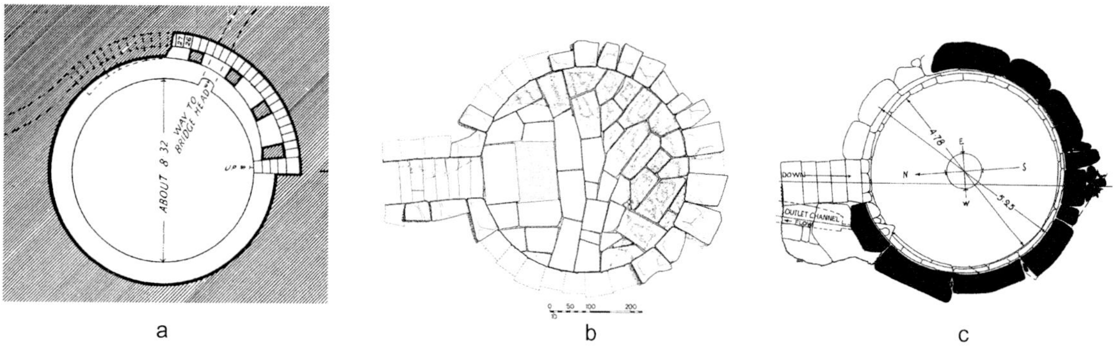


Fig. 26. Circular subterranean structures: (a) hypogaeum at Knossos (after Evans 1921–1935, I, fig. 74); (b) cistern at Zakros (courtesy L. Platon, Archive of the Zakros Excavations); (c) cistern at Archanes (after Sakellarakis and Sapouna-Sakellaraki 1997, plan 20).

Fig. 27. Cistern at Zakros. Courtesy L. Platon, Archive of the Zakros Excavations. Archive of the Zakros Excavations.

Fig. 28. Silos at the Palace of Malia, from the east. Davaras 1989a, fig. 8; © Hellenic Ministry of Culture and Sports–Archaeological Receipts Fund.

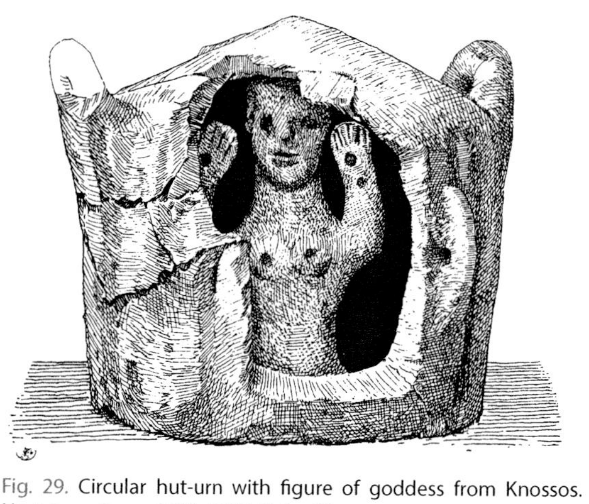

Fig. 29. Circular hut-urn with figure of goddess from Knossos. Ht. 8.5 cm. Evans 1921–1935, II, fig. 63.

Fig. 30. Circular hut model from Archanes. Ht. 18.0 cm. Sakellarakis and Sapouna-Sakellaraki 1991, fig. 9; courtesy Ekdotike Athenon S.A.

cylindrical models, known as hut-urns, are of a much later date (LM IIIC). They belong to a time corresponding to major cultural changes in Postpalatial Crete. Evans, followed by Robin Hägg, believed firmly that these objects refer to a primitive form of circular hut (Evans 1921–1935, II, 128–139; Hägg 1990, 101); that hut-urns, in other words, represent an archetypical primitive house, even though there is no material evidence for this. Rebecca Mersereau suggests that these objects were intended to make an abstract architectural reference rather than to represent a specific building type that may or may not have existed, and that they derive from the contemporary ceramic repertoire (Mersereau 1993). Vassilis Petrakis, on the other hand, moves away from the house prototype and sees the corbel-vaulted tholos tombs with circular ground plans as their only possible prototypes, at a time when an imagery of burial practices was being developed (2006, 209).

Evans embraced the view that architecture had developed from a circular hut to a rectangular building and saw in Minoan architecture the missing link between the two. Richard Dawkins too was rather biased toward the primacy of the circle: excavating at Magasa, the first Neolithic building to be found, he noted that it was "striking to find a square-built house at this period, when it might have been supposed that nothing more advanced than wattled huts yet existed" (Dawkins, Hawes, and Bosanquet 1904–1905, 263). McEnroe, on the other hand, rightly suggests that this freestanding structure, consisting of two very large spaces, may have been a sheepfold and not a house (2007, 4).

The building that provoked the most heated discussions in this respect is the so-called oval-house at Chamaizi, excavated by Stephanos Xanthoudidis in 1906 (see Fig. 111:a). Its curvilinear periphery stands out among other Minoan buildings. Its interior arrangement, however, is rectilinear and has a perfectly rectangular court at its center. Duncan Mackenzie opposed the idea that this was the missing link between the primitive circular hut and the Palace (because of its Central Court), pointing out that there was no evidence for circular huts in Crete and that it was like any other rectangular building but adjusted to the contours of the hilltop (1907–1908, 415–422). The site was reexamined by Costis Davaras in 1971, and he showed that there was ample space on the hilltop for the building to acquire a rectangular form if so desired. Moreover, there were several earlier phases below of the same curvilinear form, leading Davaras to the conclusion that this was some kind of local tradition or ad hoc choice (1972).[5]

One might rightly ask why all this fuss about the circle and the square? To tackle this question we must accept that forms are not neutral; that forms evoke emotional associations and convey meanings, some of which come natural and are ubiquitous, for they are deeply rooted in the common sensory experience of humanity (Pallasmaa 2005a, 24–44) while others are culturally generated. The circle, for example, is an introverted centralized figure that is normally stable and self-centering,

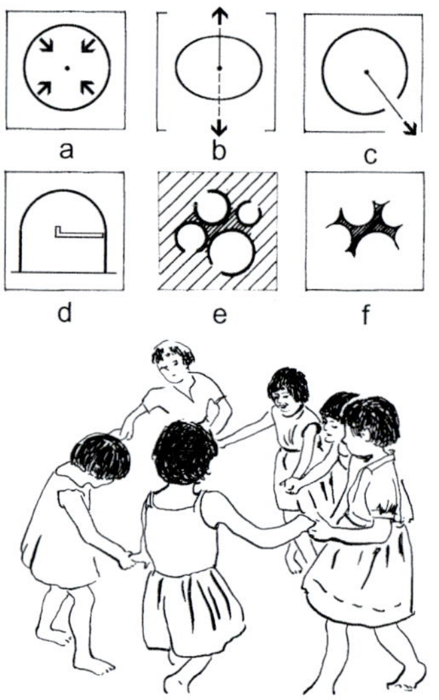


Fig. 31. Main attributes of the circle (top), showing its value as a social expression of equality and coexistence through dancing and playing (bottom). Drawing C. Palyvou.

though in association with other forms it may acquire a kind of rotary movement (Figs. 31, 32). All its parts are equal in relation to the center, and it is only the center that is privileged (Fig. 31:a). Furthermore, it has no orientation other than the vertical axis at its center (Fig. 31:b; a kind of axis mundi) and no direction except for the line that connects the center to the break of the circle at the entrance (Fig. 31:c).[6] It is a passive/static form that cannot easily evolve into something else, neither by subtraction nor division (Fig. 31:d), nor by addition (when circular units are attached to one another they retain their autonomy and their character, and they create awkward leftover spaces in between; Fig. 31:e, f).

A question arising is to what extent properties attributed to abstract geometric shapes can have timeless inherent values to all mankind, projected as far back as the Minoans. The answer, I believe, is given by the Minoans themselves in their very decision to put aside the circle for funerary use only (Fig. 33). There is no doubt, to my understanding, that this was a deliberate act of symbolic distinction, and it is therefore significant in its own right. First, by restricting the correlation between a particular form and a specific function, the communicative symbolic power of this form was highly accentuated. Second, the choice of form for the specific symbolism was very effective, taking into account the semantics of the circle presented above. The houses of the dead were thus symbolically differentiated from those of the living, and death was celebrated through its exclusive correlation with the introverted, static form of the circle.

The symbolic power of the circle is further emphasized by the contrast between the orthogonal graves and the circular outline of the tomb (Fig. 34). This is even more patent in the case of orthogonal cist burials rounded by low enclosure walls, as at Early Bronze Age Lefkada and later at Mycenae. The circular enclosure clearly has no other function than to delimit and distinguish the area allocated to the dead. On the same account, symbolism may be the reason behind the choice of form of the Mesara tombs, instead of external loans and imitations of hypothetical circular houses.[7] The fact that there are also rectangular tombs on Crete does not affect the meaning of the circular ones; they too aim at the manipulation of ancestral memory, albeit through a different symbol-making procedure.[8]

Fig. 32. Clay figurines of female dancers from Palaikastro. Ht. 11.9–13.0 cm. Courtesy Archaeological Museum of Herakleion, Hellenic Ministry of Culture and Sports–Archaeological Receipts Fund.

The power of semantic relations in architecture has been adverted by many scholars. Alberti, for one, prescribed that the most perfect forms, such as the circle, should be reserved for the church, and that public buildings in general should be carried out in the strictest conformity of formal principles. Deviations, on the other hand, were not only acceptable but also recommended for houses (Alberti [1755] 1955, IX, viii). Such conventions—very important and effective for the coherence of a community—are rather downgraded today; to paraphrase Harries, not only the "accident of location" but also the "accident of function" seems to be irrelevant in the choice of form in some contemporary post-modernist architecture (Harries 2000, 172–173). Norberg-Schulz goes as far as attributing the failure today of many architectural works to the very fact that these relations have been forgotten, and he recalls bitterly that "most of the great epochs of the past have taken it for granted that certain forms have to be reserved for certain tasks" (Norberg-Schulz 1997, 88–89 [on Alberti], 107 n. 95). Adolph Loos, to add yet another sensitive voice to this discussion, describes trenchantly the semantic power of architecture: "If we were to come across a mound in a woods, six foot long by three foot wide, with the soil piled up in a pyramid, a sombre mood would come over us and a voice inside us would say, 'There is someone buried here.' That is architecture" (Loos 2007). One might perhaps imagine a similar response for the Minoans (and the Mycenaeans) when confronted with the circle and the dome.

Fig. 33. Aerial view of tholos tomb at Kamilari. La Rosa 1992a, fig. 14.2.

The other pole of the binary in question, the square, is the basis of all rectangles, for they can all be considered variations of the square through accretion or division (Fig. 35:a–d). The square is a rational shape with an apparent center, almost as powerful as that of the circle (Fig. 35:a). It too is static and neutral, though its corners may be perceived as thrusting outward (Fig. 35:c). It has no prevalent direction, yet it is clearly oriented in relation to the four cardinal points. In comparison to the square, rectangles are dynamic forms, for they are both oriented and directional (Fig. 35:b). Furthermore, rectilinear boxlike forms may easily evolve into composite compounds through accretion, both horizontally and vertically, or by dividing their inner space into units that still retain the properties of the rectangle (Fig. 35:d). Thus, they facilitate evolution from the single-room house to a complex multi-space building, and, most importantly, they almost invite the construction of an upper floor. The latter was an early choice in the Aegean, attested already at the end of the third millennium B.C., and it remained a typical feature of Aegean architecture throughout the Bronze Age (Marthari 1997). The rectangle, in other words, is an organic form, easily adjustable to the needs of the living, as opposed to the static, finite form of the circle that alludes to archetypal elements such as the cave, the womb, and the heavens.[9]

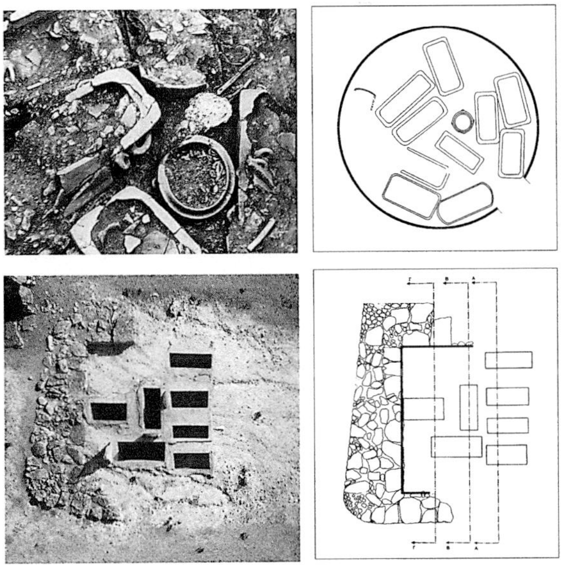

Fig. 34. Note the combination of circles and orthogonal shapes in funerary architecture at Archanes. Top: Tholos Tomb Gamma (Sakellarakis and Sapouna-Sakellaraki 1997, fig. 134, plan 45); bottom: Mycenaean burials (Sakellarakis and Sapouna-Sakellaraki 1997, fig. 141, plan 48).

In Minoan architecture quadrangular forms triumph, and among the infinite

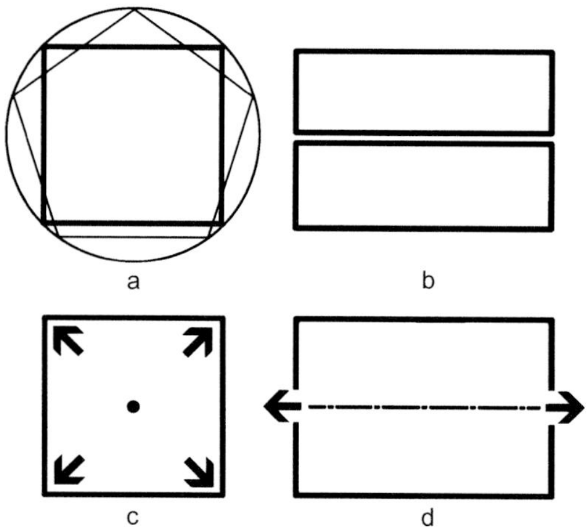


Fig. 35. Main attributes of the square. Drawing C. Palyvou.

variety of rectangles and polygons the square holds a special place. This is attested both in domestic and formal architecture, as we shall see in the following chapters. It is most apparent in the Room with a Central Column, the traditional hub of the Minoan house, and in the square-within-a-square design concept that Preziosi first discerned (see Fig. 109; Preziosi 1983, 26–27). It also exists, in a latent, albeit powerful manner, in the design process of the Palace: in the way the Central Court, the hub of the Minoan world, is defined by the act of dividing a square into two equal rectangles. Last but not least, the predominance of the square had a definitive role in the choice of centrality as a design principle, instead of linearity. These fascinating topics of forms and choices will be further elaborated in the following chapters, especially in discussing principles of design in Minoan architecture.

## Endnotes

1 According to his latest research, sedentary life in many parts of the ancient world began with settlements of circular huts, like those of the preceramic Near East and, closer to the Aegean, the settlement of Choirokoitia in Cyprus.

2 Settlements of circular huts—or "compounds" as Flannery prefers to call them—were later replaced by rectilinear houses corresponding to village societies. Whereas Saidel and others see in this transition a linear evolution and a catalyst for this to happen, however, Flannery is more interested in the social and economic differences between the two, based on type of storage commodities and family bonds (1993).

3 Not all scholars are of the same opinion. In her meticulous and exhaustive research on circular buildings in the prehistoric Aegean, Yiannouli attributes special value to the perishable nature of the hut, noting that this was not due only to technical failure but also to a cultural choice based on semantics revolving around the notion of earth (2009, 90–91). She then argues in favor of the primacy of the circle, though admitting that there is very little in the way of archaeological material data, and she concludes that pit-house architecture is related to incipient Neolithic settlement and sedentism in the Aegean, as it was in other parts of the world.

4 Schmid is doubtful about the dome of the Malian silos and suggests that the central pillar was a low structure probably holding a raised timber floor (pers. comm., August 2005). Preziosi, on the other hand, sees similarities with the silos found in Egypt and suggests influence from Egypt (1983, 108–109, nn. 174, 175). It is worth mentioning here that the term dome refers to the house, regardless of the form, whereas tholos refers to a building with a circular plan, regardless of its function (Palyvou 2009b, 40).

5 For discussion and references on Chamaizi, see McEnroe 2007, 5–6 and Lenuzza 2011.

6 Frederick 2007. For the possible relation of this line with the dawn light in the Mesara tombs, see Goodison 2004, 340–342.

7 Yiannouli is of a different opinion: "The Messara tholoi . . . may be seen as preserving a tradition of round building alive and flourishing in Minoan Crete, by transporting it to funerary grounds, in sharp contrast to the rest of the Aegean" (2009, 97). I see no convincing reason, however, why the primordial form of a house in the shape of a circular hut that has failed to appear in the archaeological record may lie behind the choice of form of the Mesara tombs.

8 Cadogan, discussing the house-type mortuary complex at Myrtos Pyrgos, remarks that this was an elite choice, and that by denying differences between dead and living they created "a focus of the resurgent, nucleated community" (2011, 46).

9 The qualities of the rectangular forms led Acar to formulate a cosmological argument, according to which the change from the circular hut to the rectangular building reflects the development from temporary to permanent settlement: "[S]edentary settlement eventually aligns the four corners of the house with the four corners of a universe that is perceived from a stationary point" (2001, 13).

# 4

# Boundaries and Connectors

## Insulation and Communication

*Civilization is . . . the insulation created by man, an artefact which mediates between himself and the world of nature. (Renfrew 1972, 13)*

Architecture, as one of the artifacts of civilization, fits very well the above definition: it is indeed the insulation humans created to protect themselves both physically, from climatic extremes and external threats, and spiritually, from being exposed to or contaminated by the other (Fig. 36). All that separates, however, is at the same time a means of communication in that it functions as a sign. Architecture, therefore, should be appreciated for its protective, utilitarian nature as much as for its communicative properties. The same is true for the cloths that enwrap our bodies.

Physical protection is of primary importance: the very existence of architecture "is founded in the deficiency of the world, first apparent in the need for physical shelter" (Harries 2000, 195). In Oscar Wilde's provocative tone, "If Nature had been comfortable, mankind would never have invented architecture" (1909, 4). The deficiency alluded to in both instances is that of human nature. This handicap is also acknowledged in Greek mythology, in the very creation of mankind: when Prometheus's anguished plea to his father Zeus to improve the pitiful, fragile creature he had created was turned down, he took fire from Hephaistos (energy)

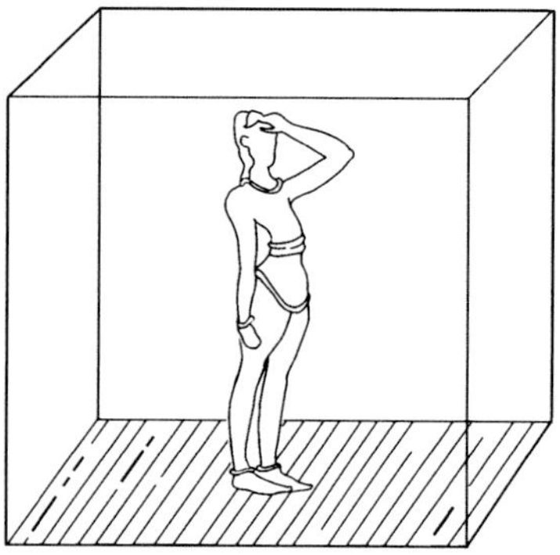

Fig. 36. Architecture is the insulation humans created to protect themselves both physically and spiritually; clothing is another such means of insulation. Drawing C. Palyvou.

and skillful wisdom from Athena (technical knowledge) and gave them to humans as a remedy to their shortcomings so that they would develop the arts of civilization, and in doing so acquire the means for the insulation and protection they lacked, a gift for which Prometheus paid dearly.[1]

Delimitation for insulation, protection, and communication is the archetypal goal and the true origin of architecture (Norberg-Schulz 1996, 412). Delimitation is the marking of boundaries; it is Daidalos drawing on the ground a circle to designate the place where Ariadne was to dance. A boundary, Heidegger explains, is "not that at which something stops but, as the Greeks recognized, the boundary is that from which something begins its presencing" (Heidegger 1997b, 105). The boundary, therefore, gives meaning to that which is contained and at the same time communicates this meaning to those beyond.

Boundaries come in a variety of forms: they may be linear, marked on the ground with a painted line, a row of stones, or a ditch; planar, such as a wall, a row of trees, or a curtain; or they may consist of single markers (Fig. 37). An example of the latter are the stone stelae with the word ΗΟΡΟΣ (limit) inscribed on their surfaces placed at the entry points to the Athenian Agora as markers defining the area beyond which certain citizens were excluded. For the Minoan world, a case of this sort may have been the mason's marks that seem to have denoted the boundaries of certain areas within the Palace at Knossos (Begg 2004, 220–222). On a different scale, the peak sanctuaries may be an instance of single markers delimitating a region. Boundaries may even be intangible, as the acoustic boundary surrounding the sacred oak tree at Dodona, created by chains emitting a sound that kept evil spirits away. In fact, immaterial boundaries can be most effective, as in a sacred grove that is respected solely through fear and awe toward its divine proprietor and its undisputed, omnipresent, and albeit invisible power of control.

Fig. 37. Archetypal boundary: a stone fence on a Cycladic island. Konstantinidis 1975, fig. 43.

The rich variety of boundaries should not escape our attention when dealing with spatial issues. In the context of this book, however, we shall narrow the discussion to those boundaries that are immediately understood as partaking in the creation of architectural space—that is, to the three planes that encapsulate the human body in action:

(1) The floor, which mediates between our body and the earth we live on.

(2) The walls that define the area of action and therefore adhere to the verticality of the body.

(3) The roof, which is the overhead plane that completes the encapsulation and mediates between the humans and the sky, where most cultures place the dwellings of their gods.

The floor and the roof correspond to the ground and the sky, while "in the wall . . . earth and sky meet" (Norberg-Schulz 1980, 66). Because of this close correlation between nature and manmade space, the treatment of the three planes can be quite revealing as to the ideology of a specific society in regard to the forces of nature. Intentional breaks or anomalies in the boundaries, for instance, are meaningful (on the deeper meaning of "breaking the roof," see Eliade 1961, 57–58, 172–179). At the Erechtheion on the Athenian Acropolis, there is a gap on the elegant marble paving of the floor of the north porch, as if some slabs are missing. This, however, was clearly intentional: there should be no boundary, no isolation at this specific point, because this was allegedly where Poseidon hit the ground to produce water when competing with Athena for the patronage of the city (the signs of his trident are supposedly visible on the exposed rock). That there is a corresponding gap on the ceiling above comes as no surprise. The breaks in the two boundaries—floor and ceiling—allow for an axis mundi to be empowered at this specific spot, commemorating Poseidon's divine act of marking it with his trident. A similar break in the ceiling is attested in a cylindrical clay model of a hut from Archanes. Such annihilation of the boundaries provides undisputable proof of the function of architecture as insulator (see Fig. 30).

## Bounding Elements

### *Floors*

Floors, in archaeological contexts, are valuable boundaries of space as much as of time. From the architectural point of view, floors declare a person's appropriation of a piece of land. They function as insulators from the rough surface of nature, an attribute that is further acknowledged by the foundation deposits and rituals addressed to the chthonic elements residing at the other side.

A floor is architecture in its own right. A threshing floor, for instance, like the one depicted in the Miniature Frieze from Akrotiri, though nothing but a floor, is nevertheless a strong boundary in itself in that it defines a piece of land as other than the surrounding ground (Fig. 38). Its circular form, specific dimensions, and hard pavement are straightforward inferences to "form follows function." When it is in use, the bodies of humans and animals in action define the intangible third dimension (very much like the body of Ariadne dancing on

Fig. 38. Modern threshing floor (left) and threshing floor depicted in the Miniature Frieze from Akrotiri, Thera (right). Left: Konstantinidis 1975, fig. 23; right: Doumas 1992, fig. 28.

the circular platform). Even when not in use, the threshing floor is a strong marker in the landscape, a sign of humanity's benign presence in the natural environment. Similarly, any distinguished paved area is a marker and a boundary in itself: a paved platform in a cemetery; a paved rectangle at the center of an earthen floor; or the raised causeways that cut through a loosely defined public area.

Floor treatment can play an important role in the manipulation of a boundary. In Minoan domestic architecture, for example, the lobby at the main entrance of a building is almost always paved. In the less elaborate houses this is probably the only area at ground floor level with such floor treatment. Even though practical reasons dictated choice of material in the first place, such as the need to protect from wear, this differentiated treatment emphasizes the point of penetration into the house and adds to the liminal character of the entrance lobby. At the other end of the spectrum, the lavish paving of almost all ground floor rooms in some elaborate houses (e.g., Nirou Chani) creates a strong, coherent, and uniform boundary that dissociates the totality of the house from the dusty world beyond.

In some cases the pavement of the entrance lobby extends outside onto the public space in front of the door. This may not be simply "to embellish parts of the street" (Driessen and Schoep 1995, 657) but a way to mark the entrance to the house and highlight its performance as a place of transition between public and private domains. By spilling out, so to speak, what belongs to the private domain, a transitional area is symbolically created, providing a sign announcing the entrance. A similar treatment is seen at the West House of Akrotiri, Thera, where the elaborate pavement of Room 5 invades Room 3, creating a preparatory space for those entering Room 5, announcing the importance of this room (see Fig. 49). A similar effect can be achieved through the application of color or whitewash, practiced commonly in vernacular architecture, treatments that unfortunately would have left no traces in prehistoric ruins (Fig. 39).

An instance of anomaly of floor treatment is the Lustral Basin (see this vol., Ch. 5): the discontinuance of the floor level is clearly meant to function as a discontinuance of the boundary—that is, as a sign of an abrupt change in the relationship between manmade space and the natural ground it has appropriated. The downward direction of this change is perceived as the earth acting as a magnet that draws toward her the manmade structure; hence, the chthonic character attributed to the Lustral Basin by Evans (Evans 1921–1935, III, 12).

The opposite, a protruding floor, is equally meaningful. This is the case, for example, with the raised causeways. The protrusion accentuates the visibility of the causeways and assists in the perception of architectural space by literally raising movement above pause and arrest. Such small protrusions, however, can also be experienced as obstacles, reinforcing the boundary effect. Floor protrusions are also attested in the form of slightly raised pavements at the center of certain rooms, as in the House of the Frescoes at Knossos. Most conspicuous are the raised platforms found in open public spaces, such as those at Kastelli and Galatas (Rethemiotakis 1992–1993, 36–37); here symbolic connotations of distinction and sublimity are patent.

Fig. 39. Walking through the narrow alleys of this Cycladic settlement on Mykonos, one feels almost obliged to avoid stepping on the colorful pavement that defines the limits of the private domain. Lavvas and Philippidis, eds., 1983–1991, II, fig. 34; courtesy Melissa Publishing House.

Minoan architecture has a rich array of floor treatment: floors are made of beaten soil, paved with stone slabs or terracotta tiles, covered with lime plaster (with or without color and decoration), or made of timber beams and planks (Shaw 2009, 107–108). Floors of beaten soil are weak boundaries in that they do not contrast strongly with the ground itself (the floor of nature). Lime-plastered floors are stronger boundaries, but their fragile nature implies restricted and cautious use; paved floors make the strongest boundaries. A type of floor treatment peculiar to the Minoan world is the strip design, as Shaw calls it, found at Archanes, Galatas, Zakros, Palaikastro, and Pseira (Shaw 2009, 150–151). These floors consist of slightly projecting strips of lime plaster forming grid patterns that were filled in with some perishable material.

Prestige and monumentality are often summoned as the reasons behind an elaborate floor treatment, mainly because of the time and labor involved and the aesthetic appeal of the materials. But prestige and monumentality are not the only issues at play. In the case of paved floors, for example, why emphasize the center in one instance and choose a grid pattern in another (see Fig. 41)? Materials and labor consumption are more or less the same in both instances. The answer lies in the communicative symbolic attributes of the center and the grid, respectively: through the appropriate choice of floor treatment, the corresponding attributes are passed on to the whole of the room, enhancing its function and meaning. An analysis of the various modes of floor treatment, therefore, is crucial to the discussion of what architecture has to offer.

The most common floor treatments follow (Fig. 40).[2]

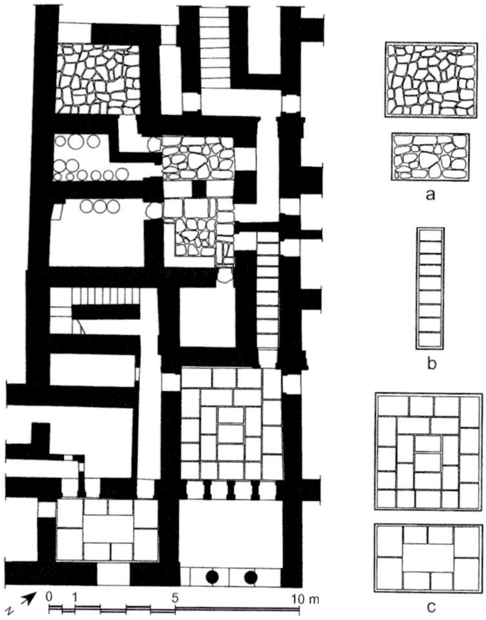


Fig. 40. Plan of Nirou Chani (left) and three types of floor treatment utilized there (right): (a) neutral; (b) directional; and (c) delimiting. After Evans 1921–1935, II.1, fig. 167.

(1) Neutral, or the carpet effect, such as a floor made of beaten soil, a plastered floor, a mosaic floor, or a floor paved in a crazy pattern (Fig. 40:a).

(2) Directional, such as the raised causeways or a floor paved with rectangular slabs laid in rows (common in corridors). These patterns promote movement (Fig. 40:b).

(3) Delimiting, in which case the floor, and hence the room, is autonomous and self-contained (for example, pavements that emphasize the center of the floor) (Fig. 40:c).

(4) Illusionary, when treated in imitation of something else. This is the case of painted floors in imitation of rug designs or stone pavement, for example.

The delimiting floor is by far the most common in many buildings of the Neopalatial period (Fig. 41). It evokes a centripetal, self-contained, and highly concentrated ambience of space. It comes in a variety of forms, the most common consisting of rectangular slabs defining the central part of the room, surrounded by concentric zones of similar slabs. In other instances only the central part of the floor is marked out with rectangular slabs or terracotta tiles (Zakros, Palaikastro, and Malia; Shaw 2009, 139–140), in sharp contrast to the surrounding zone of beaten soil or lime plaster.[3] At Nirou Chani, Room 5, the central area of the floor is further distinguished through color: it is laid with slabs of dark limestone against a crème-white peripheral zone. In all these cases the central part of the floor emerges as a distinct figure against a neutral background. Such treatment activates centripetal forces and highlights centrality. It also promotes pause, as opposed to the neutral and the directional types of floor that invite movement.

### *Walls*

Zucker writes of a German Romantic novelist, Jean Paul, who came up with a story that describes,

> [A] poor poet who inherits a piece of land but has not the money to build a house. All he can afford is a wooden wall with a window cut into it [Fig.

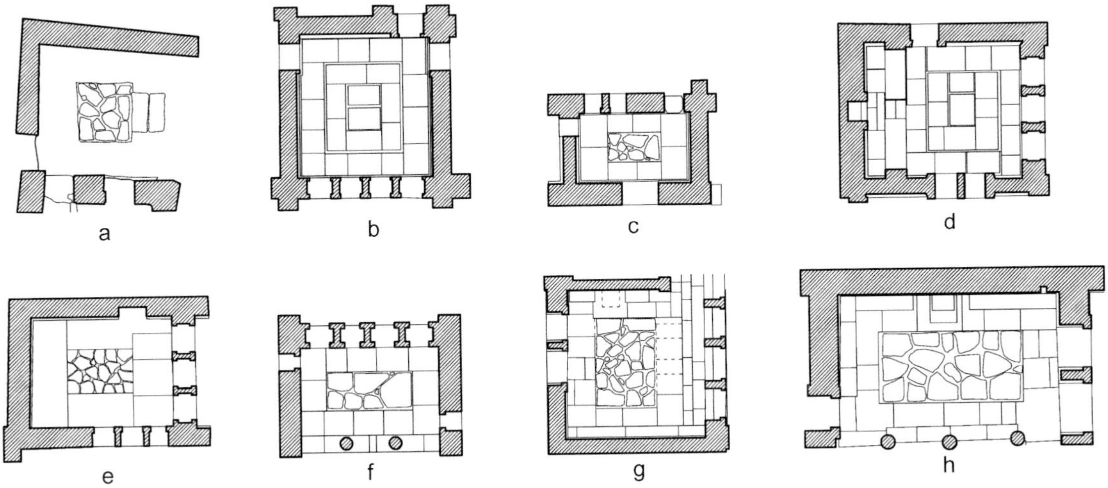


42]. This wall he puts up in the middle of his land, seats himself behind the window, and now enjoys what was before simply nature under the aesthetic aspect of a landscape. . . . The poet behind his houseless window has performed the primeval act of architecture, the separation of an inside from an outside. . . . This effect he accepts as the substitute for the house he cannot afford. (Arnheim, Zucker, and Watterson 1966, 7)

Fig. 41. Examples of delimiting floors in Neopalatial architecture: (a) Stratigraphical Museum, Knossos (after Warren 1984b, 50); (b, c) Nirou Chani (after Evans 1921–1935, II.1, fig. 167); (d) House of the Chancel Screen, Knossos (after Evans 1921–1935, II.2, fig. 224); (e) Royal Villa, Knossos (after Evans 1921–1935, II.2, fig. 227); (f) Hagia Triada (after La Rosa 1997, fig. 1); (g, h) Throne Room, Knossos (after Hood and Taylor 1981).

Such is the power of the wall as the archetypal architectural element for bounding space, both literally and symbolically.

The strong expressive power of the wall lies in its capacity to present in a concrete form the existential struggle between an attacking exterior and a secure interior (Thiis-Evensen 1987, 116). The openings determine the degree and character of the control of penetration. Walls conform to the erectness of the human body and define the third dimension of space in accordance with its use. Dimensions, proportions, and texture are therefore of great importance.

Wall treatment in Minoan architecture is rich in variations: there are walls plastered with clay or lime mortars, white or painted; walls with timber linear elements punctuating their surfaces; walls with dados emphasizing their base; and walls made of ashlar, dividing the surface into horizontal stripes. There are also walls with recesses or protrusions and with cornices and ornaments, and there are massive or blank walls as are there highly perforated ones. The topic is far too diverse to be presented in its own right. Throughout the present work, and especially in Chapters 8 and 9, there is ample discussion on the formal properties of walls, especially as facades of buildings. Here, we shall take the opportunity to discuss a specific category of walls: fortifications and enclosure walls.

Fig. 42. Wall-and-window, representing in architecture the primeval act of separation or communication between the interior and exterior space. Drawing C. Palyvou.

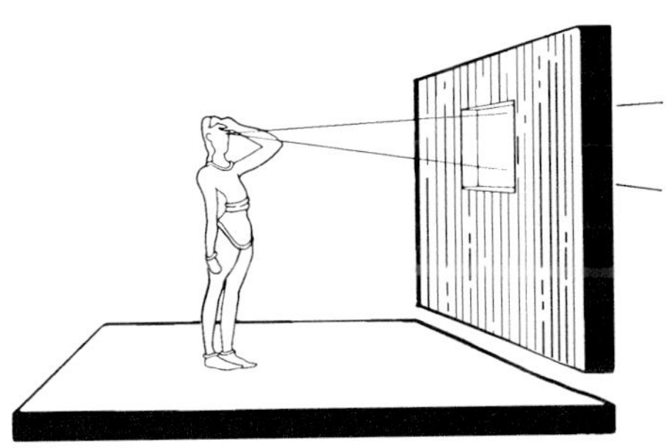

A fortification wall is a boundary par excellence and, as such, it has attracted the interest of intellectuals of all kinds. Franz Kafka, to name but one, in *The Great Wall of China*, talks about a wall built on suspicion, whose role, while purportedly being to keep out the other, is in fact to bond those protected by it and to fan allegiance to the emperor (Kafka 1983, 235–248). The role of the wall is indeed primarily to "lend . . . a sense of identity to what is enclosed within its boundaries, while engendering a sense of alterity towards what is outside" (Leach 1997a, xix). Such is the importance and power of the fortification wall as an identity symbol that Homer has Ulysses looking in vain for the city walls of the Cyclops as the symbol of the presence of civilized humanity.

The Minoan world is famous (or should we say notorious?) for its absence of fortifications walls, at least during the Neopalatial era. In the preceding EM and MM periods there are indications of defensive systems, though there is still much ambiguity as to their exact nature. Driessen has compiled the relevant information in a comprehensive article dealing with access systems (Driessen 1995b), which I selectively reference and comment on below.

(1) Hagia Photia is a MM I fortress; it has a uniquely regular plan inscribed in a clearly defined wall with bastions (Fig. 43). This is indeed an undisputable case of a fortification wall and a unique instance of an enclosure wall, referring however to a building compound and not a settlement. Driessen associates it with the Cyclades where fortification walls (of settlements) have a long tradition (1995b, 71).

(2) Myrtos Pyrgos, also of Protopalatial date, preserves impressive terrace walls with at least one tower (possibly two). Gaps near the towers have been interpreted as gates that were later walled. It is located at the periphery of the settlement, at the base of the hillside, and it is therefore understood as protecting the settlement (Driessen 1995b, 71–72).

(3) Malia presents another possible instance of a Protopalatial enclosure wall, possibly protecting the settlement. Today partially visible, it was traced to a significant length (175 m). A paved causeway led from the southeast entrance of the Palace eastward toward the entrance gate of this wall; it was dismantled in the Neopalatial period (Driessen 1995b, 72–73).

(4) Petras preserves large walls of the Protopalatial period, conspicuously located at the foot of the hill, including a robust structure, bastion, or tower. According to the excavator, they were probably retaining walls but "could fulfill also a defensive role" (Tsipopoulou 2002, 137–138).

(5) There are also some LM IB possible fortification walls at Gournia, Hagia Triada, Petras, and Vathypetro, though the data is inconclusive and all assumed gates are practically gaps in the walls (Driessen and Schoep 1995, 656).

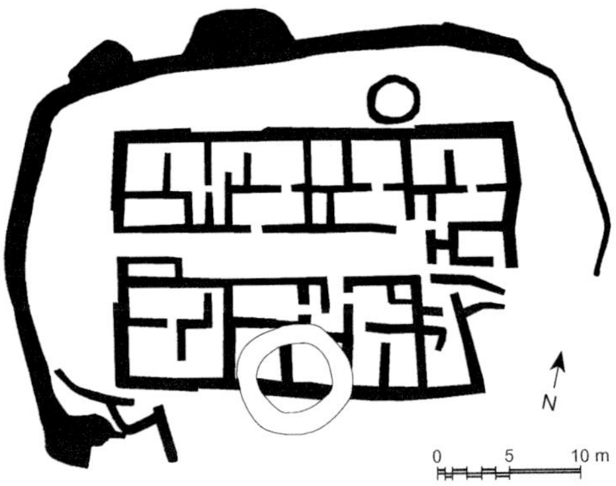


Fig. 43. Plan of Hagia Photia. After Tsipopoulou 1992, fig. 6.3.

It is clear from the above that we are talking about three different kinds of walls, in terms of what they are possibly protecting: (a) an isolated building compound (Protopalatial Hagia Photia); (b) a settlement (Protopalatial Myrtos Pyrgos and Malia); and (c) a Palace (LM Petras, and possibly Knossos and Phaistos). What is bounded and protected is, of course, of great significance, and the above variation is rather puzzling. Should we assume, for example, that Palatial settlements might have had two rings of protection, one at their periphery and an inner one at the borders of their Palaces? Or, are bounding and protection requirements to be understood differently at each site?

The archaeological evidence is for the time being scarce and inconclusive, as Driessen also observes (1995b, 74). A note of caution is that it is easy to mistake a sturdy retaining wall for fortification. Apart from Hagia Photia, which speaks of a military installation, and the evidence from Petras, there is no clear proof as yet of an all-encompassing fortification wall as such, only bits and pieces of enclosure walls that form rather weak local boundaries.

The question therefore remains: How are we to interpret the absence of fortification walls during the acme of the Minoan world in light of the significance of strong boundaries as a means to strengthen common identity? Obviously, there are other means, material and immaterial, for ensuring common identity and strengthening social coherence apart from fortification walls. If some form of political coherence existed in Crete during the Late Bronze Age, as some believe, then the boundaries are to be identified with the coastline of the island supported by a strong navy. The great sea isolating Crete was an effective buffer zone for her protection and at the same time her way of communication with the world beyond. This world, unlike Crete, was a world of bounded communities where fortifications played an important role, as attested in Melos and Kea. The same is true for her long distance neighbors in the Eastern Mediterranean. Only Thera may have had been unfortified, following the Cretan model, but this remains to be verified. The absence of fortifications—if indeed proved to be so—is a very significant differentiation that sets Crete apart, and it has many implications in regard to social structures and architectural manifestations of power.

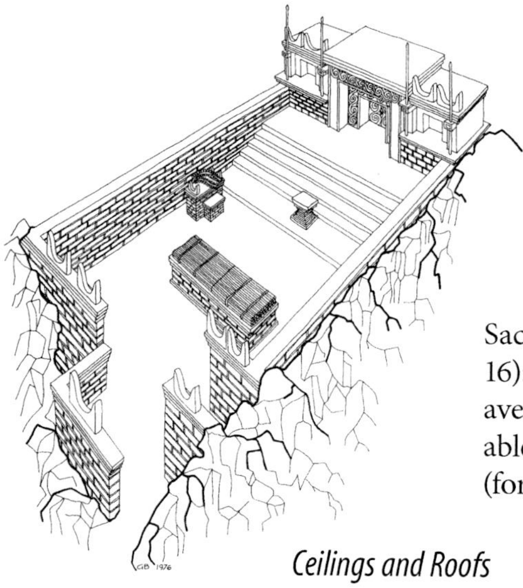

Fig. 44. Sacred enclosure depicted on the Zakros rhyton. Shaw 1978, fig. 9.

Archaeological data is much more reliable when it comes to enclosure walls. These were walls of relatively low height that delimit an area without protecting it effectively from trespassing. Their function was to demarcate areas that had specific properties or proprietors. To demarcate means to convey information regarding what is enclosed, what is included and consequently what is excluded. Sacred enclosures are of this type (Fig. 44; see also Fig. 16): though usually weak boundaries, in that they do not avert access, their presence was nevertheless indispensable for marking out the sanctity of what they contained (for sacred enclosures, see Lebessi and Muhly 1990).

### Ceilings and Roofs

Of roofs and ceilings we have sadly little to work with in prehistoric archaeology. We do know, however, that Minoan buildings had accessible flat roofs and that some ceilings were plastered and even decorated with paintings.

Flat roofs are rather weak boundaries. This is best comprehended when compared to pitched roofs, such as those preferred in the Mycenaean world: a pitched roof is a strong boundary that holds the building together and emphasizes its individuality and self-contained character by creating a vertical axis of symmetry that points to the sky above. The oblique planes that comprise the roof are in constant tension, in contrast to the horizontal planes of flat roofs that rest passively and may be projected infinitely (Fig. 45).

Evans suggested that some rooms may have had been open above, as in the case of the Lustral Basin next to the Throne Room at Knossos and the Royal Villa, both of which were actually "reconstituted" in this way (Fig. 46; Evans 1921–1935, II, IV, 402, 922, 924, figs. 227, 897). This would have been a strong discontinuity of the horizontal plane that delimited the room above. There is hardly any evidence for this, however, and Fotou has shown that it was surely not the case for the Royal Villa (1997, 35–38, fig. 2:a, b). Such design concepts (if verified) would represent a major event in the history of architecture, a foretaste of

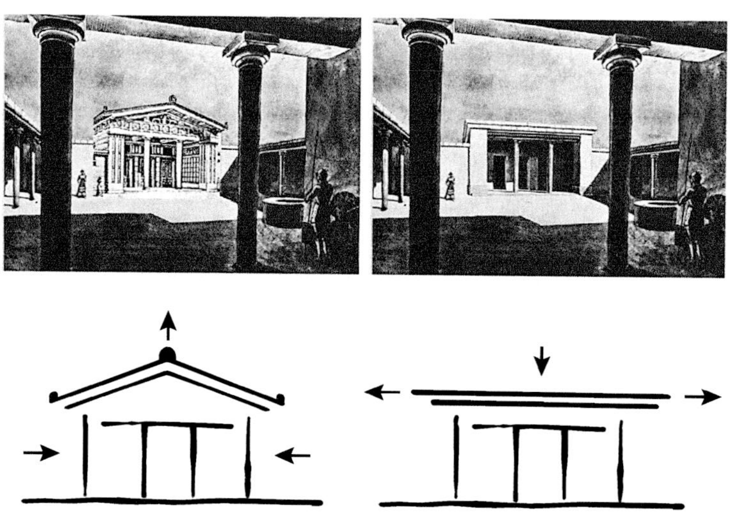

Fig. 45. Difference between a pitched roof and flat roof exemplified by two alternative reconstructions of the Megaron at Tiryns. Top left: after Müller 1930, pl. 42 and von Reber 1898, pl. 2; top right: after Müller 1930, pl. 42; bottom: drawings C. Palyvou.

the fluidity of space endorsed by the 20th-century A.D. architecture of the Modern Movement.

The manner in which floors, walls, and ceilings come together to encapsulate a space-cell dictates to a large degree the character of this space. The transition from one plane to another, horizontal or vertical, may be subtle, aiming at coherence and uniformity, or it may be abrupt and even disturbing, aiming at prioritizing certain surfaces and creating special effects. Nirou Chani, Room 5, for example, has the central area of the floor laid with slabs of dark limestone against a crème-white background, as mentioned above. The latter is continued on the vertical as well, in the form of dado slabs of the same crème-white color, promoting coherence and continuity between the two bounding surfaces, the floor and the walls. On the other hand, at Akrotiri, Thera there are several instances of plastered surfaces that continue uniformly from the floor to the wall, curving softly, at the joint of which a thin black line or a barely visible incision has been drawn in order to differentiate them (Palyvou 2005a, 163).

Fig. 46. Evans's reconstitution of the Throne Room at Knossos. Photo Gordon Gahan, National Geographic Creative.

## Connectors

### *Doors*

*The door, therefore, serves as the key for understanding the whole question of limit and transgression, of openness and exclusion. . . . [It] does not deny the concept of the boundary. Indeed it is precisely part of that boundary. (Leach 1997a, xx)*

All boundaries have points of penetration, "channels of intrusion and communication" (Arnheim, Zucker, and Watterson 1966, 11). To put it differently, there is no boundary without a break, a way in and out to the other side; otherwise there can be no life (as in a sealed tomb). Paradise acquired boundaries and gates only when the humans were thrown out; only then did an inside begin its presence, when the gate became. The ancient Egyptians, on the other hand, were quite confident about the temporality of the other world and their return to this world. For this return to be possible they fabricated so-called false doors in their tombs. The false door does nothing but declare symbolically the potential of communication. On a more real note, these doors include an actual break in the form of tiny holes that allow for communication between the two domains.

The door is indeed the most archetypal connector, a manifestation of how separating and connecting are two sides of the same act (Simmel 1997, 67; to the Sumerians it was valuable enough to follow a bride as part of her dowry [Norberg-Schulz 1997, 110]). A door is an opening that may or may not be equipped with means of control of access (e.g., door leaves, locks, guards) as well as signs communicating what lies beyond. The need to differentiate between different types of doors is reflected in the Ugaritic texts of the 13th century B.C., where there are separate names for the entrance door of a house (*tgr*), the door with leaves (*sgrm*), and the simple opening (*pth*; for further information and references, see Palyvou 2009c).

At Akrotiri, Thera there is ample evidence of doors with door leaves. In Crete there are instances of thresholds with traces of door leaves, but for the most part the evidence is indirect, through the numerous stone bases of doorjambs that are in the form of a capital L, T, or double-T. These bases indicate not only the presence of door leaves but also the direction they opened, usually toward the innermost room (Schmid 1983, 712, fig. 17). The effectiveness of the door as connector depends on its means of control; information we lack for the Minoan world. Though we know that locks existed in Minoan architecture, thanks to Graham's identification and representation of one such case (Graham 1972, 175–176, fig. 112), we will never know for sure which doors could actually lock and, of course, who had the keys.

Fig. 47. The location of the door(s) in a room defines its circulatory pattern and useful (shaded) areas. Drawing C. Palyvou.

The location of the door is of great importance, especially for the resulting circulatory pattern and the use of the room (Fig. 47). It is interesting to note that Minoan architects adopted from the beginning the practice of placing the door at the end of a wall—that is, next to the corner of the room (Fig. 47:a–d)—instead of at the center of the wall, as was the custom in the northern Aegean and the Greek mainland (Fig. 47:e; Palyvou 1999a, 324, 367). There are few exceptions to this rule, such as an Early Neolithic (EN) II building beneath the West Court at Knossos. Furthermore, doors seldom face each other (Fig. 47:c). The result is striking, for the openings establish circulatory paths that are constantly

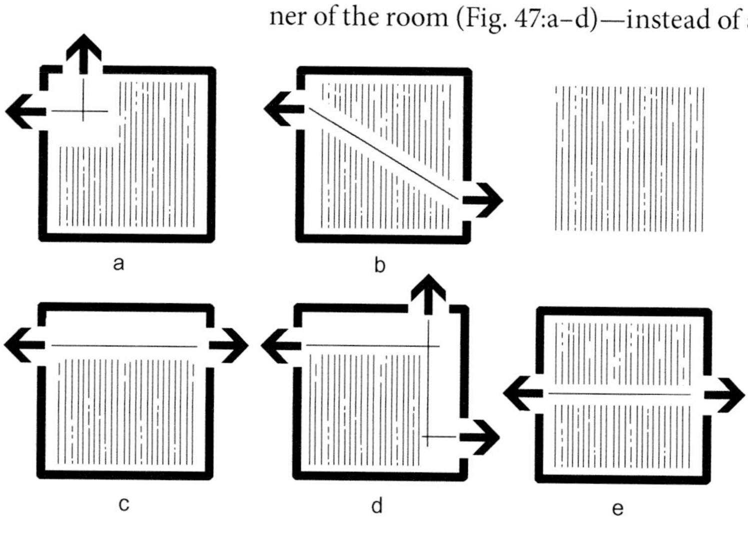

changing direction, somewhat like slaloming. In such a situation, the user is kept alert, for visibility of the space to be entered is restricted and there is no advance notion as to the existence of another exit/entrance. Furthermore, the resulting lines of communication create useful spaces within the room that vary in size and form. When placed at the center of the wall, on the other hand, as in the case of Mycenaean architecture, the doors provide circulatory patterns with little or no suspense, for there is ample visibility not only of the room entered but also often of more rooms beyond. In this case, the useful areas within the room are divided into two invariably equal parts. The Minoan design concept, as expressed through the position of the doors, is versatile and defines movement implicitly, as opposed to the axial system of the Mycenaean that is far more rigid and explicit.

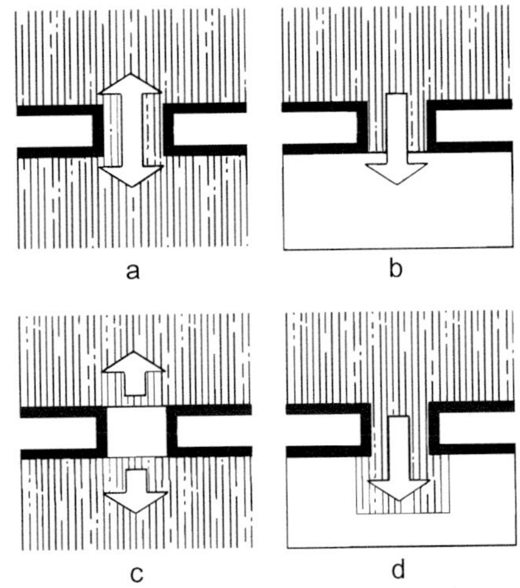

Fig. 48. Treatment of thresholds in relation to the floor pavement of the adjoining rooms. Drawing C. Palyvou.

Information missing in our archaeological records, such as texture or color of the door leaves and signs written or attached to the door, will always hamper our understanding of the contribution of each door to the function and architectural ambience of a building. Thresholds, on the other hand, have survived, and they play an important role in conveying meaning. There are four possible treatments of their surface (Fig. 48):

(1) When the two interconnected rooms have the same floor treatment then the threshold, as a rule, is also of the same type and fluidity of space is maintained (Fig. 48:a).

(2) When the two rooms differ, then the threshold usually follows the treatment of the more important room (Fig. 48:b).

(3) A third possibility, not common in Minoan architecture, is for the threshold to be different from the floor treatment of either one of the rooms it connects (Fig. 48:c).

(4) Finally, an interesting case is the West House at Akrotiri, Thera, discussed above: the pavement of the elaborate Room 5 extends beyond the threshold, into Room 3 (Fig. 49). This spillover emphasizes the importance of Room 5 and creates a preparatory space prior to entering (Fig. 48:d).

## *Pier-and-Door Partitions*

One of the most ingenious architectural elements of Minoan architecture—one we could easily place at the top of the list of its diagnostic features—is the so-called pier-and-door partition, as Graham dubbed it (Graham 1959, n. 4).[4] It consists of a three-dimensional loadbearing timber framework that substitutes a wall, in the form of a row

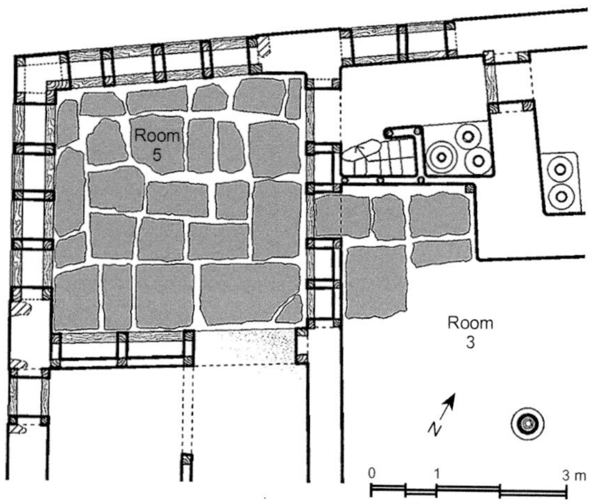


Fig. 49. Plan of the West House, Akrotiri, Thera. The pavement of Room 5 extends into Room 3, forming a liminal area that prepares entrance to the elaborate Room 5. Plan C. Palyvou.

of three to six, but more commonly four, adjacent doors, all of which could close with double door leaves.

The system could be more accurately described as a pier-and-opening partition where the opening may be treated as a door (Fig. 50:a), a window (Fig. 50:b), or a (Fig. 50:c) cupboard. This was easily done by filling in different parts of the wooden frame accordingly: a cupboard, for example, is created by blocking the back side of the opening with a thin mudbrick wall, whereas a window is created by building a low parapet to form the sill (Fig. 51). At Akrotiri, Thera combinations of all three are attested in Room 5 of the West House (Figs. 52, 53).

Pier-and-door partitions are usually identified by the I-shaped stone bases embedded in the floor as foundations for the intermediate jambs (Figs. 54, 55). It is very rare for such bases to be preserved in situ at the upper floor level, though it is common for stone bases to be found within the debris fallen from above (e.g., at Sklavokampos, Nirou Chani, and Prassa). At Akrotiri, Thera, on the other hand, pier-and-door partitions are miraculously preserved in situ not only on the first but also on the second floor above ground (Palyvou 2005a, 59–61).

The majority of pier-and-door partitions are found in Central Crete. There are several in eastern Crete as well (e.g, at Malia, Gournia, Palaikastro, and Zakros), and there are also some at Chania in the west. Their distribution is not related to regional parameters but to the type and elaboration of the buildings (McEnroe 1982, 6; for distribution patterns, see also Driessen 1989–1990, fig. 6). To the Cretan cases we may add the impressive pier-and-door partitions found at Akrotiri, Thera, and those discovered at Trianda, Rhodes, which are very interesting because of their early date.[5]

Fig. 50. Pier-and-opening partition. It is a three-dimensional timber frame that can accommodate doors (a), windows (b), and cupboards (c) in various combinations. Drawing C. Palyvou.

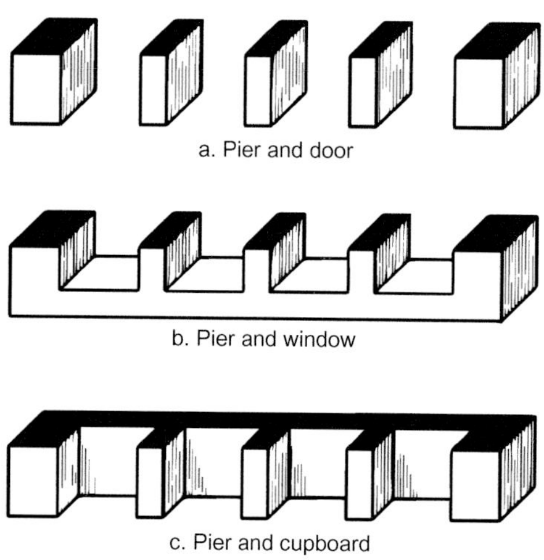


The function of the pier-and-door partition is twofold: it is both a load bearing element and a circulatory control system. Depending on which doors are open and which remain shut, the partition can provide a large variety of intercommunication patterns and can function as (Fig. 56:top):

(1) A barrier,[6] or a wall (all doors closed).

(2) A switch, or a wall with a door (one door open).

(3) A dimmer when some of the doors or door leaves are open (there are numerous combinations since each door comprises two door leaves).

Fig. 51. Graphic reconstruction of the Queen's Hall at Knossos by P. de Jong. This well-known drawing has been modified to include the indispensable horizontal timber beam at lintel level missing from the original drawing as well as from Evans's actual restoration. After Valavanis, ed., 2007, 172, fig. 34.

Fig. 52. Room 5 at the West House of Akrotiri, Thera is an excellent example of the systematic application of the pier-and-opening partition system. Palyvou 2005a, color pl. 3A.

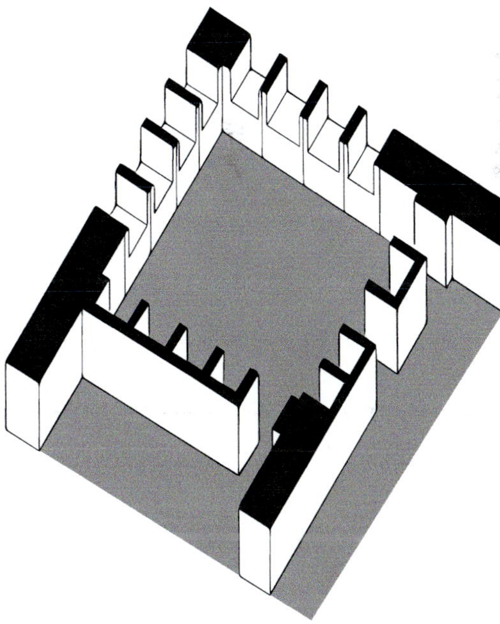

Fig. 53. Isometric drawing of Room 5 at the West House of Akrotiri, Thera. Drawing C. Palyvou.

Fig. 54. Stone bases of a pier-and-door partition at Amnissos, looking south. Photo C. Palyvou.

Fig. 55. Stone bases of a pier-and-door partition at Tylissos C, looking east. Photo C. Palyvou.

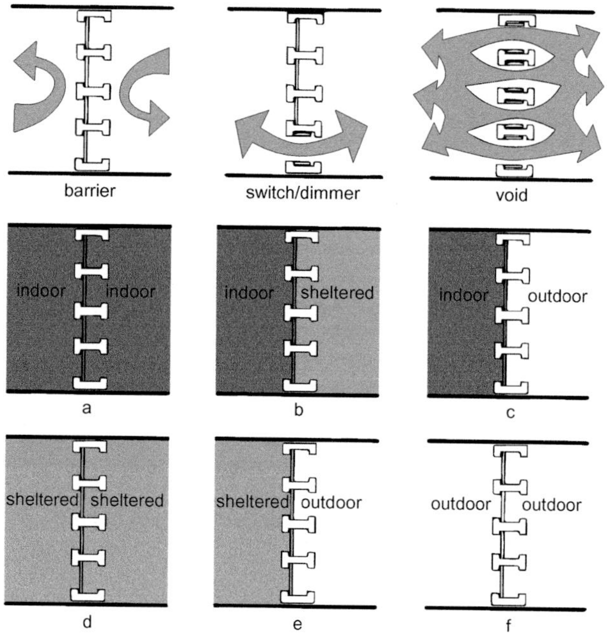


Fig. 56. The pier-and-door partition can function as barrier, switch/dimmer, or void (top), and it can provide a large variety of intercommunication patterns. Drawing C. Palyvou.

(4) A void, or the closest one can get to abolishing the wall/barrier, when all doors are open (in the absence of a wall there is no door either).

A pier-and-door partition, therefore, functions as a kind of mutable barrier, comparable to the modern sliding door or the Japanese sliding walls, providing a rich range of in-between situations and soft gradations. This ingenious device may be used in various ways and combinations to relate (Palyvou 1987, 198–200):

(1) Indoor to indoor spaces (typical in Polythyron Halls but also used to create corridor-like passages; Fig. 56:a).

(2) Indoor to semi-outdoor or sheltered spaces, typical in Minoan Halls (Fig. 56:b).

(3) Indoor to outdoor (Fig. 56:c). (Very rare; the Throne Room at Knossos is such a case, but of a later period [see Fig. 4]. Another instance is the Southeast House at Knossos, but it is due to the very small size of the Minoan Hall.)

(4) Sheltered to sheltered, sheltered to outdoor, outdoor to outdoor spaces (no such examples exist; Fig. 56:d–f)

The variety of its applications shows that Minoan architects found in the pier-and-door partition a flexible and multi-purpose architectonic tool, a true breakthrough for the time, both structurally and architecturally. In this brilliant achievement there is no influence from the East; or, on a more cautious tone, I would say that no matter who or what inspired the idea of the pier-and-door partition, the Minoans elevated the concept of the mutable barrier to the highest level of sophistication, far beyond anything that existed in their time. It is just as striking that the idea did not go any further either; the Mycenaeans had very little use for the pier-and-door partition, as discussed in Chapter 11.

### *Door-less Spaces and Basements*

Not all space-units with archaeological evidence of use had doors, which can only mean that they were approached by trapdoors from above (unless permanently sealed after having deposited the artifacts). The majority of these door-less units were underground compartments in the form of storage cists appended to the rooms above, though information is not always clear in the publications (McEnroe 1982, 12).

These intriguing space-units need detailed documentation to be properly examined and understood. The absence of drawings of sections in most publications does not allow for correlations with the ground level beyond the building. The general impression from the available data is that these spaces—at least most of them—were not designed as such but resulted from a dense network of foundation walls, some of which did not extend above ground floor level. This is the case, for example, with the houses at Gournia where the foundation walls had to be reinforced to cope with the strong inclination of the hillside. The decision to make use of these spaces, instead of filling them in or simply ignoring them, was a logical one in the context of maximum space exploitation; long-term storage was the best option for obvious reasons (climatic conditions, less light needed, casual visitation). Furthermore, such spaces are better protected from trespassing, because access through trapdoors and ladders is made difficult or even concealed if so desired. Trapdoors, on the other hand, obstruct the use of the room above because they take up floor space.

Though underground door-less spaces are common in Minoan architecture, they should not be related to the concept of the basement because the latter implies an autonomous underground level of intercommunicating spaces (yet another misuse of an architectural term). A rare instance of a true basement is the Hypostyle Crypt at Malia; it is of an early date and quite unique (Fig. 57). Once again, the restricted use of a term (in this case the basement) is in itself meaningful and might be imbued with symbolism. Basements, and underground spaces

in general, allude to caves: both are hollows within an overpowering mass, they have no exterior (no facade), and they are experienced as spaces literally interred in limitless mass and darkness. It comes as no surprise therefore that structures of the cave-type were used in Crete for the architecture of the dead, as exemplified by the underground rock-cut tombs at Poros and the Temple Tomb at Knossos.

Fig. 57. At Malia, the Hypostyle Crypt is a rare instance of a true basement (looking west). Photo C. Palyvou.

## *Windows*

As a break in the boundary that is the wall, the window is a weaker connector than the door, in that it serves all communication purposes but one: physical passing (unless in the form of trespassing). In its primal role as light and air conduit, it may be nothing more than a loophole in the wall, as in the earliest habitations of the Near East. In later times, however, the window acquired a much more sophisticated role.

Fig. 58. Sector Delta-East at Akrotiri, Thera. The facade of the building includes a variety of window types. Drawing C. Palyvou.

The window is more than a path merely for the eye, for it allows other senses to contribute to its communicative role: scents of flowers swarming inside the house through an open window inform the spring season, while a meal prepared inside sends tantalizing odors to the passer-by, reminding him or her of the time of the day. The same is true with the sounds of voices of children coming back from school or peasants returning from a day's work in the fields. Infiltration of odors and sounds through an open window is almost uninhibited; visual communication, on the other hand, is limited to what one can see through the window and how this view is framed. Where shutters exist, communication is controlled.

Fig. 59. Window looking into the light-well at Tylissos A, looking west. Photo C. Palyvou.

Windows are rarely found in prehistoric excavations, with the great exception of Akrotiri, Thera, where more than 80 windows, distributed in all three stories, are there to be seen and examined (Fig. 58). In Crete, only larger windows are sometimes detected and reported, usually found in Palaces and large mansions (Fig. 59). The pier-and-window partition, well attested in Thera, is also present in Crete at the Queen's Megaron at Knossos, for example, and at Malia House Δγ of an earlier date.

What is missing in the excavation records, however, abounds in art. Windows constitute a conspicuous feature where architecture is depicted, and they are often rendered in great detail as to their form and construction. Even the lattice blocking the window opening is clearly visible in some cases, as in the Archanes clay model of a house and the faience plaque from Knossos (Figs. 60, 61). Evans did not miss the importance of windows for such an early time in history and noted in amazement their "extraordinary anticipation of modern civilized usage" (Evans 1921–1935, I, 303). Mumford also made a strong point: "[T]he great novelty in Crete is the window, for here Knossos leaves behind the dark window-less dwellings of Sumer, lighted only from a narrow courtyard or a clerestory, if at all" (Mumford 1966, 145).

Fig. 60 Lattice blocking the opening of the window, clearly visible in two views of the clay model of a house from Archanes. After Lebessi 1976, figs. 6, 7.

A logical question to ask is what brought about such an extravagant development of the idea of the window in Minoan Crete, especially since there was not much around to inspire it. To attempt an answer we need to go back to the phenomenology of the window and elaborate on the qualities of comfort it provides. As connector, it appears in the same variations as the door: it may function as switch or dimmer, regulating communication between the inside and outside, from an absolute barrier when closed to a void when all windows are open (assuming there were shutters). But here we need to contemplate what is outside for Minoan architecture. Private courtyards are rare (except for those related to the Minoan Hall), which means that almost all windows opened onto public domains, streets, and squares. The sheer number of windows, therefore (again, judging from Akrotiri and art depictions), is proof that communication between the private and the public domains was culturally acceptable, perhaps even promoted. The communicative role of the window is further underlined by the many depictions of men and women looking out through windows.

Fig. 61. Ivory plaque from the Royal Road at Knossos. Ht. 4.5; w. 5.5 cm. Hood 1971, pl. 23.

Looking out may indeed be the main role of the window, but looking in is often unavoidable or perhaps even desirable in certain cases (Paliou 2011). On the upper floor of the West House at Akrotiri, Thera vases with flowers were painted on both jambs of a window, to the delight not only of the residents but of the passers-by as well. The decision to decorate the jambs of a window in this way implies that the Therans had some kind of understanding of the liminal nature of the window, as an element lingering between the private inside and the public outside domain.

In many Minoan buildings there exist space-cells deep in the fabric of the building that have no direct access to the outside. In these cases light and air are borrowed from adjoining rooms through windows opened in the intermediate walls or through a clerestory window above the door. Evans reconstructed all pier-and-door partitions at Knossos

with such openings (Fig. 62). This, however, has been proven false: as Akrotiri has shown, clerestory windows were used only where absolutely necessary so that the structural performance and the rigidity of the timber frame are not jeopardized (Fig. 63). The numerous wall paintings in the form of friezes deriving from such walled-in zones above the lintels of doors and windows, give proof of this.

Fig. 62. Hall of the Double Axes. Evans restored all pier-and-door partitions at Knossos with clerestory windows above the door lintels. Michailidou 1981, fig. 37; courtesy Ekdotike Athenon S.A.

## *Staircases*

The history of architecture includes a vast array of staircases, serving not only the main goal of moving in the vertical from one level to another, but also of regulating performances according to the function of the building (Fig. 64).[7] The specifics of a staircase—its form, dimensions, materials, texture, and so forth—play an important role in defining its ambience and use. Its breadth and slope—to take only two of its specifications—dictate to a large extent the way it will be used, for they impose a certain rhythm of stepping up or down that invites for a corresponding body posture and way of movement (Thiis-Evensen 1987, 89–113). Steep stairs are arduous and require effort, evident in the way the body leans forward to overcome gravity and the heart beats faster, whereas stairs with gentle slopes are easier and body movement is more relaxed. "Steep stairs address the heart, whereas gentle stairs echo the rhythm of our lungs" (Pallasmaa 2005a, 65).

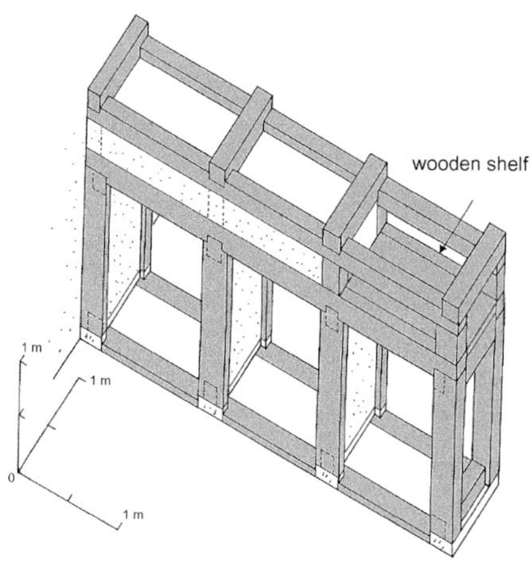


Fig. 63. Isometric plan of wall of Xeste 3 at Akrotiri, Thera, showing clerestory windows providing light and air to an inner room that has no access to the outside. After Palyvou 2005a, fig. 213.

The Minoans were obviously aware of these effects and, as Akrotiri, Thera has shown, they were very careful in designing major staircases, keeping dimensions standard and user friendly. Service staircases, on the other hand (such as the one at the West House), were designed ad hoc and were often very steep with steps of varying heights. Breadth is important: a narrow staircase, wide enough for one or two persons, is perceived as private space as opposed to a broad public staircase. The exceptionally low and broad steps of the Propylon at Phaistos, the Stepped Porch at Knossos, the Loggia at Malia, and the steps of Palatial Theatral Areas give proof of the sophisticated use of staircases to manipulate ascent, for they slow down the pace of movement and impose a solemn body posture, thereby implying formality: "One 'skips up' a narrow staircase but 'strides' up a broad one"

(Thiis-Evensen 1987, 93). Such effects are well exemplified in Minoan staircases and were surely applied purposefully.

The sheer number of staircases in Minoan architecture, the numerous levels they serve all the way up to the roof, and the variety of forms and the technical skills involved in designing, laying out, and constructing a staircase speak of a long tradition that goes hand in hand with multistory construction. This is evident in the architecture of MM II houses at Malia (Fig. 65): despite their small size, these houses comprise more than one staircase each (Poursat 1996, 93–95, fig. 53).

Fig. 64. Steps leading to a roof in vernacular Aegean architecture. Lavvas and Philippidis, eds., 1983–1991, II, fig. 198; courtesy Melissa Publishing House.

Just as with doors, staircases too may be grouped in similar categories on the basis of their performance; staircases, after all, are doors in the vertical. The categories are as follows (Fig. 66):

(1) Connector staircases with free access.

(2) Switch staircases with double doors fixed on the first step.

(3) Multiple-socket staircases, a combination of two staircases or a staircase that gives additional access to in-between levels.

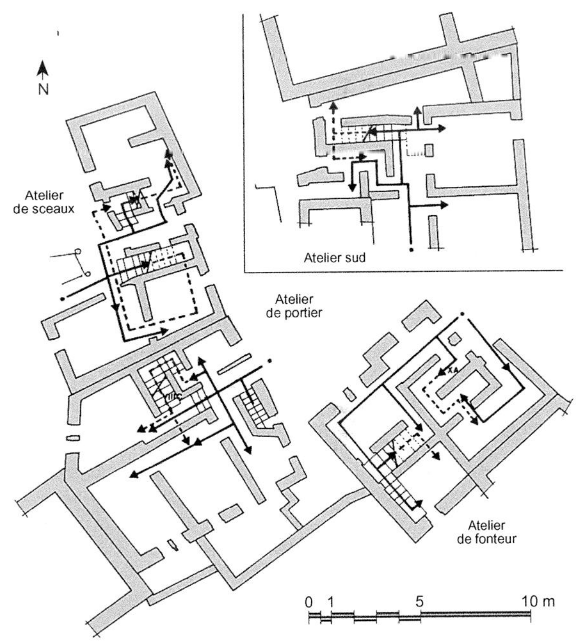


Fig. 65. Middle Minoan II houses at Malia, Maisons-Ateliers, Quartier Mu. Despite their small size, they comprise two adjacent staircases each. After Poursat 1996, fig. 53.

The difference between a staircase with free access and a staircase with controlled access (switch) can hardly be emphasized enough, and if it is not taken into account—as in the case of mechanistic spatial analyses of the Space Syntax type—the assumptions regarding circulatory patterns may be entirely misleading. The presence of a door on or next to the first step of the staircase is not difficult to detect: apart from dowels and imprints of the timber frame or even scratches on the surface of the step from hanging door leaves, it is sometimes betrayed by the larger width of the first step in order to accommodate the double leaves. At Akrotiri, such doors probably existed in all the main staircases located at the entrances of the buildings, to control access to the upper floors (Fig. 67).

Minoan staircases are situated inside buildings and connect spaces belonging to the same building distributed in different levels. There are very few examples of outdoor staircases (e.g., Malia, Palaikastro) situated

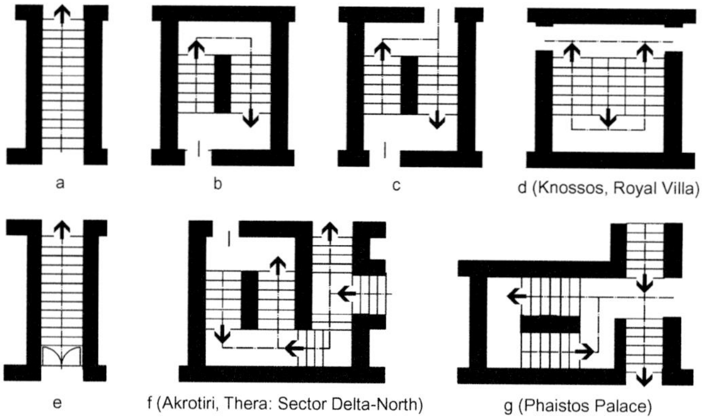


Fig. 66. Types of Minoan staircases: (a–d, f, g) connector staircases with free access; (e) switch staircases with double doors fixed on the first step; and (c, d, f, g) multiple-socket staircases, a combination of two staircases or a staircase that gives access to several intermediate levels. Drawing C. Palyvou.

at the periphery of the building and connecting the upper floor directly to the public domain of the street. There is also a limited number of staircases connecting the upper floor to a private court (e.g., Quartier Mu, Atelier des Sceaux).

The degree of sophistication in the design of staircases is attested not only by the fact that they reach two and three stories up, but also by the intricate combinations of flights and intermediate landings (the multiple-socket type) that could provide an amazing variety and hierarchy of inter-circulation. The most common form of staircase is in the shape of a Greek Π, with the area underneath the second flight used as storage space. There are several cases where the middle landing gives access to an intermediate level—especially at Akrotiri, Thera (Figs. 66:f, 68)—and there is also the impressive staircase of the Royal Villa at Knossos that splits at the middle landing in two juxtaposed flights (Fig. 66:d). This staircase is redolent of monumentality, probably because it alludes to similar staircases we know from the Italian Renaissance, yet the intention behind this design may have been primarily of a practical nature, such as giving access through the same staircase to two or more different zones on the upper floor. The whole system may be compared to a lobby comprising several doors. There are probably more such tripartite staircases that have gone unnoticed and are worth exploring. Tylissos House A is such an instance, and also possibly the Grand Staircase of the South Propylaeum at the Palace of Knossos as well as a staircase next to the Minoan Hall at the Palace of Galatas (Fig. 69). At Knossos, in particular, though the actual evidence at the so-called South Propylaeum is meager, its key location invites for a tripartite staircase that would provide access to the west and the south wings of the upper floor. These staircases are recognized by their massive built foundations at ground floor level that were meant to carry the loads of the flights above. If properly identified, these multiple-socket connectors can be of great help in understanding the distribution of functional zones on the upper floors and their relation to the ground floor compartments.

Fig. 67. Plan (left) and photograph (right) of the traces of the double door on the first step of the staircase from Akrotiri, Thera, Sector Delta-North. Palyvou 2005a, fig. 211.

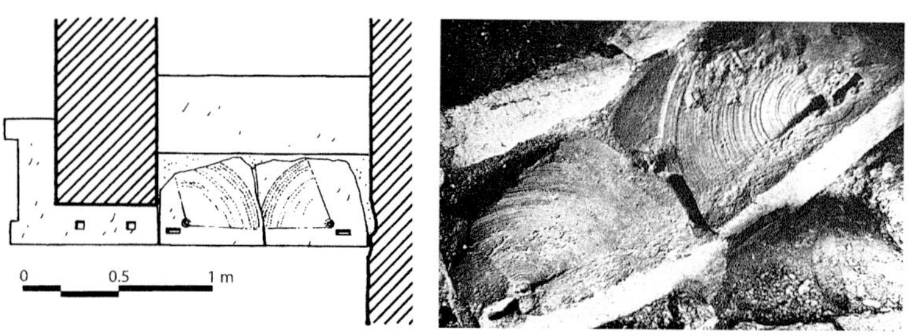


The sophisticated, extraordinary combinations of staircases are endless, all of which indicate multiplicity of choice of movement—not complexity—and hierarchy of circulation. An impressive example is the set of three interconnected staircases at the north wing of the Palace of Malia (Graham's [1979, ill. 8] graphic restoration does not acknowledge all their potential): the circulatory combinations they provide through the numerous possibilities of interconnection are stunning and give proof to the high standards of space articulation and control that the Minoans had achieved (Fig. 70).

Fig. 68. Impressive multiple-socket staircase in Sector Delta-North, Akrotiri, Thera. Palyvou 2005a, fig. 110.

Interior staircases are treated very much like doors connecting two adjacent and functionally related spaces that are superimposed, instead of being set one next to the other horizontally. As will be discussed in Chapter 10, in relation to zones, many staircases close to one another is an indication that they constitute part of the same zone that extends in the vertical. To appreciate the performance of a staircase as a connector comparable to the door, one may compare the Minoan practice to other alternative uses of the staircase. If a staircase was meant to connect two different superimposed zones, then one staircase would suffice (see this vol., Ch. 10, p. 208). Circulation would then have been distributed horizontally at each level through corridors. If the components of a zone are distributed in different levels, then more staircases are needed, each one connecting directly superimposed rooms that are functionally related. The resulting circulatory pattern ensures quick and direct communication without crisscrossing and with minimum interference among zones. Many would have envied even today such advanced awareness of three-dimensional space articulation! The only disadvantage (to our miser eyes) is an extravagant waste of space for circulation purposes.

As a consequence of the above, the location of staircases within a building is wisely thought out. A typical place for a staircase is within or near the entrance vestibule. In some instances the vestibule coincides with the staircase, as at Akrotiri, Thera. There is good reasoning behind this practice: the entrance door, combined with the staircase, acts as a direct channel of communication between the public domain outside the building and the domestic/reception area on the upper floor of the house. Access to the service rooms on the ground floor is thus kept separate. In some small houses this is the only staircase—or, to put it differently, if there is to be only one staircase, this will be situated at or by the entrance. This staircase is usually the one that continues all the way up to the roof, as attested at Akrotiri, Thera and depicted in art, especially the Town Mosaic and the Archanes model. Quite often, however, there is need for a second staircase, as mentioned above. This is the case even in relatively small buildings, as the Maisons-Ateliers of Quartier Mu, Malia (Poursat 1996). Its location is dictated by the distribution of zones and is decided ad hoc. Take for example House Δα at Malia (see below, p. 120): the second staircase is located not far from the main staircase in the entrance lobby and is appended to a small

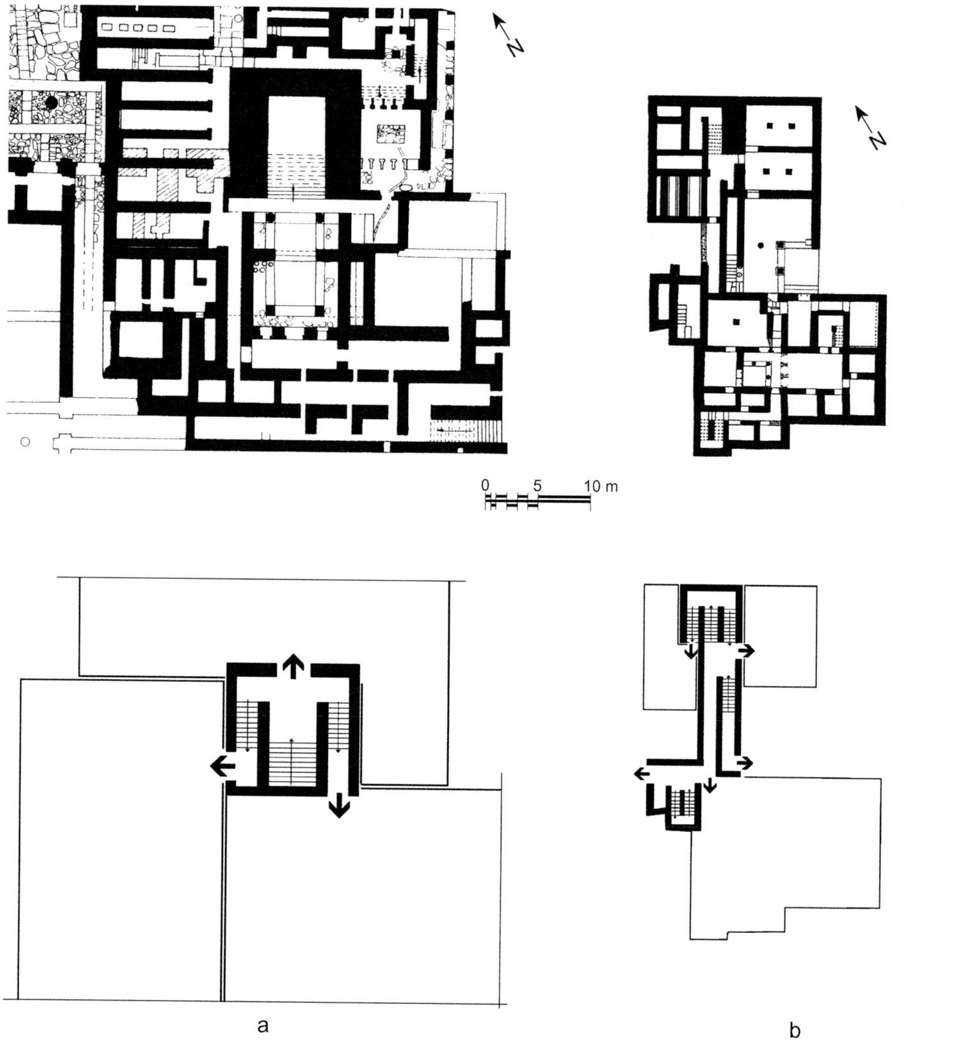


Fig. 69. Possible tripartite staircases: (a) Knossos (after Cadogan 1992, fig. 17.3); (b) House A, Tylissos (after Graham 1972, fig. 19).

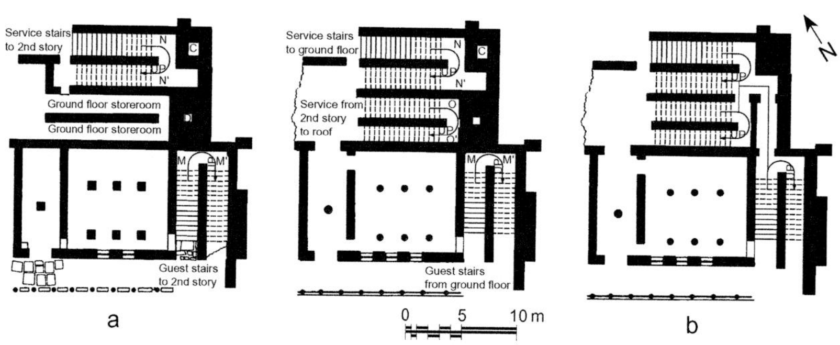


Fig. 70. An intriguing combination of three staircases at the Palace of Malia, probably communicating through their middle landings: (a) according to Graham; (b) author's modified version of Graham's second story. After Graham 1978, fig. 8.

corridor that connects the Minoan Hall to the storage area. This line of communication runs parallel to the main corridor leading from the entrance and the main staircase to the Minoan Hall. So why double the circulatory pattern? The answer is that the latter has a formal character and therefore needs to be segregated from any other movement within the house. The second line of communication is the one that allows for the residents of the house coming from the upper floor to appear or leave the Minoan Hall or visit the storage area without crossing paths with the visitor. Such arrangement is, in fact, common in houses comprising a Minoan Hall.

A special engagement of staircases is attested at Knossos and Tylissos. In both cases two related buildings—the Little Palace and the Unexplored Mansion at Knossos and Houses A and B at Tylissos—are separated by a street but joined at the upper level by a bridge (Fig. 71). Staircases are attached at the two ends of the bridge (presumably covered), one on each side; this way intercommunication between the two buildings is facilitated on both levels and in all possible combinations.

In conclusion, it seems that the communication system—horizontal and vertical—was designed with the following priorities in mind: (a) to connect directly the entrance to the upper floor; (b) to connect directly the entrance to the Minoan Hall; (c) to reach the storage areas with least interference with the previous lines of communication; and (d) to ensure privacy for the residents.

## Corridors

The corridor is the architectonic manifestation par excellence of movement, as the term itself implies (the runner, from the Italian *correre* [to run]). Its linearity and elongated form denote unobstructed straightforward movement, while its width is just enough to

Fig. 71. Separate buildings joined at the upper level by a bridge and a network of corridors and staircases: (a) Little Palace and Unexplored Mansion, Knossos (after Cadogan 1992, fig. 17.6); (b) Houses A and B, Tylissos (after Vasilakis 1992, fig. 40.1).

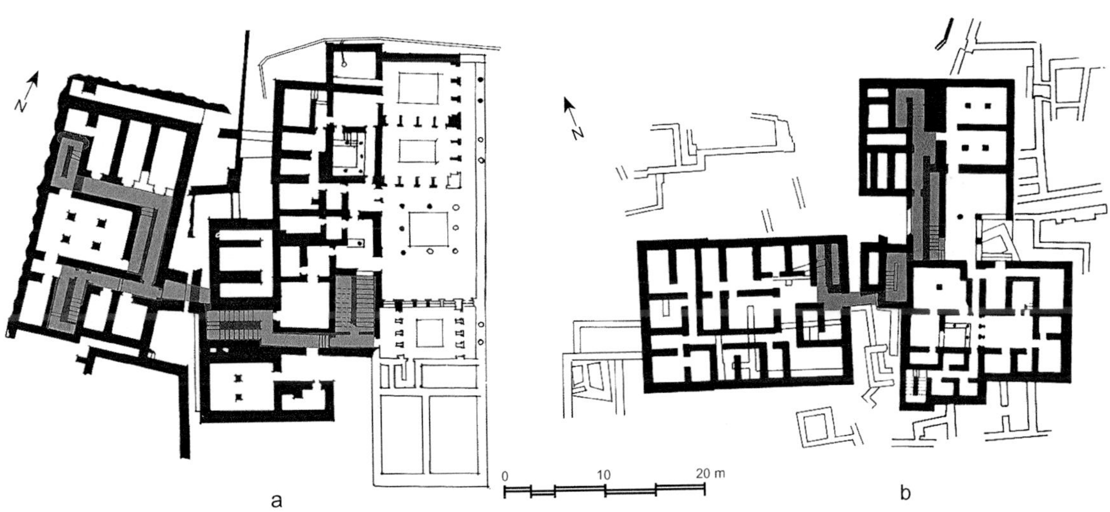

accommodate two people moving in opposite directions—that is, 1.15 m or more if the people using the corridor are carrying bulky objects, as is the case of corridors in storage areas (Fig. 72). Here, form literally follows function.

Corridors provide controlled and directional flow of movement and function as connectors as much as separators. They are the means par excellence, therefore, for managing space articulation. A corridor usually accommodates a number of spaces; if it connects only two space-cells it is like a door with elongated jambs and threshold, so to speak. Its full value lies in its ability to function as a multi-socket system, providing access to several rooms. The number and variety of possible intercommunication patterns between rooms attached to a corridor is what makes the difference.

In the context of Minoan architecture, corridors could be grouped in two categories (Figs. 73, 74): (a) main corridors that connect the entrance of the building to focal space-cells inside the house (thick lines); and (b) secondary corridors that serve space-cells within the building, regardless of the entrance (thin lines). It is often the case that the main corridor connects the entrance with the Minoan Hall (where it exists), no matter how far away it may be located, as at Tylissos House C. This allows for direct communication between the public realm outside the house and the semi-public domain of the house that is the Minoan Hall. Like an umbilical cord, the main corridor converts the geographical distance into topological proximity. Secondary corridors are used as local shortcuts allowing for direct communication between functionally related space-cells.

Simple, rational, and almost self-evident though it may seem to us today, the concept of the corridor should not be taken for granted. The corridor is missing in many early examples of architecture; space-cells are juxtaposed and movement to and from one another is served not by a distinct architectural element exclusive to movement, as is the corridor, but through the distribution of doors that define the pattern of circulation within the building. The result is much crisscrossing and interference that reduces privacy and affects the functional capacity of the rooms. This is the case in several Minoan buildings: there are numerous instances where intermediate rooms can hardly house any other task but movement. In the history of architecture, therefore, it was a big step forward when circulation was acknowledged as a task in its own right and was given a specific architectural form and name. In

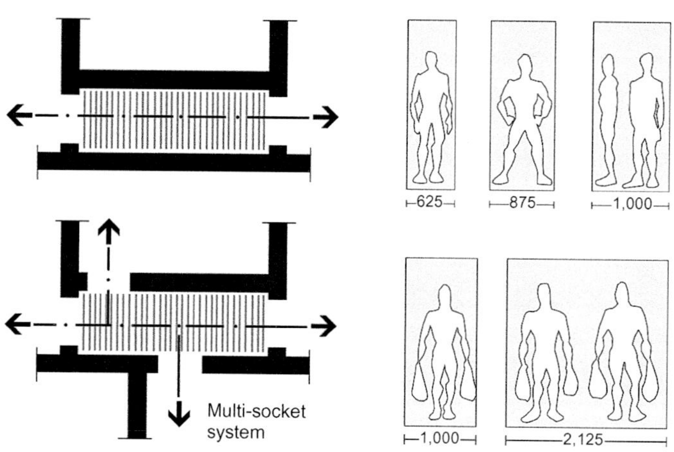


Fig. 72. The corridor functions as a multi-socket system in the circulatory system. Its width is ergonomically defined. Measurements in mm. Left: drawing C. Palyvou; right: after Neufert 2000, 17.

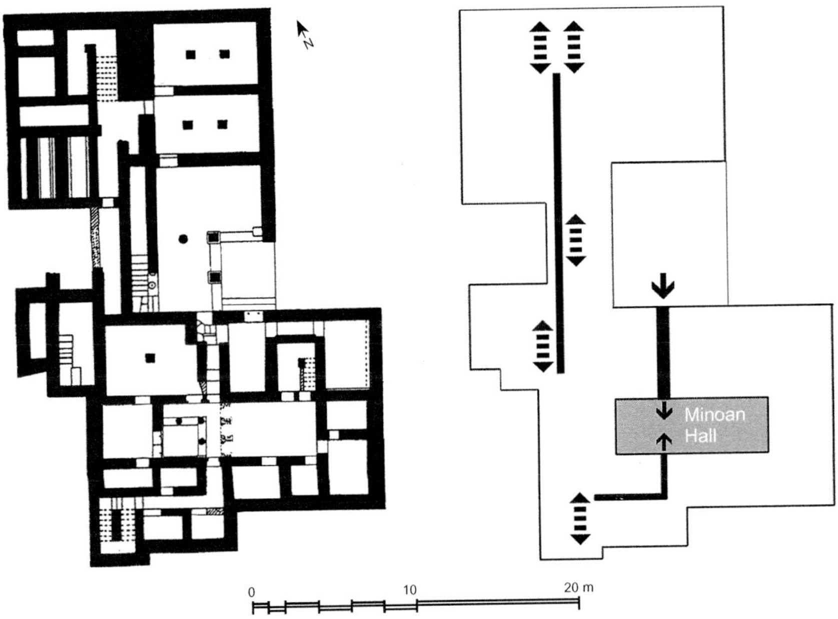


Fig. 73. Types of corridors at Tylissos House A. The main corridor (thick line) connects the entrance of the building to major space-cells inside the house, and secondary corridors (thin lines) connect space-cells within the building, regardless of the entrance. The two types correspond to the visitors and the residents, respectively. The Minoan Hall is typically connected with both types of corridors. After Graham 1972, fig. 19.

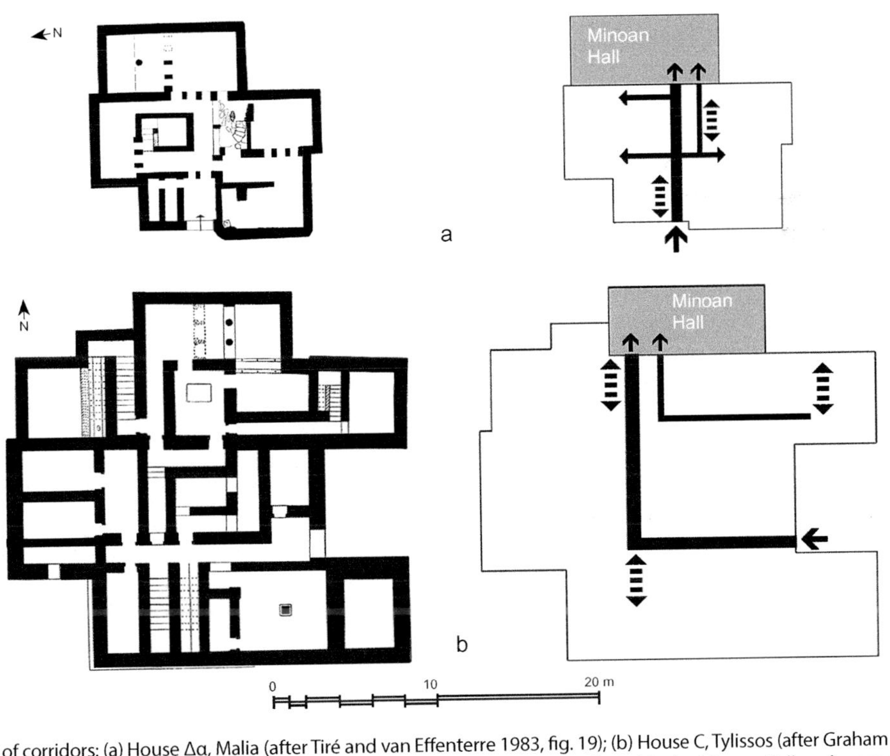


Fig. 74. Types of corridors: (a) House Δα, Malia (after Tiré and van Effenterre 1983, fig. 19); (b) House C, Tylissos (after Graham 1975, fig. 20). The main corridor (thick lines) connects the entrance of the building to major space-cells inside the Minoan Hall, and secondary corridors (thin lines) connect space-cells within the building, regardless of the entrance.

Minoan architecture, corridors appear sporadically until the Neopalatial era, before they are crystallized as part of the sophisticated architecture that marks the acme of the Minoan civilization.

## Hierarchical Circulatory Patterns and the Curse of the Labyrinth

*Labyrinth means order . . . supported by the ability of knowledge . . . not until later do confusion and hopelessness become the primary features of the labyrinth. The horrors of the way, the moment of surprise, the frenzy of perception, the step into the forbidden.* (Miller 1982)

*The walls themselves are not important. They serve only to delineate the way and the motion which carries the true meaning.* (Kern 1982, 10)

The task of architecture is to serve and facilitate movement, pause, and arrest; to offer, that is, space for movement and places for pause and arrest. All movement is linear, directional, and purposeful (even when seemingly spontaneous and erratic); it has a starting point, a sequence, and a destination, all of which leave imprints on the ground, temporal or permanent (for the configuration of the path, see Ching 1996, 252). Pause is also specific to purpose; it may be a brief lingering before entering a building, it may be an ephemeral pause, or it may require time and contemplation. Arrest, finally, corresponds to tasks that require time and space; these are tasks carried out solely or collectively, and usually repeatedly either in the short or long run of time.

To those who study Minoan architecture it is patent that communication and circulation were issues of major importance. The sheer variety and number of connectors that participate in a building in the form of doors, corridors, and staircases, regardless of its size or complexity, is a straightforward statement of the priority the Minoans placed in facilitating, channeling, and controlling circulation. This is indeed an architecture of maximum interconnections of spaces in interchangeable roles that promotes mobility and values highly the principle of least interference.

Minoan architecture nevertheless has been inextricably associated with the myth of the labyrinth, whose meaning has become almost synonymous to deliberate intricacy and confusion—a curse still haunting our understanding of the Minoan world. This is far from true: quite the contrary, circulation within a building compound derives from careful planning and designing aiming at providing alternative routes. These routes or paths comply with a hierarchy of movement corresponding to the varying identities of the users and the tasks they are involved in. Though it is difficult to speak of identities in the absence of written records, one may consider at least two different groups of users: the residents and the visitors.

A common problem underlying many interpretations of circulatory patterns is that scholars tend to describe them—and mentally imagine them—in a way that was never true. In other words, they either identify themselves indiscriminatingly with both categories of users, or, more commonly, they identify exclusively with the visitor (which indeed they are, to some extent, even if several centuries later). This however is a nosy visitor who starts from the entrance and penetrates the building crossing one threshold after the other until he or she reaches the innermost compartments. Bifurcations and alternative options are dealt with ad hoc, whereas when confronted with a staircase there is frustration and confusion, for there is seldom any clue as to where it leads.

The two sets of users need to be separated. The residents, once inside the building, are no longer concerned with the entrance/exit of the house. Their movement corresponds to everyday mundane tasks, such as food preparation and consumption, sanitation, working, socializing, and sleeping. Religious and ritual tasks may also be undertaken in a mundane context. Some tasks take place in privacy and isolation whereas others are communal and correspond to gathering places. Accordingly, circulatory patterns are wisely designed to serve these tasks effectively: as mentioned above, there are shortcuts, bypasses, and alternative options allowing for a flexible circulatory pattern that may be adjusted to varying needs.

Storage, to take an easy example, requires unobstructed yet controlled contact with the entrance of the house for obvious reasons. In the more elaborate houses of the Neopalatial era storage facilities are grouped in a separate zone with its own access from the entrance. In these cases it is interesting to observe how this zone relates to the circulatory pattern of the other parts of the house. Take Tylissos House A, for example (see Fig. 73): at the interface between the domestic zone (south) and the storage (north), there is an amazing network of interrelated horizontal and vertical connectors that allows for undisturbed interactions of all sorts, the input of materials and goods, and the output of products or waste.

Visitors comprise an entirely different group of users. The casual visitor is constantly aware of the entrance/exit of the house, connected to it psychologically through an invisible umbilical cord. As a carrier of the public realm, his/her movement within the private domain of the house needs to be restricted or guided. Visitors depend entirely on the residents (there can be no visitor without a resident to receive him or her—the opposite would be trespassing). Visitors arrive at the entrance and announce their presence by knocking on the door (giving the first handshake, as Pallasmaa calls the door handle of the building [2005b, 56]). Inside the house, the visitor's common destination would be a space-cell designated for reception. For the Neopalatial elaborate houses this seems to have been the Minoan Hall.

In several instances, the encounter of the visitor with the resident in the Minoan Hall is represented architecturally by two routes arriving from opposite directions (Palyvou 1987): one for the visitors coming from the entrance, and the other for the residents arriving from the inner compartments of the house (see Figs. 73, 74). The latter is usually associated with a staircase so that the residents may reach the meeting place from any part of the house without crisscrossing with the visitor's route. Since there is a staircase by the entrance as well, there is a further advantage in this circulatory arrangement, for all lines of communication are repeated on the upper floor.

This extraordinary and extravagant system of circulation control is unique to the Minoan world and must be fully acknowledged for its outstanding sophistication. Simon Unwin, in *Analysing Architecture* (2009), has included in his 10 case studies, along with the works of Robert Ventouri, Peter Eisenman, and Hans Scharoun, the Royal Villa at Knossos, emphasizing the ingenious layout and circulatory system of the building aiming at aggrandizing one person. He observes three differentiated accesses, culminating at the throne: one for the high official, one for his supporters, and one for the supplicants. "Like the board of a game, this small building is a clear example of how architecture can set the rules of the relationships between the various players in a ceremony" (Unwin 2009, 229–230). Preziosi has eloquently compared the phenomenon to that of railway shunting yards "which allow the maximum and most economical interactions between zones . . . without interference with each other" (Preziosi 1983, 105). This is indeed a fascinating system adhering to the principle of least interference that allows for unobstructed synchronic use of the building by people of varying identities involved in varying tasks. It speaks of hierarchy of use and, above all, of an ingenious mastermind capable of conceiving, designing, and constructing such complex spatial networks of communication.

## Endnotes

1 That craftsmanship and technology constitute the basis of the Greek myth of the creation of the human race is quite unique among early cosmologies. The idea may have its roots in the Aegean Bronze Age, alluded to by the connections between Hephaistos and Daidalos (Morris 1992).

2 Thiis-Evensen (1987, 36–87) discusses at length "[w]hat the floor does," presenting its various themes under titles such as Directional, Delimiting, Supporting, Attached/Detached, and Sunken/Rising.

3 Examples of pavements with a distinct rectangle in the middle are to be seen at Knossos in the House of the Frescoes, the South House (crazy pattern surrounded by rectangular slabs), and the Little Palace, and at Archanes (four

identical rectangular slabs in Room 3 and crazy pattern in Room 10) and Nirou Chani (central pattern in Minoan Hall and smaller one in Room 5).

4 The term refers to the structural system. The Greek word polythyron is often used as synonymous to the pier-and-door partition. Its meaning, however, is not always clear, for sometimes it is used to refer to the room (or set of rooms) comprising such structural systems. It is preferable, therefore, to use pier-and-door/window partition as a technical term referring to the structure itself, and the term Polythyron Hall to refer to a room or a set of rooms comprising such elements (see Palyvou 1999a, 343 nn. 557–561; 2005a, 144 n. 28).

5 The sheer number of pier-and-opening partitions found at Akrotiri is striking and can only be compared with those of the Palaces and Villas of Crete. The bold and extravagant applications, such as those attested at Xeste 3, can only result from a long experience with wood as a building material, probably deriving from Crete and dating back to the Middle Bronze Age.

6 The notions of the barrier, the switch, the filter, and the connector were introduced by Norberg-Schulz (1997, 113) to describe the role of architectural elements in the physical control and the "exchange of energies."

7 For examples of staircases in monumental, secular, or sacred contexts in various cultures, see Thiis-Evensen 1987, 89–113.

5

# Configuration of the Constituent Parts

## The Way: Approach and Departure

*Each architectural place, each habitation has one precondition: that the building should be located on a path, at a crossroads at which arrival and departure are both possible. (Derrida 1997, 319)*

The first act when aiming at crossing a boundary is to locate its break, its point of penetration. To those familiar with the specific boundary, this is already known, but to others it may require preparation, research, anticipation, alertness, and vigilance. More than the ultimate point of penetration, it is the way that matters: the path that guides the approach. The way consists of a sequence of movement and pause/arrest situations that begins long before the actual crossing of the boundary and continues thereafter (Fig. 75).[1] It is a process that mobilizes the mind as much as the body. Before overcoming the inertia of the body, it starts as a mental journey, with all the senses scouting the terrain—real, memorized, or imagined—anticipating the potential encounters one might come across along the path that is to be followed (Michelis 1964, 141).[2] It is a process that consumes time, space, energy, and emotions.

Architecture plays an important role in guiding the way, both physically and emotionally. First by the manner the route is traced on the ground: it may be a beaten track produced by the repetitive passage of many, or a magnificent well-built walkway; or it may be winding with

Fig. 75. In anticipation of the entrance long before crossing the boundary. Drawing C. Palyvou.

limited visibility or it might be straight and conspicuous, flanked by trees, statues, porticoes, and so forth. It may also be short or long, narrow or wide, or axial or lateral, and it may be level, descending, or ascending (Fig. 76). The configuration of the path is crucial in formulating the ambience of the way and plays an important role in the emotional preparedness of those approaching an entrance.

The history of architecture has a vast array of fascinating approach and penetration systems corresponding to varying physical and spiritual states of mind. At Karnak, to give an example, there is a strictly defined procession walk leading to the entrance of the temple, flanked by statues of reclining rams that define and emphasize the axis of movement; the same axis permeates the whole complex to its very end, the Adyton. The rams literally fix their glance on those moving along the path, for they seem to make direct eye-to-eye contact with the humans. This is, in fact, a very powerful axis, for it extends across the river, all the way to the other bank of the Nile and to the west, reaching out to the world of the dead. There it is materialized once again as an architectonic axis in the form of a sumptuous ramp leading up to the temple of Hatshepsut. Two loci of high spiritual significance—the crypt of the god to the east and the crypt of the dead pharaoh to the west—both define this compelling line of material and allow for spiritual communication. A person moving along this axis cannot but yield to the aura and the drawing forces of the divine path.

Axial approach and frontal access are typical of formal architecture in many cultures and periods of history, as for example the Hellenistic and the Roman. In classical Greece, on the other hand, movement and approach systems were designed in a subtle and implicit manner. One did not move along a precast path but among a constitution of free-standing, yet wisely interrelated volumes, placed obliquely so that they inhibit frontal views and promote lateral movement. The route to the Propylon of a temenos, and from there to the temple or the altar, was often unrestricted and seemingly unguided, yet the direction of movement was subtly implied by the volumes of the surrounding buildings, especially the Stoas whose colonnades generated strong perspective views. The result was a highly individualized experience in both the built and the un-built space.

Fig. 76. Configuration of the path determines body posture and emotionally prepares those approaching an entrance. Photo and drawing C. Palyvou.

Minoan architecture also favors lateral approach. The direction of movement toward an entry point is usually oblique in relation to the facade hosting the entrance. Such an approach bears tension on the incomer and demands alertness, since information regarding the specifics of the entrance is gained gradually; this is opposed to an axial approach where it is all out there from the beginning. Lateral approach applies to domestic as much as to formal architecture, especially the

Palaces discussed in Chapter 10; here we shall confine to the approach and penetration systems of houses.

Minoan town planning is beyond the scope of this book, yet suffice it to point out that there is a latent order in the layout of many towns, such as Gournia, Malia, and Palaikastro. This is not the result of a premeditated design but of an organic response to physical and social laws, such as the simple rule of following the contours of the land as well as not obstructing the function of neighboring houses (Palyvou 1986). Streets and open public spaces were not conceived as autonomous elements of design; they acquired their identity as urban features through the volumes of the buildings that gradually encroached the sides of what was originally a path or an open area. Their loosely defined geometry was counterpoised, however, with the aid of two very powerful and effective tools of urban design: the indentations and the raised causeways, discussed in Chapter 8.

Fig. 77. Steps leading up to the entrance of a house at Gournia, facing northwest. Davaras 1989b, fig. 10; © Hellenic Ministry of Culture and Sports–Archaeological Receipts Fund.

Within the dense and marginally ordered urban environment, access to the individual houses was ingeniously signaled. Entrances are often located in recesses or indentations of the facades, which provide a welcoming space. Furthermore, they are of high visibility value since they can be spotted from a distance (Athanasiou 2011). At Gournia, due to the inclination of the ground, access to the houses is sometimes via a small flight of steps, and the street widens just before the steps to provide space and avoid obstructing the traffic (Fig. 77). Intermediate transitional spaces, however, are not always available. There are several instances of entrance doors opening directly onto narrow streets (e.g., at Chania, Palaikastro, Akrotiri, Thera). In these cases the location of the entrance door is marginally marked from some distance by a voluminous threshold that projects into the street (Fig. 78). Such seemingly minor details give proof to well-established urban laws of communal behavior.

Fig. 78. Graphic reconstruction of LM I houses flanking a narrow street at Chania. Hallager 1990, fig. 5.

Access and penetration systems are less clear when it comes to large buildings of the Villa type, such as Tylissos, Sklavokampos, Nirou Chani, and Amnissos, which seem to include major open-air spaces within their boundaries. Unfortunately, information regarding approach and penetration systems is obscured by the fact that excavation has stopped short after reaching the outer limits of the building, and there is no clue as to the existence of intermediate, semiprivate transitional spaces between the public realm and the actual entrance to the building. This is a serious handicap when assessing their function and their integration in the urban environment.

## Entry and Egress: Crossing the Threshold

*Walls and closed doors have always been experienced as invitations to trespass. (Harries 2000, 168)*

The approach is completed when the entrance has been reached. There, just outside the door, is the place and the time to pause, to check and be checked, and to contemplate and prepare for the final and irreversible act of crossing the threshold. Architecture, once again, provides the setting and guides both the body and the mind. Since there are few intermediate transitional spaces between the private and the public domain in Minoan architecture, this is served by the local widening of the street. In some cases (e.g., Pseira Building BC, Vathypetro, Palaikastro, and Akrotiri, Thera) there are built benches next to or near the entrance door (Fig. 79). This is a common feature in Aegean vernacular architecture and a strong manifestation of social life enacted outdoors. The bench emphasizes arrest rather than pause since one may sit out as long as desired, to see and to be seen. In that sense, the bench is the earliest theatrical seat, just as the street is the oldest theater in the world.

The entrance door partakes in the concept of the boundary, accentuating its function as a barrier. Sometimes it even takes precedence: an immaterial or weak boundary may be announced or reinforced through a powerful entrance. Such is the case of the Roman triumphal arch, for example, or the Japanese Torii, both of which correspond to immaterial boundaries (on the Roman triumphal arch, see Giedion 1971, 91–135). Could this also be the case for certain isolated, detached gates depicted on rings? Two such rings from Mycenae show more or less the same picture: three women (the number three implies a row, hence a procession) moving toward a gate that looks like a Single-Column Porch (Fig. 80). Though the structure is nothing but a gate, it is undoubtedly understood as alluding to a boundary marking the distinction between two domains, physical and spiritual. The scene on the two rings is most probably an abbreviated representation of a rite of passage that involves ritual approach as much as ritual passage. The three women represent a group of females in a common state of mind, preparing to cross over to the otherness implied by the gate.

Fig. 79. Built bench next to the entrance door of Xeste 3 in Akrotiri, Thera, marking the liminal zone between public and private domains. Image C. Palyvou.

The manner in which the entrance door is incorporated in the building has a strong impact on the way one perceives and experiences the

act of entering. Thomas Thiis-Evensen describes eight different entrance motifs (1987, 285–297):

(1) The frame motif of entering through.

(2) The split motif of passing between.

(3) The deep-set motif of passing into.

(4) The baldachin motif of passing under.

(5) The directional motif of proceeding alongside something.

(6) The side-tower motif of passing by.

(7) The path motif of entering on something.

(8) The stair motif of entering up or down.

Fig. 80. Golden rings from Mycenae depicting processions of women moving toward gates that imply boundaries. Top: 1.6 x 2.8 cm; bottom 1.6 x 2.5 cm. After Mylonas 1983, 184–185, figs. 137, 138.

Most of the above motifs are attested in Minoan architecture. The deep-set motif, in particular, is common in urban houses, whereas in palatial architecture the directional and the path motifs prevail. A special type of entrance articulation is the Minoan porch, discussed below. It results from the combination of the frame, the deep-set, and the baldachin motifs.

The final act of penetration is performed by crossing the threshold. The verb cross emphasizes the movement of the body in a direction perpendicular to the boundary that is to be penetrated. It is a symbolic act of violation of the barrier, a voluntary invasion, and a conscious decision to move from one place or status to another. This symbolic connotation of the threshold is exemplified by the traditional ritual of the husband carrying the bride over the threshold of her new house, by which act she is only passively accepting, perhaps even involuntarily, her passage to the new locus and status, while all the burden and responsibility for this transfer is literally and metaphorically carried by the husband.

The symbolic importance of the act of crossing the threshold and penetrating a boundary was understood by the Minoans, as evidenced by the rituals that took place prior to placing the heavy threshold of the entrance door in its position; these rituals presumably aimed at protecting the unavoidable break of the boundary from invaders, corporeal or spiritual (Boulotis 1985). It should not escape us, however, that all entrances are potential exits as well, and, from the phenomenological point of view, the experience of crossing the threshold upon leaving the house is equally important (for an eloquent description of entering vs. exiting a Gothic or Romanesque cathedral, see Simmel 1997, 68–69).

One might even suggest that threshold rituals were also meant to protect those leaving the security of the house to roam out into the unknown as a kind of amulet against agoraphobia.

## In Between: The Porch

*[T]he scene of the gift of admittance and meeting.* (Mugerauer 1993, 125)

The transitional and preparatory character of the entrance area is best manifested in the architectonic form of the porch. From the utilitarian point of view, a porch shelters and insulates by holding out undesirable forms of weather or by opening up to moderate breezes; in other words, it is an ingenious means for reconciling outside and inside space. Its symbolic value, on the other hand, lies in its mediating character as a place lingering between the private domain of the house and the public space outside.

The porch is a place of pause rather than arrest, of prolonging the act of crossing the threshold and entering the building. It is here that the act of admittance takes place each time a person seeks to enter the house. Admittance presupposes acceptance and reception, which is precisely what the porch offers (Mugerauer 1993, 125–126).

Entrances with porches are to be seen in only a few Minoan buildings, all of considerable size and elaboration. They employ well-known principles of Minoan architecture but do not conform to a specific architectural type. Many porches are but one of the rooms of the house that opens toward the street. The result is a U-shaped space that provides inward focus and at the same time outward orientation. Some of the best known Minoan porches are worth mentioning separately.[3]

Tylissos House A has an atypical porch in the form of a broad sheltered area with free access (Fig. 81; see also Fig. 73). Two pillars and a column carried the ceiling and presumably the upper floor. This is a unique arrangement in that it consists of a broad sheltered area situated before the proper entrance to the house. Access to the interior of the house is provided by three doors: one leads to the formal sector of the house to the south and another gives access to the storage area to the north, whereas the third to the west is a staircase that led to the upper compartments of the house. At the beginning of the staircase there is a small balustrade with a column at its end (this means that there was no door, and therefore the actual entrance door was on the upper floor). The porch, in this case,

Fig. 81. Elaborate entrance porch of House A, Tylissos, looking northwest. Photo C. Palyvou.

functions as a major circulatory nexus, channeling access to different parts or zones of the building.

At Palaikastro, Block B, Room 14 has a large porch in the form of a Room with a Central Column opening toward the street. Block X, House 1–17, on the other hand, has a porch in the form of a portico (for the definition of this term, see this vol., p. 159) supported by a row of four columns. The portico is broad and deep, with a stone bench along the inner wall (Fig. 82). A similar portico with one corner column is attested at the Atelier de Sceaux at Malia, and one with two columns is attested at Building B in Quartier Mu also at Malia.

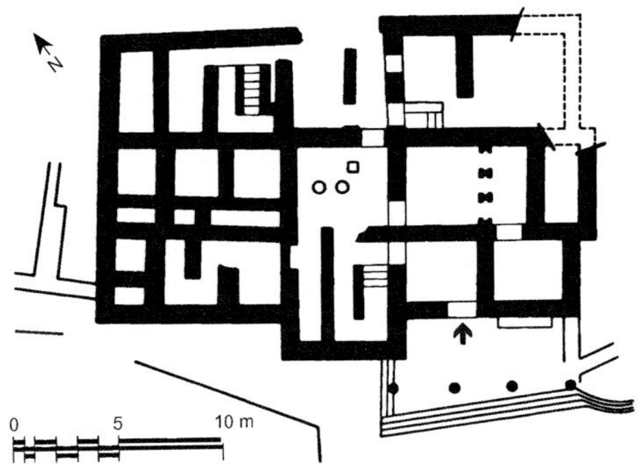

Fig. 82. Entrance with portico at Palaikastro, Block X, House 1–17. After Preziosi 1983, fig. II.20.

Zakros House G has a marked entrance. It is in the form of a small paved porch with a column at the center of its facade (Fig. 83). The two walls flanking the column protrude slightly outward like piers. This kind of Single-Column Porch with pronounced framing was probably more popular than acknowledged hitherto (similar projections exist in House Δβ, Malia and probably Chamaizi). Gournia, House Aa, Room 4, seems also to have had a porch with a central column along its open side. Malia House Δα possibly also had a porch of the same type: the broad entrance (approximately 1.80 m) asks for a central support, and there is a stone in the middle of the opening that may have functioned as the base for a central column (see Fig. 111:b)

The Caravanserai, though inadequately excavated, is of special interest because of its association to water running from a nearby spring (Fig. 84). The entrance to the building is in the form of a room open on one side. There is a single column in the middle of this facade and a few steps that give access to the porch. The porch has wall paintings on all three walls that imitate pier-and-door partitions crowned by a frieze. At the back wall, by the corner, there is the actual entrance door, integrated in the illusionary, full-scale pier-and-door partition painted on the walls (Palyvou 2000).

Nirou Chani is a large building consisting of two wings that communicate. The southern wing comprises the most elaborate rooms, among which a typical Minoan Hall opens onto a broad paved court. The excavator dubbed the porch of the Minoan Hall a "Propylon" and designated it as the entrance to the building, an assumption accepted by most scholars (Xanthoudidis 1922, 5; Hiller 1980, 227; Fotou 1997, 41–46). This, however, is most unlikely and, as Graham observes, "very unusual, if

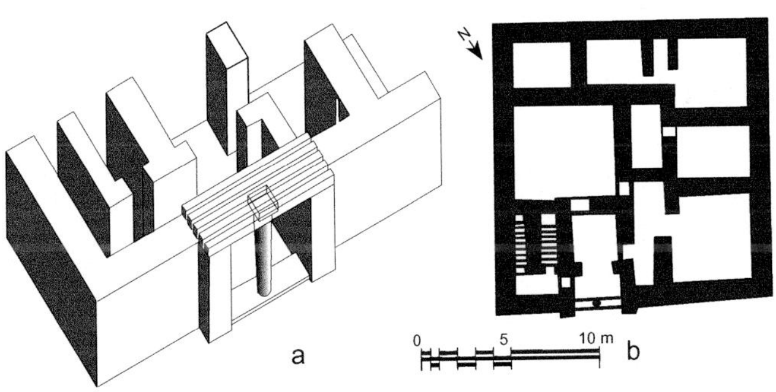

Fig. 83. House G, Zakros: (a) isometric drawing of entrance porch (drawing C. Palyvou); (b) plan (after Platon 1974, fold-out plan).

Fig. 84. Single-Column Porch of the Caravanserai. Evans 1921–1935, II, fig. 55.

not unique" (1972, 59). The interpretation of the porch of the Minoan Hall as an entrance porch to the building was based on two assumptions: first that the paved court in front of the porch is public space; and second that there is no other entrance to the building. The latter is in fact true as things stand today, but excavation is far from being complete: the west boundary of the building has not been fully exposed. The same is true for the paved court, since its outer limits are not yet defined in all directions.

Moreover, by identifying the pier-and-door partition of the Minoan Hall with the entrance to the building, two serious misconceptions ensue: one regarding the character of the Minoan Hall; and the other regarding the concept of the entrance. In Minoan architecture there are certain unmistakable norms: the Minoan Hall has an indisputable introverted character involving a private open-air space and a pier-and-door partition in the role of a mutable barrier. The entrance, on the other hand, is clearly defined as a door with a single door leaf. A pier-and-door partition consisting of three doors with double leaves each cannot act as a main entrance, just as the introverted Minoan Hall cannot open directly onto a public space. Archanes is a similar case: the Minoan Hall is also referred to as the entrance to the building. Such an access system would have been a major irregularity in the context of Minoan architecture. Amnissos is another instance: its impressive "entrance," consisting of a porch with two columns, may prove to be an exit to a private court. In all these cases, excavation is far from complete, thus important information regarding the real identity, public or private, of the adjacent open-air spaces is missing. Hence, a note of caution is necessary: premature judgement based on inconclusive data might disrupt seriously our understanding of Minoan architecture.

## The Vestibule: An Arriving-Leaving Place

What lies immediately beyond the entrance door is the first encounter with the content of the building and its inner, hidden character. It is yet another place for pause or arrest, as before crossing the threshold, another place of transition where new decisions must be made and for which the incomer needs directional clues or human guidance. On leaving the house, it is equally a place for contemplation and preparation before entering the public realm outside.

In medium- and small-sized Minoan urban houses the entrance door leads to a small lobby that serves as a node for distributing circulation and controlling access to the inner parts of the building. As mentioned while discussing forms of floor treatment (see this vol., p. 52), the lobby is often the only room at ground floor level that is paved, a treatment that links this space to the street at the other side of the entrance. It also alludes, however, to permanence and endurance. The entrance lobby, after all, is the showcase of the house, a point of arrival and departure where residents and visitors interact in their social roles, even more so in Minoan domestic architecture where porches are rare.

The entrance lobby should reveal, implicitly or explicitly, the space articulation of the building and the way to penetrate its inner zones. In many Minoan houses, the lobby presents the incomer with three options of movement, two horizontal and one vertical. One of the horizontal connectors is a corridor that leads to major formal rooms on the ground floor. The other is a door leading to the storage and service zone. The vertical connector is a broad staircase that is either incorporated within the lobby proper or attached right next to it. This staircase leads to the upper floor where the domestic compartments and reception areas are most likely to be found. The identity of the incomers will determine their choice of movement.

In many average houses the entrance lobby is more than just a circulatory node; it houses functions that need frequent and direct access to the outside public space, such as small mill installations or fresh water containers. Some lobbies, despite their restricted floor area, even had oil-pressing installations (Zakros: Houses B and J; Gournia: Houses Ac and Dd). The utilitarian aspect of these lobbies does not render their social function any less. At the other end of the spectrum, the larger and more elaborate houses have no lobbies of the type described above. The entrance area is adjusted ad hoc to the circumstances of each building, as already hinted in the previous section while discussing buildings with entrance porches.

## The Room with the Central Column: Marking the Center

This type of room is easily recognized by its squarish form, large size, and central column. The latter is identified by a stone base embedded in the floor or found in the debris of the room. The sides of the room range from 4 to 6 m, the most frequent dimension being 4.9 to 5 m (this can be spanned by two beams supported by the central column). It is one of the largest rooms in Minoan architecture—larger than the Minoan or the Polythyron Halls.

The Room with the Central Column has a long history in Crete, and it became the nucleus of the Minoan house from very early times

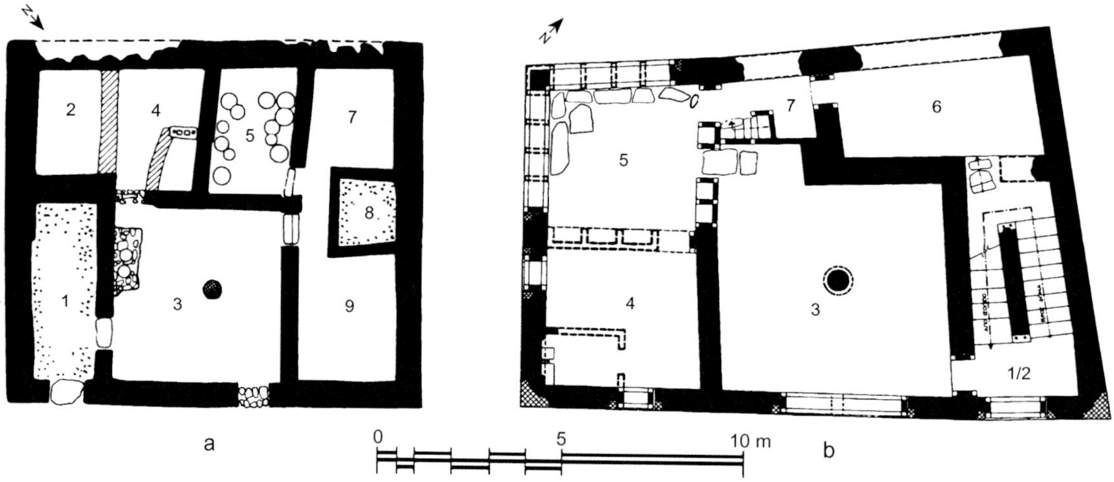


Fig. 85. Rooms with a Central Column: (a) Hagia Varvara (after Hood 1971, fig. 31); (b) Akrotiri, Thera (plan C. Palyvou).

(Fig. 85). Michailidou has elaborated at length on the form, the origins, and the possible functions of this room (Michailidou 1987).[4] The following is based largely on her work; what might be new is that whereas the interest until now has focused on explaining form primarily through function—on the basis of the form follows function dictum—the scope here is to elaborate on the architectural properties of this space-unit from a phenomenological point of view.

The most striking feature of this room is of course its form: a square with a pronounced center. Its location within the house is equally central, with easy access from the entrance. A further observation is that it typically has more than one door; in other words, it is never an end in its own right. There are usually at least two diagonally located doors, one of which is indirectly related to the entrance/exit of the building and the other to inner rooms. There is also at least one large window, as far as one can tell from the available archaeological data, especially at Akrotiri, Thera. The kind of activities that such a space unit allows or invites are twofold: circulation and activities taking place around the column at the periphery of the room, such as weaving (Tzachili 1997, 183–193). One may well imagine upright looms leaning against the walls and weavers working with their backs turned to one another as well as to the focal point of the room, the column. Though visual contact among them was not possible or needed while working, chatting was. With the weavers at rest and their bodies turned toward the center of the room, the situation would change into gathering and socializing, perhaps in the company of other people as well. The square-like form and the large size favor such gathering, but the column in the middle does not; it is an obstacle.

Why, then, a room with a central column? A first answer would be that it provides a spacious place for which the central support is structurally indispensable.[5] There are, however, other ways of obtaining large spaces by applying, for example, two or four columns, as is the case with the Mycenaean Megaron. On second thought, therefore, it may be that the choice of the single support was dictated by the symbolic value of its singularity. This is corroborated by the popularity of the single-column motif among the Minoans, both in architecture and art (see the discussion on the Single-Column Porch, pp. 198–199). A single vertical post is a kind of axis mundi that renders the room, and hence the whole house, an *imago mundi*. This is a well-known practice in many civilizations worldwide (Eliade 1961, 53).

The Room with the Central Column is one of the most resistant architectural types in prehistoric Crete, and it remained the hub of the traditional house for a very long period of time, from MM IB to LM IA (ca. 400 years). In the innovative era of the Neopalatial period this type of room was overshadowed by a new type: the Minoan Hall (discussed below, pp. 92–94). Michailidou assumes that some of the activities housed in the Room with the Central Column were transferred to the Minoan Hall, reflecting a change in the lifestyle of the people, especially in regard to issues of community and privacy. It is interesting to note that many houses were remodeled during this period in order to incorporate the new type of room, without, however, eliminating the older one. Such examples are Houses Zα and Zβ at Malia and the house at Achladia, but there may have been more if we assume that both types may have existed on the upper floor as well.

The two types of rooms, each with its special characteristics, are very well represented in the Archanes model of a house (Fig. 86). In fact, the model consists of just these two and an entrance lobby with the main staircase leading to an upper level (or roof). Storage and service facilities have been omitted. The Room with the Central Column is very pronounced and much larger than the Minoan Hall. The latter is entered directly from the entrance, while the Room with the Central Column is approached only through the Minoan Hall. The absence of a second door is due to the abbreviated rendering of the typical house (a door coming from the entrance lobby would have been a greater anomaly).

Fig. 86. Minoan Hall and Room with a Central Column in the Archanes clay model of a house. After Lebessi 1976, fig. 2.

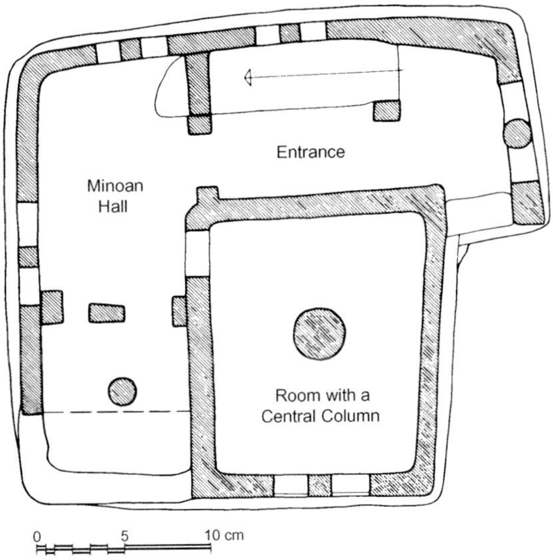


The Room with the Central Column is often found on the upper floor, as is the case at Akrotiri, Thera. Examples of this sort are attested at Knossos (Royal Villa, South House) and Tylissos (Houses A and C), but there were certainly many more. Akrotiri presents an interesting situation in regard to this type of room worth mentioning here. There is clear evidence in at least two instances that such a room was created *a posteriori*, after the seismic destruction of the settlement in the beginning of LM IA (Palyvou 1984). It is well attested that this misfortune was met by the inhabitants of Akrotiri as an opportunity to reform their houses by using the most up-to-date building technology coming from Crete. In doing so they also chose to include a type of room well embedded in the Cretan tradition yet foreign to their own: the Room with the Central Column. This they did at a time when the specific type was running rather out of fashion in Crete in favor of the Minoan Hall. The absence of the Minoan Hall at Akrotiri may indicate that this new type of room had not reached Thera yet (Palyvou 1999b, 613).

## The Minoan Hall: Symmetry, Order, and Gradation

The Minoan Hall is one of the outstanding diagnostic features of Minoan architecture, just as the Megaron is for the Mycenaean world. It consists of three units in juxtaposition (Fig. 87): a room (the hall), a forehall (portico), and an open-air space, usually in the form of a court (the light-well). The room and the portico are connected with a pier-and-door partition that allows for flexible communication between the two spaces. As discussed in the previous chapter, this ingenious architectural element provides a large variety of indoor/outdoor communication patterns and a rich range of intermediate situations. It is indeed the epitome of gradation and in-betweenness.

The name Minoan Hall was coined by Graham, and it is widely accepted today (1972, 94; for further discussion and references, see Palyvou 1999a, 344). The three parts of the Minoan Hall exhibit the following typical characteristics:

(1) The hall is usually a squarish room of medium size, it is well paved, and it has at least one blank wall.

(2) The portico, which communicates with the hall through a pier-and-door partition, is a semi-open sheltered space, its roof supported by one or more columns.

(3) The so-called light-well is a small open-air space, usually enclosed, though there are several variations as to its form and size (on the misuse of the term light-well see below, pp. 103–104).

The Minoan Hall has three fundamental spatial properties: symmetry, order, and gradation. The gradation is achieved through the pier-and-door partition(s) that allows for soft transitions: closed/semi-open/open; dark/shaded/luminous; and mass/perforated/void (Fig. 88).

The key to understanding the Minoan Hall lies precisely in the in-between situations it provides. The outdoor space, in particular, plays an important role in this respect. In almost all instances, the open-air spaces that have been dubbed light-wells are, in fact, small courts that provide not only light and air but most importantly privacy. This is evident from the fact that they are located at the periphery of the building and the rooms they are appended to are amply lit by windows. That privacy is the main goal is also evident by the tall wall separating the court from the public domain beyond. Examples of this sort are the Minoan Halls at Knossos, Tylissos, Achladia, and Malia Houses Zα and Zβ. It is also explicitly represented in the Archanes clay model of a house (see Fig. 86). Minoan Halls opening on courts situated at the edge of a cliff, like those at the Palaces of Knossos and Phaistos, do not require walls; privacy is ensured physically.

This means that it is not so much the outdoor space as such that is useful—to sit out under the sun, perhaps—but the fact that the parapet walls allow for the main hall to open up all its doors for the inhabitants to enjoy a cool breeze in privacy, without being exposed to the eyes of those passing by outside. In other words, the court provides a buffer zone between the private and public domains, and it is the sheltered portico that matters most, as a means to control the amount of sunlight entering the hall according to the season. This is well-known practice in classical Greek houses but also in many instances from other parts of the world with similar climate (see Fig. 87). Consequently, the orientation of the porticoes of most Minoan Halls in domestic architecture is to the east and south, a few to the west, and very rarely to the north (House Δα, Malia). Graham, therefore, was right in assuming thermal comfort and climatic control as the main functional virtues of the Minoan Hall (1972, 56).

The other two properties of the Minoan Hall, symmetry and order, are testified by the arrangement and distribution of the doors and the columns along a latent grid motif. The overall effect, however, is not axiality, as one might assume at first, but rather centrality. This is implied by the square form of the main hall and the floor treatment that follows a centripetal design.

Centrality is also patent in the composite Minoan Halls of the Palaces and palatial compounds, such as the Little Palace and Hagia

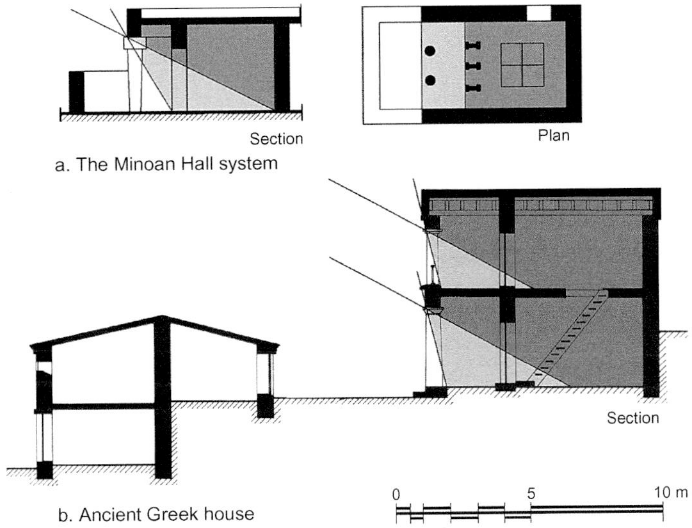


Fig. 87. The Minoan Hall provides an ideal system for controlling seasonal penetration (top), similar to that of ancient houses (bottom). Top: drawing C. Palyvou; bottom: after Hoepfner 2009, 19.

Fig. 88. Pier-and-door partition as mutable barrier at the Royal Villa, Knossos. Michailidou 1981, fig. 60; courtesy Ekdotike Athenon S.A.

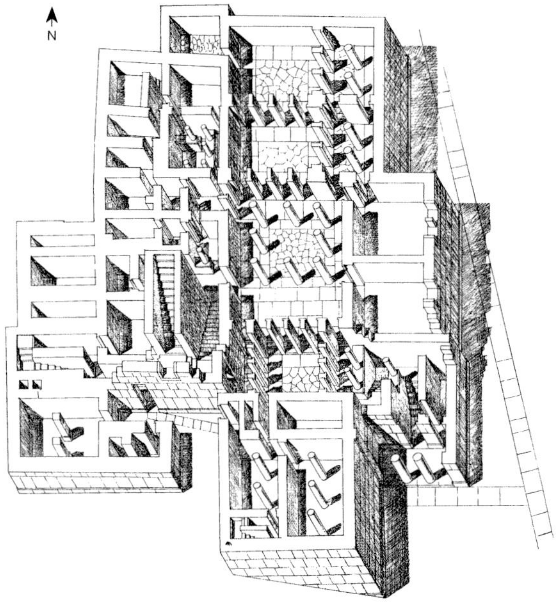


Fig. 89. Isometric drawing of the Little Palace. Evans 1921–1935, II.2, 516, fig. 317.

Triada. They are composed of two or more overlapping typical Minoan Halls that are differently orientated as if pivoting around the main Hall (Figs. 89–91). The composite Minoan Halls, therefore, should not be regarded as typological deviations but as fusions of more than one main unit (Palyvou 1987).

## The Polythyron Hall: Mutability

Pier-and-door partitions are typical of, but not exclusive to the Minoan Halls. They appear in different contexts as well, most conspicuously in sets of two or more rooms connected to each other through pier-and-door partitions. These complexes, commonly called Polythyron Halls, have none of the characteristics of the Minoan Hall described above (no columnar porch and no related open-air spaces). They too are characterized by order along a latent grid, but there is no clear focal space and no directional emphasis. Their main vantage is mutability and flexibility: the numerous doors that partake in such compositions can provide an amazing variety of space combinations and interrelations.

Examples of Polythyron Halls are to be found at the Palace of Zakros and at Akrotiri, Thera: in Xeste 3, five pier-and-door partitions connect six space-cells at ground floor level, and when all doors are open (18 in total) a Hall approximately 80 $m^2$ is created (Fig. 92). There are four pier-and-door partitions on the first floor connecting five rooms, and there were at least two more on the second floor. Because of its good state of preservation and ample available information regarding the second floor, this edifice is stunning proof of the innovative space configuration advanced by the Minoans and the bold timber technology it entailed.

## Lustral Basin and Pillar Crypt: Back to the Archetypes

The Lustral Basin, or Adyton, is a well-defined architectural unit peculiar to the Minoan world (Fig. 93). It is a small space, approximately 2.5 x 3 m, sunk into the ground ca. 0.80 m below floor level. It is accessed through a few steps winding around a parapet or a pillar. The floor is usually paved and the walls are veneered with upright slabs. This

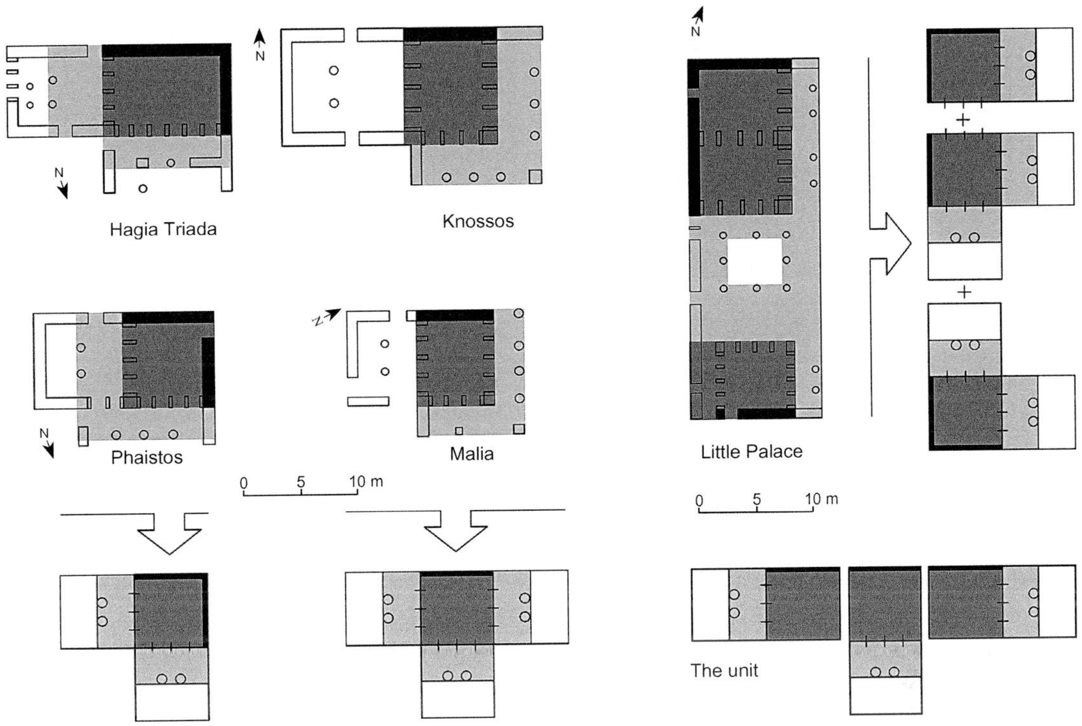


Fig. 90. Composite systems of Halls consisting of juxtaposed or superimposed Minoan Hall units. Dark shades correspond to interior space and light shades to sheltered, open-air spaces. Drawings C. Palyvou.

Fig. 91. Pier-and-door partitions at the Domestic Quarter of the Palace of Phaistos. Chatzi-Vallianou 1989, fig. 26; © Hellenic Ministry of Culture and Sports–Archaeological Receipts Fund.

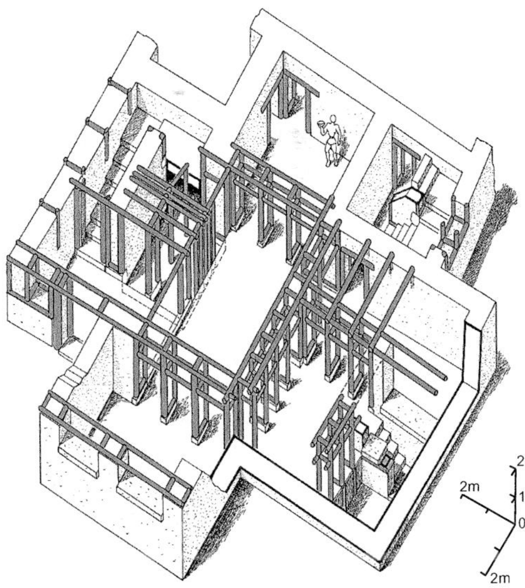


Fig. 92. Isometric drawing of Xeste 3, Akrotiri, Thera. More than 12 pier-and-door partitions distributed in three different levels existed in this building. Drawing C. Palyvou.

peculiar architectural unit is, as a rule, incorporated in a larger space through which it may be viewed.

Lustral Basins are related primarily to the Palaces, but they also exist in some Neopalatial mansions (there are 24 in Palaces and 10 in other buildings).[6] It is generally assumed that the earliest example is at Quartier Mu, Malia, though it is much larger and deeper than the later type.

The name was coined by Evans and caused much misunderstanding as to the use of water it implies.[7] There is no doubt, however, that such spaces were not meant to carry water. It is quite evident that they served some sort of ritual bearing chthonic connotations, as mentioned in discussing floor treatment (see this vol., pp. 52–53).[8] The small size and the possibility of indirect participation by viewing from above imply varying degrees of involvement (Fig. 94). Viewing downward over a balustrade emphasizes the exclusiveness of the inner space and adds to the element of performance by which some people are acting and others are gazing or participating in some other way. Going down means coming up again, so the performance could refer to submerging as much as emerging from the earthly receptacle that is the Lustral Basin.

This highly idiosyncratic space is an excellent manifestation of the power of certain functions to generate innovative and exclusive forms. This is a clear case where form follows function. Such forms are less liable to adapt to changing conditions or different functions (see this vol., pp. 176–177), for they can hardly house any use other than the one for which they were initially designed. Hence the reasonable assumption is that the reason why several Lustral Basins (e.g., South House at Knossos, Amnissos, Houses A and C at Tylissos) were filled in sometime in LM IA was because of the discontinuation of the ritual they were designed to serve (Driessen 1982). Filling in obviously deactivated the downward power of the magnet earth and cancelled their fundamental chthonic property related to that ritual.

Unlike the clear status of Lustral Basins, that of Pillar Crypts is blurry and ambiguous. In fact, very few can be readily recognized as belonging to a distinct architectural type corresponding to a specific function. Many more simply look like Pillar Crypts, basically because they include one or more pillars (which may well have been necessary for structural reasons).[9] Pillar Crypts are generally believed to be a

a b c

Fig. 93. Lustral Basins: (a) Malia (courtesy I. Swindale); (b) Phaistos (Chatzi-Vallianou 1989, fig. 25; © Hellenic Ministry of Culture and Sports–Archaeological Receipts Fund.); (c) Zakros (courtesy L. Platon, Archive of the Zakros Excavations).

Knossian phenomenon of the Neopalatial period, marking the particular identity of the Knossian region, as Evans suggested (Fig. 95; Evans 1899–1900, 32–43). They are found in the Palace as well as some of the surrounding houses (i.e., the Southeast House, the House of the Chancel Screen, the South House, the Royal Villa, and Hogarth's House B). They have ashlar walls (rare for interior spaces) carrying masons' marks and special floor treatment, including cists or channels appropriate for libations. They are deliberately windowless and hence dark, even when located at the periphery of the building, as in the Royal Villa, and they often include movable items that refer to rituals.

Fig. 94. Lustral Basin in Xeste 3, Akrotiri, Thera. A low parapet allowed for visual contact with the Lustral Basin. Palyvou 2005a, fig. 243:top.

The size of the room does not readily justify a central support; the pillar, in other words, was not statically necessary. The reference to the archetypal cave is indeed unmistakable, as was suggested initially by Evans. Eleni Hatzaki has argued convincingly in her lectures that the Pillar Crypt in the so-called Temple Tomb at Knossos may indeed represent a tomb in the form of a cave dug out from the rock, like those excavated at Poros, all of which include pier-like masses of rock supporting the ceiling of the cave.

Fig. 95. Pillar Crypt of the Royal Villa, Knossos. Michailidou 1981, fig. 62; courtesy Ekdotike Athenon S.A.

## Storage and Service

Almost all activities—mundane or ritual or ephemeral or repetitive—call for the use of objects that need to be stowed away when not in use. These could be: (a) incoming goods and materials; (b) tools, containers, and other equipment necessary to carry out the task; and (c) outgoing products. Storage facilities therefore may entail quite a complex network of items, movable or fixed, from a wooden chest and a bin to a cupboard, or a storage room, or a whole set of storage units (magazine). Circulation is crucial: access from the public domain outside the building should be easy but controlled, and intercommunication between the storage area and the area where the corresponding task takes place should be as direct as possible, with least interference between one another. Time, frequency, and ergonomic factors define the location, size, and form of storage spaces.

The Minoans, it seems, were very much aware of these requirements. The design tools they developed to deal with such complex demands were zoning and multiple connectors. Zoning ensures separation and rational distribution of functions, whereas multiple connectors allow for organizing movement by mapping distinct lines of communication with minimum crisscrossing. These are discussed in more detail in Chapter 4.

Storage facilities adhere to two design principles: ergonomy and economy. The intention to economize space is evident in the many ways the Minoans have contrived to exploit every possible inch of space, be it under the staircase, below the floor, in shelves on the walls, or on hooks hanging from the ceiling beams. Pithoi are lined up neatly against the walls and storage rooms of standard size are set in rows (Fig. 96). Ergonomy is essential to architecture and even more imperative in designing storage spaces where time, effort, and efficiency are absolute priorities. These are further discussed in Chapter 10 in relation to Palaces, but the logic is the same for domestic architecture as well. Tylissos House A, for example, has a separate storage zone wisely interconnected with the main house, with magazines that were probably intended for long-term storage, perhaps for surplus to be traded. Other storage facilities within the house proper would have served the everyday tasks.

A brief reference to service areas related to sanitation is pertinent here. The manner in which a society deals with this issue is indicative of the living standards of its people. In this context, Bronze Age Crete scores very high indeed! Drainage and sewage systems are attested almost everywhere and from very early times. There is even evidence for fresh water in the Palace of Knossos running in ingeniously designed clay pipes. Some large water reservoirs may have functioned as swimming pools, as the one in the Palace of Zakros and possibly another at Archanes (see Fig. 26). But, more than that, there were toilets! To be more precise, there were indoor toilets, and not only for the elite residing in the Palaces—as is the so-called Queen's toilet in the Domestic Quarters of the Palace of Knossos—but also for ordinary people living in ordinary houses, like the perfectly preserved toilet on the upper floor(!) of the West House at Akrotiri, Thera (Graham 1972, 108–110; Palyvou 1997; 2005a, 51–53; Bradfer-Burdet and Pomadère 2011).

Fig. 96. Storeroom with pithoi fixed in built benches in Sector B, Akrotiri, Thera, looking west. Palyvou 2005a, fig. 84.

Two points regarding the sanitary installations should be emphasized here: first, their incorporation within the fabric of the building that provides easy access and privacy (until only a century ago toilets were located outside the houses for sanitation reasons); and second, the amazing technology that allowed them to be located indoors—in other words, their connection to a communal sewage network instead of a local cesspit and the installation of some kind of smell-trap (an early form of siphon has been identified at Akrotiri). Suffice it to point out here that the hydraulic knowledge required for giving each part of the system its appropriate shape, dimensions, gradient, interconnections, and so forth, as well as the maintenance that such a communal network demands, is indicative of a well-organized community and high standards of technological knowledge accumulated through time and experience.

## Places with No Names and Tasks out of Place

The rooms discussed so far are those that in the long run of Minoan studies have been more or less identified as distinct types. There are however many more anonymous space-cells within a building compound, be it a Palace or a house, which have nothing special or identifiable about them. Names have been given only to those units with standardized characteristics corresponding to specific architectural types; name giving therefore reflects the degree of standardization of Minoan architecture. These nameless spaces are all case specific and cannot be discussed on a common basis, yet some general points can be made.

The raison d'être of such spaces can vary considerably. First, since we are dealing almost exclusively with ground floor spaces, some of these cells may have resulted from requirements concerning the upper floor, as we know well from Akrotiri.[10] Second, in the absence of corridors in most houses (the corridor is an advanced concept of space-connector) several cells act primarily as circulatory nodes or nexuses. Third, some of them are closely related to identifiable spaces, like those described in the previous paragraphs, in which case they might have had an auxiliary function as annexes. Finally, the need for storage, especially short-term casual stowing, is very demanding, as mentioned above. It may well be, therefore, that their primal role was of this sort, as a wardrobe, for instance, or a place to stow away ritual paraphernalia when not in use. Most likely, however, their use was flexible and interchangeable.

At the other end of this inquiry there are some very common everyday tasks in a household that we do not know with certainty where they took place. Strangely enough, this is the case with the three most mundane tasks of all: cooking, eating, and sleeping. Of eating there are some suggestions, mostly regarding formal eating and banquets in palatial compounds. Of sleeping there are only a few platforms in early buildings that may have served as beds (Kopaka 1990). There are also the casts of five wooden beds from Akrotiri, all of which (except perhaps the one in the room with the Spring Fresco) had been relocated after the earthquake. The situation is most bizarre in relation to cooking, especially if one thinks of the large amount of cooking and eating vessels recovered from the debris, along with the smoke and the danger of catching fire while cooking. The circumstances of these finds do not allow for safe conclusions (McEnroe 1982, 9; Muhly 1984; Shaw 1990;

Brogan and Barnard 2011; Letesson 2015; on kitchens and the difficulty of their identification, see Graham 1972, 137; on LM IB–II hearths at Kommos, see Rethemiotakis 1999). In many instances cooking took place outside, which could also mean on the roof. In general, fixed hearths were more common in the Old Palace period, whereas braziers and portable hearths became popular in the Neopalatial period, both in palatial and domestic contexts. These tantalizing questions present the opportunity to offer a word of caution, for they reflect the problems and the frustration that entails when attempting to read use through form, and also the ambiguities with regard to the meaning of function (see this vol., Ch. 9).

## Outdoor Spaces

*Greeks built their houses so they can live out-doors! (Konstantinidis 1975, 311)*

This eloquent phrase, written by a perplexed anonymous traveler to Greece in the early 19th century A.D., is a perfect introduction to the importance of outdoor living in a land with mild climatic conditions such as Crete. It is also an excellent comment with regard to the inextricable relationship between inside and outside. Indeed, there can be no outside in architecture without it being associated with an inside. The "interplay between inside and outside is the fundamental aesthetic theme of all architecture. It is the dialectical tension between the attempt at concealing the inside from the outside and yet revealing it, between barring the intrusion of the outside while simultaneously taking account of it" (Arnheim, Zucker, and Watterson 1966, 12).

Having said that, we must clarify and correct the common preconception that life in Greece is outdoors. Aris Konstantinidis, a famous Greek architect with phenomenological insights, remarked emphatically that life in Greece is semi-outdoors (Fig. 97; Konstantinidis 1975, 310). For those who have visited Greece in the summer, the urgent need to take shelter from the blazing sun is as strong as the desire to stay outdoors as long as possible. The effects on the vernacular architecture of the island are more than evident.

It is precisely in such semi-outdoor spaces that Minoan architecture thrived and developed its unique character: interlocking elements that bridge the rifts between inside and outside and provide a rich range of in-between situations became the basic tools for the innovative, imaginative, and integrated architectural style of the Neopalatial era. One should constantly be reminded, however, that such a style would never have been promoted had it not been backed by the appropriate sociocultural ideology; had it not served effectively the Minoan lifestyle, in other words. Cultural factors play a very important role in the form, distribution, and use of outdoor spaces, hence there is much to be gained by studying the relationship between indoor and outdoor domains.

Fig. 97. Life in Greece is semi-outdoors. Lavvas and Philippidis, eds., 1983–1991, II, fig. 230; courtesy Melissa Publishing House.

### *Attached: Balcony, Veranda, and Roof*

Many Neopalatial buildings are highly perforated on the outside and comprise several open and semi-open spaces in the form of projecting balconies and verandas. In addition to that, roofs are flat and functional, and they were most probably provided with light timber shelters. Walking through a Minoan town, therefore, would have been a lively interactive experience, with people peeping out of windows or sitting on the balconies and verandas, with others watching from the roof. The fascinating, extroverted nature of Minoan architecture is by no means to be taken for granted for such an early period in history, especially when compared to its eastern Mediterranean neighbors.

Balconies are attested only in art: the balcony of the Archanes model is shown in exemplary detail and there is one more in the Theran Miniature Frieze (Fig. 98; see also Fig. 136:a). What is important to note is that in both cases the balconies project at the level of the roof. They constitute, in other words, an extension of an open-air space. This is quite foreign to the modern notion of a balcony, which is understood as being attached to an indoor space. The modern balcony has its roots in egalitarian multiple-family housing. In early high-rise buildings the upper floors were thought to be disadvantaged because they lacked outside spaces; this was overcome by the extension of the floor outward in the form of balconies. Due to technical restrictions, balconies could be quite long—as long as the facade of the building—but their width (the projecting part) was limited. Consequently the use of the open-air space they provided was confined to people sitting or lining up next to each other, not gathering together. The main use of a balcony, then, was to see and to be seen, and, in many cultural contexts this has been the role of women. For the balcony to provide space for gathering and socializing its width must be at

Fig. 98. Clay model of a house (31.0 x 29.0 x 18.0 cm) with a balcony and light shelter on the roof (left), and traditional house in Veroia, northern Greece (right). Left: Sakellarakis and Sapouna-Sakellaraki 1991, fig. 36; courtesy Ekdotike Athenon S.A.; right: Lavvas and Philippidis, eds., 1983–1991, VII, fig. 46; courtesy Melissa Publishing House.

least 1.80 m. Such dimensions, however, became possible only recently, thanks to the advanced cantilever technology of our time.

The Minoan examples discussed here are of an entirely different nature: they are surely not meant to provide open-air space, since they are not attached to indoor spaces. Furthermore, it is of great interest that in both balconies the protrusion that characterizes the balcony is attested not only in the horizontal but in the vertical as well (in the Archanes model three steps lead up to the balcony from the roof level, and in the Theran fresco the balcony is set slightly higher than the line demarcating the roof). The Theran balcony, in fact, protrudes symbolically, not only in relation to the building to which it is attached, but to the town itself! Finally, in both cases there is a conspicuous female figure occupying the balcony. In the Theran painting she is emphatically depicted in size and gesture.[11]

The peculiarities of these two rare cases of balconies point to some specific function, perhaps not entirely secular. In both instances the balcony forms a pronounced platform of small dimensions, meant for one person only. The person (female) standing on the balcony is thus distinguished from other people possibly standing on the roof. In Minoan architecture, therefore, the balcony is not an egalitarian feature as we know it today, but quite the opposite: an exclusive place for promoting a single female figure (a kind of "balcony of appearance," as suggested by Hägg [1987, 132–133] in a slightly different context).

A veranda is an open or semi-open (sheltered) part of the house, usually elevated above ground. Since upper floors have rarely survived, there is only indirect evidence for the presence of verandas in Minoan architecture, mostly from architectural depictions in art and, in some instances, from the form of the ground floor.

The artistic evidence is once again compelling (Palyvou 2005b). Sheltered verandas are depicted in the Miniature frieze at Akrotiri in at least two instances (Fig. 99:b, c). The first is identified by the white background and the ashlar pier supporting the shelter. Two or three men are standing under the shelter looking out from the veranda: only their tops are seen, while the lower part of their bodies is concealed by a wooden parapet. The second veranda consists of a shelter carried by two ashlar piers and an intermediate wooden (yellow) post. Five men are depicted on a white background that indicates open air. The lower part of their bodies is here too concealed by a wooden balustrade. A fragment of a wall painting from Knossos also shows a woman standing behind the wooden balustrade of a veranda (Fig. 99a; Evans 1921–1932, III, 59, fig. 35). Such sheltered verandas have not been identified in the archaeological record, but they have been rightly suggested for several buildings.[12]

Roofs were flat and functional in Minoan architecture. They were reached from within the house via the main staircase located at the entrance lobby. Of real roofs we have very little direct evidence, mostly from Akrotiri (Palyvou 1999a, 216–220). They were evidently an important part of the house, especially in urban environments where courtyards were missing. It is very probable that roofs had permanent or provisional light shelters to protect from the blazing sun, as the Archanes model of a house has shown and as restored by Schmid at Malia (Fig. 100; see also Fig. 98).

Fig. 99. Sheltered verandas depicted in fresco fragments: (a) Threshing Floor Deposit, Knossos (after Evans 1921–1935, III, fig. 35); (b) Miniature Frieze, Akrotiri, Thera (after Doumas 1992, 85, fig. 48); (c) author's restoration of Miniature Frieze, Akrotiri, Thera (after Doumas 1992, 85, fig. 48).

### *Appended: Light-Well, Court, and Garden*

That light-wells are a characteristic feature of Minoan architecture is a leitmotiv repeated in many textbooks. This however is not so true—at least not if we use the term for exactly what it means. The loose use of the term started with Graham, who wrote, "the distinction between a court and a light-well is a matter of size, and so must to a certain extent be arbitrary" (1972, 167 n. 10). He thus introduced a misunderstanding and established the idea that Minoan architecture was full of light-wells. As a starting point, therefore, we need to discuss the term itself. The word well implies, metaphorically, a hole that has been drilled out of a mass—in this case the mass of a building—in order to provide light and air to rooms that have no other means of obtaining them (Fig. 101). As such, the well implies limited horizontal surface and accentuated verticality, and no other intended use other than bringing light and air.

Fig. 100. Model of Quartier Mu, Malia. Etienne, ed., 1996, 28.

True light-wells do exist in Minoan buildings, mostly in relation to staircases, like the three light-wells of the Domestic Quarter at Knossos, all of which provide light to staircases embedded in the fabric of the building (Fig. 102; see also Fig. 188).[13] A true light-well is also found at Akrotiri in the House of the Ladies, again next to an interior staircase (Palyvou 2005a, 83–85). This is no coincidence: even by modern standards, staircases have strict regulations regarding lighting conditions for safety reasons. The Grand Staircase at Knossos—and its miniature version at Myrtos Pyrgos—is an ingenious response to this demand, both as an architectural conception and a technical achievement: the idea to substitute the outer wall of the staircase with superimposed colonnades flanking a light-well not only brought maximum light to the staircase but also created a unique feeling of

Fig. 101. A light-well is a hole drilled out of the mass of a building in order to provide light to rooms that would otherwise be blind. Drawing C. Palyvou.

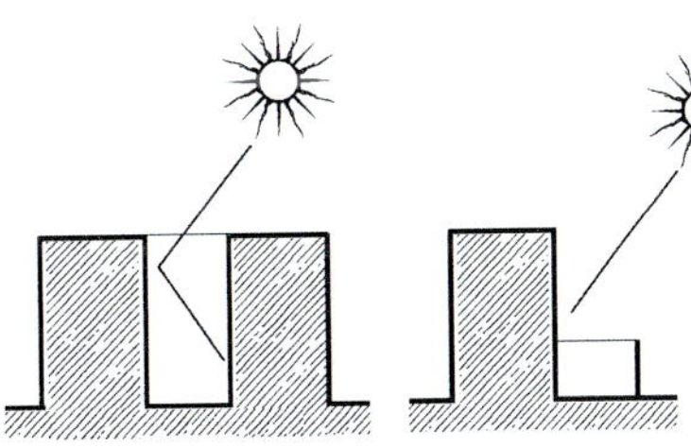

Fig. 102. Grand Staircase, Knossos. Light-wells exist in Minoan architecture often in relation to staircases. Davaras 1986, fig. 31; © Hellenic Ministry of Culture and Sports–Archaeological Receipts Fund.

lightness, transparency, and fluidity of space. As a true light-well, the space at the bottom had no specific use; it is the shaft that mattered.

It is important to reserve the term light-well for true examples of this sort, for we thus gain a more accurate understanding of the rich nuances of outdoor spaces in Minoan architecture and avoid being misled by comparing different forms of space under the same name.

A court is an enclosed open-air space within the boundaries of a building compound. Topologically, it may be situated either at the periphery of the compound, separated from the public domain beyond by a fence, a parapet, or a wall of some height, or it may be located within the fabric of the building, surrounded by private indoor space-cells. The latter is typical of the so-called court-house, an introverted design concept where the court has a focal role in the function of the house. The court-house has been popular at all times and places (Fig. 103),[14] all but the Bronze Age in Crete. The fact that the Minoans chose not to adopt this type of housing, at least not on a large scale, needs some explanation. But first we need to review the data.

The court-house type is attested in a very limited number of cases, all of an early date, such as the Prepalatial compound at Hagia Photia (which is, in fact, a broad corridor rather than a court) and possibly even earlier in the Neolithic houses at Knossos (Evans 1921–1935, II, 1–21). Strangely enough, the term court-house fits best the MM house at Chamaizi, a building that has drawn attention for its curved outline rather than its central court. The larger and more complex houses, representing 11% of the total number of excavated Neopalatial houses (McEnroe 1982, 7), comprise a variety of open-air spaces, yet few in the form of an introverted central court that functions as the focal point of the building (the houses with Peristyle Courts at Palaikastro may be considered such a case, and the very large House E at Malia).

From the Middle Bronze Age onward, houses become compact and extroverted; they relied exclusively on their periphery for light and air, hence the large number of windows.[15] Where courts exist, they are in the form of open-air spaces attached to the periphery of the house, like at Rousses, Vathypetro, and probably Sklavokampos.

The absence of the court-house type may be associated with the following factors:

(1) The function of the court in this type of house is often related to social requirements and gender discrimination: the courts provide outdoor private domains meant primarily for the women of the house. Their absence in Minoan architecture, therefore, may be indicative of a nondiscriminative society on the basis of gender.

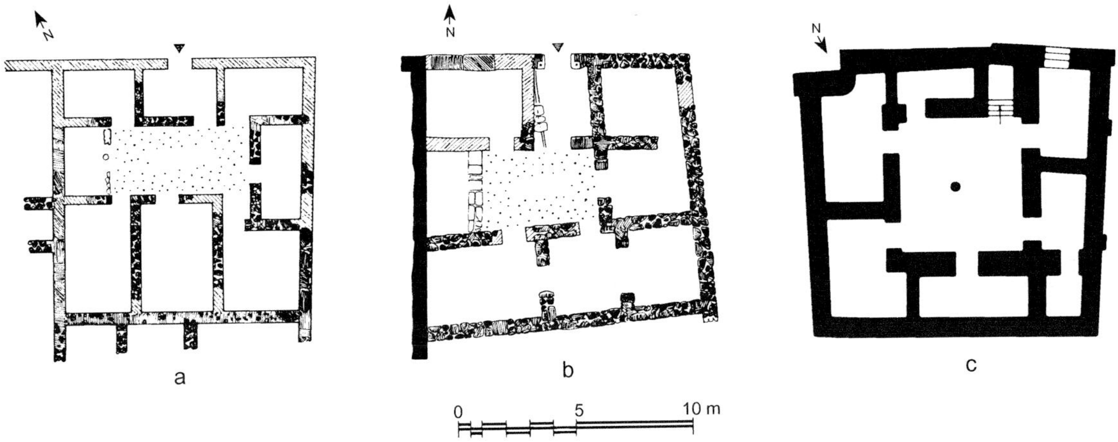


Fig. 103. Court-houses: (a) Athens, fifth century B.C. (after Travlos 1993, fig. 104); (b) Athens, 12th century A.D. (after Travlos 1993, fig. 104); (c) Ur, Mesopotamia, second millennium B.C. (after Frankfort 1970, fig. 117).

(2) In the absence of courts, the next option for outdoor activities is the roof or the veranda, both of which are exposed to the public eye. Since this is indeed the case in Minoan houses, it means that such exposure was socially acceptable at the time.

(3) The court, and even more so the garden, may be understood as a patch of the landscape appropriated by the manmade environment. Its absence therefore may reflect distinct and separate roles for the countryside and the urban environment, respectively.

The absence of the court-house in Crete is even more interesting in the light of the importance the court acquired in the Minoan Palace (see this vol., Ch. 10). Yet there may be a misuse of the term court here, because we are probably comparing two very different situations with only superficial resemblances. The Central Court of the Palace is an autonomous, powerful space that generates forces that hold together its components; it is one of the zones of the Palace, as discussed in the relevant chapter (see this vol., Ch. 10). Its origin should not be sought in the archetypal house and its court but in the architectural concretization of communal activities that traditionally took place outdoors. Indeed, there is nothing to suggest that the early "court buildings," as Schoep calls them, have any relation to the Late Bronze Palaces, as she also concludes (2004, 245–255).

A garden, finally, is a fragment of nature tamed and formulated so as to give pleasure and satisfaction to the residents of the house, a kind of negotiation for the physical environment that has been appropriated through building. That gardens did exist in relation to Minoan buildings is quite probable, as Maria Shaw has shown for the Residential Quarters of the Palaces of Knossos, Phaistos, and Malia, as well as Zakros, Palaikastro, and Hagia Triada. The garden at Phaistos, in particular, is a private open area attached exclusively to the Residential Quarters of the Palace (Shaw 1993; on gardens in art, see Tzachili 2011, 258).

## Endnotes

1 The three stages of this process are eloquently expressed in the Greek language with the verb βαίνω (to go) and three prefixes that define explicitly the sequential activities and the corresponding state of mind: πρόσ-βαση (going toward), διά-βαση (going through), and μετά-βαση (gone to; Palyvou 2009c).

2 From Michelis 1964, 141:

> "It is a fact that before overcoming the body's inertia by a forward movement, man first casts a mental glance along the line of his course, projecting it to its terminus. In other words, he gets there mentally before he arrives physically; he foresees his destination and the course he is to follow. And something more: he extends this axis to the infinite. Thus, the intersecting axes of a building which he may come across in his path, even if they do not cause him to alter his course, will be extended in his imagination, and so he will begin to perceive the main directive lines of its composition."

3 For more information regarding these houses, with references to the original publications, see Driessen and Macdonald 1997, 121–247.

4 There are several examples of this room in the architecture of the Middle Bronze Age (MM IB–MM III), both domestic and formal, as at Quartier Mu. Michailidou sees an early parallel of this type of room in the large room with circular hearth typical of the EM III/MM IA houses located south of the Palace at Malia.

5 It is interesting to note that one of the dimensions of this room is typically around 4.90 m, which divided by two gives the average spanning length of a beam (2.45 m).

6 At Knossos: Chancel Screen, South House, Southeast House, and Little Palace; at Malia: Houses Δα, Ζα, and Ε; at Tylissos Houses A and C; and at Chania. There is also one at Akrotiri, Thera (Xeste 3).

7 To avoid any allusion to a bath or a cistern, S. Marinatos preferred the term Adyton instead (1976, 24–25), also adopted by N. Marinatos and Hägg (1986, 60) and Andreadaki-Vlazaki (1988, 58).

8 For an account of Lustral Basins and the various functions that have been proposed since Evans, see McEnroe 1982, 5. These include purification rites prior to entering a compound, initiation rites, and chthonic rites alluding to cult caves.

9 Evans coined the term Pillar Crypt assuming that pillars are representations of stalactites and stalagmites worshiped in sacred caves. He regarded as Pillar Crypts almost all rooms with pillars. For general discussion and references to Evans and other scholars, see Lloyd 2011, 170–172, table 15.1.

10 See, for example, Sector Beta-South at Akrotiri, Thera: the narrow spaces B2a and B2b resulted from the division of the initial room into two parts so as to accommodate a large Room with a Central Column on the upper floor (Palyvou 2005a, 64–68).

11 The Archanes model of a house has a semi-cylindrical piece of clay added to the inside of the parapet of the balcony. According to Rethemiotakis (1998, 144), it is the lower part of the body of a female figure. The piece was identified and added at a later time, and it therefore does not appear in Lebessi's detailed publication of the model. For further discussion on these balconies, see Palyvou 2004.

12 Verandas on the upper floors have been identified with some certainty at Hagia Triada, Sklavokampos, Palaikastro (Lebessi 1976, 30 n. 1), Chania (Hallager 1990), Malia (Poursat 1996, 89–97), Myrtos Pyrgos (Cadogan 1977–1978, 77),

and Zakros (Platon 1990, 387 n. 18), and they could be suggested for many more buildings at Knossos, Vathypetro, Amnissos, and elsewhere.

13 Evans assumed there was a light-well next to the staircase at the Royal Villa, but Fotou has shown that it did not exist (Fotou 1997, 35–38).

14 The court-house is typical of the Greco-Roman period, and it remained so to a large degree throughout the Middle Ages up to the 19th century (Travlos 1993, 154–156, fig. 104). Rapoport writes that this type of house ensures separation of domains and is prevalent throughout the world "in cultures which are both crowded and hierarchic"; it also provides space for outdoor activities protected from indiscrete eyes (1969, 81–82).

15 Michailidou has suggested that the Room with a Central Column may have derived from the open-air central court of earlier rural houses, such as at Vrachnou or Lakkos, even though not many such examples exist (Michailidou 1987, 522).

# 6 Design and Execution

## The Commissioner, the Architect, and the Process

To reiterate from the preface of this book,

> It took indeed two legendary figures for the miracle to happen in Crete in the second millennium B.C.: a king Minos, representing the commissioner, the client, or the patron, and an ingenious Daidalos representing the architect, for Daidalos did not act on his own behalf, and he did not create magnificent edifices for their own accord. He was following orders and satisfying desires, some explicit, others implicit, and some even lustful. (p. xxxii)

A work of architecture begins with a need, a desire, and a vision (not always in that order); not those of the architect—at least not until our day—but those of the client or the patron. More than that, society also makes demands "which transcend the understanding and wishes of the individual" (Norberg-Schulz 1997, 15–16). The architect, therefore, is the agent and interpreter of the will of the many, hence his capacity to envision situations of human life is more important than his skill to imagine space (Pallasmaa 2005a, 189). The initiator, on the other hand, is the commissioner, the client, and the people in need of architecture for insulation, both literally and metaphorically. It is the client who chooses the architect and summons his services, either from within the local community or from elsewhere, if his status so permits or dictates.

It is also his choice not to employ an architect if he thinks that the architecture in question is within the limits of his own abilities or with a little help from his friends.

Looking at the grandeur and complexity of Minoan Palaces, one cannot help but marvel both at the skills of the architects who built them and the strong will and vision of their clients. When social status and prestige factors are at stake, the choice of architect is important. In the myth, King Minos could only have asked for the best architect, one he could afford to bring from far away, this in itself being a manifestation of status. Daidalos was a perfect choice: he was eponymous, his fame preceding him and his name discussed among circles of King Minos's equals.

The realities of the Minoan world, on the other hand, will always escape us. The client was a king, according to Evans, but new theories have put forth other identities, including so-called faceless polities—that is, societies organized into corporate groups (Driessen 2002). Whatever the sociopolitical background of the time (and the corresponding identity of the commissioner) for a building compound of the size and complexity of the Palaces of Knossos, Phaistos, or Malia to come into being, there was need for a well-articulated building program formulated by the commissioner and a mastermind who will coordinate, supervise, and keep the building process under control. This is true for any large-scale technical project, like Stonehenge for example, even if no reference to these masters has survived.

The architect—the first (αρχή) in order—is a multi-talented person in control of all the intricacies of the building procedure, from planning and designing to implementing what the client has required. It is he who divides and allots physical space and materials so that the builder can then join and combine them in harmony to create architectural space. He is the primeval cutter who "cuts something of which people who are used to material stuff are not even clearly aware" (Arnheim, Zucker, and Watterson 1966, 8).

The mythical Daidalos is the archetypal architect that meets the above description. The same is true for the first real architect recorded in history, Imhotep. Working in Egypt in the mid-third millennium B.C., he was a man of many duties who was raised to the status of a semigod. Closer to the Minoans, a talented architect is mentioned in an epic poem from Ugarit: the eponymous legendary crafts god Kothar-wa-Hasis (Skillful-and-Wise), who was summoned from Kaphtor (identified by most scholars with Minoan Crete) to build a splendid Palace with silver and gold for Ba'al. The commissioner in this case was a god, and his choice of architect was one among his own kind. Whatever the identity of Kothar and his relations to Daidalos or Hephaistos, the allusion to a highly respected master architect is straightforward, and so is the allusion to highly esteemed Cretan craftsmanship (Morris 1992, 73–100; on the role of the architect, from high priest to profession, see Roth

2007, 119–135). Furthermore, Kothar, like Daidalos, seems to have acquired his expertise through his connections with more than one place (he is also related to Egypt), a characteristic of an itinerant builder.

Somewhere between myth and reality one may assume that the Late Bronze Age architects and artisans, at least the most qualified, moved around while practicing their métier, a profession that involved learning as much as teaching. The archaeological data bare proof of such mobility through the striking similarities and standardization of architectural forms and building techniques all over Crete and beyond in Thera and Rhodes. After all, since architecture cannot travel in a boat for people to see and copy as a vase does, it must be the people who travel and diffuse technical knowledge and architectural styles.

One thing is for sure: the sophistication and complexity of Minoan architecture and the high level of building technology it requires could not have been coped with by non-experts, as Maud Devolder also concludes (2013). This is true for the most elaborate elite buildings as much as it is for two- and three-story urban houses, such as the West House at Akrotiri, Thera. Craftsmen, artisans, and artists alike were most certainly trained professionals and probably formed bodies of specialized artisans or guilds moving from place to place as demands arose, exchanging knowledge and experience.[1] What is of interest is that this knowledge, though normative by character, was not restrictive; it allowed for experimentation, innovation, and the creation of new variations of established models. One might even suggest that it thrived on initiatives of this sort and promoted innovative approaches. We are witnessing, that is, an era of versatile thinking and uninhibited creativity, a time when new ideas were being born out of a long-lasting tradition. Proof of this permeates all portions of this volume.

The production of a work of architecture, be it the construction of a fence, a house, or a Palace, goes through three consecutive phases: (1) planning or programming—that is, thinking about and classifying user requirements and aspirations in light of sociocultural norms, economic restraints, and technical specifications (what Norberg-Schulz [1997, 131] describes as formulating the tasks); (2) designing—that is, conceptualizing and attributing to the above tasks specific geometric forms and materials, calculating their dimensions, and setting their spatial associations; and (3) executing—laying out on the ground and implementing the above design (Fig. 104).

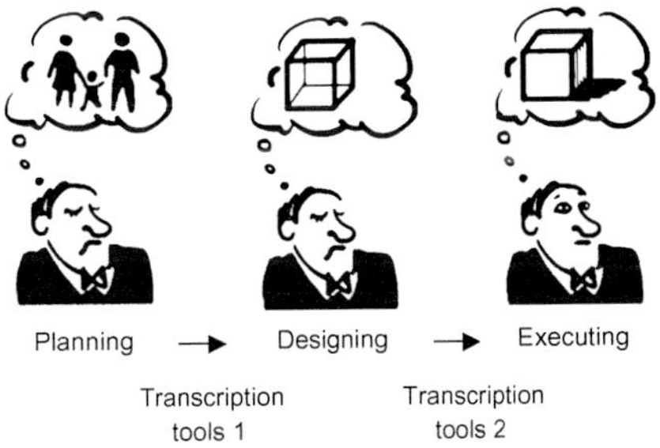


Fig. 104. Planning, designing, and executing. Drawing C. Palyvou.

These three consecutive phases require two corresponding sets of tools: the first is a set of design tools for transcribing physical and spiritual needs to geometrically and topologically defined forms; the second is a set of measuring and laying out tools through which to give definite dimensions to and materialize the design on the ground. There is lastly a set of actual, physical tools for shaping the materials to their specific size and form and joining their parts to create the whole that is the building. The first two tools are discussed below in reference to Minoan architecture. For the actual building tools, the reader is referred to J. Shaw's pioneer work on Minoan building materials and techniques (Shaw 2009).

The *chaîne opératoire* presented above is a polyparametric problem-solving procedure that involves numerous variants, some generic and others idiosyncratic, and they are more often than not in conflict with one another. In a situation like this, compromise and optimization are of primal importance. Architecture is "complex and contradictory," to use Robert Ventouri's famous phrase, because of "its very inclusion of the traditional Vitruvian elements of commodity, firmness, and delight" (1977, 16). Function, structure, and form (the modern rendering of the Vitruvian triad) are indeed the godmothers of architecture, enviously demanding priority and privilege over each other, and it is the architect's job to compromise, optimize, and hopefully satisfy them all so as to ensure a harmonious result and avoid the revenging curse of the less pleased. This is why all three elements should be invited to the party. Not all works are successful in this respect, yet another parameter we need to keep in mind when tempted to look at the past in pious admiration.

After construction begins, there is little space for modifications or corrections along the way: when laying out the foundations, the form, and the structure of the entire edifice and the loads to be transferred to the ground must be already determined, for there is no way one can go back to change things as construction proceeds. So planning ahead and making sure that the implementation of the design is carried out properly and accurately are crucial factors in a work of architecture.

## Composition and Design Tools

*Compositional systems . . . must be conceived beyond the mere geometry as a pattern of forces. (Arnheim 1983, 140)*

The process of architectural design cannot be easily grasped and described (or taught, for that matter). There is considerable literature on this tantalizing topic but very little consensus among writers; almost all methods of analysis and categorizations of design practices proposed so far have been disputed one way or another. Architectural design problems are indeed known to be "wicked problems" in that they have no definitive formulation, no explicit "stopping rule," they have more than one plausible explanation, and their solutions cannot be strictly correct or false (Rowe 1982, 18).

One such categorization is Geoffrey Broadbent's "deep structures," a concept borrowed from the field of linguistics (1980). Broadbent concludes that there are only four kinds of design that, either independently or combined, cover all possible ways of architectural production. The pragmatic and the iconic correspond to the trial and error process and to the tradition-based typological design discussed below, whereas the canonic or geometric is based on the use of strict principles, such as axes and grids. The fourth kind, the analogical, is produced by analogy to something else. In Minoan architecture, the first two are the most easily recognized, the canonic design based on the grid (proposed by Preziosi) has been disputed, and the analogical may be assumed for a few instances, such as the Pillar Crypt designed in analogy to the tree and/or cave archetypes.

## Models and Variations

*[A]rchitecture is not the field of creative freedom some have imagined it to be, but a system of rules for giving society what it expects in the way of architecture" (Eco 1997, 194).*

Since the architect is the agent who will materialize other peoples' visions, it is necessary that they understand each other as best as possible so that the built space produced is properly integrated in its social environment. In tradition-oriented societies such an understanding is based on repetition and standardization. Rules guiding the production of a work of architecture are based on "already worked-out solutions, codifications yielding standardized messages" (Eco 1997, 194). They are based on well-established formulae that have resulted from long experimentation through trial and error and have proved their efficiency in the context of a specific sociocultural and natural setting in the long run of time. Thus, in designing a new building the architect need not start from zero, but just fill in and adjust the non-fixed variables of the formula, such as the specifics of the ground and the immediate environment (Palyvou 1990).

This procedure, typical in anonymous architecture, has been described in many different ways. Amos Rapoport, for example, speaks of a system of "models and variations," a simple scheme that applies to most traditional societies, whereas Norberg-Schulz prefers "theme and variation" (Rapoport 1969, 22; Norberg-Schulz 1980, 180). Letesson's "genotypes and phenotypes" are also more or less along the same line of thought: the genotypes are the underlying common structures, whereas the phenotypes are their varying physical expressions (2009).

The model or theme, same as Benevolo's formula and Eco's codification, consists of a set of generic forms and techniques arrived at collectively and accepted by the community as the optimal solution to standard requirements—that is, the most efficient in terms of operation and costs. Diffusion of knowledge may take place in the form of apprenticeship, while communication among architects, masons, and clients is facilitated through collective knowledge of models and prototypes. In Eco's words, "the codes of architecture would then constitute a rhetoric in the narrow sense of the word: a store of tried and true discursive formulas" (Eco 1997, 195).

Such formulas, or models, become building codes that acquire the power of unwritten laws within a community. These laws are enacted collectively through social acceptance or rejection, and they may be reinforced through prejudice and fear. Examples of the latter are echoed in the Mesopotamian omen texts that speak of the severe punishment of those who do not comply with fundamental building codes, such as not trespassing on public property or obstructing a neighbor's access. Punishment comes not from a mundane human agent but from the gods themselves and is therefore not negotiable. To give an example of such a text: "If a house blocks the main street in its building, the owner of the house will die; if a house overshadows (overhangs) or obstructs the side of the main street, the heart of the dweller in that house will not be glad" (Frankfort 1950, 111).

In Minoan architecture, building codes as models or formulas are readily recognized in the standardized forms and construction techniques of elements (e.g., door, staircase, roof) and the standardized articulation of space-cells (e.g., entrance vestibule, Minoan Hall; Fig. 105). Minoan houses as totalities, on the other hand, do not conform to clearly defined formulas or models. Compare, for example, a Minoan house with the standardized paratactic megaroid house or the introverted court-house (Fig. 106:a). The difference is that the court-house and the megaroid type come in the form of all-inclusive paradigms that guide planning, designing, and construction of the part as much as of the whole, leaving little space for variations, whereas the Minoan norm (Fig. 106:b; see also below) presents the architect with not one but many sets of codes that need to be combined and synthesized to produce the totality that is the house. Sets of codes apply at different levels. Take, for example, the entrance door: there are codes of appearance, performance, and structure prescribing how it should look, operate, and be constructed (e.g., wide opening, monolithic threshold, timber frame, and so forth); there are codes of location indicating its placement in the periphery of the house in relation to an indentation of the facade; and there are codes of association indicating its relationship with other space-cells within the house (e.g., a staircase). The design of a Minoan house is therefore a very demanding process of composing sets of such codes, step by step, while handling a large number of variants.

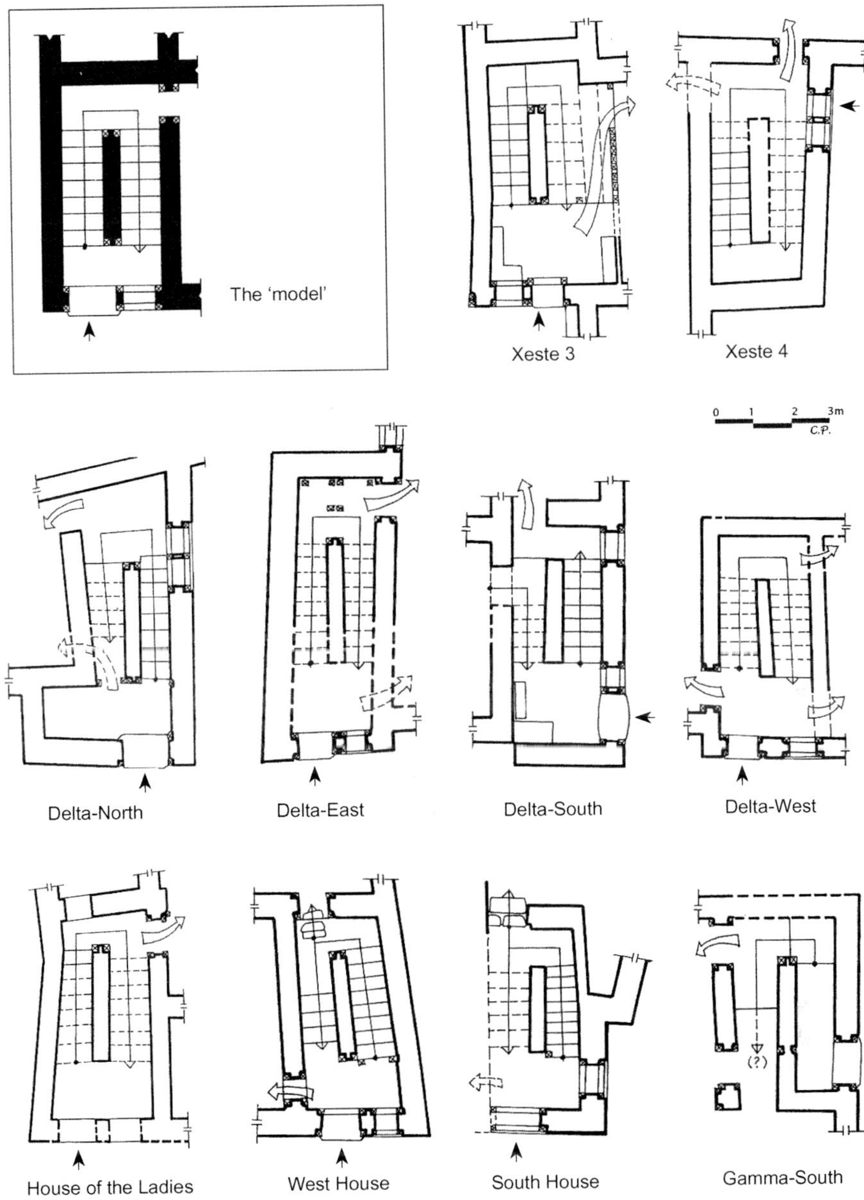


Fig. 105. Plans of main staircases at Akrotiri, Thera, demonstrating a model (bottom left) and its variations. Drawing C. Palyvou.

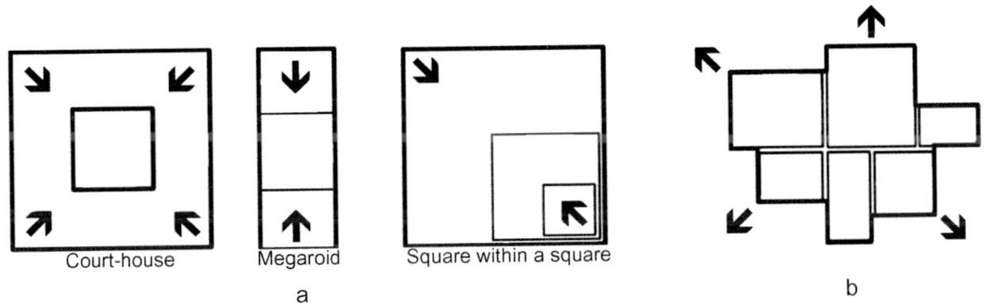


Fig. 106. Design process by subdivision: (a) within fixed outlines, or (b) by addition in the form of clustering, resulting in free outlines. Drawing C. Palyvou.

The result is a highly individualized process that ends up with a large number of variations.

The Minoans, in other words, chose a rather difficult and idiosyncratic approach to architectural composition; one that demanded expertise, versatile thinking, and imagination, as much as discipline and order. From the architect's point of view, theirs is by far a more challenging and creative involvement compared to the restrictive, repetitive court-house or megaroid-type building. The fascinating variety that results from this process is what mesmerizes modern scholars who often join their voices in exclamation and mystification, asking how is it that no two houses are alike? Yiannouli, for one, wonders, "Why does . . . the very diversity of form conceal a generally comparable content? Why is the phenomenon particularly accentuated in Crete?" (1992, 183; on the individuality of Minoan houses, see also Preziosi 1983, 484). The answer, I believe, is that variety and diversity are possible at a higher level (the whole) because powerful codes and patterns of association exist at a lower level (the parts). Thanks to the standardization of the parts, all Minoan buildings exude a characteristically Minoan aura while at the same time retaining their individuality. Minoan architecture and art have this in common.

### *Clustering or Zoning*

Design process in vernacular architecture, according to Rapoport, is of two types (see Fig. 106): clustering, resulting in free outlines, and subdivisions within fixed outlines (Rapoport 1969, 36). Examples of the latter are the court-house and the megaroid-type house discussed above. Minoan architectural design is primarily of the clustering type; design by subdivisions is less common. Of the clustering type is the square-within-a-square design procedure proposed by Preziosi (Fig. 107; Preziosi 1983, 26–27). It is a simple idea consisting of two squares sharing a common corner; the smaller, which represents a large room or a court, is subtracted from the larger. The L-shaped space surrounding the small square is then further subdivided into space-cells. This design applies to a broad range of Minoan buildings of all periods, such as Tou Vrachnou o Lakkos, a MM house in the Mesara Plain (the inner square was probably a court); Rousses (MM III; the inner square is a Room with a Central Column); House A at Achladia; House Zα at Malia (MM IIIB–LM IA); the farmhouse at Chalinomouri, Mochlos; Hagia Photia; and a few more. One may even add to the above examples the Neolithic houses at Knossos that follow more or less the same logic.

The clustering design procedure is more popular in Minoan architecture, as is evident in the large variety of buildings with free outlines. This should not be mistaken for the arbitrary agglomeration of space-cells that results in ad hoc outlines. Such misconceptions were common in the early writings on Minoan architecture, where additive or clustering design was pejoratively described as "agglutinative," a kind of juxtaposition of space-cells that are held together by magic. The clustering design process is based on norms and rules that need to be revealed and deciphered.

Clustering design in the Minoan world was first recognized by Evans in the Palace of Knossos, which he described as consisting of so-called insulae (Evans 1921–1935, I, 203). In these, however, he did not recognize a design concept as such; instead, he attributed different insulae to different times of construction. The idea of clustering was later advanced by Graham, who spoke of units or blocks, and also Preziosi, who preferred the term zones (Graham 1972; Preziosi 1983). They both rejected Evans's explanation of different building phases and spoke of a synchronic overall design scheme.

The benefits of this design concept are quite apparent, especially in the case of Palaces and large building complexes: clustering or zoning allows for breaking down the architectural project into smaller entities, thus facilitating the design process. Each entity corresponds to a specific function—or a set of related functions—and it is treated as a design object in its own right. What remains to be examined is what guides the process of clustering and holds together the whole composition.

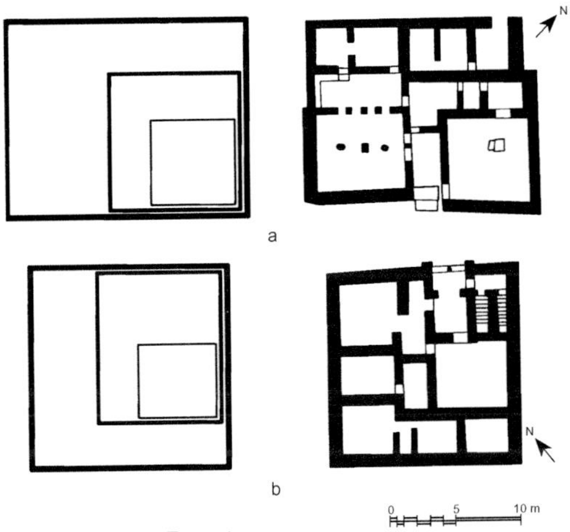


Fig. 107. Square-within-a-square design formula: (a) House A, Achladia (after Platon 1997, fig. 4); (b) House G, Zakros (after Platon 1974, fold-out plan).

## *The Binding Formula: Regulating Lines of Design and Communication*

For the various zones or clusters to come together in an integral whole there is need for a binding formula: a method of conceiving and laying out the building that will guide the overall process from its first steps. This formula does not readily reveal itself: though zones are more or less easy to define a posteriori, the way they are initially conceived as such and the way they come together is rather obscure.

After careful observation of several Minoan buildings—houses, mansions, and Palaces alike—it eventually became clear that the binding formula is, naturally, a simple one: zones come together, and at the same time are segregated, by means of a limited number of Regulating Lines of design and lines of communication consisting of corridors, doors, and staircases. These lines channel and control circulation while providing buffer zones. They also guide the layout and construction of the building. Each compartment or zone becomes thereafter a design object in its own right with new, secondary Regulating Lines applied as necessary.

The use of such lines in Minoan architecture was already implied by Evans (1921–1935, I, 203). Graham (1972, 224–229), Preziosi (1983, 485), and Schmid (2011, 117) went one step further and proposed a numeric order in the way the zones are subdivided based on the Fibonacci series.

Such practice does not exclude the Regulating Lines system; on the contrary it could well have complemented it.

The concept of Regulating Lines is not new; this is an age-old tool of design. Le Corbusier argued that they are an inevitable element of architecture, a necessity for order and "a guarantee against wilfulness" that has guided all great architecture of the past (1986, 67). This is not a recipe, he adds, but a means to an end. Therefore its choice and the modalities of expression given to it are an integral part of architectural creation.

This simple design formula may provide the key for decoding Minoan architectural design in its genesis. Regulating Lines of design and communication can be attested in many Minoan buildings. They cross in the form of a capital T or H, and they are recognized by the fact that: (a) they correspond to major wall alignments; (b) they create compartments that correspond to distinct functional zones; and (c) they correspond to lines of communication (corridors) to which main staircases are appended. These lines are generated from the core of the building and each compartment extends outward as needed (hence the free outline at the periphery of the building; Figs. 108–111). Interestingly, Regulating Lines are not an innovative feature of the Neopalatial period, nor are they exclusive to urban environments; they permeate Minoan architecture throughout its long history, as far back in time as the Neolithic period and in as disparate buildings as the idiosyncratic Chamaizi.

Tylissos House A presents a good example to illustrate the above (Fig. 110:a). The building consists of two very distinct zones (or clusters) of more or less equal size and geometry: the one to the south houses domestic activities while the other to the north houses storage and service activities. The two zones are united by an amazing system of interrelated horizontal and vertical connectors embedded at the interface between them; more than that, this circulatory node is the interface! Such arrangement allows for a variety of tasks to take place simultaneously with minimal crisscrossing of the corresponding communication lines.

Regulating Lines are more patent in the design of the Palaces, as Graham already observed in the 1970s, stating that the planning of the Palace of Phaistos is based on "a pair of straight lines crossing one another at right angles . . ." (1972, 237). Preziosi writes that the Palace of Knossos was "laid out initially from this core" (1983, 420), and Shaw joins his voice in agreement (2010). Schmid, on the other hand, has proposed a design system for House Δα at Malia based on the concept of the square and working inward from the periphery of the building (Schmid 2011).

Regulating Lines play an important role in controlling the third dimension as well because they (1) correspond to lines of communication that include staircases, and (2) extend into the vertical as regulating planes defining the basic walls of the upper floors and hence the structural system of the overall building. Regulating Lines and planes may provide the key to understanding Minoan architects at work, because of

Fig. 108. Regulating Lines of design and communication at Knossos, generated from the core of the building define functional zones and guide the design process: (a) Southeast House (after Evans 1902–1903, fig. 1); (b) House of the Chancel Screen (after Evans 1921–1935, II.2, fig. 224).

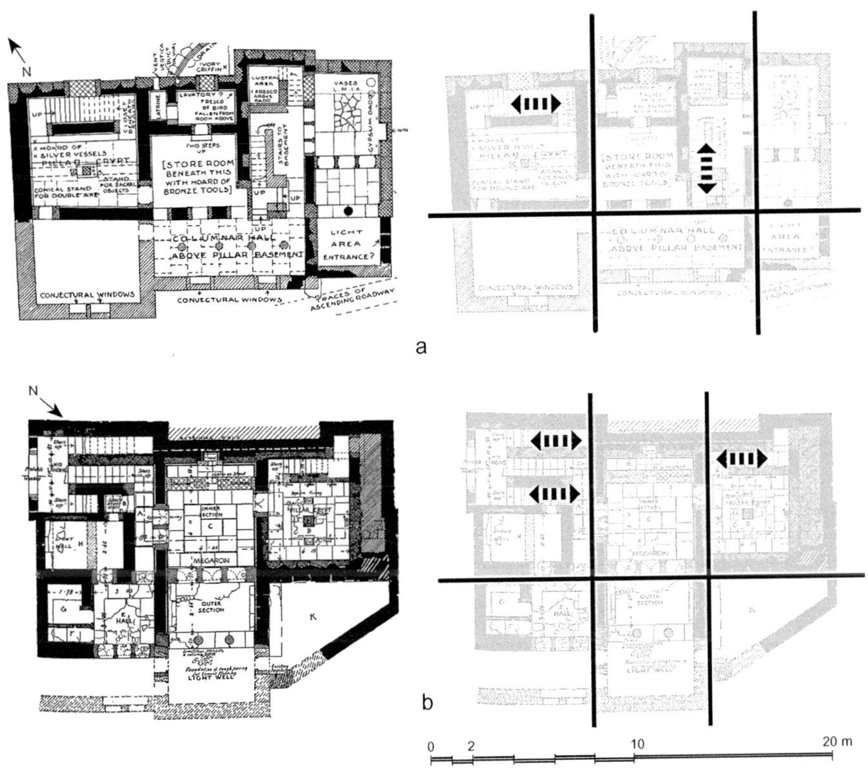


Fig. 109. Regulating Lines of design and communication at Knossos: (a) South House (after Evans 1921–1935, II.1, fig. 208); (b) Royal Villa (after Evans 1921–1935, II.2, fig. 227).

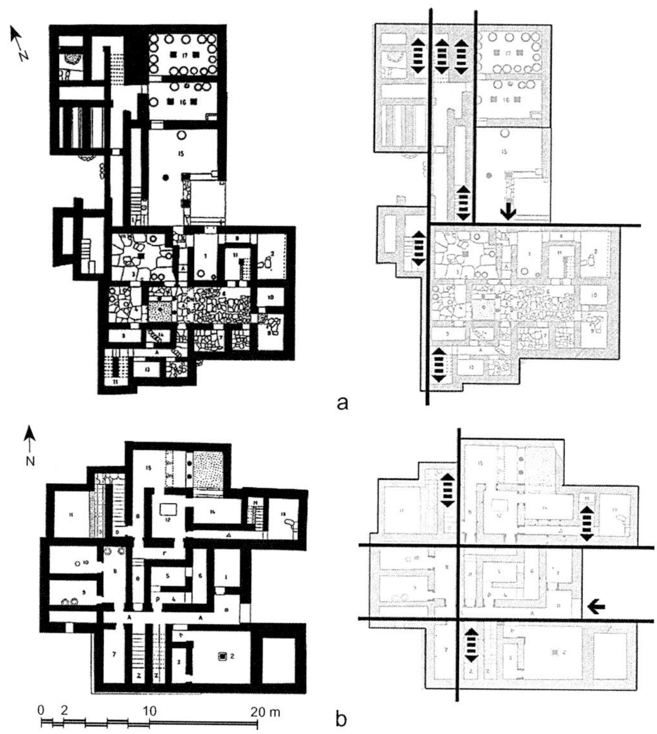


Fig. 110. Regulating Lines of design and communication: Tylissos Houses A (a) and C (b). After Graham 1972, figs. 19, 20.

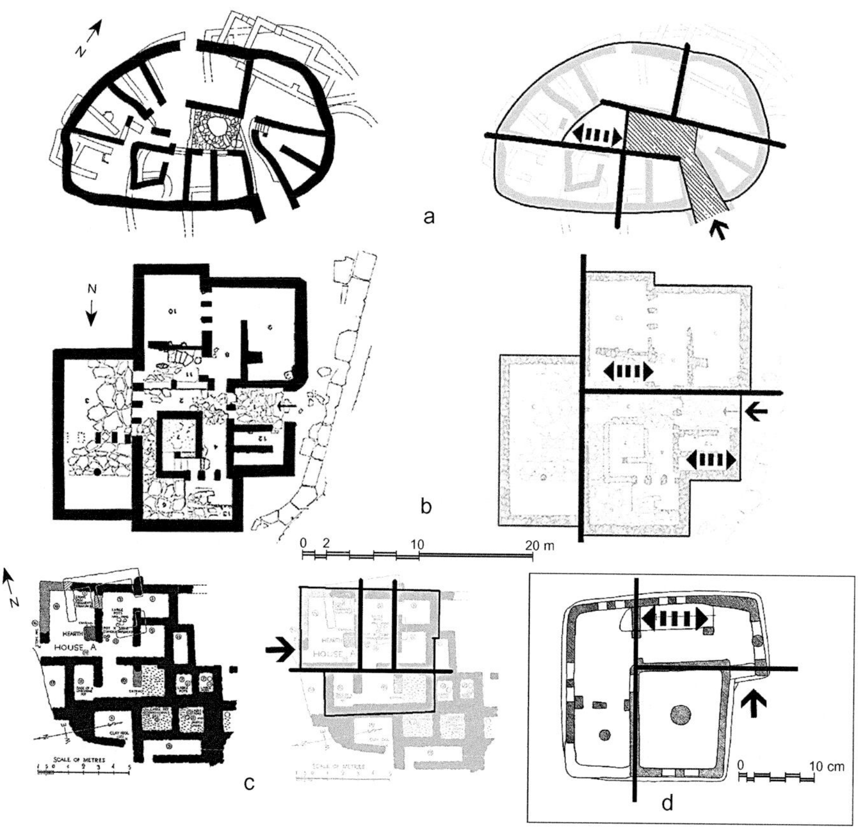


Fig. 111. Regulating Lines of design and communication: (a) Chamaizi (after Davaras 1992, fig. 8.1); (b) House Δα, Malia (Tiré and van Effenterre 1983, fig. 19); (c) Neolithic house, Knossos (after Evans 1921–1935, II.1, fig. 8a); (d) Archanes clay model (after Lebessi 1976, fig. 2).

the way they managed to conceptualize in advance such multistory and complex edifices as well as materialize their vision on the ground and keep control of its implementation.

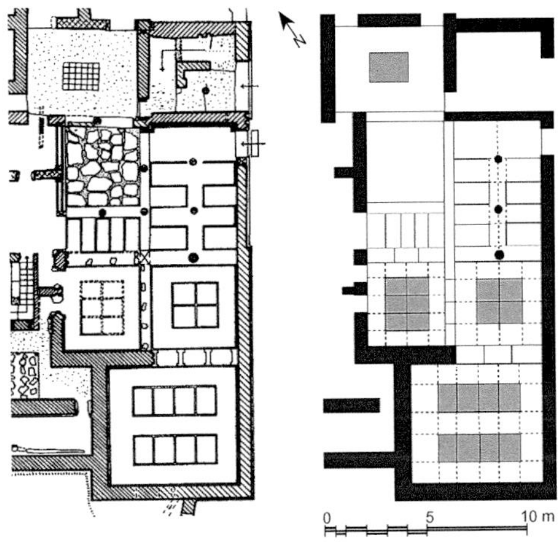


Fig. 112. At the Palace of Zakros, floor patterns adhere to individual grids that emphasize the center and the autonomy of each compartment. After Platon 1974, fig. 43.

## *The Grid*

The grid is an absolute version of the system of Regulating Lines; it is an abstract, mental tool based on the infinite repetition of a module. Preziosi has suggested that the Minoans used the grid to design and lay out their buildings (Preziosi 1983). One of his arguments was that the notion of the grid existed in the Minoan world, as verified through art where one can literally see the underlying grid in certain design motives.[2] It is also attested in architecture in the layout of the pavement of certain floors and in the so-called strip design pattern at Archanes, Palaikastro, possibly Pseira, and at the Palaces of Zakros and Galatas (Figs. 112, 113; Shaw 2009, 151–152).

The question, however, is whether the grid was used as a design tool for the whole of the building, as Preziosi has proposed. Such totalizing application of the grid has been received with skepticism, mostly because of the far too many deviations it presents in practice (McEnroe 1984). It is rather extravagant, however, to think of the Minoans laying out a perfect grid on the ground only to adjust their walls at will in situ, and it is even more extreme to think of the workers improvising along the grid laid out by the architect, as Hitchcock has suggested (1997). It is far too difficult to control a design process of this sort on undulating land (laying out the grid would have been the first step prior to any other action of land leveling or trench digging), even though numerical accuracy need not be the case.

What may be said with some confidence, however, is that in Minoan architecture the grid was applied to parts of the building, especially in relation to the pier-and-opening system whose underlying grid concept is inherent since it is based on the unit (module) that is the door, even though it is applied approximately. This is evident in the composite Minoan Halls and the Polythyron Halls.[3] The western wing of the Palace of Zakros is another example of systematic application of the grid (Figs. 112, 113). As is typical for the Minoan world, though the notion of the grid permeates a large part of the building it is applied piecemeal; in other words, there is not one but many individual grids, each one adjusted to a specific area. Furthermore, the grids (plural) end up supporting centrality and promoting the

Fig. 113. Floor patterns at the Palace of Zakros, facing north. Courtesy L. Platon, Archive of the Zakros Excavations.

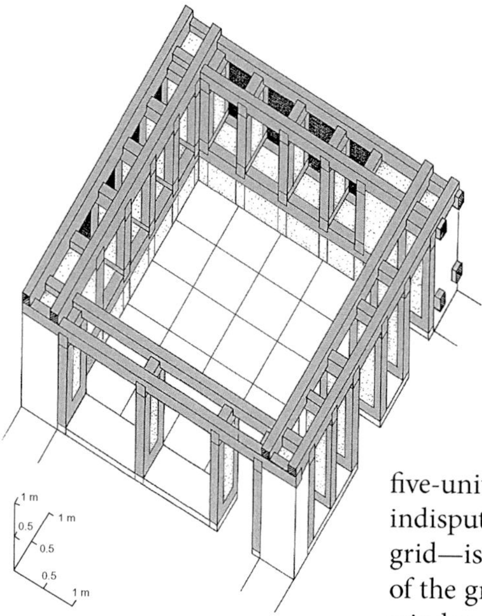

Fig. 114. All-inclusive, three-dimensional grid of Room 5 on the upper floor of the West House at Akrotiri, Thera. Drawing C. Palyvou.

individuality of each component rather than providing a unifying theme.

The most conspicuous and all-inclusive application of the grid is attested in Room 5 on the upper floor of the West House at Akrotiri, Thera: it applies to all three dimensions of space and consists of a three-dimensional timber frame articulated along a grid of 5 x 5 units (Fig. 114; see also Fig. 53). The two exterior walls of the room consist of pier-and-window partitions comprising four openings each, while the fifth unit at each end corresponds to a mass of wall. The other two sides of the room consist of doors and cupboards arranged along the five-unit grid. What is of special interest in this case—and is indisputable evidence of the awareness of the merits of the grid—is the way the artist followed and highlighted the logic of the grid by completing the visual effect below the sill of the windows with painted stripes in yellow ocher, imitating the timber elements of the frame. The result is a sophisticated space articulation that promotes the idea of self-contained space and centrality, along with openness and transparency (Palyvou 2012).

## Canonic versus Organic Design

Regulating Lines and grids belong to the canonic type of design that presupposes orthogonal forms and right angles. Though Minoan buildings are almost exclusively rectilinear, they are not always entirely of the canonic type; quite a few examples are polygons in plan that have no true parallel walls or right angles. This is organic design adjusted to local circumstances. Canonic design presupposes sets of tools, such as Regulating Lines and grids, which can produce strictly defined geometrical forms, since such forms do not come naturally. Organic design, on the other hand, may be implemented empirically and ad hoc, yet always with a prototype in mind.

Both types appear in Crete from the very beginning. The Neolithic houses Evans excavated at Knossos are quite remarkable for their canonic design. They show that already in the Neolithic era Cretan architects had solved the problem of producing right angles and parallel lines (see Fig. 111:c); or, rather, what we should emphasize is that they had already addressed this as a goal to be pursued and a problem to be solved. Though the exact way such regularity was materialized eludes us, we need not be overly impressed by the fact itself, for there are many empirical ways of producing right angles (nature herself provides right angles through gravity, and the Egyptians had a wooden "angle" in their kit of building tools long before the Minoans started building). Not all Neolithic houses were designed this way, of course; many more were of the organic type.

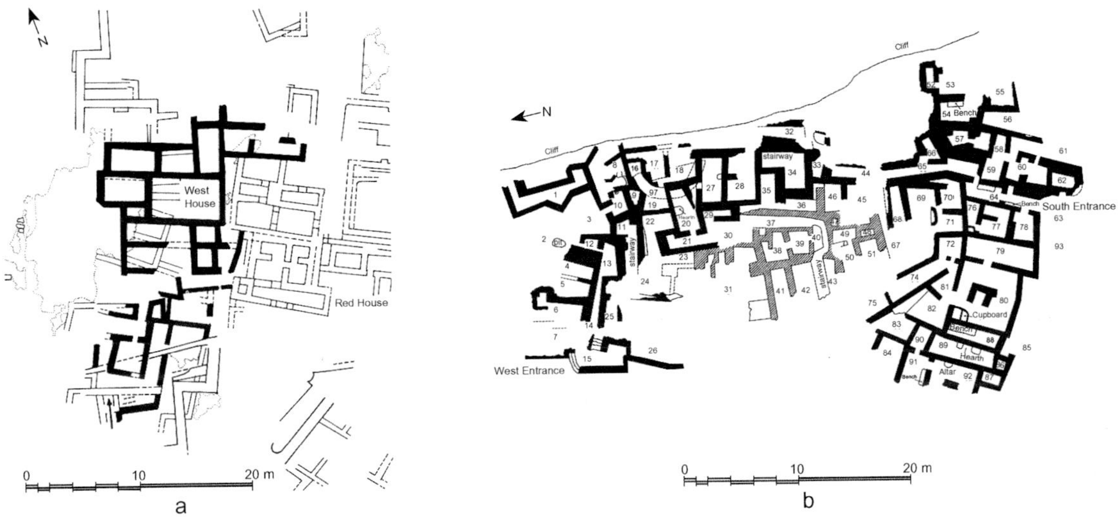


Fig. 115. Typical examples of the two opposing design practices: (a) canonic at Vasiliki (after Zois 1992, fig. 41.1); (b) organic at Myrtos Phournou Koriphi (after Cadogan 2011, fig. 4.3).

Since the two types of design, canonic and organic, coexisted from the beginning, the question arising is what guided choice of one type of design over the other? Myrtos Phournou Koriphi and Vasiliki, both of the Prepalatial period, are typical examples of the two opposing design practices (Fig. 115): Vasiliki is of canonic design, complying with a carefully planned and well executed system, whereas Myrtos Phournou Koriphi is the result of organic design. The differences between the two contemporary sites reflect different socioeconomic paradigms. Myrtos Phournou Koriphi is a rural settlement consisting of small single-story houses built ad hoc by the inhabitants themselves. Vasiliki is a building compound that seems to have served formal functions. Design process in the first instance is gradual, through accretion, whereas in the second it has been conceived from the beginning as one entity, even if it may have acquired additions or alterations through time.

## The Quantitative Aspect of Architecture

### *Taking the Measure*

*[E]verything spatial, as something for which space is made, is already in need of the dimension, that is, that into which it is admitted. (Heidegger 1997b, 114)*

Architecture has two fundamental quantitative conditions: the first is dictated by ergonomic requirements—that is, efficiency of space in relation to the human body and the task involved (Fig. 116); and the second is dictated by physical constraints and presupposes good knowledge of materials—that is, their properties, their strengths and weaknesses, and their load bearing capacity in relation to the structural system applied (for further discussion, see this vol., Ch. 7). Ergonomic demands define

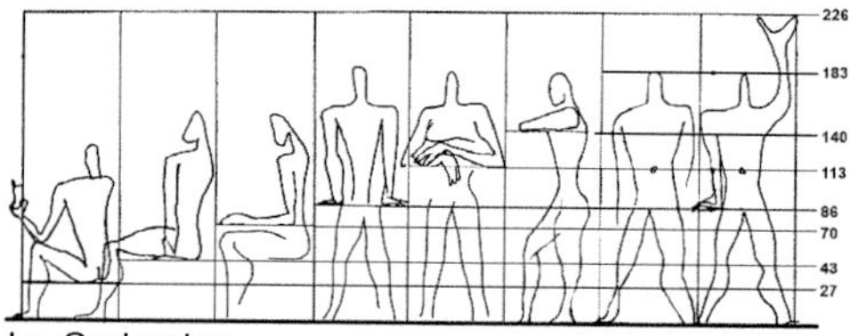


Le Corbusier

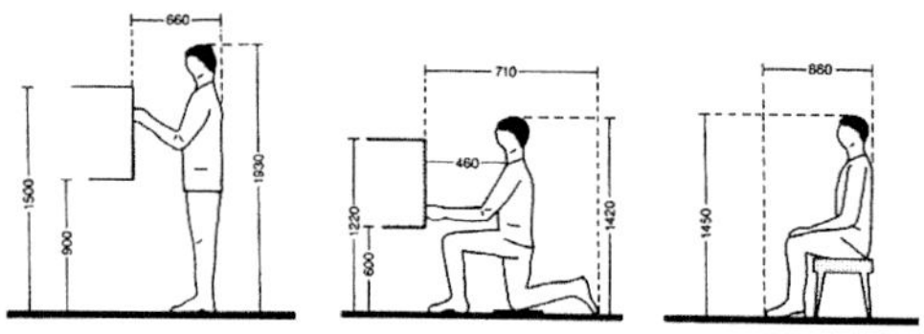

Neufert

Fig. 116. Architecture has a fundamental quantitative condition: dimensions should comply with ergonomic requirements dictated by the human body and the task involved. Top (cm): after Le Corbusier 1954, fig. 26; bottom (mm): after Neufert 2000, 16.

dimensions of space elements (e.g., the height of a door, the width of a corridor, the dimensions of a staircase, and so forth), whereas physical constraints prescribe dimensions of building parts (e.g., size of timber beams, thickness of walls, inclination of drainage channels, and so forth). Both are by their nature universal and diachronic and only slightly influenced by local conditions. Also, they are inextricably interrelated: the process of designing and constructing a building is a series of decisions and choices based on the outcome of a constant dialogue, or tug-of-war, between the two quantitative conditions. This interaction is mind provoking, and it can trigger innovative technological developments, as in the case of the Minoan pier-and-door partition.

Whatever the design procedure in Minoan architecture, calculations and measurements were surely applied, even if in a rough manner using ones own foot or palm as a provisional unit. Measuring, after all, was an important practice of everyday life, and the human body provided the rule, be it length, weight, volume, or even time (on the sophisticated weighing systems, see Michailidou, ed., 2001). To take a measurement there is need of a unit and a system of reference. The units used in Minoan building operations are difficult to detect because of the ruinous and fragmentary state of preservation of the buildings. In addition, there are far too many unknown parameters at play: the status of the people working in the building industry and their training and equipment, the relationship between the work site and the place of provenance of the building materials (quarries of stone, for example), and many more. It may be that different groups of builders used different measuring units, especially if they worked as itinerant artisans. This is in fact clearly implied at Akrotiri by the varying sizes of mudbricks: they tend to remain standard within the same building but differ from one building site to another, indicating that each work team was more or less autonomous (Palyvou 1999a, 174–176).

That metrical calculations were indeed practiced in Minoan architecture is attested in various instances. The Square Room with the Central Column, for example, has one dimension typically very close to 5 m. This dimension most probably derived from the empirical knowledge of the maximum length that could be spanned using one intermediate timber support. Staircases are another instance where measurements and calculations play an important role, this time for ergonomic reasons. The width of the flight and the dimensions of the step (rise and tread) must comply with the proportions of the average human body. Ernst Neufert explains that climbing stairs takes seven times as much energy as walking on the flat, and he concludes that from the physiological point of view the "least climbing effort" is achieved with an angle of incline of 30° and an optimum rise/tread ratio equal to 17/29 (Fig. 117; Neufert 2000, 191–193). He then goes on to explain how to calculate the width of the staircase depending on its use: 0.55 m for one user, 1.25 m for two, and so forth. Neufert's handbook, first published in 1970, has accompanied many generations of architects, and the calculations arrived at by the Minoans are not very different from those included therein. Furthermore, all the steps must be of the same height, because the act of climbing a staircase is repetitive and automatic and dimensions should conform to such expectations. This rule is well adhered to in main staircases; auxiliary staircases, on the other hand, have steps that vary, which makes the use of the staircase precarious.

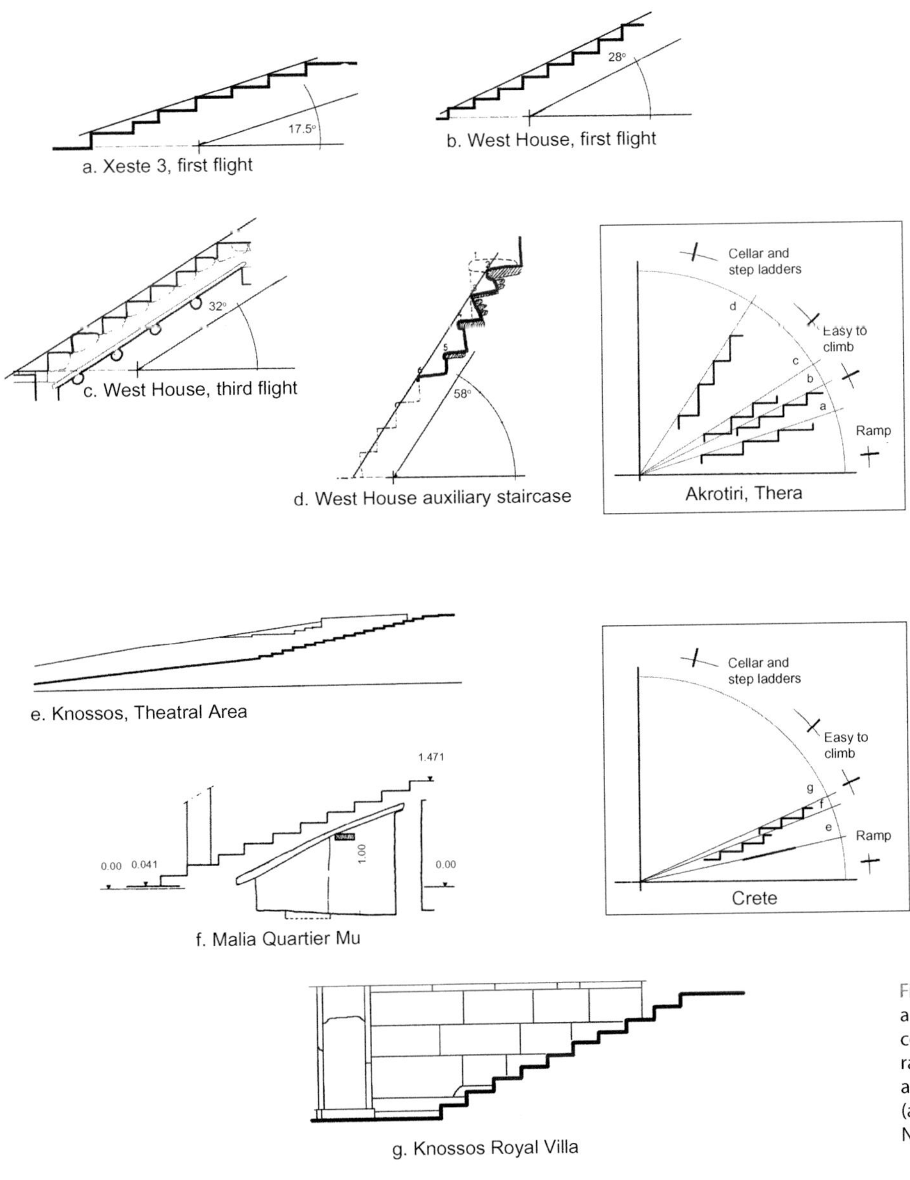


Fig. 117. The gradient of a staircase defines the conditions of its use from ramp to step ladders. Examples from Akrotiri, Thera (a–d) and Crete (e–g). After Neufert 2000, 191–193.

A brief review of the metrical units that have been proposed for Minoan architecture is presented below:

(1) Graham estimated a unit equal to 30.36 cm (1960a, 1968).

(2) Preziosi suggested that the Minoans were using two units: a shorter and a longer one, ±27 and ±34 cm, respectively (Preziosi 1983, 486–493). He generally relates Minoan planning, laying out, and construction techniques to those of the Egyptians and emphasizes the importance of modular working (as important as writing).

(3) At Akrotiri, a common height for the topmost row of blocks in an ashlar wall is 27 cm (Palyvou 2005a, 156–158). It is interesting to note that this dimension coincides with the "short" value of the Minoan foot proposed by Preziosi (1983, 483–493).

(4) Cherry has calculated a unit equal to 46.8 cm (the highest peak in his quantal analysis of dimensions deriving from 87 buildings), but he remains skeptical as to the existence of uniform units throughout Crete (Cherry 1983).

(5) Peter Warren, commenting on the standard width (1.40 m) of the raised walkways at Knossos, concludes that it was based on a metrical unit that fits well with Cherry's unit (Warren 1994, 206).

(6) Schmid is in favor of a harmonious model of design based on the square rather than a metrical system, and of an Egyptian and Anatolian derivation of metrical systems in the Aegean (Schmid 1985, 64).

(7) Despoina Vallianou and Symeon Parcharidis, working on the Acropolis of Smari, came up with two units, 34 and 27.2 cm (Vallianou and Parcharidis 1999, 876 n. 18).

(8) Eleni Mantzourani, Giorgos Vavouranakis, and Chrysanthos Kanellopoulos follow Graham's foot, 30.36 cm (Mantzourani, Vavouranakis, and Kanellopoulos 2005, 757–758).

(9) Giuliana Bianco, working with data from Kommos, estimated a unit of 32.55 cm for the Neopalatial period (Postpalatial buildings have a different unit), and she argues that the Minoan foot was based on two hands outstretched, hence the minor differences from place to place (Bianco 2003).

With so many different numerical estimates, one is tempted to ask, paraphrasing the title of Flannery's paper, "Will the Real [Unit] Please Stand Up?" (1993). Though it is not my intention to take sides as to which metrical unit is the best, it is necessary to comment on the very discrepancy of the proposed estimates: either all scholars (but one?) are mistaken or all are right, in the sense that there was not one common unit for the Minoan world but many, decided ad hoc at the work site itself. There is also the possibility that planning, designing, and laying out a building were based primarily on geometrical principles, as suggested above, rather than on numerical calculations. What is certain, however, is that Minoan architects were very competent in conceptualizing and materializing architectural space, and for this to be possible they had to rely on effective tools and methods of design and construction, which might even justify David Romano's bold suggestion of Minoan "surveyors" at work (Romano 2003).

## Approximation

*Du monde de l' à-peu-près à l'univers de la précision. (Koyré 1948)* [4]

Assuming that the Minoans did have specific metrical units, the next question is where and how they used them. Accurate measurement does not seem to have been a goal in itself, but only in very few instances concerning important parts of the Palaces, such as the facades. The scarcity of accuracy is, in fact, the main reason why it is so difficult to detect metrical units. The rule is approximation, typical of the architecture as much as the art of the Minoan world. This approximation, however, was not due to incompetence: accuracy, it seems, was put aside for special use only.

A casual reference to structures based on fairly accurate measuring might provide some clues for further discussion:

(1) Indentations of palatial facades (see Fig. 175);

(2) Pavements, such as at Malia, Archanes, and the Palace of Zakros (see Figs. 112, 113);

(3) Curvilinear bases like those found at Archanes (see Fig. 127);

(4) Ashlar facades with identical heights of rows at Akrotiri, Thera (Fig. 118);

(5) Raised causeways with constant width throughout.

The fact that accurately measured structures do exist in a variety of instances shows that the Minoans possessed the appropriate means for this—that is, measuring tools and metrical units adhering to a specific system. But why then is approximation and not precision the rule?

First, a brief note on the two terms. Precision can only be intentional, as a kind of mental exercise aided by tools of design and implementation that allow for control, adjustment, and verification. Precision is easy to detect and to identify in the archaeological record. Approximation, on the other hand, is not synonymous to haphazard or random; it too is intentional in its own way. Approximation is in itself a process toward a prototype or an ideal; it means approaching this ideal

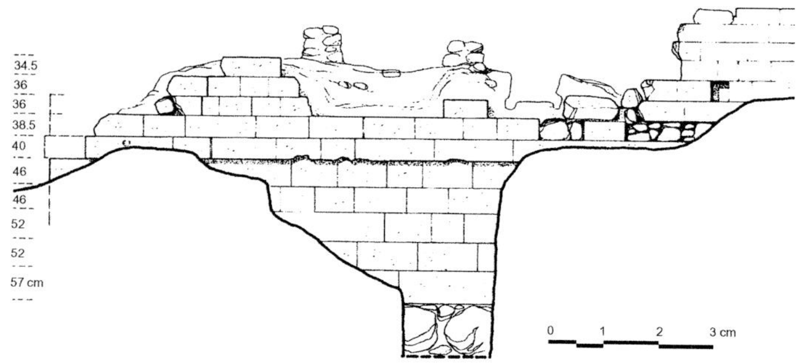


Fig. 118. Calculations are evident in the ashlar facade of Xeste 4, Akrotiri, Thera. Every two rows of blocks have the same height. Palyvou 2005a, fig. 235.

but not exactly arriving there. So, for approximation to be enacted, an ideal needs to exist. To give an example: several urban houses at Gournia, Palaikastro, and other Minoan towns exhibit an approximate geometry in their layout (walls are not exactly straight and parallel and perfectly right angles are rare). By referring to the plans of these houses as approximate, we infer that the initial intention to produce an orthogonal plan was compromised by the peculiarities of the specific urban environment.

Another example of numerical approximation with an underlying precise ideal is the pier-and-door partition. This structure has an innate order that derives from the standard unit, the door. This unit is repeated three or more times so as to span the distance between two walls. Such procedure encourages or even asks for precision, yet this is rarely the case in reality. A possible reason for this is that visual order, as opposed to metrical precision, was sufficient and easier to apply; minor deviations, after all, are not apprehended and do not interfere with the general perception of order.

Certain divergences, however, may be intentional. In the Throne Room at Knossos, for example, the openings of the pier-and-door partitions are not of standard width. Being an architectural space of such significance, it is hard to see this as the result of negligence. Goodison noticed this and suggested that such an architectural anomaly, as she calls it, may have been dictated by ritual demands: in this case, to allow for dawn light effects (Goodison 2004, 343). Similarly, it is possible that the discrepancies in the widths of the doors of the pier-and-door partition between Rooms 3 and 4 of Xeste 3 at Akrotiri, Thera are intentional: the wider doors in the middle allow for better visibility of the wall paintings beyond, as Paliou has shown (Paliou, Wheatley, and Earl 2011). There are many more examples of this sort, such as the differentiated inter-columnar dimensions of some palatial porticoes (see Fig. 151).

Bronze Age architecture, on the whole, is characterized by approximation, as opposed to the precision that permeated later Greek monumental architecture. Even the Palaces and the large Neopalatial mansions exhibit a degree of numerical and geometric approximation, despite their canonic design. Precision is time and labor consuming and implies a certain expertise. Could it be, then, that it was regarded as a special treatment to be applied in special cases, perhaps as a symbolic statement of order, status, or hierarchy? As with the circle versus the rectangle, by restricting precision to exclusive cases its symbolic power would have been enhanced.

It is important to stress that this world of approximation—Alexandre Koyré's *monde de l' à-peu-près*—is not a lesser world; it is an organic response to the desire for order. It is pertinent to recall Koyré's thoughts on this topic, as he asks: Why were mechanics not born in ancient Greece, instead of the 17th century A.D.? Though the obvious answer is that statics had to come first before dynamics—just as Archimedes had to precede Gallileus—the reason why the Greeks did not seek to go any further was that they did not believe it was possible to mathematize the phenomena of everyday life; the mundane was the domain ("*du mouvement, de l' imprécis, de l' a peu près*"; Febvre 1950, 25). For Koyré, the Greek spirit did not want to accept that mathematical order could be of this mundane terrestrial world; such order was of the celestial world alone. It seems that Minoans too felt that approximation was good enough for the mundane world, whereas precision should be reserved for special cases (celestial or not). On a final note, it is important to keep in mind that the significance of accuracy versus approximation may have been perceived differently then. For us today, accuracy is primarily a matter of technical thinking that goes along with standardization and prefabrication; notions not entirely unknown to the Minoans, as discussed below.

## *Size, Scale, and Proportions*

A brief comment on the terms size, scale, and proportions seems appropriate, for they are often used indiscriminately as coterminous. To clarify: size is an absolute value, measured in relation to a standard metrical unit, whereas scale is relative and has many meanings; its value is calculated proportionally in relation to a conventional unit or model established ad hoc. This model needs to be clearly determined each time there is reference to scale, even when referring to human nature: "Man, as man, has always measured himself with and against something heavenly. . . . The godhead is the 'measure' with which man measures out his dwelling, his stay on the earth beneath the sky" (Heidegger 1997b, 114).

Scale can become problematic when the unit of reference is not sufficiently clarified, as for example when referring to a building as being big, small, or monumental without specifying, "Big in relation to what?" or "What is monumental within a specific context?" In these cases, it is generally assumed that the unmentioned unit of reference will be retrieved automatically from our shared experiences in the world. This notion, however, is too broad and nebulous to perform as a standard, especially when projected to a remote past.

The most common unit is the human body. When we speak of a work of architecture as being human in scale, we all understand that its main characteristic is that its parts can be easily gauged proportionally, in analogy to the human body. Hence, small and big in architecture are also understood in analogy to what is human in scale. Minoan architecture can be described as human in scale because its individual parts are within our comparative understanding as humans. Egyptian architecture, on the other hand, is big in the sense that it transcends human scale. But to refer to a work of architecture as monumental only because it is big, is not correct; it takes more than size to use this term (for further discussion, see this vol., Ch. 9).

### *Laying-Out Techniques*

There is no clear indication as to how the Minoans realized a design concept on the ground, but there is ample evidence from Egypt, from which the Minoans have borrowed technical know-how in many occasions. The Egyptians were indeed very advanced in this respect: they had elevated design to an autonomous task that involved some kind of drawing board, away from the work-site, and they consequently developed media to transfer the abstract drawing to the ground: namely, the scaled grid. There is no clear evidence that the Minoans had a similar use for the grid, despite Preziosi's strong views on this topic discussed above. It may be assumed, nevertheless, that they too used ropes to lay out straight lines, perhaps with knots like those we see in Egyptian art, and that they mastered simple techniques of how to extend a straight line and create a perfectly horizontal or vertical surface or a right angle.

Laying-out techniques go hand in hand with the design procedure: if the plan of a house was conceived along a set of Regulating Lines, as suggested above, then laying out on the ground followed the same logic: the Regulating Lines would be the first to be traced on the ground with the use of ropes and pegs, starting from the center of the site outward. These lines defined compartments that corresponded to different zones of the building. Each compartment could then be treated independently with the aid of secondary lines (see Figs. 108–111). Such laying out techniques are detectable in canonic as well as organic design procedures, perhaps even more so in the latter instance: the design and laying out in such cases aims at keeping as orderly as possible the core of the building while confining irregularities to its periphery. This is the case, for example, with the almost triagonal plans we see at Palaikastro and Gournia at certain crossroads: the irregular outer boundary has resulted from maximum exploitation and in-fill growth of the town that has come to its limits. The interior of the house, nevertheless, is fairly canonical and follows the logic of Regulating Lines.

On a rather personal note, finally, I wish to add that for a trained architect who has had her share in designing and building, Minoan architecture shouts out loud that it is the product of highly sophisticated planning, designing, and laying out systems, consistently applied at each building site. A casual glance at the plan of the Palace of Knossos, with its perfectly aligned walls spreading over a highly undulated ground of more than 25 acres, suffices for this, as Macdonald also points out (2002, 49). The fact that the Palace of Knossos, as we see it today, represents a long history of modifications and building phases only proves that its fundamental design logic was understood and adhered to at all times. Seen in its three dimensions and multistory construction, the whole design endeavor is breathtaking, especially since space articulation on the upper floor is no mere repetition of the ground floor, as Akrotiri has clearly shown. Most remarkable in this context is the design of the intricate communication systems, horizontal and vertical: staircases, connecting two and three stories, provide access to intermediate levels through their middle landings and appear in combinations, which produce ingenious inter-communication systems, even by modern standards. A glance beyond the Aegean may help appreciate the situation even better: Egyptian temples and Mesopotamian Palaces may be of a much larger size and very canonical in their design, but they lie on flat land, they are mostly one story high, and, most importantly, they are designed along far more simple ordering principles, such as symmetry and axiality.

## Endnotes

1 Such guilds could rely on local workmanship for simpler tasks. The manufacture of mudbricks, for example, does not ask for a high degree of specialization, as Devolder rightly points out (2005–2006, 80). On Minoan itinerant builders and specialized craftsmen, see also Cummer 1980; Driessen 1989–1990, 17–21.

2 A rare and early instance of the use of the grid should be mentioned here. It is in the form of a row of rectangles traced on the wall of Building A at Quartier Mu, Malia. Schmid assumes that they represent a harmonic system of design (1985).

3 The effect of the grid may be compared to what Arnheim describes as the Cartesian or grid compositional system, in opposition to the centric or cosmic: "Viewed dynamically, the grids consist of vectors oriented not toward internal but toward external centers, by which they are attracted or for which they strive" (1983, 140). The columns beyond the pier-and-door partitions seem to materialize this outward thrust of the grid.

4 The title of Koyré's seminal essay, first published in *Critique* 1948.

# 7 

# The Art of Building

## Building as Technology

The construction of a building is a multi-task operation that involves many different materials and technologies, all of which need to concur harmoniously to efficiently serve the form and function specified for the edifice. This means that structure is not dealt with on its own accord after function and form have been defined; quite the contrary, structure is an impartial partner in the poly-parametric problem solving process that results in architectural creation. This process entails formulating the tasks, checking requirements versus constraints, and making choices and decisions based on optimization and compromise, none of which should jeopardize human lives.

Vitruvius described architecture explicitly as involving on equal terms the three conditions of building well. It is no coincidence, of course, that *firmitas* (structural stability) was first in his list, for if a building is in danger of collapse its form or use will not save the lives of the people. The other two conditions, *utilitas*, as appropriate spatial articulation, and *venustas*, as attractive appearance, have been shifting levels of priority in the design process. For a long time after Vitruvius, beauty, style, and ornament prevailed, putting use and structure in secondary roles and taking for granted that they would perform their standardized roles (function).

With the Industrial Revolution, and the new ideas of an egalitarian society that came with it, the Vitruvian triad was reevaluated, and the new dogma granted function the leading role; form simply followed. Though structure is not mentioned explicitly in the famous dictum of the Modern Movement—form follows function—the implication is that it goes hand in hand with form. This was a time of glorification of technology. In the age of machinery and engineering, when Le Corbusier spoke of the house as "a machine for living in," materials and construction techniques were of primal importance in any architectural creation (1986, 95). This was positivist thinking in its prime, and building technology was viewed as the asocial application of scientific truths (Moore 2001, 133).

Though this is not the place to elaborate further on the adventures of the three Vitruvian conditions that define architecture, suffice it to say that many scholars are still engaged in a tug-of-war between the pragmatics and the aesthetics of architecture. This confrontation is noticeable more than anywhere else in the education of architects today. Just as many, however, endorse the all-inclusive nature of architecture, refusing to accept any distinctions or priorities between the poetics and the tectonics.

For a remote past like the Minoan, technology is understood primarily as knowledge gained in the making, through craft and tactile empirical experience (Watson 1997). Experience is an accumulative intergenerational process that goes hand in hand with experimentation, observation, and constant reevaluation. It goes back to humanity's earliest attempts to manipulate nature, when the need to tame and manage the land arose. The stepped cultivation terraces, for example, are technical achievements in their own right (see this vol., p. 20; Fig. 11), which entail many of the basic principles of the art of building: they require good knowledge of the properties of different building materials, their baring capacity and performance in respond to different types of stress, their endurance in time, and their vulnerabilities. Furthermore, they require knowledge of the techniques of acquisition and formulation of raw materials (e.g., quarrying, trimming, cutting) and their transportation to the site, and, above all, knowledge of binding techniques that will bring the parts together to produce an operative whole.

Building technology, of whatever scale or purpose, is integral to architectural design. It is also culturally defined, for it is challenged by social demands and environmental restrictions and empowered by transcultural interactions. Bruno Latour's notion of technological networks thrown over space describes well the spatial character of building technology as the result of mobilization of human and non-human resources within a broader region (Latour 1993, 118). The spatiality of technology is an important tool for prehistoric studies that has been applied in many fields, though less in relation to building technology (for an innovative approach to the energy, manpower, and costs required in a building project, see Devolder 2013).

## Building Materials

In preindustrial societies building materials—mainly stone, clay, and timber—are provided by nature, and there is a reasonable preference for materials that are locally available. Clay and mudbricks, for example, are more popular in Crete in loamy lowland regions such as Malia, whereas stone is dominant in the rocky outcrops of Phaistos and the Cycladic islands. Environmental determinism, however, is not the only, nor necessarily the primal criterion for the choice of materials; parameters of social or cultural value, such as tradition, fashion, prestige, and religious beliefs, may overpower physical demands. This is attested in Crete from the Middle Bronze Age onward, when most local communities became affluent enough to import raw materials from far away if they so needed or desired, especially within the context of the conspicuous consumption of an incipient elite clientele.

There is nevertheless an overbearing technical aspect in the choice of materials that should not be underrated: building materials are ultimately selected on the grounds of their expected performance according to their role within the structural system of the specific building. Their physical efficiency is of primal importance and is carefully evaluated based on prior experience and acquired knowledge that has set norms and specifications. Exceeding the limits or violating the norms will sooner or later result in structural failure, as Akrotiri, Thera has shown (Palyvou 2005a, 137).

Stone, clay, and timber went hand in hand from the earliest habitation on Crete (see Shaw 2009); the same artisans worked with all three materials, their expertise being equally fed from all. Wood, however, has a certain degree of primacy over the other materials. The very name given to architecture has its root in carpentry and wood joining, as the Greek word τέκτων (*te-ko-to* in Linear B) implies. Daidalos too was originally related to carpentry (Morris 1992, 73–100).

Stone is abundant on the island and was used from the Neolithic times onward as the main building material. The land of Crete provides a rich variety of stone for building purposes—limestone, schist, sandstone, gypsum, and so forth—which has been used wisely for wall construction, paving, or veneering according to its physical properties, including color and appearance.

Clay is used for many purposes: to lay out floors, to plaster walls, as a bonding material in stone walls, and to construct walls made of prefabricated mudbricks. Mudbricks were used in Minoan architecture from the Neolithic times. In later periods they were applied in two different ways (Figs. 119, 120): (a) set upright within timber frames as infill material to create light and thin partition walls; and (b) in horizontal layers, placed flat, to create load-bearing walls of some width. The former could be applied on the upper floors, resting on ceiling beams (see, e.g., the

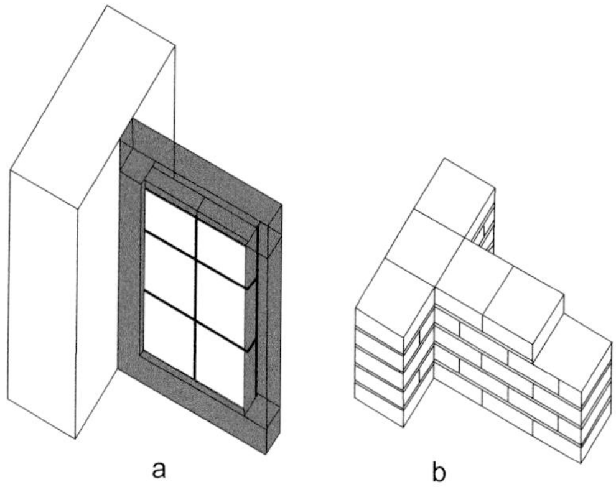


Fig. 119. Mudbricks were applied in two different ways: (a) set upright within a timber frame to form thin partition walls and (b) in horizontal layers. Drawing C. Palyvou.

West House at Akrotiri, Thera). The mudbricks in this case had no load-bearing function; the timber frame played this role.

It must be emphasized here that it is important to distinguish between building materials participating in the structural system at a primal level, materials used for the construction of load bearing elements, and materials used at a secondary level as infill or veneering. The use of mudbricks at a primal level, in the construction of load-bearing walls, is in fact limited. Yet, in Minoan scholarship there lingers the notion that mudbricks were broadly used in the construction of the upper parts of the buildings, presumably in load-bearing walls.[1] Quite often, excavators arrive at this assumption through only the presence of a few fragments of mudbricks found in the debris of a building. But these may well belong to the second category described above—that is, thin partition walls that must have been very common on the upper floors, as we know them to have been from Akrotiri.

The readiness to interpret the bits and pieces of mudbricks as proof for adobe load-bearing walls on the upper floor may have to do with the fact that it is assumed to be an easier (i.e., cheaper and lighter) way to build upper stories. Furthermore, this kind of construction was common practice in many prehistoric sites of the Near East, and in the Aegean studies there is always an eye looking east for inspiration and origins. But there should be no hasty assumptions, and there is surely no reason to think that the Minoans made their choices based on easiness. Akrotiri, Thera, for one, is standing proof of the existence of three-story buildings made almost exclusively with stone. On the same account, the use of the term *pisé* in Aegean bibliography, with or without a cast, is inappropriate. Again, though this technique was popular in the Near East, it is doubtful that it was ever used in Crete; disintegrated mudbricks may sometimes give a false impression of *pisé* during excavation.[2]

Fig. 120. Thin partition walls made of mudbricks set upright within a timber frame in Sector Alpha, Akrotiri, Thera. Palyvou 2005a, fig. 120.

## *Wood: The Inconspicuous Hero*

By the time the second Palaces were being built, the Cretans had developed a sophisticated lifestyle mirrored by an equally sophisticated architectural style, which, in turn, asked for a bold and innovative building technology. Wood became the protagonist of this new technology. Evans recognized the importance of wood in Minoan Neopalatial architecture

played an important role in the adoption of massive structural systems and the invention of vaults. True massive systems, however, are rather limited, and the history of architecture shows a constant struggle to liberate structures from their limitations.

Fig. 122. Valley Temple at Giza. Though made of massive stone elements, it is of the skeleton structural system. Photo C. Palyvou.

The skeleton system represents what Louis Kahn described as "the momentous event when the wall parted and the column became" (from his talk at the American Institute of Architects, when presented the 1971 Gold Medal, quoted in Roth 2007, 29, 32). This system, also known as post and lintel or trabeated (*trabs* in Latin means beam), is timeless in that it has no origins and no end. Skeleton systems are not exclusively of wood; Egyptian architecture, for example—purely of the massive system when it comes to the pyramids—exhibits a skeleton system in stone in the Valley Temple at Giza (Fig. 122; Roth 2007, 32). Timber, however, is the prevailing material in the skeleton system, hence Norberg-Schulz's assumption that "the wooden constructions have played a more important formative role in history than structures in stone" (Norberg-Schulz 1997, 164, n. 14).

The skeleton system implies cutting and joining; *dieresis* and synthesis. To connect one must first divide, and in this process the joint—the seam or the interstice (αρμός)—is what will ensure the harmony and integrity of the building. The way individual elements come together is crucial for their performance within the system, and their proper collaboration depends largely on the effectiveness of the joint. Greeks called the result of this joining *harmonia* (αρμονία). Quite appropriately, Harmonides in the Iliad was a skillful builder (τέκτων) who built the ship in which Paris carried away Helen (Hom. *Il.* 5.60). Last but not least, the skeleton system asks for order and repetition—preferably prefabrication and standardization, as discussed below—and it gives back in return flexibility of articulation and a variety of space configurations.

After this rather long introduction, let us turn now to the structural systems applied in Minoan architecture. Minoan building materials and techniques have been amply studied by Shaw and others, and they need not be reiterated here. Addressing the construction techniques of individual parts such as floors and walls is, however, only part of the question. What is urgently needed is an overall appreciation of the structural logic that guarantees the collaboration of all the parts and keeps the edifice standing. What is also needed is an awareness of the tensions between function, form, and structure, for it is only by studying their interaction that a work of architecture can be truly appreciated in its totality and its character revealed. Between the form that serves a given function and the structural challenges this choice implies, there lies much contention and compromise. Practicing architects know this

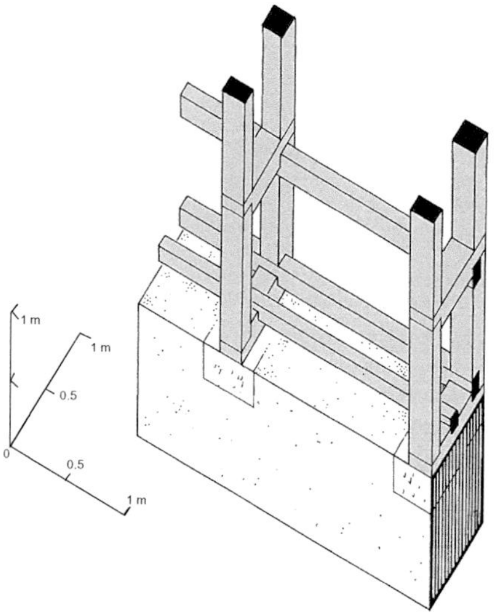

Fig. 123. Vertical timber reinforcement in Xeste 3, Akrotiri, Thera. Palyvou 2005a, fig. 132.

well, and, as Spiro Kostof remarks, "the special excitement of architectural intention lies in the tug of war between the structural and formal systems" (Kostof 1985, 9).

With regard to the two systems described above, exclusive massive systems were very limited in the Minoan world, probably restricted to the Mesara (tholos?) tombs and some relatively small structures such as the silos outside the Palace at Malia and the metallurgical kilns. The debate regarding the structural system of the missing upper parts of the Mesara circular tombs is ongoing (Warren 2007). It has been suggested that some of the larger tombs may have been covered with a flat or conical roof made of timber beams, in which case the building was of the composite system. Exclusive skeleton systems were equally rare, presumably applied to the few known instances of early huts. Otherwise, the majority were composite systems—that is, structures made of massive stone walls with or without horizontal timber reinforcement (this does not affect the massive character of the wall) and ceilings/roofs made of timber beams in the skeleton type.

The use of vertical timber elements in the load-bearing system of a building (columns and vertical timber reinforcements of the walls) was a significant step forward in the building technology of the time (Fig. 123). The great breakthrough, however, a true leap in the history of building technology, came with the introduction of the pier-and-opening partition that allowed for the skeleton system to be autonomized. Tsakanika-Theochari has given a detailed account of this innovative structural system, which is based on what she calls the "pier system" (Tsakanika-Theochari 2006). This system is, in a way, the perfect skeleton system, the architect's dream tool that makes it possible to create flexible boundaries consisting of doors, windows, or cupboards that can provide numerous varieties of flow of movement, intervisibility, and light and air circulation. The Domestic Quarters of all major Palaces present exquisite examples of the resulting style of architecture.

Speaking of an architect as anyone other than a civil engineer, by the way, is only a matter of speaking that reflects our own, long-established division of the profession. In the context of the prehistoric world, it is merely a way to refer to the many duties of the all-inclusive craft of the builder. Through history, combined knowledge of architectural design and building technology have proven to be extremely fruitful, as is evident in the works of great builders such as Buckminster Fuller and Luigi Nervi, two civil engineers who produced innovative and challenging architectural forms (not to mention Leonardo da Vinci). The work of architect Santiago Calatrava is another example of the marvelous forms good knowledge of structural engineering can produce.

The question arising in regard to the pier system described above is how this ingenious idea came into being. A ready answer would be that it was the work of a Buckminster Fuller or a Luigi Nervi of the prehistoric world. This is always a possibility that should never be underestimated. But archaeological thinking is suspicious of wishful arguments of this sort, so we need to follow more conventional ways of thinking and look for precedents and inspirations—after all, Fuller and Nervi also worked with previously accumulated knowledge, and so did Da Vinci, who studied in depth the great Alexandrian engineers.

Scholars long have been concerned with the origins and development of the pier-and-opening partition, and the idea that has prevailed is that the three-dimensional timber frame was first invented and applied as a means to build frames for walls made with mudbricks (assumed to be an early practice). Actual evidence for this, however, is very slim. I will therefore risk a different line of thought based on the treatment of the openings (Fig. 124). Doors and windows were initially treated as breaks in the masonry that needed only to be spanned with timber beams. At some point in time, however, openings became autonomous, acquiring a load-bearing structure of their own in the form of a three-dimensional timber frame encased in the masonry. This was a momentous technical event, because builders were dealing for the first time with a vertical plane (a wall) consisting of two different structural systems in juxtaposition: the massive system of the masonry and the skeleton system of the opening. Having autonomized the structural system of the opening, it was one step further to add more such systems, one next to the other, and to substitute completely the mass of a wall. The pier-and-opening partition was thus born.

The invention of the pier system and the pier-and-opening partition was not a matter of deterministic technological process; it was triggered by the strong urge to produce an architecture of openness and fluidity in accordance with the lifestyle of the Minoans. The challenge for the Minoan architects was enormous, for the openness they were asked to provide was the worst possible choice for an earthquake-prone land. The amazing result is trenchantly epitomized by Tsakanika-Theochari in the ending paragraph of her dissertation: "Where other civilizations add mass to support up to two stories, they [the Minoans] take out mass to support even four stories" (2006, 254, my translation).

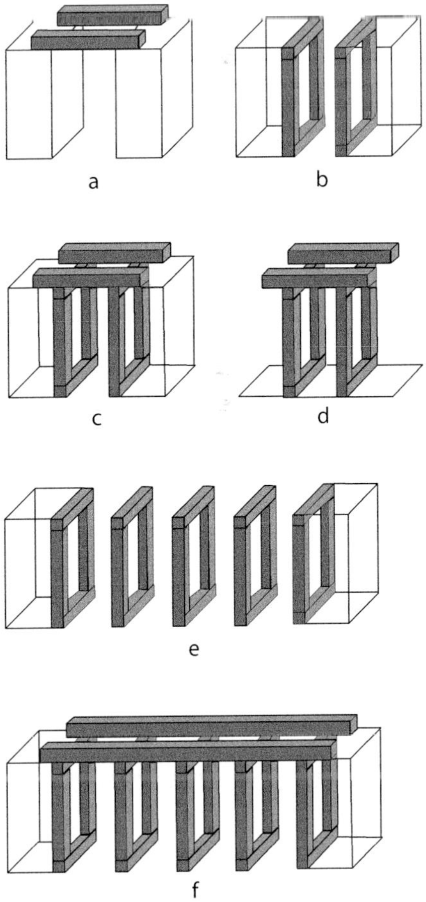


Fig. 124. Evolution of the door (a–d) and genesis of the pier-and-opening partition system (e, f). Drawing C. Palyvou.

## Multistory Construction

Multistory construction began very early in the Aegean, as the Early Cycladic settlement of Skarkos, Ios demonstrates (Marthari 1990), and it remained a standard feature for both domestic and formal architecture throughout the Bronze Age.

Building a second story is not something that comes naturally, for it requires extra effort and technical skills. Building a third and a fourth story is an event in itself! It is of special interest, therefore, that multistory construction became almost standard practice for urban houses in the Minoan world, whereas it was abandoned in the Dark Ages, along with many other advanced technological achievements of the Bronze Age, to be regained in the classical era, albeit in a much more limited manner than before.

The factors that facilitated and generalized multistory construction in the Minoan world are primarily the adoption of the flat roof and the mild Mediterranean climate that has always promoted outdoor living. The absence of court-houses is another strong factor: in an urban context of closely packed houses with no courtyards, the flat roof offers a perfect substitute for outdoor activities. The fact that activities taking place on the roof were exposed to the gaze of the neighbors and the passers-by obviously did not inhibit the Minoans. One might even assume that the tolerance of the Minoan society encouraged the use of the flat roof as one more level of habitation, and that it led eventually to the development of the two-story house.

As Aris Konstantinidis rightly contested, life in Greece is semi-outdoors; in other words, there is always need for shelter (see this vol., p. 100). A shelter of this kind—typical in the vernacular architecture of Greece—is seen on the roof of the Archanes model of a house (see Fig. 60). It is interesting to note that the shelter was supported by robust wooden columns in the Minoan style, an indication of aesthetic concern and permanence that heralds the second story. After the second floor was fully established, the idea of the functional roof was not abandoned; it was carried higher up, leading eventually to more stories.

The second story therefore came about not by the division of an interior space but by the duplication of the ground floor in the vertical. This explains perhaps the rather heavy construction of the upper floors, in imitation of the roof, with an unnecessarily thick layer of clay above the supporting beams (this layer offers insulation in the case of the roof). At the same time, the wise diminishing of the thickness of the walls on the upper floors, well attested at Akrotiri, Thera, shows that they were aware of the static issues involved in multistory construction.

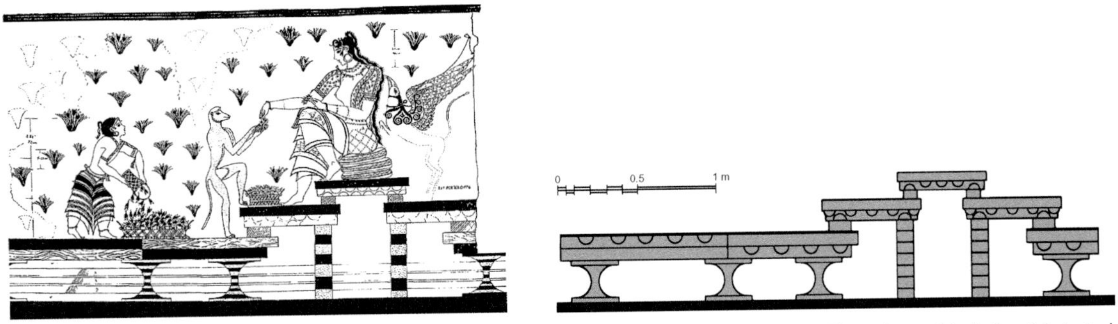


Fig. 125. Tripartite stepped platform depicted almost full-scale on a wall painting in Xeste 3, Akrotiri, Thera. It consisted of prefabricated, standardized elements. Image C. Palyvou.

## Standardization (and Prefabrication?)

It is quite likely that the people who developed a building technology of the quality and complexity of the Minoans also understood the values of standardization and perhaps even prefabrication. Standardization helps organize the worksite and manage the project, while prefabrication facilitates the building process.[3] True standardization is indeed manifested in the Minoan world in many instances, for example in pottery production. In architecture, however, standards are of the model-and-variation type, discussed in Chapter 6: the model is prescribed in terms of the optimal materials, form, dimensions, and so forth, ranging within given sets of values. But their variability excludes standardization in the full sense.

The development of the pier-and-opening partition favored—if not demanded—standardization and prefabrication. To give an example: Rooms 3 and 4 on the first floor of Xeste 3 at Akrotiri, Thera required ordering and manufacturing 18 stone bases, 52 timber posts, and 36 lintel beams, all very similar in form and size.[4] So, even if there is no absolute standardization in Minoan architecture, it is clear that the prehistoric builders were thinking not only in terms of flexible models but also in terms of standards and prefabrication.

Fig. 126. Isometric representation of the Theran tripartite stepped platform. Reconstruction C. Palyvou.

There is, however, an instance where true standardization and prefabrication is the case. It is evidenced primarily in art but is also corroborated by archaeological findings: it is the tripartite stepped platform with a woman seated at the topmost level. One such platform is depicted almost full-scale on a wall painting at Xeste 3 at Akrotiri (Figs. 125, 126). A detailed study of this

Fig. 127. Curvilinear stone bases, like those depicted on the wall painting in Xeste 3, Akrotiri, were found at Archanes, set one next to the other (looking south). Sakellarakis and Sapouna-Sakellaraki 1997, fig. 62.

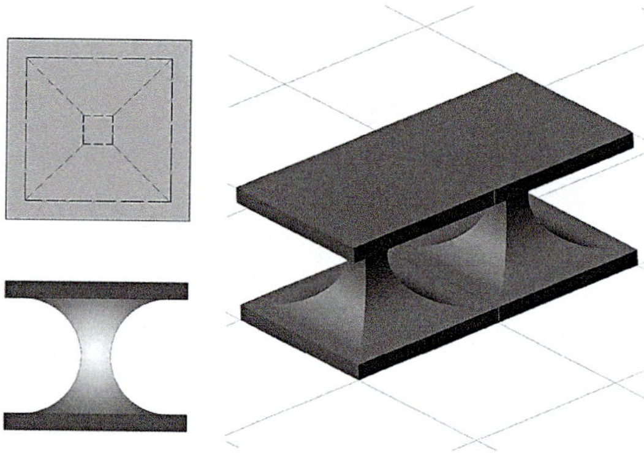

Fig. 128. Sketch of standardized curvilinear stone bases. Drawing C. Palyvou.

structure has shown that this was a prefabricated mobile installation consisting of a number of timber beams and stone bases in the form of the so-called curvilinear altar, all of which were standardized in form and dimensions (Palyvou 2006). These objects were carried to the site when the occasion arose—presumably for a ritual performance to take place in the countryside—and they were arranged to form the tripartite platform. The structure was dismantled and stowed away when the event was over to be reused in the future.

Curvilinear bases are known from many depictions in art but also from a small number of real ones found in excavations. The most stunning are the four stone bases found at Archanes (Figs. 127, 128): they are identical in size and form (and theirs is not an easy form to produce), and they were found placed next to each other, fitting perfectly together so as to create a square platform. The form of these bases is absolutely symmetrical in all directions, thus facilitating their combinations in many different ways. This is a true case of absolute standardization and mass prefabrication! It also bares proof of the dexterity of the Minoan craftsmen and their ability to produce perfectly accurate and standardized forms, if so desired. That theirs was nevertheless a world of approximation was a matter of choice rather than inability to achieve precision, as discussed in Chapter 6.

## Responding to Seismic Threat

Builders of all times have set as their primal goal the creation of edifices that will endure and be safe for their users. This indeed they have achieved: standing buildings are the norm and failures the exception. For this to be the case, good knowledge of structural engineering and laws of nature are a prerequisite, even if empirical.

Among the natural phenomena that might threaten human lives, none is more frightening than the earthquake: it is unpredictable and comes suddenly, whereas all others allow for some time to prepare, both physically and emotionally. As contradictory as it may sound, earthquakes have become even more frightening since architecture came into being, because earthquakes are mostly felt, and far more dangerous, when one is inside or very close to a building. In the open air—out in the fields, in the sea, or, nowadays, in the air—one might not even sense them at all.

Natural phenomena become hazards when injury occurs. Hence, disasters are not physical but social phenomena. Though builders and engineers know, more or less, what makes buildings stand, they cannot always tell what makes them fall (not even today; see Levy and Salvadori 1994). When designing a building, all its parts are calculated so as to transfer loads safely to the ground. In other words, gravity is the main force in question, taking for granted that the ground receiving the loads is steady. In case of earthquake, however, the ground is no longer steady and lateral forces coming from all possible directions are activated. This kind of stress is difficult to predict and calculate.

The question arising, therefore, is to what extent were the people of a remote past like the Minoan aware of the effects of an earthquake on their buildings, and, if so, what did they do about it? Can we speak of an earthquake-resistant technology in Minoan architecture, as Driessen positively argued in 1987 (Driessen 1987)?

Judging from the architectural style of the Neopalatial period, one might argue that in an era as prolific as the Late Bronze Age, the challenge to build multistory edifices pierced with numerous openings on a land with high seismic activity became a stimulus for technological achievements and excellence. This was an affluent society sparing no time and labor in improving its means; a society exhorting able artisans to experiment and invent. In times as opulent and creative as these, the dialogue between style and technology can only find a happy outcome and trigger a feedback process that enhances and promotes both.

One of the factors that may have accelerated technological developments is the frequent recurrence of catastrophic events. If a builder had the bitter opportunity to live through a number of severe earthquakes and judge for himself how the structures he had built behaved under extreme stress, he may have had a better understanding of the mechanisms of strain and collapse and may have detected the vulnerable points of the edifice. It would have been easier, then, for him to correct and improve his own techniques.

To give an example from Akrotiri: the diagonal timber beam that ensures rigidity of the corner of a wall (a well-known practice today) is attested in only two instances, in two buildings located near each other; this means that this salutary practice was not part of the local building tradition but the ingenious initiative of one brilliant mind (Palyvou

2005a, 122). It was the work of a man who understood that "a design problem is not something to be overcome, but an opportunity to be embraced" (Frederick 2007, 98). Though we cannot tell how he came up with the idea, a possible scenario is that he realized the importance of ensuring a rigid corner by observing failures after seismic events. An observant builder would have understood the beneficial properties of wood for earthquake protection. Its elasticity and its ability to absorb forces of tension through deformation is a great advantage over stone in case of lateral forces.

But for wood to be fully effective there has to be proper collaboration among the different members of the timber structure as well as between the timber parts and the other elements of the building (i.e., stone walls). This is indeed attested in the careful bonding of the timber elements through special cuttings and joints, and above all in the system of mortises and dowels that ensured cooperation between timber and stone elements: wooden pegs (dowels) run through the timber beam into the cavities (mortises) of the stone, fixing it to the wall and preventing dislocation in case of lateral movement. These details are common in most Minoan sites but are best understood at Akrotiri, Thera, the building technology of which is Minoan in more than one way (Fig. 129). As fibrous material, timber responds well to tensile stresses and allows for a building to be deformed to a state that may be irreparable but does not collapse, thus giving time to the residents to escape danger (Fig. 130). This is very important proof of technology in the service of society.

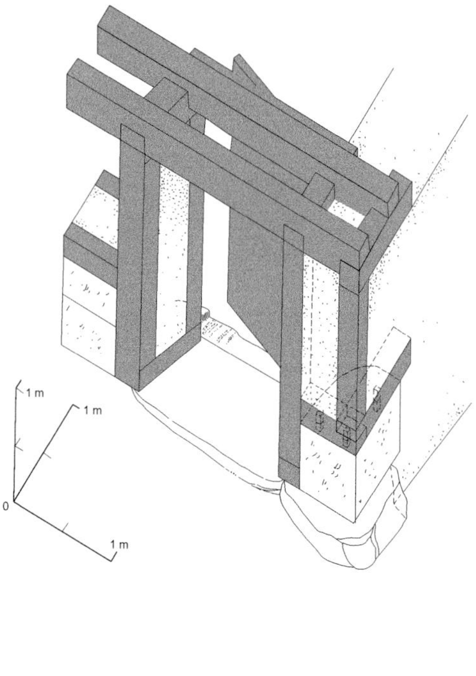


Fig. 129. Timber elements of this door frame in Sector Delta, Akrotiri, Thera, carefully joined and fixed onto the corner stone with dowels (wooden pegs) inserted in mortises (cavities in the stone). After Palyvou 2005a, fig. 199.

An early example of the system of dowels and mortises is to be seen on the upper surfaces of the double orthostates at Knossos. The cuttings on the stones are in the form of dovetails meant to receive wooden clamps (Shaw 2009, 109–110). It is quite probable that the Cretans picked up this technique from Egypt, along with other details regarding tools, the dressing of the stones, and the ashlar technique in general. This specific technique of holding together stones in the horizontal, however, has no other parallels in Crete. The mortises and dowels that prevailed in Minoan architecture are of a different logic: they were intended almost exclusively to anchor timber beams onto ashlar stones—that is, to connect timber to stone so as to protect the timber beams from being displaced in the event of lateral forces enacted through earthquakes.

Experimenting with timber began early in the Bronze Age, and the builders had all the time to develop new and innovative uses of this valuable material, of which their island provided abundant species and supplies. Wood was indeed the material that played the most definitive role in the formation of the unique Minoan architectural idiom: the colonnades, the numerous doors and windows, the floors, the staircases, and above all the pier system and the timber reinforcement of the wall are all based on wood. The ingenious use of wood is what allowed for the sophisticated architectural idiom of the Minoan Neopalatial era to take its form; and, vice versa, it was because of the demand for such an architectural idiom that timber technology reached such unprecedented levels of achievement.

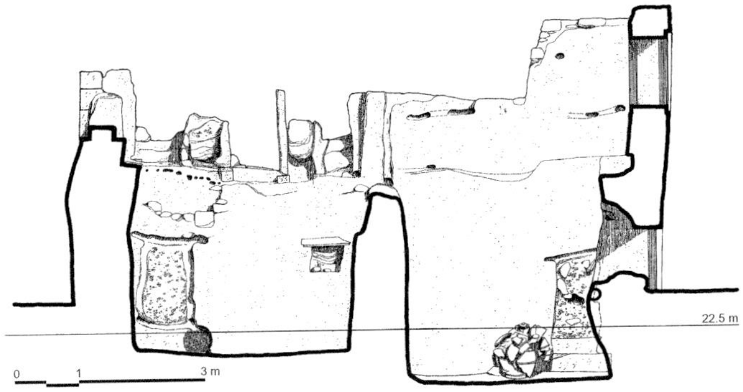


Fig. 130. Section through the West House at Akrotiri, Thera, showing a wall (right) deformed to a state of no repair without it collapsing, thus allowing the residents to escape danger. After Palyvou 2005a, fig. 53.

As mentioned above, disasters are not only physical phenomena but also social. It is interesting, therefore, to observe the people's reactions to such threats. These are vividly demonstrated at Akrotiri, Thera, in the systematic evacuation of the city in the face of an oncoming disaster after people tidied up their houses and removed their valuables (Nikolakopoulou 2003). Clearly, they had previous experience of earthquakes and had spotted the safer parts of the house; this explains why basements are found literally packed with vases and other objects, and pithoi are neatly stowed under the timber frames of doors and windows. One may even glimpse the sensitivity of a resident of the West House who placed a small straw mat between a wall and a vase to protect it. The universal, deeply rooted, existential need to believe in one's return is clearly manifested in these fretful yet disciplined reactions to a crisis. The Chinese describe eloquently crisis as a combination of danger and opportunity (Frederick 2007, 98); in other words, if the Therans were given the opportunity to return, they would have excelled once more, just as they did after the seismic destruction of their town some 50 years prior to its volcanic end (Palyvou 1984).

## Endnotes

1 Shaw (2009, 127–134) gives a detailed account of the various uses of mudbricks throughout Crete and quotes Evans who, referring to the South House at Knossos, writes that "From the amount of clay deposit in the lower rooms and basements it may be inferred that the upper part of the house walls was largely composed of sun-dried bricks . . ." (1921–1935, II, 390). Other excavators have made similar assessments. For reservations regarding the extent of use of mud bricks in Crete see Palyvou 1999a, 112; Tsakanika-Theohari 2006, 237–241.

2 For a detailed discussion on this topic, with references to various misunderstandings, see Aurenche 1977, 40–42, 119–122. Shaw (2009, 57 n. 330, 157 n. 1019) also points out that the term *pisé*, used originally by Evans, should be avoided in relation to Minoan architecture. On the use of soil in Minoan architecture, see Devolder 2005–2006.

3 For an interesting account of time, labor, and costs in the Minoan building industry, see Devolder 2013.

4 It is interesting to note that a Linear B tablet from Pylos mentions six wooden door beams that may well correspond to one door and not to two as Chadwick assumed, presumably misled by the form of the frame of a modern door (1976, 139). The tablet also implies prefabrication and standardization reflected in the manufacturing and supply of materials.

# 8 

# The Art of Appearance

*[A]rt is nothing if not the art of allowing things to appear through it. (Michelis 1964, 142)*

Of the three Vitruvian principles, *firmitas, utilitas*, and *venustas*, the third has blessed architecture with attributes immediately appealing to our senses, especially to the privileged sense of vision. Yet, what we see is at the same time what limits and obstructs our vision. In every composition, Panagiotis Michelis points out, there is an art of display and an art of concealment, the combination of which facilitates perception, promotes hierarchy (the primary is exposed in full, while the secondary only partially), and ultimately provides the composition with a plot (1964, 142).

For the plot to unfold, formal clarity is required. This depends on the relationship between the whole and the parts, the interplay between mass and space, the way a building stands on the ground and its figure is projected on the background, the articulation of the bounding surfaces, and much more. In between mass, through space and under the light, people's actions add time to the ever-changing angles of perception. These infinite viewpoints and corporeal experiences, in which all senses partake, add up eventually to the apperception of a work of architecture as a totality. Minoan architecture, as we shall see below, exhibits a high degree of formal clarity; what is more, in some cases such clarity seems to be a conscious and intentional goal. But first, let us step back to examine the broader picture.

## Undulating Ground, Indented Facades, Stepped Skyline

Within the wet and volatile boundaries of Crete, ragged mountains alternate with mild hillsides, narrow gorges with broad valleys, and deep bays and cliffs with long stretches of sandy coasts in a perpetual succession of rest and unrest, permanence and change. Human habitats in Minoan times seldom rested on flat land, though strong inclinations were equally avoided. Even when inhabiting highlands up on the mountains, as at Zominthos or Syme, the buildings themselves stood on a pocket of relatively temperate and gently sloping land (cf. the post-Minoan choice of precipitous sites such as Karphi in eastern Crete).

Upon this land, boxlike buildings were set to conform closely to the relief of the ground (Graham 1972, 239). In the vertical, this is reflected in the way all buildings, domestic and formal compounds alike, stand on the ground: neither elevated nor sunken, they follow the contours of the land by adjusting the levels of their ground floors accordingly. To appreciate such a down-to-earth choice of setting, especially in regard to formal architecture, we need to look briefly into the history of architecture to see that elevated ground floors—buildings standing on raised platforms—were common, either as a means of protection (e.g., from inundation) or as a way to distance the building and its context from the mundane world. Such setting evokes awe and a subordinate feeling. The difference of height, in other words, is symbolically experienced as a difference of status. It is quite notable, therefore, that Minoan buildings stand even with the surrounding land, providing easy and undifferentiated transitions from the public to the private domain.

Though elevated ground floors are not the case in Minoan buildings, their bases are often visually accentuated. Means to this end are the krepidoma (κρηπίδωμα), or plinth, and the orthostates (Shaw 2009, 59–65). The former is a slight projection at the base of the wall, implying strong foundations firmly embedded in the ground. The visual effect of a broad base provides reassurance that the building will not sink under its own weight (Figs. 131–133). In a few cases, as in the Unexplored Mansion, the effect of stability is further highlighted by the stepped formation of the facade: a wall that gradually broadens toward its base is a steady wall.

Orthostates (with plinths) appeared in the First Palace period in major facades, such as the West Facade of the Palace of Phaistos. There are also some examples of a later date at Kommos and Galatas. Early orthostates consist of a row of large blocks with well-dressed faces, ranging in

Fig. 131. Krepidoma and orthostates in the West Facade of the Palace of Knossos. Evans 1921–1935, I, suppl. pl. I.

Fig. 132. Krepidoma and orthostates in the Palace of Galatas. Photo C. Palyvou.

Fig. 133. Plan of krepidoma and orthostates in Building T at Kommos. After Shaw and Shaw, eds., 2006, pl. 1.43.

height from 0.65 to 1.00 m. Whatever the composition of the wall above (rubble, mud bricks, or ashlar), this row stands out as a robust base for the whole building. Apart from their structural role in adding firmness to the building, therefore, orthostates also carry explicit symbolic messages of power and permanence.

The undulation of the ground is taken up in the horizontal as well, through the so-called indentation of the facades. This is a well-known, age-old characteristic of Minoan architecture that may have originated in the East where it has an even longer tradition (Palyvou 1986, 192–194). Indentations, as a rule, are shallow (20–60 cm), and they are applied at relatively short distances (3–5 m) extending over several abutting houses. This allows for a long street facade to be adjusted to the contours of the ground while retaining the volumnar clarity of the buildings involved (Fig. 134).

Indentations do not always correspond to transverse walls inside the building, as one might expect: they also occur at intermediate points of the wall, in a rather awkward manner and without any obvious reason at first sight (e.g., Tylissos House B, Malia House Zα, Knossos, Rousses, Makrygialos). Moreover,

Fig. 134. The so-called indentation of the facades is the result of adjusting rectilinear forms to a curved route following the natural contours of the ground. Drawing C. Palyvou.

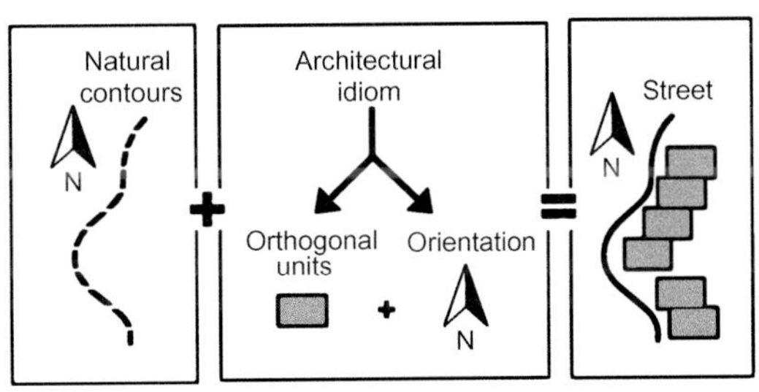

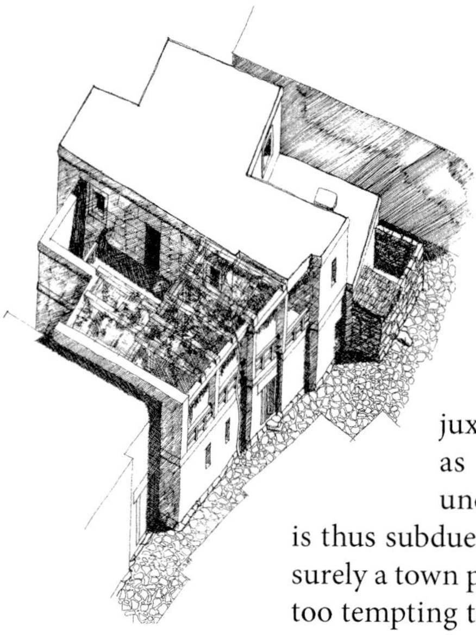

Fig. 135. Wall indentations in House I at Chania project the volumes of the building while subduing their individuality to the street facade. Hallager 1990, fig. 6.

sometimes the two walls meet at their edges with no bonding between them whatsoever. It is quite clear from these instances that the raison d être of these indentations is not always to stabilize a long wall, as has been suggested, or to project the inner structure of the building. Quite often, indentations do not refer to the building at all; rather, they have been designed as a special morphological treatment signifying an important public space (Fig. 135). Furthermore, indentations have a strong unifying effect: the facades of juxtaposed individual buildings are no longer distinguished as such, and they blend into one another forming a long, undulating street facade. The individuality of each building is thus subdued to the overall composition of the townscape. This was surely a town planner's tool—and a conscious one at that—and it is only too tempting to think of it as a means toward an egalitarian treatment of the public image of the town.

If the base links the edifice to the earth, it is against the light and the emptiness of the blue sky that manmade forms acquire their strongest presence, and it is here that they meet with infinite space where the divine dwells. The treatment of the uppermost boundary of a building—its silhouette or skyline—is therefore a significant part of its identity and often heavily imbued with symbolic meaning. The importance of the sky as an integral part of the cosmos should not be underestimated, Goodison points out, warning against the western model of dualistic thinking that sharply separates earth and sky, body and mind, and matter and spirit (Goodison 2004, 346).

The skyline is one of the most characteristic features of urban environments, a unique image marking out the townscape of each city; it is a fondly familiar figure for the local people and a condensed ideogram of what is to be explored for newcomers. The true Minoan townscape, as the blending of the manmade environment and its natural background, will unfortunately always escape us, though Akrotiri, Thera is preserved well enough to offer some information of this sort. A phenomenological approach to this issue, therefore, will have to rely largely on imagination and extrapolation from images of towns as perceived by the Minoans themselves and rendered through their art (Fig. 136).

From the limited information regarding the Minoan townscape, one may envisage a gentle and gradual transition from the natural horizon to the manmade outline of the buildings. This we infer from the close conformity to the contours of the land that was presumably repeated on the upper floors and the roofs, as Akrotiri, Thera has shown it to be. The undulation

Fig. 136. Skylines of building compounds depicted in art: (a) Right Town, Akrotiri, Thera (after Doumas 1992, fig. 35); Left Town, Akrotiri, Thera (after Doumas 1992, fig. 35); (c) Sacred Mansion Ring (after Rethemiotakis and Dimopoulou 2003, fig. 1); (d) Master Impression (after Hallager 1985, fig. 11).

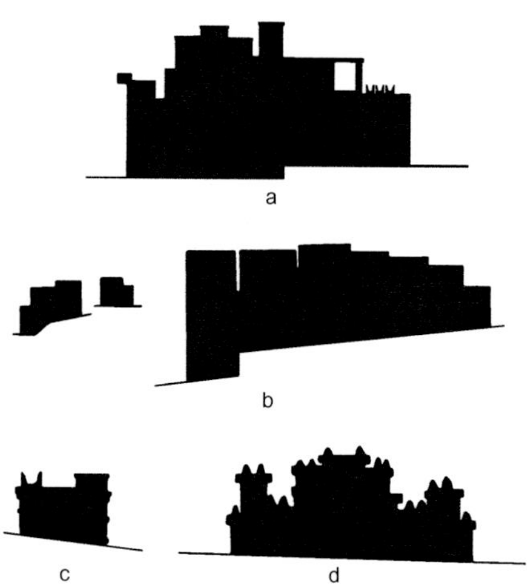

of the land was thus repeated a few meters above ground in the stepped skyline of the buildings. In this skyline horizontality prevails, punctuated with only a small number of vertical elements, such as the projecting tops of the main staircases leading up to the roofs, a distinct feature of the Minoan urban townscape (Figs. 137, 138).

Fig. 137. The verticality of each individual house is subdued to the horizontality of the street facade. Drawing C. Palyvou.

Several depictions of architectural compounds in art show roofs crowned with Horns of Consecration, either single or in rows. Such objects, made of stone, have been found in the archaeological record in palatial, ritual, and urban contexts (Fig. 139). They all seem to be related to entrances. A single pair of horns standing high on the roof above an entrance can be quite a commanding sight (Alexopoulos 2008, 395–396). When observed from a close distance, the two symmetrical vertical projections thrusting upward to the sky denote a strong axis, corresponding to the axis of the entrance (Fig. 140). Seen from far away, on the other hand, as part of the townscape, the horns punctuate the skyline denoting the location of entrances to (specific?) buildings. Some very large Horns of Consecration, over 2 m high, such as those found at Knossos and Mt. Juktas, were meant presumably to be seen from an even bigger distance—that is, their symbolic function performed at a regional level.

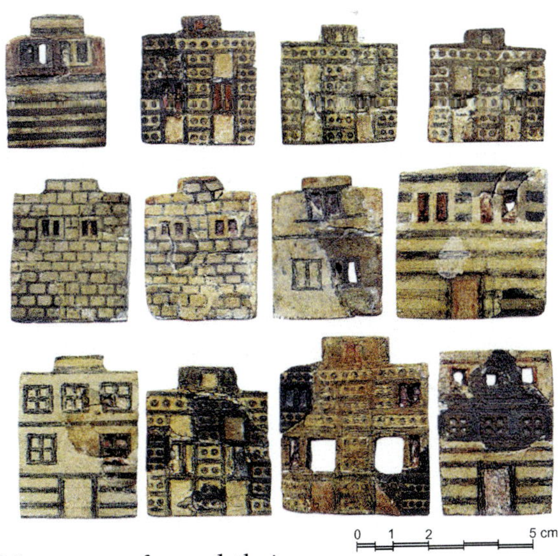


Fig. 138. Faience plaques of the Town Mosaic. Courtesy Archaeological Museum of Herakleion, Hellenic Ministry of Culture and Sports–Archaeological Receipts Fund.

Horns of Consecration, mostly of medium size, have been found in several sites (D'Agata 1992). In art they often appear in large numbers, arranged in rows crowning the tops of walls. If this was the case in reality as well (despite the absence of archaeological evidence so far), then they would no longer emphasize verticality: repetition and row formation would have transformed their vertical figures into a horizontal undulating line (Fig. 140). Plenitude and rhythm would have prevailed, and the emblematic symbolic power of these objects would have been amplified.

In an urban environment where private open air spaces in the form of courts were limited, the roof was an important functional annex to the house proper, and we can safely assume that many roofs had light shelters like the one on the Archanes house model (see Fig. 98; see also this vol., Ch. 5). These pergolas would have added to the skyline a kind of decomposed upper boundary, an interlocking element mediating between the enclosed, bounded volume of the house and the unlimited space beyond. Moreover, the Minoan skyline was inhabited: this we

Fig. 139. Horns of Consecration at Knossos. Evans 1921–1935, II.1, 159.

deduce from the archaeological evidence of the various activities that took place on the roof, especially from Akrotiri, Thera and from "people on the roof" depicted regularly in art.

On a closing note, we should add that apperception of a building, both in its totality and in its details, relies greatly on the distance from which it is viewed and the direction of movement (Letesson and Vansteenhuyse 2006). As one moves closer to a building its volumes lose their coherence and are perceived in a fragmented way, to be dissolved eventually into planes and individual bits and pieces. Direction of movement also plays an important role: frontal, lateral, and oblique views promote planes, volumes, and perspectives, respectively. These were well-known tools of architectural design in later periods (Scully 1962; Martienssen 1964). Minoan architecture favors oblique views that promote a feeling of suspense and anticipation, but there is seldom adequate viewing distance to allow for full apprehension of the volumnar qualities of a building. Moreover, the prevailing horizontality and the way buildings tend to spread out in all directions make it even more difficult to grasp their totality. It is indeed in the totality that formal clarity is compromised. These characteristics are best observed in the West Facades of the Palaces, discussed below in Chapter 10.

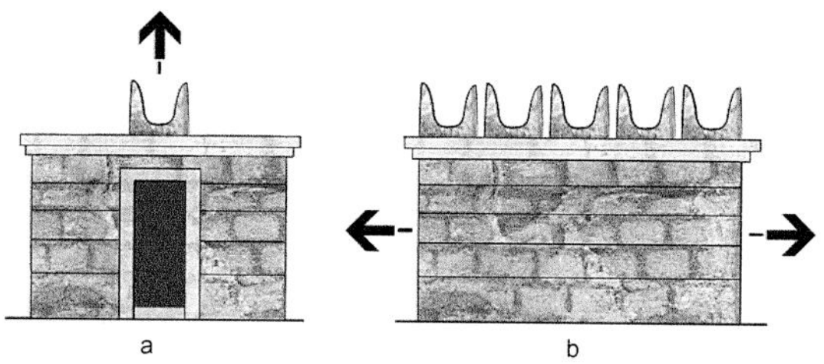


Fig. 140. Horns of Consecration standing on top of entrances emphasize verticality (a), whereas when set in a row, crowning the tops of the walls, repetition transforms this vertical figure into a horizontal undulating line (b). Drawing C. Palyvou.

## Solids and Voids

The visual balance between solids and voids—mass and space—and the mode of expression of their interface are determinant factors of the architectural style of an era. More often, form and structure mimic each other overtly. There are indeed many examples of skeleton-type structures disguised as massive-type structures and as many massive types treated to look like skeleton types (Roth 2007). In Egyptian monumental architecture, for example, solids triumph even when the structural logic is that of the frame and skeleton, as in the Valley Temple in Giza, mentioned in the previous chapter: the oversized dimensions of the individual stone elements—posts and beams, all far beyond static requirements—do nothing but declare mass (see Fig. 122). The result is an overwhelming assemblage of stone that celebrates gravity, endurance, and eternity, while space is conceived and experienced as subordinate to mass. A similar effect is attested in the hypostyle halls of the large temples at Luxor, Karnak, and Edfu. Mass and solids, in this case, are means of representing the cosmos. The dense claustrophobic effect of the marshes and the starry sky above are represented by the thick and closely placed columns in the form of plants rising from the ground. The ceiling, painted with stars, looks as if it is suspended because of the invisible blocks above the capitals of the columns that carry the ceiling slabs.

At the other end of the spectrum, but along the same lines of cosmological symbolism through the manipulation of solids and voids, Japanese architecture is a magnificent example of the celebration of space; mass is almost immaterialized in the form of slim timber frames and ethereal paper walls. The fragile, ephemeral nature of this architecture (the tectonic or forest concept) stands in strong contrast with the stone eternity (the glyptic or cave concept) of Pharaonic architecture, yet their symbolic power is equally strong.

Where does Minoan architecture stand in this tug-of war-between form and structure? Needless to say, there can be no simple answer to this question, for in the long run of time almost all concepts of space are to be found in prehistoric Crete. Morphological concerns regarding the balance between solids and voids are implied by the way Minoan architects treated facades made of ashlar versus rubble (see Fig. 138). The former inspired mass effects, they were treated as compact solids with few and relatively small windows, and discontinuity was avoided (timber reinforcement was seldom applied on the outside; Palyvou 2005a, 119). Rubble walls, on the other hand, were sometimes highly perforated, especially when adhering to the skeleton structural system.

Of great importance in this discussion are the openings: their size, form, number, distribution, and location. Such choices were made primarily on cultural grounds, and structural concerns were but a challenge to be met next. Proof of this is that the Minoans chose openness despite the fact that this was not advisable from the structural point of view because of the seismic risk of the region. Openings, in general, are perceived either as minor perforations in an overpowering mass, emphasizing enclosure and interiority, or as autonomous, clearly defined elements that negate mass and evoke exteriority and transparency. There is, of course, a rich range of situations between these two extremes. The size and form of the windows and their relation to the wall surface are important: if they are small and in the form of a niche they stress massiveness, if they are flush with the wall facade the plane effect is enhanced, and if they are very large in proportion to the wall surface they promote skeleton-type effects (Norberg-Schulz 1997, 133–134).

Though the archaeological records from Crete offer inadequate information regarding the windows, especially those on the upper floors, one can always turn to Akrotiri, Thera for evidence and firsthand experience. Minoan art also offers indisputable evidence of the conspicuity of windows in Minoan architecture (see Figs. 58, 60, 61, 138). It is indeed in the openings that Minoan architecture exhibits its unique character, leaving behind its Near Eastern mass-oriented neighbors. The unprecedented sophistication in the use of openings (i.e., doors and windows) gives the architecture of this era its very special formal qualities in celebration of space, volumes, and voids.

Minoan resourcefulness is best exemplified in the pier-and-opening partition (see this vol., Ch. 4). This ingenious device is in itself a manifestation of the triumph of space over mass. Here, mass is minimal: it only exists in the posts and beams of the skeleton, both of which are under constant, almost palpable tension. Pier-and-opening partitions appear in the facades of the buildings almost exclusively in the form of multiple windows (pier-and-window partitions) located on upper stories, as we know them from Akrotiri, Thera. Pier-and-door partitions are applied almost exclusively in interior spaces. In the periphery of the building they exist only in relation to Minoan Halls, in combination with a columned porch opening on a private open-air space. The sheltered porch protects the timber elements of the pier-and-door partition. This means that the pier-and-door partition does not participate directly in the public image of a Minoan building, with one exception: the pier-and-door partition of the Throne Room at Knossos opening onto the Central Court (see Fig. 4). It is a bizarre case, against all practical and stylistic logic, which may be due to the fact that this arrangement has resulted from a series of reformations that took place in this area at a very late date (Niemeier 1987).

According to Norberg-Schulz, mass is expressed in varying degrees of concentration, and space or volume in varying degrees of closure. Surface treatment, edges, and corners of adjoining planes play an important role in enhancing or diminishing these effects. For example, if two adjoining surfaces (facades) are morphologically alike and their common edge is curved, then the mass concentration effect is largely accentuated, whereas if adjoining surfaces differ in treatment, texture, color, or otherwise, and their common edges are broken, blurred, or differentiated, the result is discontinuity and the effect is that of juxtaposition of bounding surfaces, rather than wholesome mass (Norberg-Schulz 1997, 135).

In Minoan architecture it is often the case that adjoining surfaces are treated differently. In many instances one facade of a building is ashlar whereas the others are plastered rubble. If viewed together (this depending on the possible ways of approaching the building and the corresponding angles of vision), their differences are perceived as discontinuity and therefore the mass effect is compromised. Compare for example the two largest buildings at Akrotiri, Thera, Xeste 3 and Xeste 4: the former has only some facades made of ashlar, while the major facade looking south consists of rubble with timber reinforcement. Xeste 4, on the other hand, is the only building so far at Akrotiri that has all its facades made of ashlar. The difference is striking: large and impressive though they both are, Xeste 4 exudes a compactness that is not as apparent in Xeste 3.

# Ordering Principles

## *The Euclidean Triumph and the Supremacy of the Horizontal*

*Order without diversity can result in monotony or boredom; diversity without order can produce chaos. A sense of unity with variety is the ideal. (Ching 1996, 320)*

Rudolph Arnheim writes that "order is a necessary condition for anything the human mind is to understand" and adds that "the perceivable order tends to be manifested and understood as a reflection of an underlying order, whether physical, social, or cognitive" (1971, 1–3). The perceivable order of Minoan architecture is our next target, in the hope that we might reveal its formative principles and discover the underlying levels of order these principles reflect.

As discussed in Chapter 3, one of the intrinsic characteristics of Minoan architecture is the dominance of the square. The result is an Euclidean universe of rectilinear shapes, straight lines, and right angles. Deviations from these formative guidelines are precisely that: the Euclidean concept still prevails, even if obscured due to specific circumstances. This is the case, for example, with the skew walls of some houses in densely inhabited areas such as Gournia and Palaikastro.

There is, however, one instance where the Minoans have chosen consciously to counterpoise the Euclidean prepotency: the diagonal causeway (Fig. 141). In a realm of orthogonals and right angles the diagonal is an event, if not a scandal. The diagonal causeway simply materializes on the ground the route a person would naturally take crossing an open space and moving from one point of interest to another that happens to be directed diagonally (the diagonal line, we should be reminded, exists only in relation to a prevalent system of perpendicular lines). The diagonal lines, therefore, though they contradict and contest the Euclidean geometry of Minoan architecture, nonetheless do nothing but emphasize its supremacy. The effect did not pass unnoticed, as evident from the conspicuous depiction of such diagonal causeways in the Knossian Miniature Fresco, and it may have played an important role in enhancing their occasional formal function as Corridors of Procession.[1]

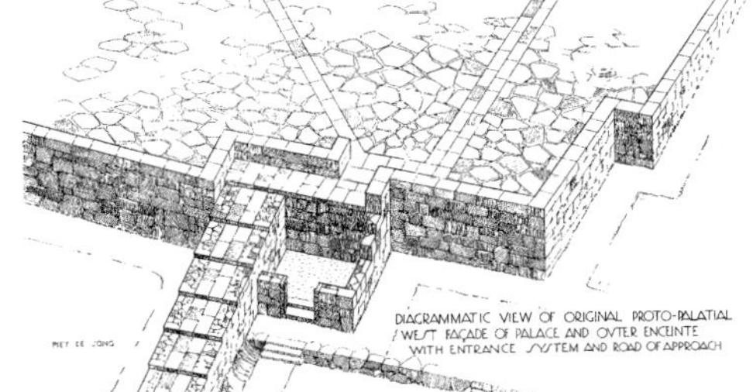


Fig. 141. Diagonal causeway crossing the West Court of the Palace of Knossos. After Evans 1921–1935, IV.1, fig. 34.

The Euclidean ordering system in the third dimension, the vertical, refers to the most fundamental principle of nature: gravity. There are architecture styles through history where verticality is the master principle of design, like the

Gothic, but there are others where horizontality takes the lead, as in the more recent work of Mies van der Rohe, for example. The difference between the two is striking, and it can be conceptualized almost physically. This is possible because of a kinesthetic, empathic bodily response to architectural forms: the horizontal is sensed as being at rest or surrendered whereas the vertical corresponds to effort and assertiveness (Norberg-Schulz 1980, 50–51; Roth 2007, 71). In between situations are perceived as instability and transition.

Fig. 142. Projecting cornices divide the facade of the building compound depicted in the Master Impression from Chania into horizontal zones (2.7 x 2.0 cm). Hallager 1985, fig. 11.

In Crete, no building has survived to a height that allows for a comprehensive discussion of the third dimension. One might assume that the fundamental and early choice of multistory housing alludes to verticality. Yet, since houses seldom stand on their own, their verticality is eventually subdued by the horizontality of the street facade (see Fig. 137). Furthermore, multistory construction in Minoan architecture is an additive process that results from the superimposition of stories and not from the inner division of a space cell. This is emphatically declared by the projecting cornices that divide the facade of a building into horizontal zones (see Fig. 118). Interestingly, they do so in a symbolic manner rather than literal, because cornices are structurally independent and sometimes do not even coincide with the floor level inside the building (Palyvou 2005a, 116). Their role is to divide the facade of a building evenly so that a viewer from the outside may conceptualize easily its many interior levels. This speaks of architectural design based on purely morphological grounds aiming at making visible the multistory reality that lies behind the facade and also at explaining its additive character. In other words, formal clarity at its best!

Fig. 143. Clay model from Knossos depicting the facade of a two-story building with a plinth at the base, a projecting cornice at the level of the first floor, and a pier-and-window partition above (92.0 x 10.0 cm). Courtesy Archaeological Museum of Herakleion, Hellenic Ministry of Culture and Sports–Archaeological Receipts Fund.

Projecting cornices are conspicuous in three-dimensional models and many two-dimensional depictions as well, such as the Master Impression from Chania and a clay model from Knossos (Figs. 142, 143). Strangely, projecting cornices are missing in the Town Mosaic, although two and three story buildings prevail in these miniature faience plaques (see Fig. 138). In some cases, for example in the Miniature Frieze from Akrotiri, projecting cornices appear only at the top of the building implying closure, as if a lid has been added to the building.

The supremacy of the horizontal in Minoan architecture is patent in many instances, as in the rows of openings and the colonnades, discussed below (Fyfe noticed this as early as 1903 and ascribed it to the method of wood-construction; 1903, 110). It is also prevalent in art: the division of a surface into horizontal zones is a well-established ordering principle, both in vase painting and wall painting. Verticality is not absent, of course, but it exists in the parts rather than the whole; above all, it exists in the emblematic form of the Minoan column. It may be assumed that it was also promoted through complementary elements, such as large double axes or flagstaffs and upright human figures as in the Master Impression (Fig. 142).

In sum, horizontality and continuity prevail in Minoan architecture, as they do in art. To this horizontality there is a strong vertical counterpoint, albeit not in the manmade environment, but in the commanding mountains that punctuate the natural environment of Crete. It may be that in a land where verticality is manifested strongly in nature there is no need to express it otherwise. In Egypt, on the other hand, where horizontality prevails in the landscape, it was the role of the architecture to counterbalance this force by creating strong and emblematic edifices in the vertical.

## Rhythm: The Colonnade

*The rhythm, with its measured flow and order, brings unity to the plot's variety; it assists the memory to foresight and apperception even of what the eye does not see. (Michelis 1964, 142)*

Michelis describes the role of rhythm and style in architecture by analogy to the way prosody and meter in poetry prepare us for the next verse (1964, 142). Rhythm is the measured flow and order of on/off situations monitored through duration in time and space; it is incident and interval, sound and pause, arrest and movement, light and shadow, and solids and cavities. As with music, in architecture there may be more than one rhythm enacted simultaneously on a building: the rhythm of the colonnade, the rhythm of the windows, and the rhythm of the indentations of the wall, all of which are meant to be apperceived together (Roth 2007, 76–80).

Rhythm in Minoan architecture is present in many different ways, but the result is often obscured because of the approximation that characterizes most Minoan works of architecture. The elusive effect of order that results from this approximation was discussed in Chapter 6; here we shall confine ourselves to the architectural element where rhythm is almost palpably perceived: the colonnade.

In the context of Minoan architecture, colonnades refer primarily to porticoes. To clarify terms, once again (Fig. 144): a colonnade is a row of columns (minimum three) of more or less equal intercolumnar dimensions. It may be associated with a porch, a portico, or a Stoa. The porch is part of an entrance system, whereas porticoes are sheltered spaces supported by columns or piers and attached to a building, yet not exclusively in relation to entrances. The term Stoa is not synonymous to the portico: if properly used in its original meaning deriving from classical Greek architecture, it is an elongated building with a wall in the form of a Π encompassing a colonnade. A Stoa is a freestanding structure, broad enough to accommodate various activities. It is not an interlocking element, as are

Fig. 144. Portico (a), porch (b), Stoa (c), and Minoan Single-Column Porch (d). Drawing C. Palyvou.

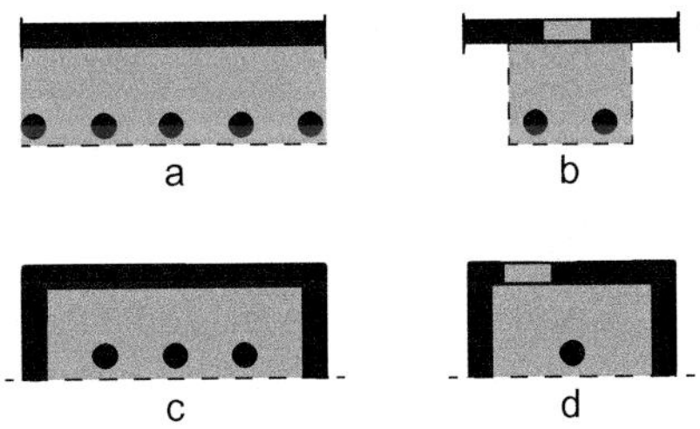

Fig. 145. North Stoa at Kommos. Shaw 1987, fig. 5.

the porch and the portico, but it is a type of building. True Stoas are very rare in Minoan architecture, with the closest examples seen at Hagia Triada and Tylissos (Hayden 1982; Shaw 1987). Another candidate—though not entirely independent—is the so-called Stoa at Kommos, a sheltered space 5.50–5.60 m wide that could hold gatherings and various activities (Fig. 145).

Before we proceed to discuss the role of the colonnade and the portico in Minoan architecture, it is pertinent to start with the formal qualities of the individual element it consists of, the column (on columns and colonnades, see Thiis-Evensen 1987, 195–219), especially since the Minoan column stands out as one of the emblematic features of the architecture of this civilization. The main reason for this is its characteristic downward tapering, unlike the great majority of columns throughout history that taper upward (Fig. 146).[2] The visual effect of such tapering is that of unbalance, for if the base of a tall object is smaller than its top one has the feeling that the object is in danger of being overturned. Another uncomfortable effect resulting from the downward thrust of the column is that it looks as if it is about to sink into the ground, a feeling quite unsuitable for an element that is meant to hold the loads of the upper structure and resist subsiding (Fig. 147).[3] Moreover, the lack of a pronounced base in most Minoan columns accentuates this effect; where it exists, it only projects a few centimeters from the ground, as if the downward pressure has indeed driven it into the earth. Furthermore, the rounded capitals—as we know them from art—declare bluntly the pressure they receive from above (this the Minoan column has in common with the early Doric capital). Admittedly, these disquieting effects are only marginally felt, for they are counterbalanced by the robust proportions of the Minoan column and by the fact that the stone base or pavement receiving the column would appear to be more resistant than the timber trunk.[4] A slight feeling of unrest, nevertheless, is lurking in the sight of the Minoan column, and it is no coincidence that this form came from nowhere and lasted only into the Mycenaean period.

Fig. 146. Stone model of a column from Zakros. Courtesy L. Platon, Archive of the Zakros Excavations.

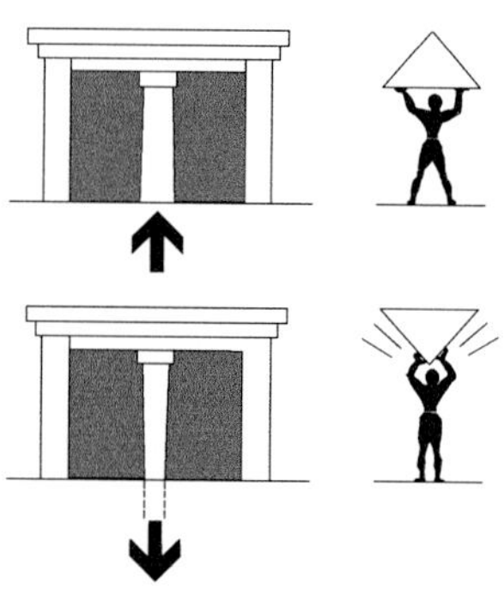

Fig. 147. Visual effects of a downward-thrusting column are instability and sinking. Drawing C. Palyvou.

A colonnade is not just a juxtaposition of vertical elements: the beams holding together the columns tame their thrusting verticality, both literally and visually, and transform them into a horizontal plane with strong rhythmical, directional, and perspectival effects. Horizontality is the main characteristic of the colonnade, as opposed to the verticality of its constituent members.

A clay model from Knossos showing three freestanding columns set closely in a row, with birds perching on their tops, is of special interest in the context of this discussion (Fig. 148). The fact that they stand apart emphasizes the singularity and the verticality of each column, and it leaves one wondering if indeed it represents a colonnade. Yet their number (three) and their orderly alignment (same size, same inter-columnar distance) speak of a colonnade.[5] Missing are the longitudinal beams connecting the three columns; instead, there are twin beam-ends over each column. This, in fact, may be correct! If indeed it implies a colonnade related to a portico, then each column is first connected firmly to the back wall, spanning the shorter distance (Fig. 149). The longitudinal beams would have been set next, above the transverse twin beams, stabilizing the structure in the third dimension. The use of two juxtaposed beams instead of one seems to have been common practice in order to ensure the desirable dimensions (see, e.g., the Archanes model of a house and the Lion Gate at Mycenae). In other words, the artist who produced this model may have presented reality faithfully, albeit partially. The result is a bizarre reading of the model both as a colonnade, which presumably alludes to palatial architecture, and as three individual columns declaring triumphantly their emblematic character. The perching birds, whatever their symbolism, counterbalance the upward thrust of the columns.

Fig. 148. Clay model from Knossos depicting three columns with birds perched on their tops (17.0 x 7.2 cm). Courtesy Archaeological Museum of Herakleion, Hellenic Ministry of Culture and Sports–Archaeological Receipts Fund.

A variation of the colonnade is a row of piers (Makrygialos, Petras). Though the rhythm in terms of number and dimensions of vertical elements and their intervals is similar, the rectangular form of the pier, as opposed to the cylindrical of the column, induces a different effect (Fig. 149:a): the pier is a more stable form than the tapering column and more fitting to the structural logic of the building—it is but a fragment of the wall. The column, on the other hand, is self-referential and autonomous, and therefore more conspicuous. It is important to keep in mind that piers were not robust monolithic vertical supports, as mistakenly restored by Evans at Knossos; they were made of a low stone base and a timber frame anchored on top (Tsakanika-Theohari 2009). They blend in well, in other words, with the timber structural system of the porticoes.

There is yet another variation of the portico of special interest because of its more complex rhythm: it is the combination of columns and piers in alternating order evidenced in the Central Courts of the Palaces at Phaistos and Malia, at Petras, and at the public court at Myrtos Pyrgos (Figs. 149:c, 150). The reasoning behind such an elaborate arrangement is not very clear. Stability does not seem to be a factor, for both piers and columns are statically adequate to perform their role. I would suggest turning for answers to formal aspects, perhaps even symbolism, and more specifically to the affirmed Minoan preference for single columns. The alternating sequence of columns and piers promotes the autonomy of each individual column, for it may be perceived as standing alone, flanked by piers, very much the

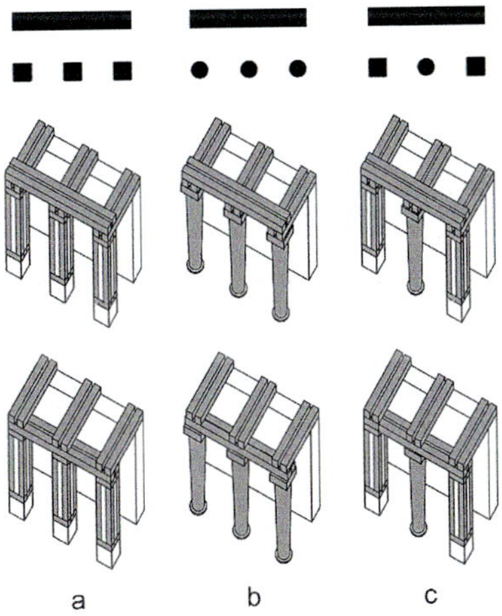


Fig. 149. Types of porticoes with piers (a), rows of columns (b), and alternating columns and piers (c). The last type promotes the autonomy of each individual column and alludes to the Single-Column Porch. Drawing C. Palyvou.

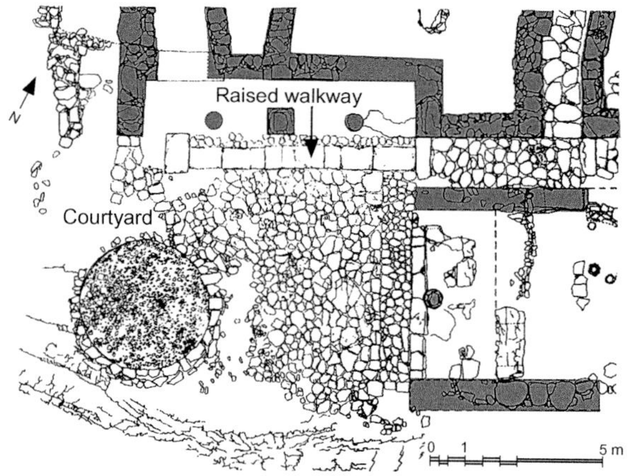


Fig. 150. Court at Myrtos Pyrgos flanked by porticoes with alternating columns and piers. After Cadogan 1977–1978, fig. 21.

way we see them in the Single-Column Porch and in several depictions in art.

Rhythm is expressed through repetition and punctuation. Yet, as is typical in the Minoan world, there are many deviations in the size of the trunks of columns and the inter-columnar distance. Within certain limits, deviations are perceived as such and do not cancel the rhythm of a colonnade. Deviations, however, are not haphazard; they all have a purpose. Take, for example, the north colonnade of the Central Court at the Palace of Malia. It consists of 11 columns arranged in more or less equal distances with two exceptions: the second column from the east has been moved to the west to allow for more space in front of the Grand Staircase that lies beyond (Fig. 151); and the second column from the western end has been moved slightly eastward to allow for more space in front of the major line of circulation through the corridor leading to the court.

For rhythm to emerge as a pattern, a certain length in space and time is required. This is not always the case in Minoan architecture: the porticoes bordering the Central Courts of the major Palaces do not enfold the court uniformly—they seldom occupy the whole length of one side, for that matter. Porticoes and colonnades correspond to specific zones only. This selective treatment undermines the power of rhythm as a unifying principle of the court facades; instead, rhythm becomes primarily a means to distinguish and project the individual zones that comprise the Palace.

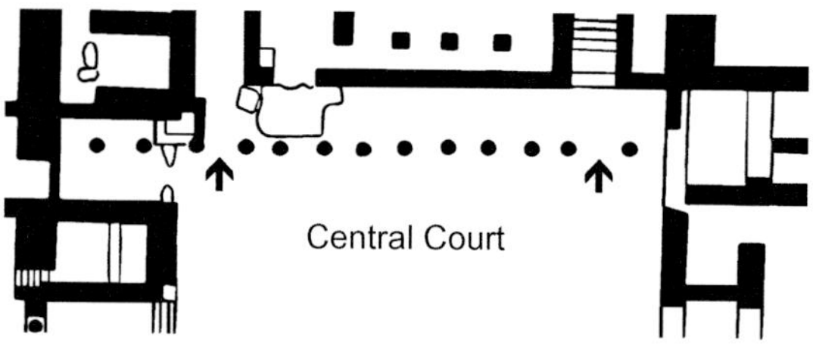


Fig. 151. North facade of the Central Court at the Palace of Malia. The intercolumnar space is broader where it corresponds to major accesses. After Davaras 1989a, fig. 1; © Hellenic Ministry of Culture and Sports–Archaeological Receipts Fund.

What happens above the colonnades is also of interest. Colonnades supporting porticoes on the ground floor correspond to balconies on the upper floor. Though we only know of balconies from art depictions, it may safely be assumed, on structural grounds, that they would have followed the same logic and the same rhythm as the colonnades below. The rhythmic effect was thus reinforced by its repetition in the vertical.

A final note, or rather a reminder, is that we are missing information crucial to the formal analysis we are attempting here: texture and color, to name but two. Wood was the main material in both columns and piers, and unless timber elements were plastered over or painted, as Evans's restorations imply, the prevailing texture and color was that of aged and weathered timber and not of stone.

## The Elusive Effect of Symmetry

Symmetry is a powerful ordering principle that "stresses the concentrated, in itself resting and complete form" (Norberg-Schulz 1997, 134). It comes in various forms—bilateral, rotational, by repetition, identical, or mirrored. The most common is bilateral symmetry, an archetypal ordering principle underlying many natural forms, most conspicuously the human body. The axis of symmetry can be immaterial, in which case the two parts are identical, or materialized in the form of a distinct element (Fig. 152). In the latter case the central figure is often privileged and the whole composition takes the form of a tripartite arrangement, well known in Minoan art (Figs. 153, 154).

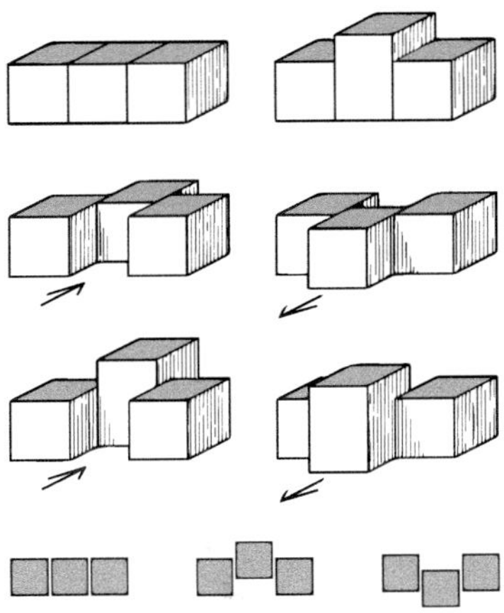

Fig. 152. Modes of bilateral symmetry in tripartite arrangement. Drawing C. Palyvou.

A typical example of this sort in art is the so-called Tripartite Shrine appearing in several depictions. Its existence in reality eludes us, except perhaps at Vathypetro (Driessen and Sakellarakis 1997). Though only the foundations of what clearly seems to be a tripartite structure have survived, they are sufficient to suggest a symmetrical compound consisting of two identical parts flanking a middle part of the same dimensions but in a recessed position (Fig. 155). If we are to assume a stepped formation in the vertical as well—in analogy to the Tripartite Shrines depicted in art—then the message conveyed through symmetry is clear: the central part, being recessed and higher than the two flanking

Fig. 153. Tripartite symmetry depicted on a golden plaque from Mycenae (7.5 x 6.9 cm). Mylonas 1983, fig. 145; courtesy Ekdotike Athenon S.A.

Fig. 154. Tripartite symmetry depicted on a rhyton from Zakros. Shaw 1978, fig. 8.

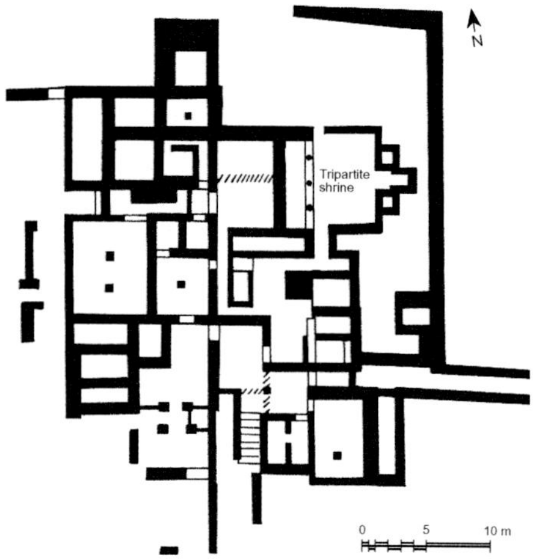


Fig. 155. Possible tripartite structure at Vathypetro. After Driessen and Sakellarakis 1997, fig. 3.

parts, is more removed from the viewer (both in the horizontal and the vertical) and hence hierarchically distinguished. A similar effect of tripartite symmetry may be detected in the West Facades of the major Palaces, though it is not immediately evident in the context of the complex sequence of recesses they partake in (see this vol., Ch. 10).

An instance of bilateral symmetry, also known as dualism, is the Single-Column Porch discussed in Chapter 10 (see Fig. 178). Dualism promotes divisibility because the beholder is forced to make a choice of direction between two equal and undifferentiated parts, a choice that is normally made for him in advance by the architect. Thus, dualism in architecture is a special state of symmetry that presents a kind of challenge to both the spectator and the architect. Symmetry applied by rotation is also attested in Minoan architecture in the Minoan Hall, especially in its composite versions, and in the Room with the Central Column.

In many early civilizations, like the Egyptian and the Mesopotamian, symmetry is a fundamental ordering principle of formal architecture. In the Minoan world, however, though symmetry is unmistakably present (if not prevalent) in artistic depictions of architecture, it is less so in real architecture. If artistic depictions of architecture are taken to represent reality in an ideal generic manner—as facades with no interiors—then the symmetry they bluntly declare must correspond to architectural intentions that have been obscured, compromised, or even obliterated in the process of real building (Palyvou 2005b). This is indeed the case with symmetrical windows in art, which correspond to the basic rule of placing the window in the middle of the wall. The same may be said for ashlar facades depicted as isodomic masonry that is never the case in reality (Palyvou 2005b, 195–196).

Absolute symmetry does exist in Minoan architecture, but only in a limited number of instances. It is attested in the Palaces, in the indentation of the West Facades, and in certain facades looking onto the Central Court, such as the northern facade of the Central Courts at Phaistos and at Galatas (see also Graham 1972, 243–244). The fact that symmetry is applied to only some of the facades, or even parts of a facade, is typical of the fragmented individualized approach that the Minoans practiced both in art and architecture. Absolute symmetry is also applied to a limited number of interior spaces: the House of the Chancel Screen, the Caravanserai Spring (Fig. 156), the Royal Villa, and the House of the High Priest, all in the vicinity of the Palace of Knossos. By restricting the

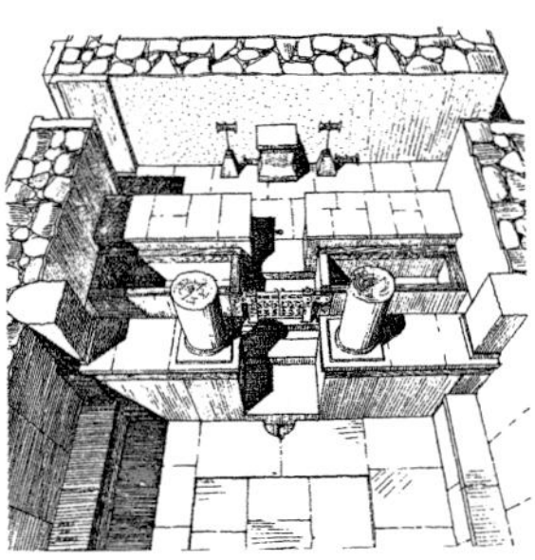

Fig. 156. House of the Chancel Screen Knossos (left) and the Caravanserai Spring (right) at Knossos. Left: Evans 1921–1935, IV.1, fig. 157; right: Evans 1921–1935, II, pl. XVI.

use of absolute symmetry to only a few instances its symbolic meaning becomes more easily identifiable.

## Ornament: The Art of Display and Concealment

Ornament is the result of prosthetic process, an accessory added for embellishment. In the case of architecture, the underlying notion of such a definition is that ornament has no structural or practical value; it is something that the building would still be fine without. A witty rendition of this definition is echoed in a layman's description of the effects of a disastrous typhoon that hit his house: "the building's fine but the architecture blew away!" (Roth 2007, 4; this also reflects the contesting definitions of architecture vs. building, discussed in Ch. 1).

The history of architecture is strewn with the corpses of a war between form, function, and structure, and the idea of ornament is more often than not caught in the middle. Hence its changing roles from a means to achieve visual Delight (Wotten's rendering of Vitruvian *Venustas*) to Loos's aphorism that ornament is crime and degeneration (1998). The term ornament, therefore, is in need of a better definition.

Architectural ornamentation works in two ways: it either promotes and underlines the structural logic of the building or it conceals and even eliminates it. An example of concealment is rubble walls pretending to be ashlar with imitations of ashlar blocks incised on the wall plaster. This is the case of light-well III 7 at the Palace of Malia. The special ornamental treatment was intended to add to these surfaces properties appropriate to exterior walls.[6] Another instance is the way wall paintings are treated depending on the structural characteristics of the room (Palyvou 2000, 415–425). If of the skeleton type, with walls highly perforated with openings, the available wall surfaces were treated as individual panels. Structural elements, such as sills, lintels, and orthostates, were incorporated into the design and their presence was enhanced. If of the massive type, with very few and small openings, then the walls were treated as a uniform surface enfolding the spectator. Massive-type effects were further promoted by concealing and almost annihilating the structural elements of the room (corners and minor openings). In other words, the artist manipulated space through the art of display and concealment, amplifying its characteristics.

A tantalizing question regarding the skeleton-type structures of Neopalatial Crete is whether the timber elements were visible, in which case the skeleton effect was explicit. In several cases there is evidence that timber elements were plastered over and concealed (this is in fact correct because it protects wood from rotting; Palyvou 1999a, 357–359). Even if concealed, the timber elements were sometimes marked out in other ways: in the Hall of the Double Axes at Knossos, the location

Fig. 157. Two views of the Hall of the Double Axes at Knossos, showing the location of the timber beam marked on the wall plaster by a narrow frieze of running spirals. Evans 1921–1935, III, figs. 221, 228.

of the timber beam of the wall is signaled by a narrow frieze of running spirals painted on the wall plaster along the line of the invisible beam (Fig. 157). The decision to provide information on the exact location of the hidden timber may indicate architectural awareness on behalf of the artist. It may also have served practical reasons: a wall painting from Knossos depicting life-sized shields hanging on the wall along the line of such a frieze of running spirals—presumably as they would have hung in reality—suggests that hinges or wooden pegs existed there, inserted into the timber beam behind the wall plaster (Fig. 157, right). One of the functions of the frieze, then, could have been to indicate the hidden timber.

At the Palace of Knossos, fragments of two limestone friezes in relief were found, depicting triglyph and half-rosette patterns (Fig. 158). Their width is 0.19 and 0.35 m, respectively, and according to Nelson the former was most probably set into a narrow horizontal slot on the upper surface of ashlar blocks as a revetment of a timber beam (Nelson 2007, 21). This would have been an effective and elegant way to conceal and protect the timber beams of an exterior wall. The painted frieze of running spirals discussed above may well be an imitation of such stone friezes. There are a few more pieces in relief, made of stucco or stone, but they are too fragmentary and their use remains obscure.

Veneering in the form of stone dadoes was another means of ornamentation popular in Minoan palatial architecture (Fig. 159). These were thin slabs, usually of high quality stone, covering the lower part of a wall. Their role was once again twofold, to serve as embellishment—as a means to provide a durable and attractive base for the wall—and more practically as a means to protect the wall from the humidity of the ground. At Knossos, Evans found large fragments of such dadoes that had their upper edges molded in relief (Fig. 160). They are preserved to a height of 0.45–0.50 m, but their total size and exact position on the building are unknown. Such fine moldings should not be taken for granted; they show an advanced aesthetic concern to provide the veneering with an upper finish, heralding the elaborate profiles of cornices and friezes of classical Greek architecture.

Fig. 158. Limestone frieze in relief from Knossos, depicting half-rosette patterns. Evans 1921–1935, II.2, fig. 368.

Floor pavement also falls in the category of revetment and embellishment. There is a variety of floor treatment in Minoan architecture, the most elaborate of which speak of painstaking efforts to embellish: these are pavements of well-cut slabs arranged in patterns, tarazza floors made of lime

Fig. 159. Veneering with upright slabs at Hagia Triada. Photo C. Palyvou.

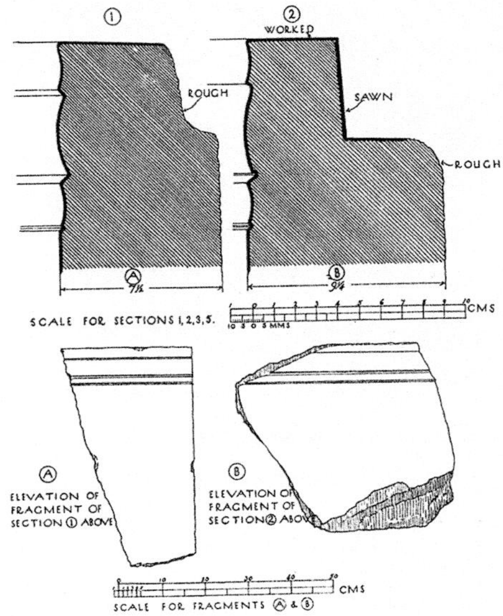


Fig. 160. Large fragments of dadoes from Knossos with upper edges molded in relief. Evans 1921–1935, II.2, pl. XXII.

and colorful beach pebbles, floors made of painted plaster, and floors consisting of stripes of lime plaster forming rectangles that were filled in with wooden planks or some other perishable material (Shaw 2009, 150–152). The corresponding visual effect in each case adds to the identity of the room, as discussed in Chapter 4.

Last, but certainly not least, there is one element in Minoan architecture that may be considered as glyptic, three-dimensional ornamentation in stone: the Horns of Consecration. They come in varying sizes, some of which truly huge, and they characterized the Minoan townscape (see Figs. 136, 139, 140). Their primal role was symbolism and not embellishment; symbolism, however, relies on modes of visual perception, hence their aesthetic value should not be underestimated.

## Color and Light Effects

Crete is privileged with one of the richest palettes that nature has provided. It comes as no surprise, therefore, that color was omnipresent in the Minoan world: in the building materials and wall paintings, the clothes people wore, the flowers in the vases, the painted artifacts in everyday use, the mats and carpets, and even the furniture. Walking through a Minoan town would have been an experience strongly imbued with color. Crete is also generous in light, and the agency of light is essential for perceiving forms, volumes, and textures, as well as accentuating the effects of color.

Minoan architecture offers ample proof of systematic, purposeful exploitation of the colorful material resources the island provided. Colorful effects, created deliberately through the combination of different building materials, are typical of Aegean architecture (Fig. 161). This is demonstrated in many floors and pavements but also in the way colorful stones have been combined at the corners of the buildings, the

Fig. 161. Antechamber of the Throne Room at Knossos. Michailidou 1981, fig. 29; courtesy Ekdotike Athenon S.A..

window frames, and the projecting cornices (these we know best from Akrotiri, Thera). To name but a few examples of purposeful combinations of colorful building materials: Palaikastro Block M has the floor paved with marron green slabs, the column bases of blue limestone, and the piers of mottled green serpentinite; at Archanes, column bases are of blue limestone combined with a beige porous threshold; and at Myrtos Pyrgos, the column bases and the walkway are of purple limestone in sharp contrast with the surrounding gray cobble pavement (Rehak and Younger 1998, 107–108).

Evans and his architects appreciated the colorful aspect of Minoan architecture from the very beginning, especially as represented in art. Evans was convinced of the polychrome style of Minoan architecture and decided to pass it on to the otherwise colorless ruins he was bringing to light through his reconstitutions. Fyfe had some reservations regarding the meaning of color in art, and he was more inclined to see it as conventional: black, he suggested, may have stood for old and seasoned wood and red or yellow for new (1903, 114; 1914, 489). Yet black, red, and yellow were the very colors used in the restoration work; the signifier, in other words, became the significant. Three years after he started working at Knossos, Fyfe wrote a paper "at Dr. Evans's request" as he explains in "Painted Plaster Decoration at Knossos with Special Reference to the Architectural Schemes" (1903, 107). This paper includes some interesting remarks on the aesthetic aspect of Minoan architecture, yet its primal purpose was to prepare the ground for the extensive colorful reconstructions that were to commence soon after, based chiefly on art. One of the paragraphs has the explicit title "Some Probable Restorations of the Palace Based Chiefly on the Miniature Frescoe."

The temporality of light accentuates or softens the effects, brings out latent qualities of texture and form, and enhances color (on light and temporality, see Norberg-Schulz 1980, 31–32). Color and light, tempered by time, are what Unwin calls the "modifying elements" of architecture (Unwin 2009, 43–56). Thanks to the numerous openings typical of Minoan architecture, light penetrates deep into the fabric of the buildings in varying angles, intensities, and qualities according to the hour of the day or the season and the orientation of the openings. Doors, however, had door leaves, and the majority of windows, if not all, had dense lattices and some perhaps had shutters. Light, therefore, was controlled and filtered through a thick web of vertical and horizontal wooden elements, especially where pier-and-window partitions were involved. As a result, it would reach the inner surfaces decomposed into horizontal and vertical stripes of light alternating with shadows. This effect would create impressive wall patterns, and when hitting painted surfaces it would enhance their appearance (or perhaps disturb it). The importance of the shadow and its levels of tonal variance should not be underestimated when imagining a space. In Pallasmaa's eloquent words, shadow inhales and illumination exhales light (Pallasmaa 2005b, 47).

When daylight was gone, oil-lamps were lit. Placed on high stands, hanging from above or carried around, these would create a different feeling of space. Sharp contrasts and dark backgrounds would bring out surface textures and irregularities that where not visible in daytime, while the colors on the wall paintings would emit an entirely different range of shades, for "the night itself is the shade, that darkness which can never become a mere blackness because as shade it is wedded to light and remains cast by it" (Heidegger 1997b, 117). These fascinating cycles of living tissues of architecture often escape us when dealing with ruins from a purely (or poorly?) archaeological point of view. For this reason, research on the role of light in the conceptualization of the Minoan built environment, like those carried out by Goodison in regard with the dramatic effects of dawn-light and Platon on nocturnal ceremonies are more than welcome (Goodison 2004; Platon 2010, 250–251).

## Endnotes

1 Marinatos 1987, 137; Davis 1987. Preziosi emphasizes, instead, the triangular areas in between the causeways as the locii of ritual, based on their representations in art (Preziosi 1983, 85). At Knossos and Malia raised walkways run parallel to the West Facades of the Palaces leading to the entrances. Letesson and Vansteenhuyse rightly observe that the West Facade acts as a barrier inciting movement along it, and that the walkways guide vision while their slight elevation obstructs and discourages the flow of movement beyond (Letesson and Vansteenhuyse 2006, 112).

2 This form is unanimously accepted today, mostly on the basis of the numerous depictions of columns in art, including a small-scale stone model from Zakros. Initially, however, there was strong disagreement between Evans and Doll, whose reservations as to the tapering of the column shaft are mentioned in a footnote and are depicted in one of his drawings (Evans 1921–1935, I, 342, n. 1, fig. 247). Others, too—Pernier, for example—were reluctant to accept this "anorthodox" form (see Kienzle 1998, 413–414).

3 A similar uncomfortable effect is produced by the V-shaped columns of the piloti (piers) of Le Corbusier's L' Unité d'Habitation (Thiis-Evensen 1987, 201).

4 That this is far from true is clearly evidenced at Akrotiri: while restoring a pier-and-door partition on the ground-floor of Xeste 3, we found that the timber posts had resisted very well the pressure from the loads of two(!) stories above. The imprints of the timber posts showed clearly that they were intact and perfectly upright, whereas their corresponding stone bases had been literally shuttered to pieces.

5 A single element—a column in this case—provides a focus and invokes centrality; two columns create symmetry and invoke axiality; three columns in a row equals "many" and conveys the notion of sequence. On the same account, the three women depicted on the gold rings from Mycenae convey the idea of a procession (Mylonas 1983, figs. 137, 138).

6 I am thankful to M. Schmid for this observation (pers. comm. June 2003).

# 9

# On Function in Architecture and Archaeology

## The Many Meanings of Function

The urge to give life to the material remains of the past—be they tools, vases, or buildings—asks for an understanding of their function, that is, of how people used them and what they meant to them. When the past in question is mute, as is the Aegean Bronze Age, then function can be inferred solely through material evidence—through the form and structure of things and the circumstances (context) of their finding. In architecture, however, form, structure, and function have had notoriously ambiguous relationships, and they are seldom transparent to one another. This ambiguity is reflected in the different ways the word function has been used in the past and still is used. Time and again its notion has changed, and today it has come to substitute a whole range of variables, such as use, purpose, destination, role, program, character, and, more recently, meaning. This variability is important in itself, as Lilly Chi points out in her paper "On the Use of Architecture," for it is suggestive of different ways of conceiving the inhabitation of buildings (1996, 18).

In view of the adventures and connotations of the word function through time, it is expedient to begin this discussion with a brief reference to its biography in the context of architecture, and the manner in which this was passed on to archaeology. This might help us understand some of the ambiguities in the way function is treated in Aegean studies and appreciate the need to exploit the subtle nuances and differentiations between its various expressions; the richer the palette the more potent the analytical tool.

According to the dictionary, the word function appeared in mid-16th century A.D. French, deriving from the Latin *functio*, which meant performance or execution. Later on it was used in mathematics, whereas as a verb (to function, perform) it appeared in the mid-19th century. In architecture it has a story of its own to tell. The earliest surviving textbook on architecture, Vitruvius's *De Architectura*, speaks of *utilitas*, referring to the practical aspects of a work of architecture. The destination or purpose of a building was implied through the headings of the chapters of the book, such as "House," "Temple," "Theater," and so forth. Function appeared in the architectural jargon, and became a topic in itself, as late as the 18th century. It was rarely used in architecture until the 19th century and certainly not consistently before the biological analogy for the systemic study of societies became commonplace. Until then, the notion that an edifice should fulfill its function was understood as a moral obligation of the totality of architecture—a duty or a character fitting to its destination—and it therefore carried sociopolitical and cultural values. The purely utilitarian aspect of architecture, on the other hand, was described as the intended use of the building, its destination or purpose (Chi 1996, 18).

The modern shift of emphasis on use is heralded in Quatremère de Quincy's words of warning (1832, 307), in the early years of the 19th century: "The domain of shared experience on which architectural expression relies has contracted to the immediate issue of use" (Chi, trans., 1996, 21). By "contracted," he obviously implies that there is much more in experiencing architecture than its use, while the reference to "shared experience" anticipates phenomenological approaches of our days. The primacy of usefulness is thereafter strengthened and finds its full expression as a mechanistic analogy in the Modern Movement of the 20th century and the concept of functionalism. The famous dogma "form [should] follow function" that became its flag implied a deterministic ahistorical and acultural notion of use (Kruft 1994, 357; Chi 1996, 31–32). To serve justice to Louis Sullivan, however, whose words were rather misused in coining this phrase, we should point out that his own understanding of function was of a holistic nature (1956, 258). To quote Hanno-Walter Kruft, he was concerned with:

> [the] natural, social and intellectual factors, the sum of human needs, that constitute the functions which determine the form of a building. . . . not structural laws. It is wrong to interpret his axiom "Form follows function" in a functionalist, technological sense, for his concept of function is Romantic and thoroughly American. (Kruft 1994, 357)

Nevertheless, it was the utilitarian, mechanistic notion that prevailed, and the word function, stripped of its sociopolitical and ethical notions, became synonymous to use. The restrictive utilitarian meaning of the word function was maintained even when the postmodernists challenged the supremacy of function and reversed the axiom to "function follows form" or invented new catch phrases such as "form follows fiction" (for a discussion on the postmodernists's self-doubt and the bad conscious of modernity, see Harries 1985, 54). The need to refer to the multiple aspects of function in architecture, however, is always there, and in lack of an appropriate vocabulary (or rather due to its oblivion) we resort today to adjectives that might clarify the sort of function we are referring to: social function, symbolic function, circulatory function, and so forth (see also Roth 2007, 11–23).

Scholars have taken notice of these shortcomings. Kostof, for one, clarifies that purpose in architecture is "the way in which a building accommodates its prescribed function" and suggests that perhaps a better word for function "would be ritual, for function tends to undermine and mechanize the concept of purpose . . . Ritual," he continues, "may be said to be the poetry of function: in so far as a building is shaped by ritual it does not simply house function, it comments on it" (Kostof 1985, 19). That a building comments on its function is a recurring idea, reflected in Harries's observations that architecture should edify (a notion that gave birth to the word edifice as a metaphor). It is also reflected in Pallasmaa's definition of the task of architecture to create "embodied and lived existential metaphors that concretise and structure our being in the world" (Pallasmaa 2005b, 71).

Another notion relevant to the function of a building is its character. This is understood as the imprint of the particular destination of a building on its form in a way that it announces the building for what it is. According to Étienne Boullée (1953), "Our edifices, above all the public edifices, should be, in some facet, poems. The images which they offer to our senses should excite in us sentiments analogous to the usage to which these edifices are consecrated" (quoted in Chi 1996, 24–25). The underlying idea of physiognomy goes back to popular character writing in the 17th century that promoted inquiries related to ethics. On the basis that any real presence is intimately linked with a character, the concept was also applied to architecture to justify its diversity in analogy to the plurality of characters (Norberg-Schulz 1980, 12–14; de Sola-Morales 1987). Character, however, is an intangible notion, and its concretization or performance relies on a set of culturally defined forms that constitute the style of an era. It also relies on the presence of a spectator as sentient body and moral actor, who will activate what Chi calls the "theatrical concept of architectural use" (1996, 23–29).

Function, as more or less coterminus to use, followed a similar path in archaeology. The "form follows function" dictum was inspired largely by the study of vernacular architecture, and it was believed to apply also to so-called primitive cultures; it was only one step farther to project the idea to extinct prehistoric cultures as well. The idea was gradually generalized, and finally archaeologists came to believe firmly, though somewhat subconsciously, that if form follows function then form should be able to lead back to function. This, however, is rather wishful thinking that reflects the frustration prehistorians experience when seeking to understand function though the only data available to them: form and structure. The underlying misconception is that form is transparent to function and that use and function are one and the same thing; yet, there is no direct correspondence between specific forms and specific functions, even when use is apparent, as in the case of storerooms, for example. Meaning is not inherent in forms but is culturally constructed through use, for "use never does anything but shelter meaning" (Barthes 1997b, 174; on forms and meaning, see also Nesbitt 1996, 44–46). Stanford Anderson, discussing the fiction of function, writes, "No description of function, however thorough, will automatically translate into architectural form. . . . It would be difficult if not impossible to find an artifact, simple or complex, that has not functioned in unanticipated ways" (Anderson 1987, 22).

Function in Aegean studies was the main topic of two symposia, one regarding the Minoan Palaces (Hägg and Marinatos, eds., 1987) and the other the Villas (Hägg, ed., 1997). They were both very productive in that they offered the opportunity to discuss a variety of related issues and many case studies. Yet, none of the papers addressed directly the varying meanings and nuances of function and the corresponding blurriness in the use of the word.

The most common problems arise when equating function to use and then seeking to associate it with form. See, for example, the difficulties that scholars are faced with when attempting to identify the architectural spaces that served the two most mundane everyday tasks: eating and sleeping. Architecture does not provide exclusive clues as to which forms are appropriate for these activities; information of this sort is culturally provided. This means that our difficulties with decoding forms the way the Minoans did are due to cultural barriers. This is also due, however, to the fact that the specifications regarding eating and sleeping were probably a weak parameter in the design procedure (see the Japanese example below). Furthermore, even if we do manage to add labels to space-cells—kitchen, bedroom, workshop, shrine, and so forth—this alone will not reveal their real function in the full sociopolitical and ethical essence of the word.

To understand how something is used does not explain why it is what it is and how it partakes in the cultural identity of the people. To give an example: while discussing the Royal Villa at Knossos, Fotou and Michailidou assume with some certainty that it combines "habitation and special function involving transactions" but admit that the "character, whether civil or religious" of the building eludes them, and they are thus left frustrated as to whether the building exudes religious sentiments or authoritative awe (2006, 93). By introducing the concept of the character of a building, what they are rightly saying is that function, as use, cannot reveal its full ambience. Habitation or transaction is information on a primary level (denotative); we need more information (connotative) regarding the people involved in these tasks, as well as specifics of the transactions taking place, in order to understand not just the use but the full essence of the building and its role in Minoan society.

Another example is Trigger's definition of monumental architecture as a work of scale and elaboration that "exceed[s] the requirements of any practical functions that a building is intended to perform" (Trigger 1990, 119). Trigger was mindful to add to function the adjective practical so as to clarify that he is referring to only a part of the full function of the building; monumentality is the functional attribute par excellence of a building in terms of intentions and performance.

In sum, function in architecture has an all-inclusive meaning; it refers to the architectural totality as a cultural phenomenon and includes use, purpose, destination, program, character, and style. In the context of this book, the intention is to treat the subtle nuances of these terms with clarity and consistency. This goal, however, may be compromised at times, because the word function is so strongly cemented in our modern minds as synonymous to use that it is sometimes almost impossible to distinguish it without causing unnecessary confusion. The true function of architecture, with all its cultural, sociopolitical, and ethical connotations, may never be completely grasped for as silent and blurry a past as the Aegean Bronze Age, but one may gain a deeper understanding of the role of architecture in the Minoan world if it is approached with a richer set of theoretical tools and corresponding vocabulary.

To further illustrate the difficult relationship between form and function, let us borrow a scene from the powerful art of filmmaking. The film is *The Gods Must Be Crazy*, written and directed by Jamie Uys (1980), and it is based on an ingenious story that, with some sense of humor, could well represent an allegory for the study of prehistoric archaeology. The story unfolds around a bottle of Coca-Cola—the symbol par excellence of western culture—which drops literally from the sky in the midst of a small village of a tribe of bushmen located in the Kalahari Desert of southern Africa. In reality, it was thrown out of a small airplane by a young American who remained completely ignorant of the troubles he was about to cause with his act. The glass bottle was an entirely unknown artifact for the bushmen who decided to embark on a painstaking effort to understand it.

In fact, the bushmen are doing exactly what prehistorians do: in the absence of direct information regarding the purpose and destination of the object from the people who produced it, they focus on its form in the hope that it will reveal its function. The bushmen soon resort to experimentation through a process of trial and error, only to find that there were many possible uses of the object: it can produce music, both as a percussion and a wind instrument; it can be used to spread pasta; it hurts if you knock ones head with it; it can function as a container; and so forth. Moreover, they determine that it was god-sent, since it came literally from the sky, so whatever its use it had to have some religious connotations as well. Each bushman comes up with a different idea, and, convinced that his or her interpretation of use is of course the most valid, claims its ownership and gives it a name. It could be argued that all the proposed uses were valid to the extent that they did actually work, but it was the principal use—the initial one for which it was created—which everybody was claiming to have found. This interpretive process ends up causing serious friction among the members of the small community. Eventually, the bushmen decide that they are better off without it, and that the Gods were careless for once, and they expel the object from the community. On a similar line of thought, archaeologists would lock such an object in the window case of a museum for all to see, allowing only a few to touch it, and all to continue fabricating new interpretations.

## Capacity, Tolerance, and Time

In designing a building, its space-cells are given their quantitative and qualitative attributes according to their anticipated use, be it temporal, periodical, ephemeral, or occasional. It is often the case, however, that a space-cell serves more than one use, varying according to the time of the day, the month, or the year. Furthermore, buildings tend to outlive their original architects and inhabitants and remain in use long after the lifestyle of the time in which they were conceived has passed away. In this context, capacity and tolerance could be described as the potential of a work of architecture to receive contents and serve lifestyles beyond those for which it was initially programmed (Fig. 162). For a work of architecture to survive the wear of time and adjust to new uses, maintenance, conservation, restoration, and rehabilitation are necessary. These tasks leave behind marks that speak of the individual biography of each building.

Some architectonic forms are quite tolerant to changing requirements, whereas others are less compromising. The capacity of a work of architecture to absorb change depends on two parameters: (a) the articulation of the new use, wherein the simpler the task, the easier it is to accommodate in a variety of spaces, whereas tasks with high performance requirements can only be accommodated in specifically designed architectural settings (Norberg-Schulz 1997, 106, 175); and (b) the articulation of the space-cell, wherein neutral or flexible architectural forms are more tolerant to changing use. Japanese vernacular architecture offers an example of the latter: most space-cells are neutral and not transparent of their use, even though they house a lifestyle deeply imbued with formality and ritual. The ingenious system of sliding walls allows for maximum adjustability of space that can meet varying performance requirements. Not all tasks require specific and fixed space attributes for their function to be enacted: aside from the entrance, the kitchen, and the bathroom, no other room has a designated use; each can serve as living room, dining room, study, or bedroom at any time.

Fig. 162. A multi-functional single-room house on Rhodes. Lavvas and Philippidis 1983–1991, III, fig. 197; courtesy Melissa Publishing House.

Minoan architects developed a space articulation system that raised capacity and tolerance to extraordinary heights. This trait distinguishes Minoan architecture from its contemporaries in the eastern Mediterranean region, as discussed in the closing chapter of this book. It is no coincidence that the crisis and fall of the Minoan world is marked by the annihilation of this very characteristic feature: many pier-and-opening partitions were indeed blocked during the troubled times (see Driessen and Macdonald 1997, 43; also Driessen 1995a, 73–74).

If form and structure are more or less tolerant to change, character is much less so; the character of a work of architecture will always speak of the initial circumstances of its design. Let us take a contemporary example: imagine, for instance, a neoclassical urban Villa built in the early years of the 20th century in downtown Athens and used today as an office building. Walking through the building, one can still identify the bedroom that has become an office and the dining room that is now the conference room (with the precondition, of course, that one is familiar with the context and character of a neoclassical urban Villa). The building has most probably adapted well to suit changing needs, and there is no difficulty in recognizing the new use of the rooms. But the character of the building, as such, has not followed this change; looking at the building one still sees a neoclassical mansion, and it is only the sign on the door that informs of its new identity. The character of the building, in other words, will always bear witness to the original circumstances of its design.

## The Symbolic Capacity of Architecture: Monumentality

*[F]unction should be extended to all the uses of objects of use . . . to the various communicative, as well as to the denoted functions . . . for with respect to life in society the "symbolic" capacities of these objects are no less "useful" than their "functional" capacities. (Eco 1997, 187)*

Discussing the semantics of the natural language of architecture, Harries considers two kinds of symbols: the natural symbol, based on timeless forms of being in the world, as is the cave; and the conventional symbol, such as the cross, which is culturally created. The latter presupposes and builds on the former, because "buried in every conventional symbolism lies a natural symbolism, which still speaks to us if we are but willing to listen" (Harries 2000, 132). Harries concludes that we must learn to read from what was once called the book of nature (2000, 133). This deep belief in the ability of all human beings to deduce meaning from their interaction with the environment Harries shares with other phenomenologists, especially Norberg-Schulz.

Symbolization is enacted when shared experiences of an idea or a thing are projected onto another medium, in which case meaning is disassociated from the immediate circumstances of its creation. The cultural object thus produced can thereafter stand on its own and be transferred anywhere. The Minoan Horns of Consecration is such a cultural object, as a conventional symbol based on natural symbols, be it the horns of the venerated bull, as most scholars believe, or the mountain peaks of a nature inhabited by gods, as Nanno Marinatos has suggested (2010, 107–110). When viewing such objects on the roof of a building, the divine power of the sacred bull or the sanctity of the mountain peaks is transmitted to the building itself and consequently to the institution it houses.

Symbolism in architecture is most prevalent in public buildings as a means to enhance their readability as embodiments of political, social, religious, or economic power. Symbolism can be enacted in many different ways: the orientation of the Central Court of the Palaces toward the cardinal points, for instance, carries symbolic connotations of cosmological order; whereas the form of the Corridor of Procession at Knossos, in analogy to the raised urban causeways, carries symbolic connotations of sociopolitical order.

Because architecture is highly visible and durable, it is an effective means to convey meaning (see Schoep 2004, 243). These two attributes—high visibility (referring primarily to size and exposure) and durability (referring to the quality and endurance of materials)—are often summoned as signs of conspicuous consumption and display and therefore as indicators of monumentality. Monumentality is in fact a common designation for many elaborate Minoan buildings. It is used, however, in a rather self-referential manner, as if the term explains itself automatically. In reality, monumentality is a broad and nebulous concept used in many different contexts. Once again, then, it might help to elaborate on the meaning of the word before we proceed to investigate the way it is used in the context of Minoan architecture.

The word monumentality borrows from the idea of the monument only some of its attributes, mostly size and elaboration, while leaving others out. The word monument (*monumentum*) derives from the Latin *moneo* and the Greek μιμνήσκω, which apply to anything that can activate memory for the benefit of the present; it is a reminder or warning of past experiences and hence a tool for programming the future. A monument therefore is a mediator between the past and the future, its values constantly reassessed by the ever-changing present. The present decides what can or should activate memory and for what purpose; in other words, it is the present that assigns attributes of monumentality. Mozart's house, for example, became a monument long after it was erected, despite the fact that its architecture is not monumental in terms of size and elaboration and there was no intention of this sort in its initial design. This is what Alois Riegl called the "unintentional monument" (Riegl 1982, 21; see also Forster 1982). Intentional monuments or memorials, on the other hand, are what people erect purposefully in their own lifetime to commemorate a notable person (sometimes themselves), an action, or an event. The pyramids were constructed as monuments/memorials of this sort.

Through time, the designation monumental retained only some of the attributes of the monument—namely, size, elaboration, endurance, and conspicuity. Thus, monumentality became a rather loose designation, fitting many works of architecture that carry such characteristics, regardless of their meaning. In this process, the issue of memory as a reminder and warning based on associations with the past has faded away. What we read in the monumentality of a work of architecture today is often raw power, for "the ability to expend energy, especially in the form of other people's labour, in non-utilitarian ways is the most basic and universally understood symbol of power" (Trigger 1990, 125). This is in fact how monumentality is commonly referred to in Aegean studies, as a means to signify status and power.

One may wonder, however, if monumentality could also be a means to activate the memory of things, people, and events that belong to the past (their past)? An ashlar facade is assumed to be monumental and a marker of status because of its time and labor consuming technology, but could it also be that it is monumental because it alludes to (activates the memory of) earlier important buildings of the same quality and appearance? Summoning the past to empower the present is very effective practice. Ashlar facades originate in the first Palaces, as Phaistos clearly shows, which means that there was a long-standing memory of this type of wall construction in association with the Palace and its institutions. This shared memory would have constantly charged what Tim Cunningham calls the social batteries: "monumental architecture works to gather, focus, store and transfer social resources—especially at a conceptual or ideological level" (2007a, 28). This is why monuments are ideal targets against group identities.[1]

Another elusive issue associated with monumentality is scale. A building—or part of a building, such as its entrance—is often described as being monumental in scale. The obvious reference, of course, is to large size, yet it is interesting to look into the choice of the word scale instead of size. The latter is an abstract numerical statement with no connotations, whereas the former is in need of a system of reference that will allow for evaluation, even if arbitrary and self-referential. One might ask, for example, on a scale of 1 to 10 how monumental is the Little Palace, implying that 10 is on the scale of the Palace of Knossos? Or, if the West Facade of the Palace of Knossos was indeed constructed of rubble and timber above the ashlar orthostates, as Shaw has persuasively shown, instead of all ashlar as Evans restored it, how many points in the above scale of monumentality would it loose? In other words, our judgments with regard to monumentality are often vague and subjective, hence noncommunicative, and they allow for misconceptions to creep in.

Size, elaboration, and endurance of materials are not the only means to convey monumentality. Another way is to selectively emphasize, for example, the vertical dimension: a dominating tall structure standing among low volumes exudes monumentality not only because it overpowers them, but also because verticality implies victory over gravity and therefore stands for life and power (see this vol., Ch. 8). This is the case of Mesopotamian ziggurats and temples that stood high above the city that surrounded them. In the Minoan world the situation is different: horizontality prevails everywhere and the sprawling stepped skyline of a typical Minoan townscape would include the Palace with hardly any differentiation in height from the surrounding houses, except for the differentiation caused by the strong inclination of the terrain in certain instances. The lack of (or limited) distinguished architectural emphasis on the vertical, however, does not exclude monumentality; the symbolic capacity of architecture provides many more means to this end. Monumentality, as a means to evoke awe and a subordinate feeling, can be achieved, for instance, by prolonging the access to a building. As Trigger asserts, "By compelling officials, visiting dignitaries, and servants to expend extra energy moving from one place to another, monumental buildings further impress people with the power of the ruler and the resources that he has at his disposal" (Trigger 1990, 127).[2] This has been common practice from the earliest times to the modern. In Crete, however, it is less evident and of a rather different kind (on access systems to the Palaces, see this vol., Ch. 10). The most conspicuous access of this sort, the Corridor of Procession at Knossos, is indeed a prolonged access that induces intimidation and even confusion due to changing directions.

Interestingly, what merits most the term monumental in Minoan architecture is in fact a void: monumentality is indisputable in the compelling vastness of the Central Court of the Palace, and in its strict proportions and standard orientation, all of which are exclusive to this architectural element—yet another way to reinforce symbolic connotations.

There are two more points pertinent to this discussion, both already hinted at above. The first is related to the architectonic continuum that characterizes the Minoan world. For symbols of monumentality to be easily conceived as such, they need to be prominent and limited to specific cases only (as is the case with the exclusive use of the circle for funerary architecture in the Minoan world). The Minoan architectonic continuum does not facilitate such a goal. Jan Driessen and Ilse Schoep have stressed that the proliferation of monumentality from the Palace to the town is perhaps "the most surprising feature that sets Minoan culture apart from contemporary civilisations" (1995, 652).[3] This proliferation, however, devalues the symbolic power of the associated architectural elements. Ashlar masonry, for example, is often summoned as an indicator of monumentality even though it was not employed exclusively at the Palaces or to the larger and most prominent buildings of a site. It was applied to town houses as well in Palaikastro, Malia, Akrotiri, and elsewhere. In an urban context the target of monumentality was most probably not the individual houses but the street facades along major arteries of the town.[4] It may also be, however, that ashlar facades in the Minoan world had a different significance: exhibiting prosperity is not exactly synonymous to exhibiting power through monumentality.

To give another example: upon approaching the Palace of Knossos from the south, architectural elements that speak of monumentality (forms, materials, elaboration, and even size) are present everywhere, in Palace structures and houses alike. Would this mean that the resulting visual impact devalues the monumentality of the Palace? In fact, it is only to the west that monumentality becomes an attribute of the Palace alone, because it is only here that the town retreats, allowing for the impressive West Facade of the Palace to communicate its monumentality. Distance is crucial in evaluating forms, sizes, and monumentality, as Letteson has pointed out.[5] Could this situation reflect two different contents and recipients of monumentality? It is quite possible, in other words, that in the first case the importance lies in the way the Town-and-Palace compound, as one entity, is perceived as monumental from afar at a regional level, whereas in the latter the message of monumentality is addressed from the Palace to the town.

The second point is monumentality in relation to materials, and more specifically timber versus stone. Though Evans had appreciated the contribution of wood in Knossian architecture from the beginning, it took a long time for scholars to understand in some depth the structural logic of Minoan architecture and to come to terms with the idea that this was an almost half-timber technology (see this vol., Ch. 7). Underlying the reluctance to accept that wood was the protagonist of Minoan palatial architecture is a latent feeling of frustration, for stone is assumed to convey monumentality better than wood. This is due to the common misconception that wood is less enduring and lasting than stone (see this vol., pp. 136–138), attributes thought to be essential for monumentality and a stereotype deriving from the classical Greek ideal in stone.

It is interesting to note that Evans too must have had some reservations of this sort, for he could not resist interfering with his findings in order to give the building the monumentality it deserved as the Palace of King Minos. He thus construed a stone monumentality, one his era could understand and relate with best. Examples of this sort are the West Facade of the Palace, where he restored an ashlar wall above the orthostates instead of rubble and timber, which was clearly the case, and also the corner piers he restored as if entirely of stone, whereas in reality they consisted of a stone base topped with a load-bearing timber frame filled in with rubble (Kienzle 1998; Tsakanika-Theochari 2006).

It is vital to restore our faith in wood and see it for what it is: the material par excellence that allowed for the innovative architecture of Neopalatial Crete to come into being. It is also essential to accept that wood played as equally an important role in expressing monumentality as stone did. After all, one of the most potent symbols of Minoan architecture, the column, was made of wood. On the same account, it is important to keep in mind that horizontality can be just as effective as verticality in producing monumental effects; it all depends on the way these attributes are used to convey meaning.

In sum, function and monumentality have multiple meanings and many subtle variations. The ambivalence with regard to the meaning and the goal of monumental architecture is exemplified in the following contradicting arguments: For Trigger, "the need to express power through the medium of monumental architecture may be greater during the formative stages of early civilizations or at times when the degree of centralized power is increasing" (1990, 127). For Mumford, on the other hand, "the more shaky the institution, the more solid the monument" (1938, 434). Neopalatial architecture in Crete may not even be monumental through choice; this was architectural style formation in progress. Architectural style is the result of a holistic process and not of a conscious effort to create a particular look (Frederick 2007, 82).

## Endnotes

1 On the reuse of the past to enhance intergenerational value, see Cunningham 2007a, 42; Driessen 2007, 86.

2 Hitler was particularly pleased by the fact that due to a 230 m walk from the entrance to the reception hall, visitors would get "a taste of the power and grandeur of the German Reich" (Trigger 1990, 127).

3 This paper discusses in detail the implications of the proliferation of palatial architectural features and the various ways the phenomenon has been interpreted, either as pointing to an integrated political organization centered at Knossos, with lower order centers repeating at a less grandiose scale the functions exerted by the capital, or as a result of interaction and emulation between independent peer polities.

4 Cunningham (2007b, 102) also remarks on the uniformity of the facades along the main street at Palaikastro as referring to the street rather than to the individual houses, but speaks of street ornamentation rather than purposeful signaling of the importance of this street.

5 Letesson and Vansteenhuyse (2006, 101) make a valuable contribution to the perception of architecture in accordance to the relative position of the viewer. They conclude that for rules of visibility to be valid there was need for much higher facades around the Central Court. Since this is not the case, they accept the position that their impressiveness may have been achieved through over-emphasized horizontality.

# 10 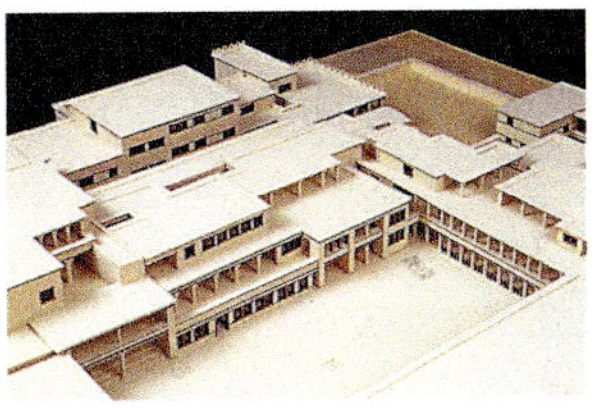

## The Minoan Palace

### Empowering the Center

## On Names and Terms (Again)

In line with the sequence of inquiries adopted in this book, we shall begin the discussion by addressing once again names and terms: in this case, a tantalizing pair of a name and a term that has been haunting Aegean prehistoric studies ever since Evans coined his discoveries at Knossos "The Palace of Minos." For Evans, the names Knossos and Minos corresponded broadly to a property and a proprietor, while the term Palace implied the identity of this property and the authority of the proprietor. It took some time for the name Minos to become an adjective and acquire the power of the generic designation of a civilization (Graham's book, published in the early 1970s, bore the prudent title *The Palaces of Crete* and not *The Minoan Palaces*).

Names and words bequeathed by Evans and his contemporaries are held responsible today by many scholars for a distorted view of the Bronze Age civilization of Crete, because of the connotations they carry in regard to function. Their response was the fabrication of new names to replace the old ones, along with in-depth inquiries as to the meaning of words: What is a Palace? Who were the Minoans? Why Knossos? Two conferences on these topics—one in 1987 and another 15 years later (Hägg and Marinatos, eds. 1987; Driessen, Schoep, and Laffineur, eds., 2002)—illustrated vividly the differences of opinion. The situation is becoming even more complex as excavations throughout Crete multiply and expand, bringing to light architectural compounds that comply with some of the properties that the indisputable major Palaces of Knossos, Phaistos, and Malia have in common (hence the provocative title of the 2001 conference "Crete of the Hundred Palaces?").

The frustration underlying name-giving is real, but it is due not so much to the ambiguity of the meaning of the word Palace as to the difficulty in specifying and describing a definite group of building compounds that may be called Palaces (or otherwise). The idiosyncratic character and the rich nuances of Minoan architecture make categorization and corresponding name-giving a very difficult and evasive task, as explained in Chapter 1.

To keep the discussion transpicuous and within reasonable limits, the observations that follow are confined to the topmost Palaces in terms of size, elaboration, and degree of adherence to a common model: namely, Knossos, Phaistos, and Malia, with occasional references to Zakros, Galatas, and other compounds. The discussion aims primarily at highlighting the main features of these building compounds from a phenomenological point of view, in the hope that such an approach will reveal their character and contribute to the tantalizing question of what is the Minoan Palace.

## The Taking Place of the Palace: Group Design

*The question of architecture is in fact that of the place, of the taking place in space. (Derrida 1997, 320)*

The taking place of architecture is a process of interaction between man and nature. It is people's toilsome efforts to appropriate a piece of land and to shape and model it so as to comply with their needs and admit the edifice that will house their family and their possessions. It requires energy and constant care, for nature has no sympathy to his needs and intentions and will take over in due time if not resisted. A retaining wall holding a cultivation terrace that was created with great effort, if unmaintained, will eventually decompose and tumble down, allowing for the initial undulation of the hillside to take back its form. The same is true for deserted buildings: in time they will ruin and their debris will add involuntary masses to the contours of the land. At Knossos, the traces of the work of many generations are there to tell this story, one of cutting the rock straight down to a depth of more than 7 m to accommodate the buildings on the eastern and southern slopes, as well as tiding-up layer after layer of debris of several millennia of habitation, adding over 10 m to the original altitude at the summit of the Kephala hill. One has to undo an ages-long process of land manipulation to arrive at the land formation that originally attracted human presence and dictated choice of location for habitation.

Turning back to the issues of terminology, an innocent reader faced with the term palace (not the name Minoan Palace) would perhaps expect it to be a conspicuous building located on a prominent site, preferably overlooking the town, both literally and metaphorically. This, however, is not the case with the Minoan Palace—to start, it hardly stands out as a building. To clarify: a building, by definition, "implies a continuous boundary (however permeable) as well as continuous internal permeability" (Hillier and Hanson 1984, 53). Minoan Palaces do not comply with this definition: outer boundaries are not always continuous or even discrete, and internal permeability between separate zones is either limited to a very small number of links or is served only through the Central Court. The main characteristic of the Minoan Palace is indeed the informal way it is embedded in the urban fabric in close relation to the town. Zakros is perhaps the best example of this inextricable bonding, but the general feeling is there in the other Palaces as well, regardless of the fact that some parts are better distinguished than others. At the outset of this discussion, therefore, the issue of the setting of the Palace is one that has to include the town as well. It is the setting of the Town-and-Palace system on a regional level that matters foremost; the setting of the Palace vis-à-vis the town comes next.

One might rightly ask, "If the Minoan Palace is not a building, then what is it?" To answer this question, we need to refer briefly to the four levels of design of the manmade environment: (1) architectural design applies to a single building and its immediate environment; (2) urban design or group design refers to a number of interrelated buildings and all the open-air spaces, private and public, that relate to their function; (3) town-planning deals with public space and land use at the level of a settlement; and (4) regional planning encompasses economic and social issues besides architecture and settlement patterns. The Minoan Palace falls in the second category. It is the outcome of group design aiming at bringing together disparate building units (zones) born from the bowels of the town.[1] The Central Court, the hub of the compound, is the magnet that holds firmly together the constituent parts through forces of repulsion and attraction, keeping the balance steady between integration and segregation.

A quick overview of the major palatial towns shows that there is no obvious consistency in terms of geographical location: the Town-and-Palace systems at Knossos, Phaistos, and Galatas are inland and seem to conform to the expectation of high land to some degree. Malia and Zakros, on the other hand, are both situated on low land and relatively close to the coast. Yet, they too are highly conspicuous from a distance: people moving from the mountainous hinterland toward

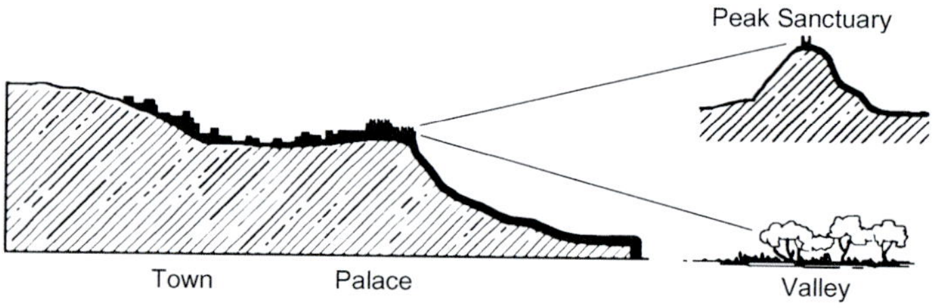


Fig. 163. Schematic representation of the Town-and-Palace and its broader region. Drawing C. Palyvou.

the coast would have had a demanding view of the Town-and-Palace system, even if looking down instead of up. It is the approach that mostly matters, the "looking at." In both instances the view is non obstructed, and it may even be surmised that visibility was guided and promoted by paths of approach designed accordingly.

Long-distance visibility is an important issue, hinted by Evans and especially by Graham, though mostly as a view directed outward from the Palace to the surrounding landscape. Lately, scholars have addressed the question the other way round as well. Driessen notes that the Palaces were perceived as impressive, robust structures standing out in the broader region as landmarks; the Palace of Knossos, in particular, looked like a ziggurat, with stepped terraces at about 20 different levels, especially to the south and east (Driessen 1999, 123–124). The same may be said for Phaistos and Galatas, for there too strong retaining walls protected the steeper sides from erosion: at Phaistos, these would have been primarily to the south and southeast where nothing survives today, whereas at Galatas such walls have been found to the north and northeast.

In fact, the Palaces at Knossos, Phaistos, and Galatas, though on high land, do not occupy the summit of the hill and are only partially visible, because the town sprawls over the hilltop, enfolding and obscuring the Palace from at least two sides. On the other two sides, however, the Palace stands out conspicuously, because it is built on the edge of steep slopes that correspond to the fringes of the town in those directions. The picture emerging is that the Town-and-Palace formation is meant to be conspicuous at a regional level, with the Palace standing out as the bow of the ship that is the town, ready to sail into the fertile green valley below (Figs. 163, 164). Visual contact with the corresponding peak sanctuary provided further affirmation of the territorial significance of the Town-and-Palace system, with the Palace as its pike. Such a setting can only be a direct reflection of the Minoan socioeconomic and political system.

Fig. 164. Aerial view of Phaistos, facing west. Photo Gordon Gahan, National Geographic Creative.

A deeper understanding of site choice in relation to physical characteristics requires meticulous observation for each specific case separately. Peter Day and David Wilson have attempted an analysis of this sort for Knossos with excellent results: starting from the port of Katsambas and working their way south and uphill to the mound of Kephala, they describe in detail the peculiarities of the landscape as it unfolds around them and discuss the reasons that may have had prompted the first colonization of this specific area and its transformations through time (Day and Wilson 2002). I am tempted to propose that this experiential exercise should also be carried out the other way around, from Knossos to the coast. This is an exemplary phenomenological approach to site matters that should be extended to other cases as well. Until such analyses are available for each site, we shall have to be confined to a more general discussion.

## Keeping the Distance: The West Court and West Facade

The West Court is part of the nomenclature bequeathed to Aegean studies by Evans. The term court, however, is inappropriate and misleading in this case, because it is used for an open public space with loose boundaries and unrestricted access. It is part of the urban fabric of the town and acts as a public square, a kind of "principal public plaza," as Preziosi preferred (1983, 107). The difference between a court (an enclosed space with controlled access) and a public piazza (a communal space with free access) is of course fundamental. Once more, however, the term has acquired the value of a name, and as such it will be used here. Moreover, the designation West is valid only for the three major Palaces: Knossos, Phaistos, and Malia.

There are no strict specifications regarding the form of this open-air space as opposed to the Central Court, discussed below. It resulted from the organic growth and infill development of the town, rather than from a formal design process. The only standard feature is that it is paved and has one well-defined boundary: the West Facade of the Palace (Figs. 165, 166). This facade acts as a plane of reference, a kind of stage scene that provides the perfect background for civic or religious activities taking place in the West Court (presumably under the auspices of the Palace, as has been suggested; Hägg 1987). This is the only place where the two domains—the town and the Palace—actually confront each other. In this confrontation, the Palace has raised an imposing and impregnable facade of an architectural ambience that calls for monumentality. The town, on the other hand, keeps its distance and retreats, instead of encroaching on the Palace as it does on all other sides. It is through

Fig. 165. West Court of the Palace of Malia, facing east. Davaras 1989a, fig. 7; © Hellenic Ministry of Culture and Sports–Archaeological Receipts Fund.

Fig. 166. Model of the Palace of Knossos at the Archaeological Museum of Herakleion, facing east. Photo C. Palyvou.

the everyday encounter with this monumental facade—the only part of the Palace exposed toward the town with such formal clarity—that the citizens are constantly reminded of the presence and significance of the institution that lies beyond. This is the true function of monumentality, discussed in Chapter 9.

For a facade to be perceived as one of the planes of the volume that is the building, clear edges and outlines play an important role. Formal clarity of this sort, however, does not apply here: it is only along the broader part of the West Court that the facade is well defined, while its two ends are rather blurred with no clear edges to frame and complete the picture. Take, for example, the West Facade of the Palace of Knossos: to the north, a deep recess obscures the continuation of the façade (Fig. 166, left). Evans and Graham assumed a staircase or ramp leading up to the Piano Nobile at this point, whereas Driessen suggests that there may have been a bridge connecting the Palace to the North-West Treasury, like the one connecting the Little Palace to the Unexplored Mansion (Driessen 1995b, 78–80, figs. 18, 19). An entrance here would have changed drastically the strict, inhibiting character of the Palace facade toward the town, while in the case of the bridge the Palace would have looked as if it were spilling over to the west in a different context and direction. To the south, the West Facade ends rather abruptly with a small projection accommodating one of the major entrances to the Palace (on a rather extravagant level of comparison, the projecting entrance is reminiscent of the entrance of the Archanes model of a house). Next to this entrance, continuing westward, there are buildings of obscure identity and long history that are not directly related to the Palace (Macdonald 2013). The West Facade of the Palace of Knossos, therefore, is not perceived as one of the planes of a volume that is the building, but rather as an autonomous screen bordering the public piazza. This is further reinforced by the indentations of the facade, discussed below.

At Malia, the situation is similar: the West Facade is best perceived around its center, whereas to the north it fades away into some sort of parapet wall screening off a garden (Fig. 167). The building compound encroaching farther north, known as the Agora, leaves a relatively narrow passage for accessing the northern entrance to the Palace. To the south, the facade ends abruptly to accommodate a group of freestanding round silos and parapet walls. The southern facade of the Palace is well defined and comprises a broad entrance with a beautifully paved corridor that leads to the Central Court. The open public space in front of this facade, however, is not exactly the continuation of the West Court: the two open spaces are connected through a narrow passage. In other words, none of the entrances to the Malian Palace were visible from the public piazza.

At Phaistos, the West Facade is very impressive but only along its central part, for it too has no clear ends. To the north it extended on a much higher level than the rest of the facade while to the south the Palace is encroached on by houses and the West Court degenerates into a narrow passage that obscures the continuation of the monumental facade. In fact, the West Facade is best perceived in relation to the Theatral Area with its impressive retaining wall situated perpendicular to the Palace facade.

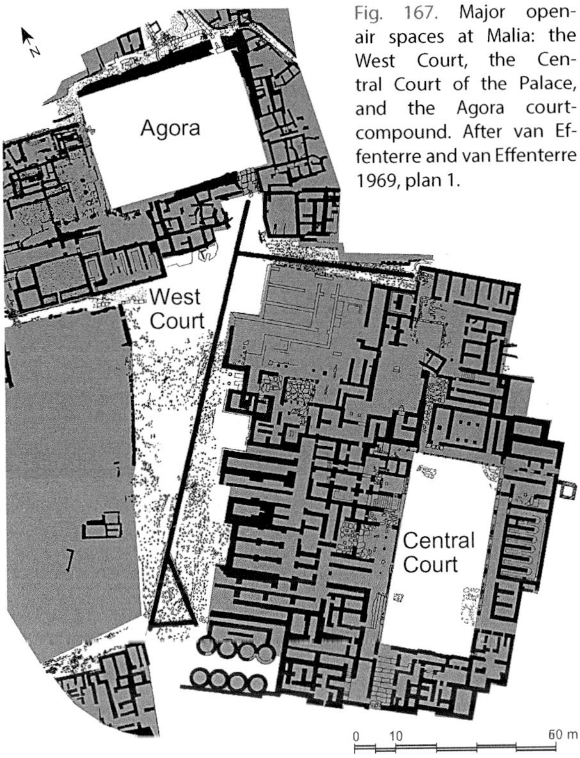


Fig. 167. Major open-air spaces at Malia: the West Court, the Central Court of the Palace, and the Agora court-compound. After van Effenterre and van Effenterre 1969, plan 1.

Needless to say, the above observations require a much more detailed treatment with regard to chronologies and building phases, for Palaces and towns have grown into each other and gone through many modifications. The overall impression, however, is that Minoan architects did not handle the West Facade as one of the planes of the well-defined volume that was the Palace, but rather as a plane or a screen in its own right that refers primarily to the public piazza and the town. Furthermore, it is clear that architects worked in a piecemeal manner (a process familiar to art as well): in designing the West Facade, their priorities lay in the segment that corresponds to the (intentionally) broader part of the West Court where visibility is at its maximum and the monumental facade can be better appreciated for what it is. This monumentality fades away on either side, and the two ends of the facade are adjusted ad hoc to the local urban conditions.

The above observations may help understand the symmetry underlying the indentations typical of the West Facade (Fig. 168). They are very regular and often accurately designed and executed, and they convey a strong ambience of discipline and order, a rare practice in Minoan architecture. Underlying the sequence of alternating recesses and projections there is a latent tripartite symmetry designed to accentuate the importance of the facade and focus attention on the portion corresponding to the broader part of the piazza. This symmetry reveals itself only when reading the facade piecemeal and in relation to the public space in front of it.

At Knossos and Malia symmetry is in the form of a projecting central part, flanked by two identical parts in deep recess (see Fig. 152). The strong thrust of the projecting part of the Palace facade dominates the public space (Fig. 168:a, b). If it projected in the vertical as well, and if

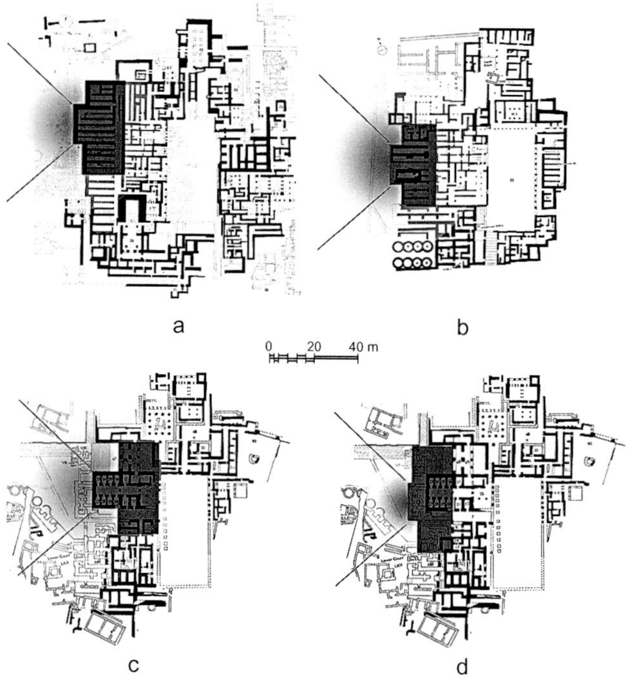


Fig. 168. West Facades of the three major Palaces—Knossos (a), Malia (b), and Phaistos first Palace (c) and second Palace (d)—where tripartite symmetry served as a means to focus attention on the thrusting part of the facade. After Palyvou 2002, pl. LVI.

there was indeed a window of appearance (or a balcony) on the upper floor of this projecting part, as Hägg has proposed for Knossos, then the person appearing there is literally coming forward to address the people gathered below (Hägg 1987). Furthermore, at Knossos there is the base of an altar located at a small distance from the facade along the axis of this projection.[2] The same holds true for Phaistos, though the picture is misleading at first glance, because the projecting part encompasses the broad staircase and the so-called Grand Propylon (Fig. 168:c). The result is a strong recess at ground floor level interfering with the way we read this part of the facade (especially since the upper part is missing).[3]

## Access and Entrance Systems

Having emphasized cogently that the Minoan Palace is not a single building but the result of an urban group-design process, we should tune our expectations accordingly and be prepared for a corresponding access/entrance system. And this is indeed the case: instead of one imposing entrance, which would signify the one and mighty power of the institution that lies beyond, there are several entry points to the compound in varying degrees of formal clarity and accessibility.

This multitude of access points has perplexed scholars, as is evident from the discrepancies in the ways they are described. Graham, for example, is not certain which is the main entry at Malia, and though it was generally assumed that it is the northern entrance, he disagrees and thinks the south is more important. For Knossos he sees two main entrances, one to the north and the other to the west, which he identifies as ceremonial. For Phaistos he states that the main entrance was in the middle of the West Facade, both in the First and the Second Palace, but when describing the Grand Propylon, only a few meters farther north, he talks of a "magnificent entranceway" with no other comment (Graham 1972, 44). The Propylon at Phaistos, in particular, has raised several questions as to its status, mostly because of the inconsistency between its size and what lies beyond. Henri van Effenterre does not think of it as a main entrance and neither does Preziosi (Graham 1972,

28–29 [Knossos], 36, 41 [Phaistos], 44 [Malia]; Preziosi 1983, 127; van Effenterre 1987 [Phaistos]).

Notwithstanding the above ambiguities, it is still expected that major entry points to a palatial compound should be announced from some distance and that access to them would be marked out. It is also expected that control and admittance of entry would be clearly expressed through the architectural configuration of the entrance area. A first glance at the larger Palaces, however, leaves us rather confused, for there is no consistency and hardly any obvious clues as to how to read the entry points. In general, moving from the town to the Palace does not have the ambience of moving toward a monumental entrance but rather as moving through its entry points toward the ultimate place of destination that is clearly the Central Court. This through-movement is actually materialized on the ground in the form of a network of well-defined causeways.

### *Ariadne's Clews: Raised Causeways*

To facilitate access through the muddy, bumpy streets and guide movement toward the entrances of the buildings, the Minoans came up with an ingenious idea: the raised causeways (Figs. 169–175). These are linear walkways with perfectly flat surfaces that cross through major streets. It may be assumed that they extend to the outskirts of the town and act as a kind of Ariadne's clew, or ball of yarn, that guides one through the meandering streets of the town, leading eventually to the Palace. Causeways are commonly discussed in Aegean studies in relation to the Palaces as ceremonial processions, but they constitute an unmistakable urban feature as well, attested in many Minoan settlements (see Driessen 2009).

Fig. 169. Royal Road at Knossos, facing east. Davaras 1986, fig. 45; © Hellenic Ministry of Culture and Sports–Archaeological Receipts Fund.

Causeways, as a rule, consist of orthogonal slabs set on a foundation of well-compressed stones that protect them from sinking. Their well-dressed surface projects from the surrounding ground a few centimeters. Their width, on the other hand, varies from a minimum of 0.60 m, wide enough for one person, to 1.00–1.20 m, wide enough for two people crossing in opposite directions. Sometimes, as at Knossos and Archanes (Fig. 171), they consist of two juxtaposed rows of slabs approximately 0.70 m wide each.

Causeways run along one side of the street, like a sidewalk, or in the middle of the street, as in the Royal Road at Knossos, in which case they exude a rather formal aura (see Fig. 169). Their strict linear form contrasts sharply with the irregular geometry of the street and acts, therefore, as a marker of the urban fabric: a circulatory

Fig. 170. Early example of a diagonal causeway at Quartier Mu, Malia, looking north. Photo C. Palyvou.

network that organizes and guides movement and sets a hierarchy of circulation. As urban signifiers, they delineate public space and avert trespassing or encroachment, though not always effectively. Furthermore, they orient and facilitate traffic in difficult situations such as rain, fog, and even darkness—probably the reason why most causeways are made of white slabs that reflect light and are easily distinguished.

Causeways partook in the urbanization process of the Protopalatial period, best exemplified at Malia where several such causeways have been revealed running through the town. When reaching the formal district of Quartier Mu, a diagonal causeway traverses the small public space, leading to the entrance of Building B (Fig. 170). Some of the early causeways were partly covered over, but, in general, they continued in the Neopalatial period (see, e.g., Palaikastro, Gortyn, Metropolis, and Chania).

The earliest evidence of a raised causeway is at Myrtos Pyrgos and dates back to the Prepalatial period (Cadogan 1977–1978, 71, figs. 4, 5). Interestingly, it is related not to domestic architecture but to a tomb or shrine: it is made of a pavement of slabs of varying shapes and leads to the entrance like a "red carpet," as Driessen dubbed the raised causeways (Driessen 2009, 45).

In the Neopalatial period causeways often appear in intricate arrangements, with several bifurcations that often culminate in triangular formations occupying broad, open public spaces (Fig. 171). This is especially evident in the areas of the West Courts of the Palaces at Knossos, Malia, and Phaistos. At Archanes and Kastelli the causeways are combined with low platforms or exedras presumably of some formal function (Fig. 171; Warren 1994, 206; Rethemiotakis 1992–1993, 36–37). The resulting mesh, with all its branches and diverging directions, makes up a redundant network of arrest and movement situations, which are also portrayed in art. Though their full function remains to be decoded, it is safe to assume that the raised causeways had a dual role: they served mundane everyday needs, and, on special occasions, they acquired a formal character acting as ceremonial or processional walkways, as Driessen and others have also pointed out (Driessen 2009, 51–52).

Fig. 171. Mesh of causeways at Archanes. After Sakellarakis and Sapouna-Sakellaraki 1997, fig. 21.

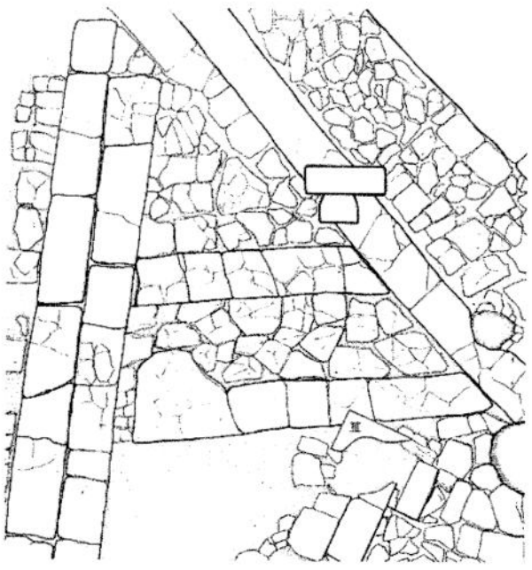

Their formal character is especially evident in relation to the Theatral Areas at the Palaces of Knossos and Phaistos (see Fig. 7). At Knossos, the Theatral Area is the ultimate destination of the formal causeway running along the axis of the Royal Road. It comes from the town, and, as it slopes gently to the east, one would have had a magnificent view of the northwest entrance of the Palace at the far back. Yet, access to this entrance is interrupted by the Theatral Area: the causeway bifurcates some distance before reaching it, producing a secondary branch that leads eventually to the entrance of the Palace, while the main branch stops short right in front of the steps of the Theatral Area. The steps, in other words, act as a kind of barrier. Since all barriers are at the same time elements of communication, it is also a meeting place for those coming from the Palace and those arriving from the town, as Marinatos convincingly suggested (1987, 139). This function is further corroborated by the unusually low height of the steps that shows that this area was not designed as a staircase; it was not a passage or a way up. In fact, the only reasonable way to use these steps is by standing upon them, one row of people above another. The 12 cm of height difference is just enough to allow for unobstructed viewing.

Fig. 172. Theatral Area of the Palace of Phaistos. Courtesy Hellenic Ministry of Culture and Sports.

At Phaistos, a network of causeways relates the Theatral Area to the entrance of the First Palace. Here, the causeway continues over the steps of the Theatral Area, leading north to an unknown point of interest (Fig. 172). Or perhaps the causeways should be read the other way around: as marking important lines of communication originating from the town and leading to the Palace. Both Theatral Areas are remarkable examples of an advanced urban design concept.

On reaching a broad, open space—a piazza or the West Court at the three major Palaces—causeways conform to the basic rule of minimizing time and effort, and they cross the area diagonally leading straight to the entrances. There, a most unexpected thing happens: some of the causeways continue straight through, inside the compound (Figs. 173–175). Since practical demands are no more at play, they are no longer raised. The message this visual continuity conveys is that one is still on the go and that, though inside the Palace, the destination point has not been reached yet. The way the urban walkway penetrates the Palace compound may be symbolically understood as a statement of the strong bonds between the town and the Palace. Causeways, in other words, act as umbilical cords bonding urban life with its womb, the Central Court, where they all stop sharp. The fact that there are no causeways within Central Courts is a strong proclamation of arrival: this is the end of the journey, or, to put it differently, this is where the Palace begins.

Fig. 173. Raised causeway at Knossos continuing inside the Corridor of Procession (looking south), emphasizing the strong bonds between the town and the Palace. Davaras 1986, fig. 9; © Hellenic Ministry of Culture and Sports–Archaeological Receipts Fund.

## Gates, Porches, Propyla, and Other Entrances

Looking carefully at the various entrances of Minoan Palatial compounds, it soon becomes clear that

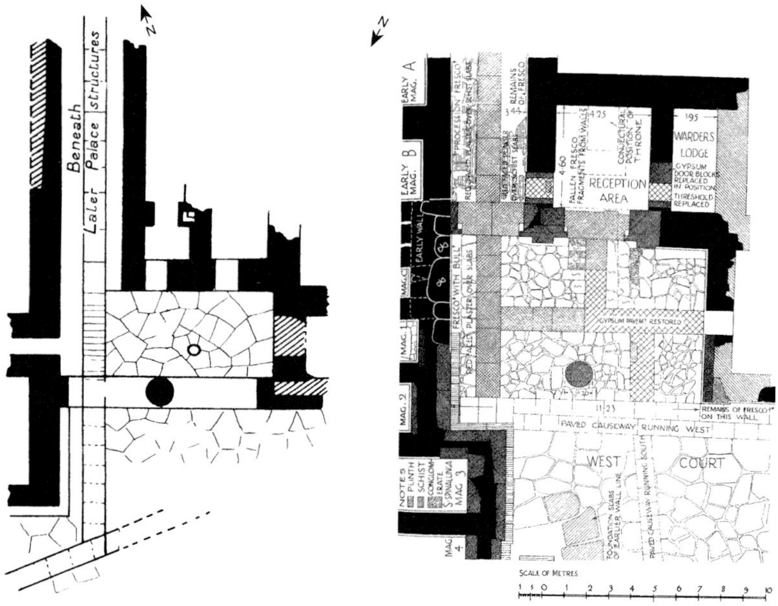


a b

Fig. 174. West Porches: (a) Protopalatial Palace, Phaistos (after Evans 1921–1935, I, fig. 159); (b) Palace of Knossos (after Evans 1921–1935, II, 427).

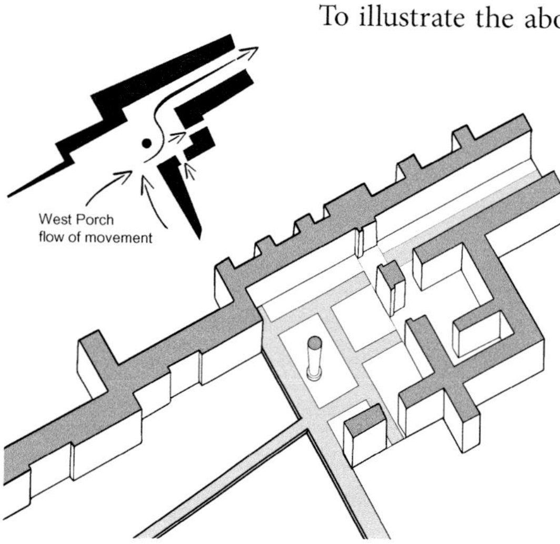


Fig. 175. Isometric drawing of the West Porch at Knossos where the entrance system functions as a circulatory node. Drawing C. Palyvou.

there is great variety in their location and treatment. This means that there was no specific type of entrance encoded in the minds of the Minoan people and no clearly formulated expectations as to the location or form of the entrance. The intention was not to design a conspicuous formal entrance to the Palace but several points of entry in varying modes of transition and degrees of formality.[4] This also explains the variety of names given by Aegean scholars to the entrances (e.g., gate, propylon, porch) and the frustration when attempting to distinguish between major entrances and secondary ones, as mentioned above (Palyvou 2009c). In fact, it is more likely that they were all main entrances to the zone they primarily served. This matches well the group design process of the Palace, as a compound consisting of distinct entities/zones, each one entitled to its own entrance. One might even suggest that they were not even conceived as entrances: the way the urban causeways penetrate the building is very telling of the liminal character of the entrance itself. What we think of as an entrance is, in fact, an intermediary stage in an integral sequence of arrest and movement situations.

To illustrate the above, we shall comment briefly on some of the entrances of the three major Palaces, starting with the West Porch at Knossos (Figs. 174:b, 175). Its position and general characteristics do not readily reveal its function as a major entrance to the Palace: it is located at a corner with limited visibility from a distance and is accessed through two raised causeways coming from the west and the north, respectively. The walkways continue inside the porch as distinct stripes of rectangular slabs (not raised) branching toward various directions, one of which corresponds to the Corridor of Procession. Despite the fact that the area has gone through modifications, the result, for such a limited space, is congestion and too much information for the incomer.

At Phaistos the West Porch of the Protopalatial period is in many ways similar to the one at Knossos, only much earlier in date (Fig. 174:a; Evans 1921–1935, II, 214, figs. 158–160). A raised causeway coming from the town penetrates the entrance leading through a rather short corridor straight to the Central Court. There are four or five doors in this small space that underline its function as a circulatory node and access control system.

Fig. 176. Monumental Propylon at Phaistos, facing north. Chatzi-Valliarou 1989, fig. 1; © Hellenic Ministry of Culture and Sports–Archaeological Receipts Fund.

A special comment is pertinent for the so-called Monumental Propylon of the Second Palace at Phaistos (Figs. 176, 177). What makes this structure so impressive, as much as puzzling, is the way we tend to look at it today: what we see is a grand staircase leading up to a grand entrance. Yet such a view is atypical for Minoan architecture and inconsequential with respect to the articulation of space beyond the two entrance doors. The doors open onto a porch and a light-well of relatively small dimensions. To the south there is a small room (a kind of porter's lodge). For the incomer there are two main options of movement thereafter, both of which correspond to intricate systems of vertical communication: (1) to the north a staircase leads to the Piano Nobile (Fig. 177:a1, a2); and (2) to the east a middle landing provides access to three locations, the Central Court (Fig. 177:b1), the Piano Nobile (Fig. 177:b2), and the eastern compartments (Fig. 177:b3). The two systems meet at the upper level (Fig. 177:a2, b2), thus completing an incredible three-dimensional circulatory system. In total, this area comprises six different staircases—it is an intricate circulatory node, a

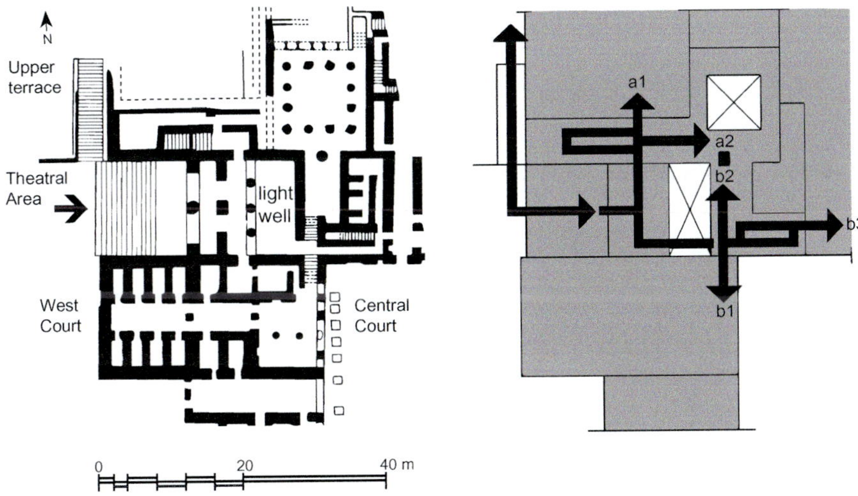


Fig. 177. Monumental Propylon of the Palace of Phaistos partaking in a circulatory nexus that distributes movement to the various zones of the Palace at different levels. After La Rosa 1992b, fig. 33.3.

breathtaking example of manipulation and control of three-dimensional space that speaks unmistakably of the hierarchical articulation of movement and circulation control that allowed for a large number of people of varying identities and tasks to move between zones and different levels with minimal crisscrossing and inconvenience.

Preziosi rightly observed that the Grand Staircase at Phaistos belongs to the Theatral Area rather than to the facade of the building (Preziosi 1983, 127; for the agreement of other scholars, see Hiller 1980, 229; Marinatos 1987, 140). It has the same geometry (with broad, low steps) and is perpendicular to the stepped structure that dominates the West Court. The intentions underlying the design of this area are further affirmed by the presence of another staircase next to the Propylon that leads to the upper terrace at an altitude very close to that of the landing of the West Porch (Fig. 176). This staircase makes no sense, for coming from the north one is obliged to descend and then ascend the same number of steps in order to reach the entrance. This absurd arrangement was clearly imposed by the Theatral Area. In conclusion, what we are looking at is not a monumental entrance as such, but rather an ingenious solution to a multi-parameter design problem: by combining the Theatral Area steps with the entrance, the architect met all requirements within the limited space allotted.

### *Minoan Single-Column Porch*

Despite the variety of entrance types, there is ample evidence from both the Protopalatial and Neopalatial Palaces of Knossos, Phaistos, and Malia, as well as from other buildings such as the Caravanserai at Knossos and House G at Zakros, that the Minoans preferred a type of entrance porch comprising only one, centrally positioned column, as opposed to the porch with two columns that prevailed throughout the history of architecture (Fig. 178).[5]

The Minoan choice of the Single-Column Porch asks for some explanation, and the best way to approach the question is by reflecting on the differences between two configurations: the Single- and the Two-Column Porch. In both instances bilateral symmetry is prevalent, but in the Single-Column Porch the center corresponds to the mass of the column and therefore denotes arrest, whereas in the Two-Column Porch it corresponds to the space in between the two columns and hence promotes movement. Movement is essential to the function of an entrance. A porch with two columns invites axial movement and evokes concentration and formality. In the case of a porch with one column, on the other hand, the person approaching the entrance is requested to make a choice of movement, to the left or to the right of the column (unless there is a causeway guiding the way). This situation presents the incomer with the possibility—or rather the obligation—to choose a course of action that generates stress. In other words, to take an initiative, unlike the case of the Two-Column Porch where direction of movement is given.

The position of the door(s) beyond the column plays a determinative role: if located at the center of the wall it results in unnecessary movements in order to bypass what will be perceived as an obstacle (the column), whereas if situated at one end of the wall it renders the other end useless (as in the Caravanserai). In many instances, however, there is more than one door within the porch and hence more than one choice of movement: in this case, the porch is no longer a momentous pause in a linear movement but a point of temporal arrest in order to reorient and choose direction.

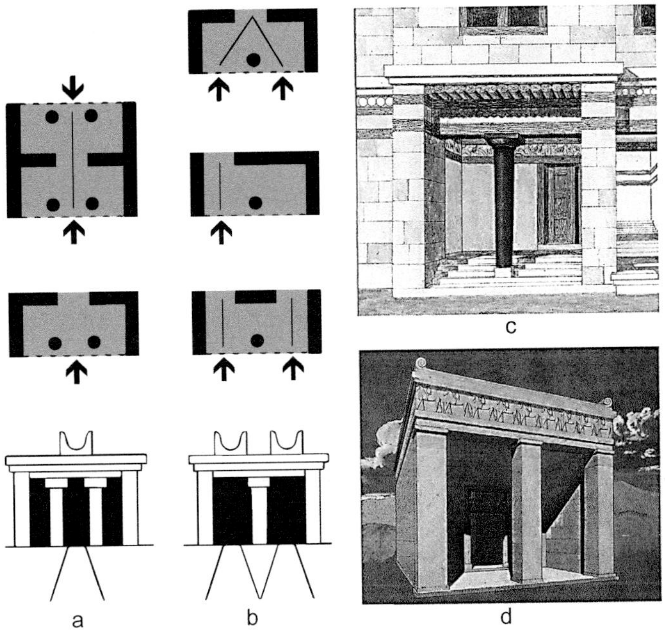


Fig. 178. Types of porches: (a) Two-Column Porch, where direction of movement is explicit (drawing C. Palyvou); (b) Minoan Single-Column Porch, where direction of movement is a matter of choice (drawing C. Palyvou); (c) Single-Column Porch at the Caravanserai (after Davaras 1986, fig. 20; © Hellenic Ministry of Culture and Sports–Archaeological Receipts Fund); (d) Greek Single-Column Porch at Prinias (courtesy Archaeological Museum of Herakleion, Hellenic Ministry of Culture and Sports–Archaeological Receipts Fund).

The Single-Column Porch promotes emphatically the idea of the column as a structural element of great importance—which indeed it is due to its load bearing properties—projecting this attribute symbolically to the institution to be entered. Such symbolic connotations underlie the depiction of single columns in Minoan art, usually in heraldic compositions, and, later in time, in the Lion Gate at Mycenae. It is possible, therefore, that the Single-Column Porch was preferred by the Minoans over the Two-Column Porch precisely because of the well-established symbolic value of the column as a single entity. Minoans approaching a Single-Column Porch may not have been preoccupied with the fact that they had to choose direction; instead, they may have even paused in reverence in front of the column before entering. Symbolism aside, however, the porch with two columns has more advantages, and it is no wonder that it prevailed thereafter, just as the even number of columns prevailed over the odd in the narrow facades of Greek temples (it is probably no coincidence that the early Cretan temples of the Archaic period at Prinias and Kommos are single columned).

## Void but Not Empty: The Central Court

*Doors and windows are cut to make a room:*
*Through their Non-Being comes the room's utility.*
*6th century B.C., Lao Tzu (2002, 21)*

The Central Court is the diagnostic feature of the Minoan Palace, the hub of the town, and the nucleus of the Minoan world. What delineates this broad, open-air space is its formal clarity. In a world of approximation, such as the Minoan, it is indeed of great importance to find a space that is strictly defined in terms of form, size, proportions, and orientation. The fact that this is an open-air space, void of any structures, reflects the great significance that outdoor activities must have had in the Bronze Age and shows that un-built space can be just as important as built space. As Lao Tzu wrote in the 6th century B.C., "Take advantage of Being, make use of Non-Being" (2002, 21)

The Central Court is truly both central and a court. The latter is attested by the fact that it is well defined on all four sides and access to it is restricted or controlled (all dictionaries emphasize the enclosed, confined character of the court). It is an architectural entity conceived in its own right, and it is perhaps the most significant of the components of a Palace, one that took priority over all the others in its design. Its centrality is topological rather than geographical, for it is situated at the core of a building compound that extends unevenly in all directions.

Access to the Central Court from the town is provided from many directions. The status of each access varies according to the significance of the corresponding entrance, and also according to the characteristics of the access itself. The Corridor of Procession at Knossos is a good example of a formal access that carries the incomer from the town to the Central Court directly, with no diversions and very little distraction.

What is clearly proclaimed in all Palaces is that the Central Court is an absolute locus (τόπος): though the town penetrates the Palace symbolically through formal corridors and causeways, they all stop short when reaching the Central Court. No causeways interrupt the unity of the space: there is no need to specify crossings from one point to another; its importance lies not in moving through space but in being there, it is a place of arrest rather than movement; and it is a destination in itself. The effect is further intensified by the impressive pavement of some Central Courts spreading out like a uniform carpet, as if the paved corridors that brought the incomers to the edges of the court spilled all over the broad, open space to mark its unity. If indeed the Central Court is depicted in the Knossos miniature frieze, with the scene of a crowd of people looking at all directions and gesturing to one another, then this is the kind of arrest suggested above; as Ellen Davis observed, the crowd itself is the subject of the painting (Davis 1987, 160; on the power of the Central Court to manipulate visual perception and communicative potential of particular rites, see also Driessen 2007, 77). The Central Court is indeed a starting point as much as an end in itself, and it is the architectural manifestation of mankind's desire "to concentrate and scatter; scatter to exploit the riches of the earth, and concentrate to make interaction and 'progress' possible" (Norberg-Schulz 1997, 116–117).

## Unifying Facades and Interlocking Elements: Porticoes and Balconies

The open-air space that is the Central Court, despite its large size, exudes an aura of interiority, a strong feeling of being inside. This "inside" is defined by the multistory facades rising on all four sides that provide the third dimension and determine the architectural character of the place. The facades, that is, belong to the buildings as much as to the court they envelop. Interestingly, it is here that we find the most ornate facades of the Palace: walls perforated with numerous openings, colonnades, piers, sheltered porticoes, balconies with wooden balustrades on the upper floors, and verandas. It is no wonder that the most sophisticated architectural depictions in Aegean Bronze Age art have been identified with these elegant facades. The emblematic image of the Palace, in other words, is the one viewed from within, from the semi-public domain of the Central Court.

Each building component of the Palace—referred to as an insula, zone, or cluster—has its own individualized association with the Central Court. This is clearly declared through the variance of the corresponding facades toward the Central Court. At the same time, there is a latent desire to promote unity and enhance the autonomy of the Central Court as the zone par excellence of the Palace. This is pursued through a common vocabulary of architectural elements such as colonnades, porticoes, and balconies, applied invariably to the surrounding facades. These elements perform a dual role: (a) they provide formal unity to the facades of the Central Court; and (b) they act as interlocking elements at the interface between inside and outside domains. That the Central Court is a semi-public space is further affirmed by the presence of entrance porches, all of the single-column type, leading from the court to the inner compartments. The one at Phaistos leads to the storage zone, while those at Knossos and Malia are in the form of Stepped Porches providing formal accesses to upper floor zones.

Fig. 179. Model of the Palace of Malia, showing porticoes, probably with balconies above, which were a common feature of the Central Courts of the Palaces. Etienne, ed., 1996, fig. 34b.

Porticoes are a common feature of the Central Courts of the Palaces (Fig. 179). They are supported by rows of columns or piers or by a combination of the two (see this vol., Ch. 8). They seldom embrace all four sides of the Central Court or even occupy the whole length of one side (such fragmentary treatment, however, is common in Minoan architecture; Fig. 180). At Phaistos, for example, there are porticoes only along the two long sides, whereas to

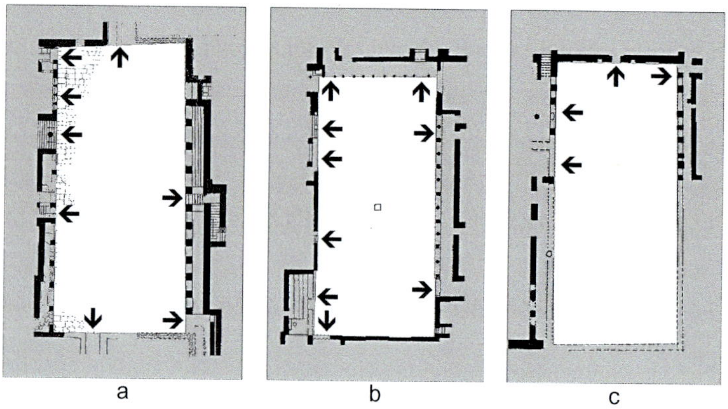


Fig. 180. Central Courts and their interfaces with the surrounding zones: (a) Knossos (after Shaw and Lowe 2002, fig. 9); (b) Malia and (c) Phaistos (after Palyvou 2002, pl. LVI).

the north there is a blank wall with two symmetrical semi-columns attached to the wall bordering the door (Fig. 181). This rare instance of semi-columns alludes to a colonnade that has been walled, and it therefore helps relate the north side of the court to the western and eastern porticoes (the south side is missing).

Porticoes should be considered an integral part of the Central Court, for the semi-open spaces they provide refer foremost to the court and secondarily to the buildings. This is evidenced by the fact that the back wall of the portico is often blank, with no or few doors. Porticoes are also applied as interlocking elements in the so-called Peristyle Courts, like those in the Palaces of Phaistos and Malia (both to the north). Myrtos Pyrgos presents a rather tantalizing hybrid, which combines both a Central Court and a public piazza: it has the aura of a Central Court partially surrounded by porticoes but the urban character of a public piazza (see Fig. 150). It is indeed an excellent example of the rich and subtle gradations of the Minoan architectural continuum.

The presence of upper floors in all the Palaces is well attested. It is highly probable, therefore, if not certain, that above the porticoes surrounding the Central Court there were balconies, as represented in several graphic reconstructions and models of the Palaces. Their presence is implied by the fact that at ground floor level there are two parallel load-bearing elements situated very close to each other: a wall and a colonnade. This redundancy is due to the fact that the colonnade was meant to carry the balcony or balconies above. The colonnade was most probably repeated on the upper floor with the inclusion of a balustrade (see Fig. 179). This would have been a long and narrow balcony, like the corresponding ground floor portico, and therefore it could not have accommodated activities that needed broad space, such as gatherings. But neither would it have served as a passage in this case. The portico below and the balcony above differ in this sense (Fig. 182): the portico is a sheltered, semi-indoor extension of an outdoor space (the movement is from the court to the shelter), whereas the balcony above is a sheltered, semi-outdoor extension of an inner space

Fig. 181. Central Court of the Palace of Phaistos, facing north. Courtesy Hellenic Ministry of Culture and Sports.

(the movement is from the inside of the building outward; for more on balconies see this vol., Ch. 5).

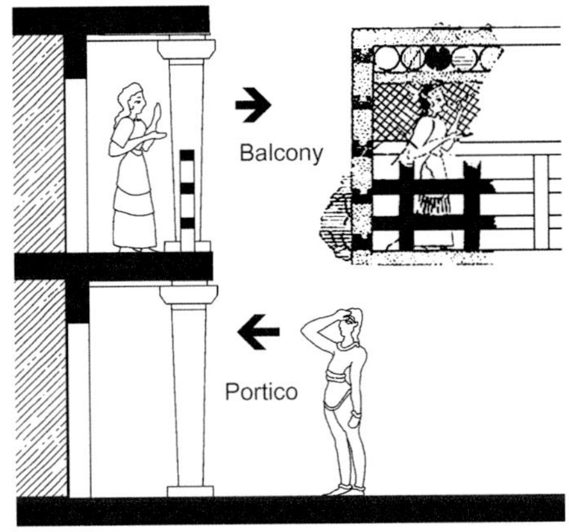


Fig. 182. The portico is a sheltered extension of an outdoor space, whereas the balcony above is a semi-outdoor extension of an inner space. Drawing C. Palyvou; after Evans 1921–1935, III, fig. 35.

## Constituent Zones

That Palaces consist of distinct zones or clusters of space-cells is fairly obvious, even with a casual glance at their plans. Evans had observed this at Knossos, and he called the constituent parts insulae. He suggested that these insulae revealed the history of the Palace, and that they corresponded to a number of individual parts that were gradually incorporated into a single coherent compound (Evans 1921–1923, I, 203). Graham rejected this progressive accumulative idea and made a strong point regarding the unity of the design of the Minoan Palace, asserting that it can only be the product of an overall more-or-less synchronic design procedure (Graham 1972, 230, 236). Preziosi was the first to look into the idea of clustering and zoning systematically (1983). Marking-out the zones does not present much of a problem, for they are quite distinct architecturally (Fig. 183). The questions that are more difficult to answer are: "Why they exist as such?" "What is the destination or function of each one?" "How do they come together to compose the whole that is the Palace?" Evans set out to answer these questions, especially those related to function, and he gave names implying their assumed use: storage zone, residential area, workshops, and so forth. In some cases this was self-evident (e.g., storage), whereas in others it was conjectured (e.g., residential). In the context of this book, the goal is to discuss the architectural properties that make zones identifiable, distinct, and different from one another, in the hope that this might shed some light on their character and performance capacity (for these terms, see this vol., Ch. 9) and, indirectly, on their destination and use. We shall therefore confine our discussion to those zones that have sufficient formal clarity in order to allow for some general observations.

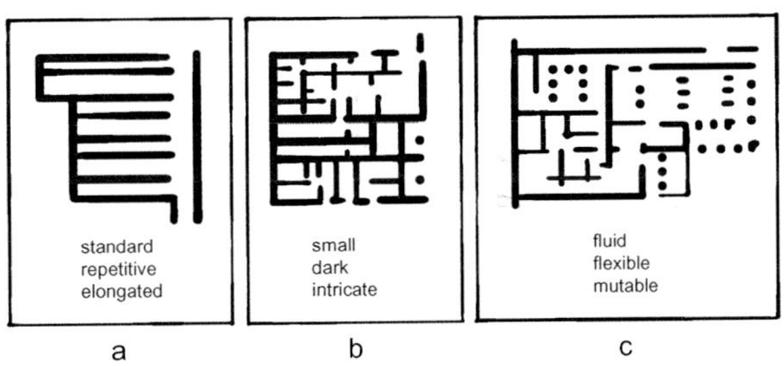


Fig. 183. Each zone of a Palace has its own attributes and distinct architectural character: (a) storage; (b) formal; (c) residential. Drawing C. Palyvou.

### *Central Court*

The Central Court is the most conspicuous and formal of all the zones, and it has already been discussed above. That this highly ordered, open-air space is a zone in itself is a fact of primal importance. All other open-air spaces—light-wells and courts (even large ones)—are

Fig. 184. Magazines at Knossos, looking west. Michailidou 1981, fig. 28; courtesy Ekdotike Athenon S.A.

integrated into their corresponding zones. The West Court, on the other hand, where it exists is an urban space related to—not part of—the Palace compound.

### *Storage Zone*

The storage zone is by far the most transpicuous, a rare instance where form is transparent of use, intentions, and purpose (Fig. 184; see also Fig. 96). Here form is a straightforward rendering of function, in celebration of the form-follows-function dogma. Starting with the choice of location, both geographically and topologically, it is obvious that it is defined by the need to protect the stored goods from both climatic extremes and trespassing. Hence, storage spaces are situated to the west, and they have indirect, controlled accesses from the main entry points of the Palace and the Central Court. The truth is, however, that a northern orientation would have been preferable based on such criteria, so this must have been the second best choice, dictated by other factors as well.

The choice of location was the result of complex, polyparametric decision-making, starting with the restrictions imposed by the most uncompromising zone of the Palace in terms of orientation and proportions: the Central Court. The result is a north wing of limited width and capacity in comparison to the west wing. In other words, had the storage zone been located to the north, it would have had to extend a very long way out to accommodate the required total space, in which case the criterion of least effort for its use would have not been met. Another parameter is the location of the administrative/ritual zone that acts as a kind of buffer between the storage zone and the Central Court. If we accept that ritual zones had to face east (as Goodison [2004] has proposed), then this is another compelling parameter that leads almost univocally to the location of the storage zone to the west, behind (e.g., Knossos, Malia) or next to (e.g., Phaistos) the administrative/ritual zone. The above reasoning may explain the standardization and continuity of the west wings of the Palaces, both old and new, which, as Donald Begg points out, present the least variation and the oldest foundations (Begg 1987, 179).

Storage zones consist of a number of standardized units set in juxtaposition. These are elongated rooms with only one entrance/exit and probably one window placed just below ceiling level. The two openings are located at the corresponding narrow ends of the room. The proportions, dimensions, and installations of a typical storage unit speak lucidly of the activities that took place there, for they mirror a sequence of movement-and-arrest situations: it is the linear movement of a person walking along a row of containers punctuated by an ephemeral pause in front of each one of them. It is a simple, repetitive act prolonged in time and space as required.

Measurements have been calculated on the basis of ergonomic factors—that is, according to the dimensions of the human body in action, including fatigue (the time variable). The aim is maximum exploitation of space combined with fast and unobstructed movement while carrying items in and out of the magazines (Fig. 185). A double row of pithoi flanking a corridor is the most effective and common type of arrangement. The corridors within each storeroom are surprisingly narrow (0.70–0.90 m): they can accommodate only one person at a time carrying a bulky object, which means that maximum exploitation of space was more important than allowing for two persons to cross inside the storeroom. The total width of a storage unit results, therefore, from the maximum diameter of the pithoi multiplied by two, plus the minimum width of the corridor—that is, approximately 1.50 m for a single row and 2.20–2.60 m for the typical double-row magazine. The length of the storeroom, on the other hand, comes in three different sizes at Knossos (13, 14, and 19 m), and it was calculated presumably on the basis of the overall quantity of the commodities that needed to be stored and the least effort principle (storage rooms should not be too long).

On the same logic, storage units are then arranged one next to the other to form a battery, accommodated by a common corridor. The width of this corridor is much larger, since it must now allow for more people and perhaps even a cart moving in and out (at Knossos the width

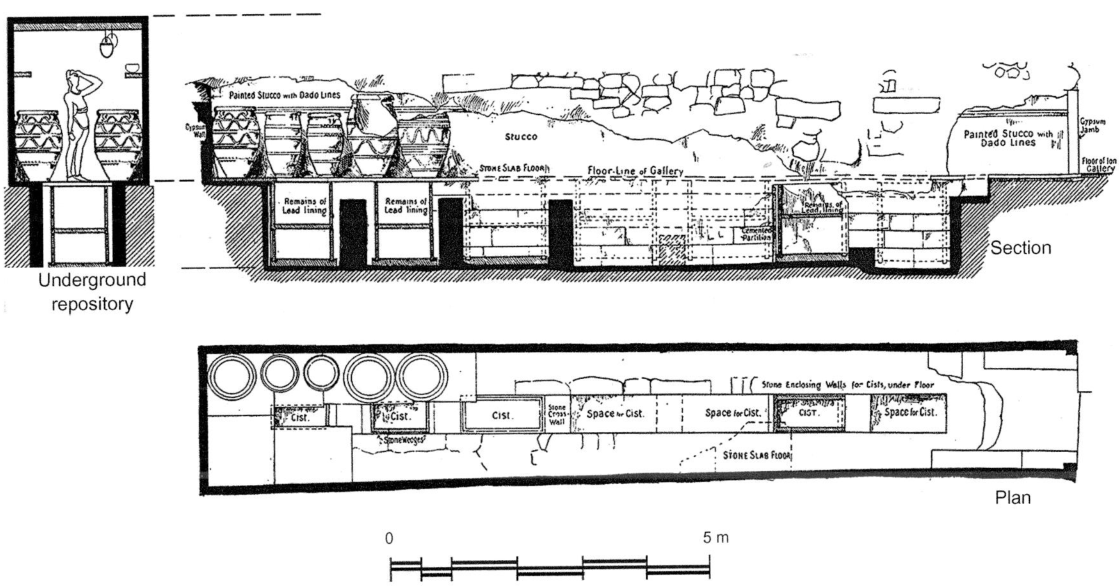


Fig. 185. Form and dimensions of the storage zone at Knossos, the result of ergonomic requirements and the maximum exploitation of space. After Evans 1921–1935, I, fig. 325.

Fig. 186. Storage zone of the Palace of Phaistos, from the east. Two sets of storerooms flank a common corridor, just as two rows of pithoi flank a common corridor within a storage unit. Chatzi-Vallianou, 1989, fig. 21; © Hellenic Ministry of Culture and Sports–Archaeological Receipts Fund.

is 3.20–3.40 m and the corresponding length 37.50 m). Staircases are strategically positioned at the ends of the main corridor to ensure direct and easy access to and from the upper floor zones. Usually, there is one row of storerooms attached to the main corridor, but at Phaistos the main corridor is flanked by two sets of magazines—that is, they follow the same concept as the storage unit with the two rows of pithoi (Fig. 186).

In the context of the form-follows-function logic and the maximum exploitation of space, it comes as no surprise that even the floors were used as storage space, specifically as underground repositories. Access to these repositories was more cumbersome, hence they were allotted to items not in daily demand or perhaps more precious. On the same account, there is no doubt that there were shelves on the walls above the pithoi and that ceiling beams were used to hang objects. Predictable, repetitive, simple functions, such as those involved in storage activities, produce standardized forms, limited in complexity and variations, hence storage spaces are more or less common in the Old and the New Palaces in Crete, as they are in Pylos and the Near East. Their architectural form alone need not be taken as an indication of interconnections or diffusion patterns.

### *Formal Zone*

Most scholars identify a kind of formal zone in the west wing of the Palaces, to which they ascribe administrative and ritual functions. Looking at the plans of Knossos, Phaistos, and Malia, one cannot help but note the striking difference between this zone and the storage zone discussed above (see Fig. 183): unlike the simple, repetitive pattern of the latter, the formal zone consists of a mesh of small interconnected space-cells with far too many doors and alternative options of circulation that actually leave very little space for tasks to be performed. If the characterization "labyrinthine" is to be used for the Minoan Palace at all, this is where it would fit best. Preziosi describes eloquently the circulatory effect of this zone as "the obverse of a courtyard standing between functional zones" (1983, 110). At Knossos and Malia, this zone acts as barrier and filter between the Central Court and the magazines. At Phaistos the situation is slightly different: the two zones, storage and formal, are in juxtaposition. The articulation of the magazines is different too, as discussed above. A probable reason for this was lack of space, especially when the West Facade of the Second Palace was withdrawn in order to leave more space for the public piazza. At Phaistos, the strong undulation of the land and the encroaching town dictated to a large extent the form of the west wing.

In all three major Palaces, the formal zone is seemingly open and easily accessible from the Central Court. On a more careful observation, however, one notes that it is only the first row of space-cells that is indeed open to the Court, whereas there is very limited and tortuous access to the rooms beyond. In other words, there is little circulatory depth. These back rooms consist of a real maze of passages and dark spaces that filter and control communication.

The west wings have surprisingly few interior staircases and only in relation to the storage zone. Communication in the vertical is very limited, in comparison with the residential zone, for example. This means that the administrative/ritual zone is self-contained and limited to the ground floor level. The autonomy of this zone and its strong, almost exclusive relation to the Central Court are very important factors in explaining its function, and it favors the idea of ritual activities directed toward people gathered in the court. The small rooms behind are a kind of backstage for these performances, whereas the invisible magazines beyond are inaccessible proof of power for which both secular and divine protection is provided.

### *Residential Zone*

Evans named a distinct zone in the east wing of the Palace at Knossos the Domestic Quarters based primarily on its architectural characteristics (see Fig. 183). His reasoning was that if domestic functions were to be expected within the Palace, this would be the most appropriate place because it provides privacy, a good view, and perfect climatic conditions. His line of thought found many followers.

Function (as use) set aside, what distinguishes this part of the Palace as a zone in itself is its architectural character, which is entirely different from the storage and formal zones described in the previous sections: it is highly perforated, it includes many open-air spaces integrated in its fabric, and it has a dense vertical communication system. Here is where the apical technical invention of the Minoans, the pier-and-door partition, is best appropriated for the lifestyle housed in this part of the Palace. Applied in various combinations, this mutable barrier offers an amazing array of alternative indoor/outdoor situations, both in terms of circulation and light/shade or cold/warm nuances. An aura of ease, luxury, and embellishment prevails in this zone, enhanced by the use of high-quality building materials (e.g., alabaster floors, gypsum dadoes, trimmed timber elements). In addition, the wall paintings that adorn several rooms manifest the intention to distinguish and impress.

The location of this zone is important in that it is carefully isolated from the other zones and activities taking place in the Palace, especially the Central Court. It literally turns its back to the Central Court. At Knossos and Phaistos these zones are located at the edge of steep slopes that allow for unobstructed, splendid views of the surrounding

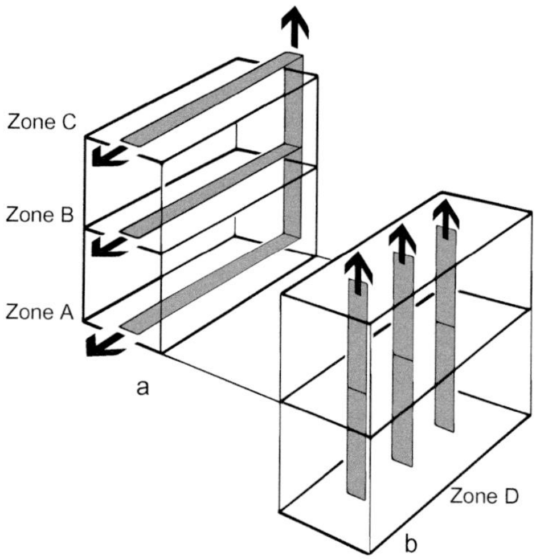


Fig. 187. The number and distribution of staircases provides proof of the articulation of the zone: (a) one staircase at the periphery indicates different zones at each level, arranged in the horizontal; and (b) two or more inner staircases indicate one zone distributed in the vertical. Drawing C. Palyvou.

landscape. At Malia where the ground is flat, it opens onto a broad open space that is assumed to have been a private garden—that is, an artificial landscape—delimited with an enclosure wall.

The residential zone extends in two or three stories—in other words, it is organized vertically as opposed to the west wing where zones are organized in the horizontal (Fig. 187). Vertical intercommunication and hierarchy of circulation are therefore important and are accommodated by a large number of staircases, each one serving a specific function. At the Domestic Quarters of Knossos, the staircases and the corresponding corridors occupy 39% of the sheltered surface of the zone (Fig. 188)! The three staircases serve three different kinds of intercommunication between stories, ranging from the most public to the most private. In other words, within the residential zone there are subzones consisting of spaces distributed in two or three stories, and each subzone is provided with its own staircase. This allows for all users to move around easily and unobstructed according to their identity and task. For example, visitors can reach the Hall of the Double Axes from the Grand Staircase, whereas the residents can approach from the other side using two alternative private staircases. The narrower staircase in the corridor that connects the two halls is the most private and allows for both halls to connect directly, and exclusively, with the upper floor compartments. This zone is indeed an architectural marvel of space fluidity combined with flexibility and hierarchy of movement.

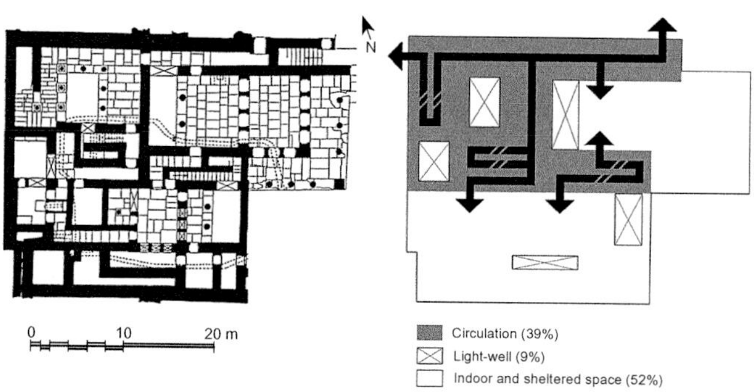


Fig. 188. Domestic Quarters of Knossos, where three staircases, set close to one another, offer remarkable flexibility of movement and hierarchy of circulation. After Evans 1921–1935, III, plan F.

### *Upper Floors*

Upper floors surely housed important parts of the Palace, yet there is very little left of them to allow for safe observations. We may assume, however, that the Minoan architects were more than capable of articulating space arrangement on the upper floor in any way they chose, regardless of the restrictions imposed by the arrangement of the ground floor walls—Akrotiri, Thera is standing evidence of that. This means that extrapolation of the configuration of the upper floor based on the layout of the ground floor is only marginally justified.

It is important to stress, once more, that the concept of zoning was applied in Minoan architecture both in the horizontal and in the vertical. In other words, there were zones occupying only one level and other zones distributed on two or more levels. Generally speaking, where there is a high concentration of staircases—as in the residential zone at Knossos—one may safely assume that this zone extended vertically. Where there are few staircases, located at the periphery of a zone, then these are most probably connectors of different, superimposed zones.

Graham envisaged an independent zone on the upper floor of the west wing—his Piano Nobile (Graham 1960b)—to which he allotted a direct access of its own. At Knossos and Malia, access is provided by a broad and elaborate staircase opening on the Central Court. The equivalent for Phaistos, I would suggest, is the Grand Propylon, even though coming from the West Court and not the Central Court, for it gives direct access to the upper floor of the west wing. All three cases are in fact stepped entrance porches of the single-column type (see Fig. 8).

## Patterns of Connectivity and Coherence

Graham was the first to discuss issues of morphology and architectural design, and his pioneering work contributed greatly to the appreciation of Minoan architecture (Graham 1972, 190–209). He was also the first to suggest that the design of the Palace began with the Central Court, and that the buildings surrounding the court were arranged according to certain lines guiding the design procedure. At Phaistos in particular, he visualized a pair of straight lines crossing at right angles at the northwest corner of the Central Court. These lines marked out the boundaries of the Central Court and generated the distribution of the various zones of the Palace, and they were measured in round numbers that he called "the Minoan foot" (Graham 1972, 237).

In the 1980s, Preziosi put forth the idea of a modular grid as the basis for the architectural design of the Palaces (Preziosi 1983, 419–464). According to his approach, the starting point is a large square divided in two equal orthogonal parts, one of which is the Central Court (Fig. 189). The other, to the west, corresponds to the ritual/administrative zone that acts as a buffer zone between the Central Court and the storage area. This design procedure is quite plausible for two reasons: first, the standard proportions of the Central Court—approximately 1:2—point unmistakably to an underlying square, and, second, there is ample evidence of major walls and structures aligned along the square (the walls of the magazines, the *eschara* at Malia, the Pillar Crypts, and so forth). Such alignments are surely no coincidence. Most importantly, a square is easy to apply on the ground; numerical accuracy and calculations are not even a prerequisite, and geometry suffices. The subdivision of the square can be just as easily implemented with the aid of the two diagonal lines crossing each other (on the use of diagonal lines to organize wall paintings, see Palyvou 2012).

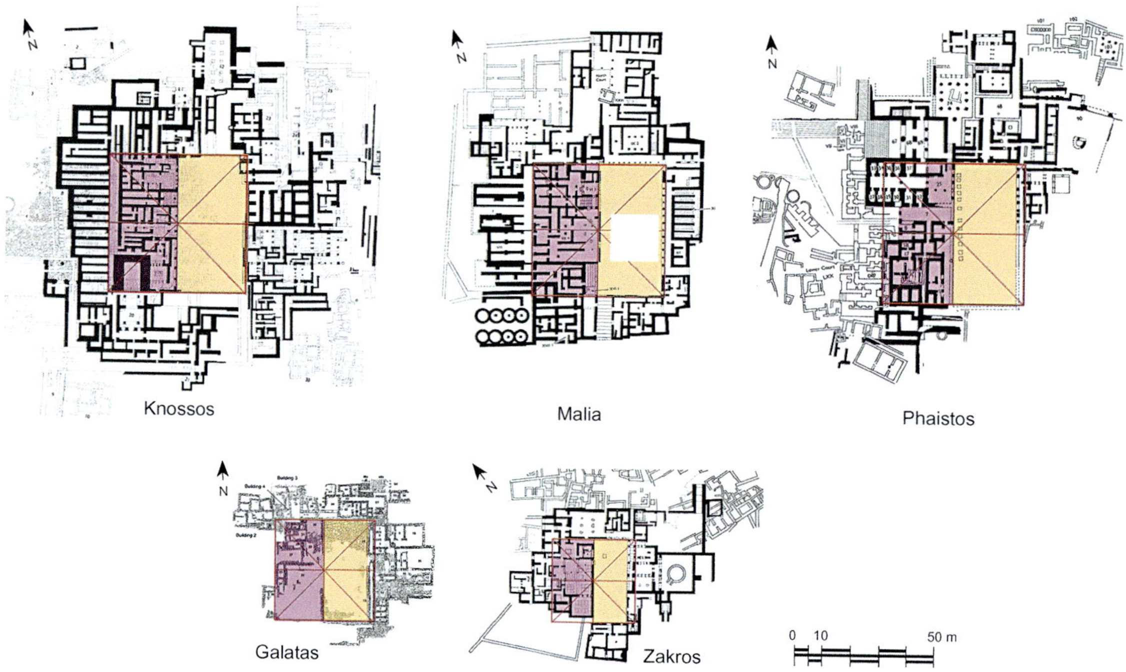


Fig. 189. Design process of the Palace, starting with a large square divided in two equal orthogonal parts, one of which is the Central Court. After Palyvou 2002, pl. LVI.

At Knossos and Malia the situation is most telling of such design process. In both cases, the western half of the initial square coincides largely with the area dedicated to administration and cult. The effect is so striking that one is tempted to read in this twin arrangement the expression of power mirrored in its outdoor versus indoor, public versus private, and mundane versus ritual manifestations. Phaistos, Zakros, and Galatas exhibit variations of the west wing that obscure the idea of the square, but there is still sufficient, even if latent, evidence for its presence (Palyvou 2002).

Having laid out the Central Court and the part of the west wing that completes the square design, the next step is to allocate the areas that correspond to the other zones of the Palace. As discussed above, each zone is delimited, contextually defined, and more or less self-contained. Careful observation of the plans of the Palaces shows that—as Graham had already detected—the delimiting lines at the interface between zones correspond to Regulating Lines radiating outward from the Central Court (Fig. 190). The design process of the Palace, in fact, is not very different from that of domestic architecture (described in Ch. 6)! These lines perform the dual role of separating and connecting, and they provide the key to understanding the layout of the Palace (for Knossos, see also Macdonald 2002, 49–50).

Most Regulating Lines also act as lines of communication, for they correspond to long corridors to which staircases are attached.[6] At Knossos, for example, the residential zone is delimited to the north by a long corridor with staircases at its two ends: one end connects with the Central Court and the other end with the adjacent zone to the north

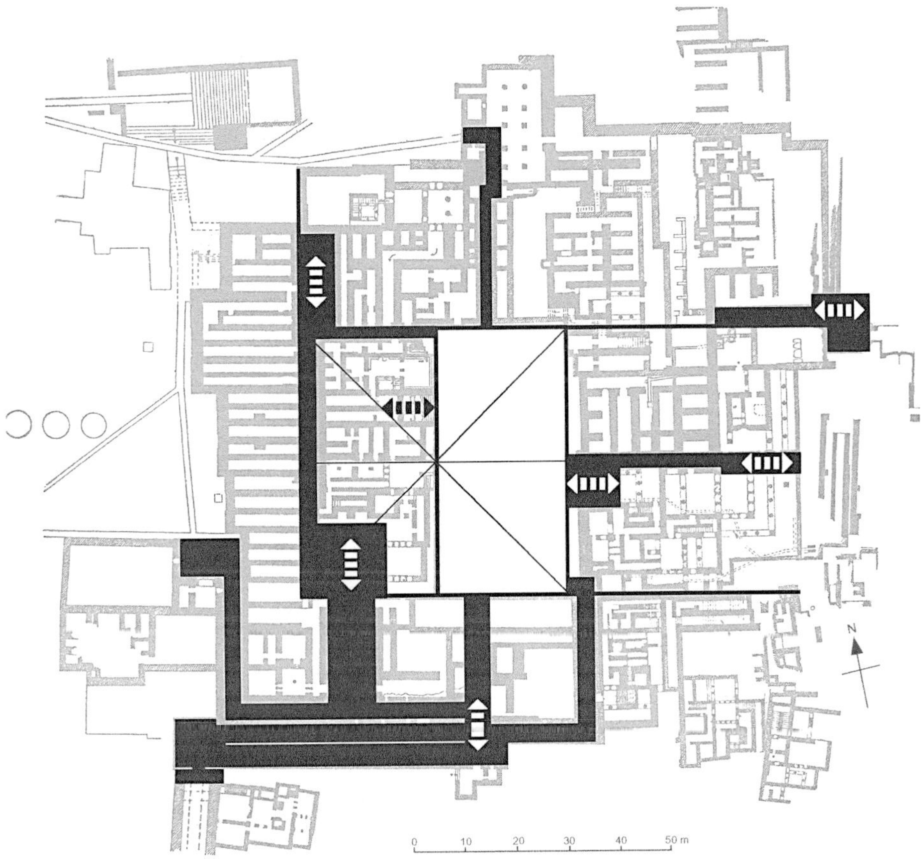


Fig. 190. Plan of the Palace of Knossos, where Regulating Lines guide the distribution of zones, the lines of communication, and the layout of the plan. After Michailidou 1981, 50–51.

(workshops?). A similar arrangement is attested at the interface between the storage zone and the administrative/ritual zone in the Palaces of Knossos and Malia: a long corridor with staircases appended at its two ends separates the two zones. Shorter corridors in the north and south wings of the Palaces also act as means of separation and intercommunication between adjacent zones. In conclusion, the design formula that guides the layout of the Palaces consists of a system of Regulating Lines that define zones and intercommunication while at the same time providing a pattern of connectivity that brings together the disparate building compartments (the zones) to produce the coherent whole that is the Palace.

## Endnotes

1 The term group design was first used by Robert Scranton to describe the correlation between sacred freestanding buildings within a temenos or an agora (1949). Giedion took over the term, defining group design as spatial harmony between independent buildings "sculpturally related" yet "spatially distinct" (1971, 9, 270). The deeper meaning of the term implies a design procedure

based on forces of attraction and repulsion that aim at creating a harmonious whole, while respecting the formal individuality of each component; in this it fits well the design concept of the Palaces.

2 Letesson and Vansteenhuyse (2006, 107–108) have elaborated at length on the ambience of this area and the visual contact between those moving on the ground level and those above, and they have suggested that the walkway running parallel to this facade may have marked the limit of intimacy.

3 Graham proposed a window of appearance above the entrance, but situated in such deep recess it could hardly function as such (1970). The steps below make it impossible for people to walk up and at the same time to look up to an assumed window of appearance. Preziosi is right in seeing both the steps and a possible window looking outward to the Theatral Area (1983, 127, 129).

4 The permeability of the Palace compounds changed through time: in the earlier Palaces of Knossos and Malia there were direct entrances from the West Court, whereas in the later Palaces these entries were cancelled and new, indirect and more restricted access systems were created (Driessen 1995b; Driessen and Macdonald 1997; Macdonald 2002).

5 The two-column portico of a Minoan Hall should not be confused with an entrance porch. There are a few more cases of Single-Column Porches from the Mycenaean world, but it is in Mycenaean Tiryns that the Two-Column Porch makes its first formal appearance, as an independent structure connecting two open-air areas—a true forerunner of the emblematic Greek Propylon (Palyvou 2009c).

6 Evans came close to such an understanding of the corridors, which he envisaged as open gangways between the insulae (1921–1935, I, 203).

# 11 

# Back to the 21st Century A.D.

## Reflections from the Future

## The Minoan Distance: Myths and Realities

The closing chapter of a book that set out to explore a broad range of issues with regard to discourse and praxis in archaeological and architectural contexts is inescapably an anadiplosis, a reflection, an introspect, and a fall back into one's own time and perseverance. From the past to the present, and from the realities to the myth, there is a distance that we can only keep crossing without it changing (Lawrence 1964; Cadogan 2004). It is a distance in time as much as in space, echoing Frank Sinatra singing "Long Ago and Far Away" in 1944, for space is cast in time.

Nevertheless, scholars of all times have firmly believed that theirs is a better understanding of the (Minoan) past than others before them, that their approach is precisely that: a step toward a goal, even if backward. As if, by definition, the longer the distance in time the closer one gets to the truths and realities of the past. Yet, time does nothing but add infinite reflections to the box of mirrors that is history, making space for intermediate times and new myths to creep in. Such is the case with Evans's time and personal myth in the early years of the 20th century A.D., yet another distance we need to cross, and hence a topic of interest and research in its own right.

As a pioneer in the field, Evans's task was to introduce this previously unknown civilization to the world. Evans, however, went far beyond an introduction, producing an all-inclusive narrative of this past, both tangible and intangible, thus leaving an indelible personal mark on Aegean archaeology. More than his verbal interpretations of the Minoan past, it was his extensive interventions on the ruins of Knossos that aroused voices of concern from the very beginning. Hogarth, for one, wrote that "Restorations like the Throne Room are not a question of methods, but of the gratifying of a desire to reconstruct tangible what must otherwise only be imagined" (letter to Evans, quoted in Bintliff 1984, 35). Evans's work at Knossos is indeed primarily a question of professional ethics within the field of management of cultural heritage,[1] an approach that is seldom embraced, with the exception of Peter Kienzle's exhaustive and comprehensive analysis that sets Evans's choices and actions within their proper perspective, as a "learning process" (1998, 448).

The closing chapter of a book that has set different lines of investigation is not the place to open this discussion. Suffice it to say that there are strong opponents as much as there are supporters of Evans's work at Knossos (Kienzle 1998, esp. 434–435; Warren 2000). A point worth making, nevertheless, is that despite Evans's affiliation to the ideas of William Morris,[2] through family connections, his attitude toward the monuments was closer to Viollet-le-Duc's theory and praxis, commonly referred to as "stylistic restoration": "To restore an edifice means neither to maintain it, nor to repair it, nor to rebuild it; it means to reestablish it in a finished state, which may in fact never have actually existed at any given time" (1854, 14–34). Viollet-le-Duc's prolific work in France during much of the 19th century was highly influential as much as controversial. Notwithstanding his extreme, purist ideas, he was among the first to establish a scientific profile for the conservator as a person who has studied in great detail the vocabulary of the architecture he is dealing with, to the effect that he can put himself "in the place of the original architect and try to imagine what he would do if he returned to earth and was handed the same kind of programs as have been given to us" (Viollet-le-Duc 1996, 317). Viollet-le-Duc, in other words, believed that the restorer should identify himself with the original master and should seek to have access to the same resources as he had. This description comes close to what Evans and his architects practiced, for they too were very well acquainted with the specifics of Minoan architecture, and their reconstitutions aimed at recapturing (to some extent, as opposed to Viollet-le-Duc's totalizing approach) the aura of the original building. Nevertheless, a correct vocabulary that is used ad hoc may produce wrong sentences with meanings that were never meant to be; it is in the synthesis that Evans has often failed, as in the West Facade of the Palace of Knossos, restored with Minoan-style ashlar that was never there.

Following the new approaches to the hermeneutics of archaeology, the debate regarding Evans—the man, the archaeologist, and his deeds—has largely intensified the past two decades. Some of the criticism has gone as far as to dispute his intentions; it has been suggested, for example, that he understood his mission in the new field of Minoan archaeology to be "to fabricate an authentic past for Europe . . . that from which modern Europeans should wish to imagine their descent" (Preziosi 2002, 32).[3] Evans's legacy is indeed often treated like a blot or a curtain we need to remove in order to reach out to the realities of the Minoans.

So, what are these Minoan realities? What constitutes the Minoan architectural style, and what is its place in the history of architecture? A preliminary synthesis of the analytical discussion presented in the previous pages leads effortlessly to what has already been observed by several scholars: a feeling of familiarity. This is due to the fact that the material remains of the "the familiar Minoans" (Farnoux 1996, 104)—their art and architecture—emit a distinct, albeit elusive aura of modernity. The effect of this Minoan modernity is indeed inescapable, and it has been addressed by several scholars who see the Minoan past as an agent in the formulation of 20th century A.D. modernity as much as the victim of interpretative tools deriving from the principles of Art Nouveau or Art Deco.[4] There is, however, a third possibility worth exploring: the Minoan modernity and the 20th century A.D. modernity may well represent two phenomena in asymptote trajectories, sharing common architectural and artistic traits with no causal connection. On this idea we shall focus below, after having discussed briefly the recurrent hermeneutic cycle of "agent/victim" mentioned above.

The reception of the material culture that Evans and his colleagues were unearthing on Crete in the early years of the 20th century was characterized primarily by astonishment. One thing was for sure: the cultural artifacts of this remote civilization were very different from—even opposed to—the classical ideals of the Greco-Roman period that had prevailed for so long. The artistic and intellectual avant-garde of the turn of the century, however, were questioning and challenging these very ideals. As a result, those in favor of the incipient new movement praised Minoan art for the very same qualities they professed as essential to Modern art and architecture. Archaeologists such as Arne Furumark, Geerto Snijder, and Guztave Glotz referred to Minoan architecture with phrases such as, "motor-optical experience of spatiality," "pictorial rather than plastic," and "the lines, surfaces, volumes join together to lend variety, movement—to take away from the mass all excessive heaviness," while Luisa Banti asserted that "It is the modern architectonic conception in opposition to the classic . . ." (Graham 1972, 246).

Evans too, though a Classicist by education, was impressed by the architecture he was bringing to light, which he described as "surprisingly modern" without elaborating any further (Evans 1921–1935, I, 306); he obviously felt it to be self-evident. Artists of the Art Nouveau and Art Deco styles in the early years of the 20th century declared with enthusiasm their admiration for Minoan art and willingly grafted Minoan iconographical themes on their art. Leon Bakst, for example, working for the Ballets Russes, spoke of Cretan art as "full of unexpected audacity . . . bold and dazzling . . . [an art] which is so close to us" (Momigliano 2017, 89). Mariano Fortuny produced so-called Knossian scarves and used the Minoan labyrinth as his trade-mark, and Charles Catteau designed vases in the Knossian marine style.[5] We should not forget, however, that the beginnings of the Modern era go back to the mid-19th century, and they therefore antedate Evans's discoveries at Knossos; in fact, Art Nouveau was fading away in the early years of the 20th century. In other words, Minoan art did not play a decisive role in the formation of the Modern Movement; its appreciation came after the crystallization of the new style.

Architectural historians, as well as practicing architects, also followed closely the new discoveries of the prehistoric Aegean civilizations from the very beginning, thanks to the publicity they enjoyed through newspapers and architectural journals (Laroche 1996). Eventually, Minoan architecture found its way to the architects' drawing boards and inspired some exponents of the Modern Movement, such as Josef Hoffmann, Loos, and Josef Plecnik (Prelovšek 1992, 154; Laroche 1996; Farnoux 2006, 362).

Greek architects did not remain indifferent either. Nikolaos Zoumboulidis (1888–1969), for example, a prominent architect of the 1920s and 1930s, was highly inspired by Evans's work at Knossos, which he followed closely (Fessa-Emmanouel, ed., 2009, 24–29). He studied architecture in Constantinople and later in Berlin at the Technische Hochschule (1910–1911). Zoumboulidis was involved in the design of many of the buildings of the National Bank of Greece. Fascinated by Minoan art and architecture, he designed the interior and the furniture of the head office of the National Bank of Greece in Athens as well as the Stock Exchange building in the Minoan style (Fig. 191). The branch of the National Bank of Greece at Nafplion, in Creto-Mycenean style, is surely his doing as well, in collaboration with the architect Michalis Kanakis who signed the drawings. The Minoan style is also present in the design of the ceiling of a private house at Ermoupolis and in his own house in Filothei, Athens (Fig. 192; Palyvou 2003).

Fig. 191. Interior decoration of the National Bank of Greece in Athens by Zoumboulidis. Courtesy M. Nomikos and M. Doussi.

Those opposed to the new trends of the early

Fig. 192. Front (left) and back (right) views of a Minoanizing villa in Athens built in the 1930s by Zoumboulidis. Palyvou 2003, fig. 15.9.

20th-century avant-garde were in fact more effective in describing the Minoan modernity. One of the most cunning accounts is by Robin Collingwood, a philosopher and historian of Roman Britain, who expressed his abomination for the architecture of Knossos for being, according to Hood (1995), "un-classical" (quoted in Cadogan 2004, 542). Visiting Crete in 1933, he spoke of boxlike forms and volumes and declared his aversion to "the surprise element in Minoan architecture," which, as Cadogan remarks, delights many of us nowadays. Collingwood's position was bluntly that "The Cretan artists were modern in the sense of being barbarously utilitarian, not Hellenically classical." In other words, he fully recognized in Minoan architecture all that glorified modernity in the heyday of the Bauhaus. The important corollary, Cadogan concludes, is that Crete was not "the forerunner of Greece" (as in the title of Hawes and Hawes 1909), "but its antithesis." As such, Knossos was considered a true scandal in the early 1920s and a severe blow to the prevailing precept of unilinear world growth from savagery to civilization.

The second component of the hermeneutic cycle has to do with the influence of Art Deco on the restorations carried out at Knossos, especially by Piet de Jong (1887–1967) in the years 1925–1930 (Figs. 193, 194). Contrary to the explicit reception of Minoan art by Modern artists, acknowledged in their own words, this assumption is only suggestive and implies a rather unconscious effect (De Craene 2006–2007, 58). It appeared in the discourse in the 1990s in the form of assessments such as "[Knossos is] a tribute to Art Nouveau and Art Deco sensitivities" (Papadopoulos 2005, 91), and it is considered to be

Fig. 193. Loggia above the Throne Room at Knossos as reconstituted by P. de Jong in 1928. Courtesy M. Papadantonakis.

Fig. 194. North Lustral Basin at Knossos as reconstituted by P. de Jong in 1929. Photo C. Palyvou.

"the best-preserved and finest examples of Art Deco and Art Nouveau architecture in Greece" (Papadopoulos 1997, 110). The result, Alexandre Farnoux concludes, is that "Evans's restoration belongs to the architectural legacy of the turn of the century . . ." (Farnoux 1996, 111).

For Farnoux's statement to be true, it has to be due to the architects working at Knossos, even if all major decisions were made by Evans personally. These architects, however, remained rather silent, and there is not much one can say about their stylistic preferences (Kienzle 1998, 380–394; Palyvou 2003; De Craene 2006–2007, 48–53). Theodore Fyfe (1875–1945) held tight to his classical education—to which he later contributed with his writings—and he was concerned with traditional materials and techniques along the lines of the Arts and Crafts Movement. He was among the few to look for echoes of classical ideals in the prehistoric past, a view he did not take any further.[6] Christian Doll (1880–1955) and de Jong were responsible for much of the reconstitution work, but they left almost nothing in writing that might shed some light regarding their position on the issue of Minoan modernity, though their background speaks of affiliations with the Modern Movement.[7] In conclusion, it is their actual work—with Evans's blessings of course—that is believed to be an Art Deco overlay to the ruins of Knossos (Farnoux 1996, 110–111; Laroche 1996; Papadopoulos 1997, 110).

On such unsubstantiated grounds and loose analogies, the issue of the influence of Art Nouveau and especially Art Deco on the restorations and reconstructions at Knossos will always remain a vague assumption. On the other hand, if we embrace the third option, as proposed above, of two worlds in asymptote trajectories sharing common architectural and artistic traits with no causal connection, we may find a better explanation why Evans and his architects were able (not just willing) to produce the Art Deco redolence through their reconstitutions. After all, would it have been possible to impose modernity on the ruins and the wall paintings of Knossos had the original material been entirely alien to such characteristics?

## Common Traits in Asymptote Trajectories

Could it be, then, that the familiarity acknowledged by many emanates from a set of remarkable similarities with no apparent causal connection? Barthélémy De Craene asks more or less the same question, pointing out that the main attributes of Minoan architecture,

> la simplicité des lignes droites, la géométrie abstraite, la volumétrie cubiste, les articulations des plans, les toits plats alternant avec de zones vides,

cours, escaliers ou puits de lumière (jeux sur les pleins et les vides) sont autant d'éléments marquant la recherche des pionniers de l'architecture moderne," to conclude that "si le monde minoen possède bien une part de modernité, celle-ci fut accentuée dans les restitutions et reconstitutions d'Arthur Evans. (De Craene 2006–2007, 56)

To test this hypothesis, a set of 10 such common traits are presented below in plain juxtaposition, free from any kind of interaction between the Minoan past and our Modern world. Their communality may be understood as a manifestation of the potentials of the human mind to arrive at similar formulations and conceptions of space in different times, places, and cultural contexts, independently of one another. As such, it does nothing but declare the timeless, transcultural (trans- meaning beyond and above specific paradigms) nature of architecture, where origins and diffusion are of less importance. See, for example, a perfectly Minoan pier-and-window partition being constructed in Tibet only a few years ago (Fig. 195)! This, it should be emphasized, is not cross-cultural comparison. There is no cross-fertilization: the architectural creation of each era abides to its own rich matrix of parameters, cultural and otherwise. Neither do similar traits necessarily result from or point to similar social, political, or other conditions.

The common traits enumerated below are all lucidly expressed in the manifestoes of the Modern Movement, with Le Corbusier's *Vers une architecture* first published in 1923 as the spearhead (Conrads 1970; Le Corbusier 1986). At the same time, they constitute a kind of checklist of the most characteristic formative principles of Minoan architecture, discussed at length in this book. They apply primarily to the best of the Neopalatial period—that is, the architecture of the Second Palaces and the large mansions that were built or reformed during the closing decades of the Bronze Age. This is represented by a considerable number and variety of buildings throughout Crete and is therefore indicative of well-established architectonic thinking and workmanship.

Fig. 195. Pier-and-window partition under construction in Tibet. According to the law, only six beams of this two-story house may derive from a protected forested region. Photo Robb Kendrick, National Geographic Creative.

### *Organic Design, Open Plan, and Asymmetry*

One of the most profound architectonic concepts of the Modern Movement is the open plan that develops outward in harmony with the conditions of its being. It is an organic design concept in which the specifics of the environment and the purpose of the building are the determinant factors (Fig. 196). The result is asymmetrical rather

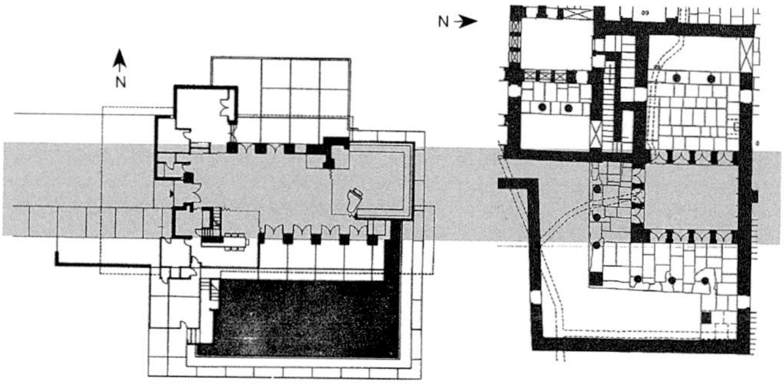


Fig. 196. Frank Lloyd Wright's Dream House for *Life Magazine* in 1938 (left) and the Domestic Quarters at Knossos (right). Left: after Chermayeff and Alexander 1963, 130; right: after Evans 1921–1935, III, plan F.

than symmetrical forms, free in outline and dynamic over stable situations.

These principles of design apply to Minoan architecture as well (see this vol., Ch. 6), and they are best appreciated when compared to different design concepts, such as the court-house and the megaroid-type building, both of which were very common in other places and other times (Fig. 197). Scholars have hinted in this direction, mostly in reference to the Palaces: Graham refers indirectly to organic design (the Minoan Palace "grew, or was planned, from the inside out, rather like a tree" [1972, 27]), while Shaw, Preziosi, Driessen, Schmid, and others have emphasized the role of the Central Court of the Palace as a starting point for its design. The open or free plan, in particular (one of Le Corbusier's "Five Points of a New Architecture," based on a grid of structural vertical supports filled in with non-structural walls that enclose spaces as desired; 1960, 44–45), is well paralleled in the Minoan Polythyron Halls.

### Formal Clarity and Transparency

That the exterior form of a building should express clearly the articulation of its interior spaces is another fundamental principle of the Modern Movement, echoed in the form-follows-function dogma. In the Minoan world, structural elements are visually enhanced and formal clarity is promoted through practices such as the indentation of the facades and the stepped skyline, which describe explicitly the volumnal composition of the building, and the horizontal cornices that project the multistory interior.

### Regulating Lines of Design and the Grid

For Le Corbusier, the revival of Regulating Lines in the 1920s was a major event, even though they were not used for their symbolic order, as in most great architecture of the past, but rather as a tool to control form and "guarantee against willfulness" (Le Corbusier 1986, 67). These lines relate significant parts of the building and are used to rationalize the placement of all features, such as doors and windows. This method of design, according to Le Corbusier, helps formalize the intuitive sense of aesthetics while integrating human proportions (1986, 64). A

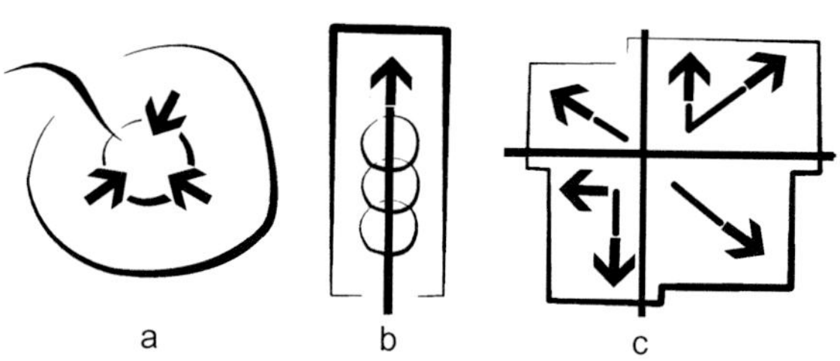


Fig. 197. The court-house (a) and the megaroid-type building (b) follow the same logic of interior subdivisions and fixed outlines. The Minoan house is of the open-plan type (c), which develops from within. Drawing C. Palyvou.

similar use of Regulating Lines is attested in Minoan architectural design, both palatial and domestic.

An absolute version of Regulating Lines, popular among the architects of the Modern Movement, is the grid. Preziosi's totalizing theory of the use of the grid in planning Minoan buildings may be an exaggerated statement, but its essence is true (1983). What is even more impressive, however, is the three-dimensional grid clearly observable in Minoan architecture, regardless of its numerical accuracy. Cases such as Room 5 of the West House at Akrotiri, Thera exude a timeless quality of discipline and order that could well have sprung from the workshops of the Bauhaus and the collaboration of geniuses such as Le Corbusier and Mondrian (Fig. 198).

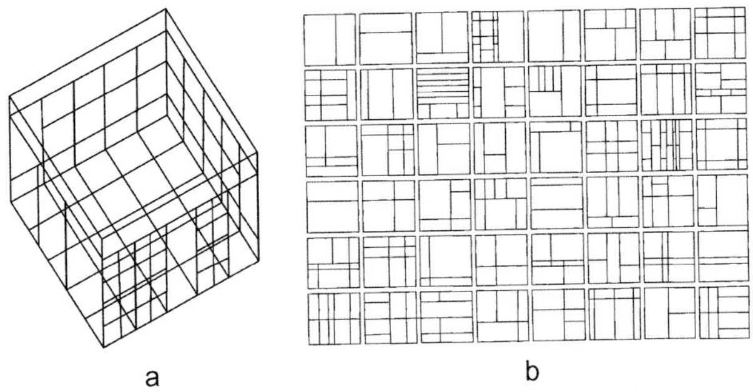


Fig. 198. Regulating Lines and grid patterns: (a) West House, Room 5, Akrotiri, Thera (after Palyvou 2005a, fig. 238:a); (b) *The Panel Exercise*, after Le Corbusier 1954, fig. 39).

## *Functional Flat Roofs and Horizontality*

Flat roofs were understood as extensions of the living space of the house and were designed accordingly (see Le Corbusier's flair for roof-gardens; 1960, 44–45). The Mediterranean climate favors such use of outdoor and semi-outdoor spaces, and in the case of Minoan domestic architecture it becomes even more imperative due to the absence of courtyards. Minoan art provides ample evidence for flat, functional roofs, and so does the archaeological record, especially at Akrotiri (see Fig. 98). A consequence of flat roofs and boxlike volumes is visual emphasis primarily on the horizontal but also the vertical lines; International Style modernism promoted both. This is also the case with Minoan architecture, especially where three-dimensional timber frames are involved.

## *Fluidity of Space and Mutable Interaction between Indoor and Outdoor Domains*

Fluidity implies interwoven spaces in dynamic equilibrium as opposed to static juxtaposition (the megaroid case, for example). Flexibility and adjustability were fundamental elements in the formulation of the Modern Movement, as expressed through Le Corbusier's "Dom-ino" house (Kruft 1994, 397), Mies Van der Rohe's "all-purpose or embracing space" that could adjust to the ever-changing needs of its inhabitants (Roth 2007, 6), and Adolf Loos' "raumplan" (Kruft 1994, 364–365). Frank Lloyd Wright promoted the idea of "flowing spaces," inspired perhaps from his study and admiration of Japanese architecture (Nute 1994; Roth 2007, 6). In Minoan architecture, fluidity of space and mutable interaction between indoor and outdoor domains is provided by the ingenious

Fig. 199. House of the Sakaro Family at the Mitsukaido Climate Museum, Joso, Ibaraki Prefecture, Japan.

combinations of pier-and-opening partitions; their functional logic is, in fact, not very different from the Japanese sliding walls and the works of the modern masters (Fig. 199). Indeed, Minoan architecture could stand well alongside the works of the Bauhaus, under what Giedion has called the "third space conception" where "interior and exterior space continually interpenetrated one another, establishing new interrelationships" (Giedion 1971, 268).

### *The Window and the Supremacy of the Void*

In the equilibrium between mass and voids, the window plays an important role, and its potentials were highly exploited in modern architecture (see, for example, Le Corbusier's horizontal "ribbon window" aiming at enhancing the view; 1960, 44–45). Windows are conspicuous in Minoan architecture too and appear in a variety of forms, sizes, and combinations. The pier-and-window partition in particular could be paralleled to the ribbon window (Fig. 200; cf. Fig. 52). The important role of windows did not escape Evans's notice or Mumford's attention: they both made strong statements in regard to the originality and modernity of windows in Minoan architecture (Evans 1921–1935, I, 303; Mumford 1966, 145).

### *Circulatory Patterns of Multiple Choices*

Circulation and movement are very important in modern architecture. In fact, modernism has often been described in terms of motion. The same is absolutely true for Minoan architecture, and it is no coincidence that the labyrinth, the archetypal symbol of Minoan architecture, is all about the way. The highly sophisticated circulatory system of multiple choices that the Minoans developed is an all-inclusive network consisting of corridors, staircases, and doors, which resembles the "board of a game [that regulates] the relationships between the various players in a ceremony" (Unwin 2009, 230).[8]

Fig. 200 The so-called ribbon windows of the Villa Savoye by Le Corbusier. After A. Fisher (CC BY-ND 2.0).

Le Corbusier's favorite practice of the "architectural promenade" as a visual and conceptual itinerary is also echoed in the Minoan world in the treatment of many access systems and in the way procession is guided through space (1956, 60). The raised causeway in particular is an innovative Minoan feature that defines networks of promenades that spread throughout the town, offering clues of orientation as much as tours for the eye.

## *Innovative Building Techniques, Standardization, and Prefabrication*

Technology was of paramount importance to the formulation of the Modern Movement: steel, glass, and concrete were potent new materials for architecture. For the Minoan world in the Neopalatial period, it was not so much the materials but the techniques that were new and innovative, and most significantly the advanced use of timber in the skeleton structural system allowed for multistory construction and for the pier-and-door partition to come into being.

The skeleton structural system went hand-in-hand with an architectural style of openness and mutability that thrived on volumes and space rather than mass and solids. It is indeed in the treatment of the skeleton type that the Minoans excelled most among the early civilizations of the eastern Mediterranean: what the Egyptians achieved through sheer mass and gravity, the Aegean people conquered through tectonics—that is, through the natural forces of tension, elasticity, and compression, qualities attributed primarily to wood and the skeleton type of construction. As for standardization and prefabrication, the few examples discussed in the relevant chapter give evidence to an incipient understanding of their significance in building construction (see this vol., Ch. 7).

## *Color and Light*

Evans envisaged a colorful Knossos (Fig. 201), a vision his architects materialized for all to see through the reconstitutions of the ruins in concrete painted over with hues of yellow ocher, red, blue, black, and white, colors that came straight from the Minoan artists' palette. The predisposition for color may have been encouraged by the work of the architects of the École des Beaux Arts and the rigorous discussions regarding the polychromy of ancient Greek architecture, both of which were paving the way for the use of color in contemporary architecture (Kruft 1994, 278–279). Even if Evans's colorful Knossos is to some extent imaginary, there is still plenty of hard evidence for the appreciation of color by the Minoan architects, especially through the choice and combination of the bright colors that the natural resources of Crete (and Thera) provided.

Light, too, is clearly a major component of Minoan architecture, manifested by the large number and variety of windows (unprecedented at the time), the light-wells, and the in-between sheltered areas, as well as by the shadows cast by the undulating surfaces. This is the kind of architecture that Le Corbusier defines as "the masterly, correct and magnificent play of masses brought together in light" (1986, 29).

Fig. 201. Color in Minoan art and in Evans's reconstitutions: (a) northern Lustral Basin, Knossos (photo C. Palyvou); (b) Grand Staircase, Knossos (Davaras 1986, fig. 31; © Hellenic Ministry of Culture and Sports–Archaeological Receipts Fund); (c) reconstruction of the Parthenon, Athens (after Fenger 1886, pl. 2); (d) detail of the Three Column Shrine fresco, Knossos (courtesy Archaeological Museum of Herakleion, Hellenic Ministry of Culture and Sports–Archaeological Receipts Fund); (e) detail from the Grandstand miniature fresco, Knossos (after Evans 1921–1935, III, pl. XVI); (f) restored room in West Wing Knossos (Michailidou 1981, fig. 27; courtesy Ekdotike Athenon S.A.).

### *No Two Houses Are Alike . . .*

This recurring comment in regard to Minoan architecture is the epitome of Minoan modernity (Preziosi 1983, 484; Yiannouli 1992, 183). The variety of house plans that adhere to a distinct style is the result of confident professionals trained to work within a framework of norms and building specifications that prescribe the parts explicitly but leave their composition open to choice and will. Embedded in these canons, and in the organic design concept discussed in the first paragraph of this chapter, is variation as a potential. This is an important observation, for such freedom of expression is rare in the history of architecture. The norm has always been to adhere to all-inclusive prescriptive styles.

## The Minoan Modernity: A True Genesis

*To the surprise of everyone, the Minoans had already invented a style that we might comfortably call modern. (Farnoux 1996, 108)*

The Modern Movement of the 20th century A.D. was born out of a complex set of parameters and developments, much of which had to do with the changes in the social conditions of production. These parameters went hand-in-hand with a reaction to the values and restrictions of the past. Its newness, therefore, was the result of a deliberate break with the past: one for one the new ideals were formulated in opposition to the old ones. The Modern Movement, therefore, exists in relation to its past, to what preceded it. In that sense, "Modern architecture was not a rupture with history, but simply a moment in the same continuum, a new episode in the evolution of the zeitgeist" (Eisenman 1984, 163), even if the Modernists did not conceive themselves then as part of this continuum.

The Minoan modernity of the Neopalatial period, on the other hand, is of a different kind. It is not the product of a subversive reevaluation of existing modes of expression; in this it differs from 20th-century A.D. Modernism. It is genuinely new in the sense that it neither follows nor rejects earlier choices; it is not innovative in the sense of challenging a convention, but a true genesis, an original conception of built space that was generated by new demands, social, cultural, and otherwise, and it is supported by unprecedented technical potentials. True genesis in architecture "is to allow architecture to be a cause; in order to be a cause, it must arise from something outside a directed strategy of composition" (Eisenman 1984, 170).

Describing Minoan architecture as a genesis does not mean that it owes nothing to what was already there within the land of Crete or beyond. The great civilizations of the East, in Mesopotamia and Egypt, were quite advanced at the time Crete was formulating her sophisticated architectural style, and there was surely much to gain from their experience. But, diffusion processes are not simple and straightforward; people choose, modify, and adapt, and it is through this intricate process that they eventually define their own character. Quoting Eisenman again, "One example of an artificial origin is a graft, as in the genetic insertion of an alien body into a host to provide a new result. As opposed to a collage or a montage, which lives within a context and alludes to an origin, a graft is an invented site, which does not so much have object characteristics as those of process . . . a site that contains motivation for action—that is the beginning of a process" (Eisenman 1984, 168).

The pier-and-opening partition is a good example of the above. It is an original Minoan invention brought about by the conjunction of technological advances and the requirements of a new lifestyle. Its graft on Mycenaean architecture, however, did not last; it was rejected as an alien body. The Mycenaeans had no use for this architectural element: fluidity of space and flexibility of intercommunication—the two fundamental properties of the pier-and-opening partition—were simply not desirable nor suitable for their way of life. The only two examples at Tiryns and Glas show that, though structurally they copy the Minoan pier-and-door partition, their role was very different: it was not flexibility that they offered, but rather a kind of emphasis on the entrance system of the Megaron (Fig. 202). Indeed, Mycenaean architecture could not have

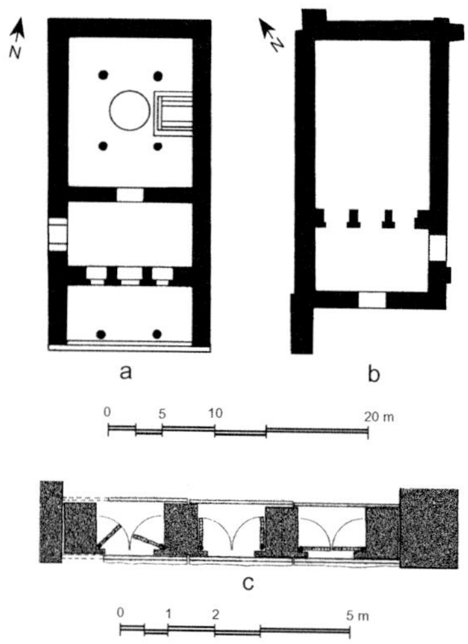


Fig. 202. Pier-and-door partitions at Tiryns (a) and Glas (b, c). After Iakovidis 1989, fig. 22.

been more different from the Minoan with regard to the fundamental principles of space articulation, regardless of the fact that it adopted many of the building techniques of the Minoans (Palyvou 2009a).

Having discussed common traits in asymptote trajectories as a way to approach the "familiar Minoans," a point needs to be made regarding the meaning of the familiar. Though I completely sympathize with Yiannis Hamilakis's plea for de-familiarization when interpreting the archaeological data (Hamilakis 2002, 19), I have to admit that dealing with Minoan architecture, no matter how much I distance myself, it is still the familiar that dominates my thoughts at the end of the day. It is the familiar in the sense of the intimacy of belonging to the same family: the familiar in the formal clarity of volumes by the way they are announced; the familiar in the way light and breeze penetrate in the most unexpected depths of the building; and the familiar in the multiple choices of movement and the fluidity of space. Just as well, the familiar is still there in the order and the soberness of the magazines, in the ingenious standardization and prefabrication of altar bases and exedras, and in the apical conception of three-dimensional timber frames that hold together two and three stories, allowing for an unprecedented freedom of interchange between solids and voids. If tempted to take the familiar into deeper levels of comparison, one might tentatively suggest that the two eras also share the following traits: intensive urbanization, transcultural contacts, promotion of experimentation, innovative technical developments, and proliferation of an elite lifestyle supported by affluent societies.

This sense of familiarity I comprehend best when I turn to Mycenaean architecture. There, the familiar is cognitive rather than sensual; this is an architecture wherein I understand its principles but do not feel at home with. Strong boundaries, axial confrontation, linear directed movement (explicit rather than implicit), and overpowering mass rather than voids are not the kind of spatial experience I can relate to. And here I must explain: the spatial experience I am referring to is that of an architect trained in the 1960s, during the heyday of the Modern Movement. Looking at the plan of a Minoan building, I have no difficulty identifying with its design logic, its underlying Regulating Lines, and its free outlines. As one of the daughters of Daidalos, I feel his shadow lingering over the drawing table of my student years. I mean nothing mystical or simmering by this remark; it is just an observation, a personal reaction to Minoan architecture, if you wish.

I will end with a coup de grace of wild imagination picturing three architects, Daidalos, Arata Isozaki, and Frank Lloyd Wright, sitting somewhere between Knossos, the Katsura Palace, and the Bauhaus, in the company of Modrian, Michelangelo, and Katsushika Hokusai, profoundly discussing the myths and the realities of art and architecture, only to conclude that "the Katsura Palace, the Parthenon, the Capitoline piazza [and Knossos] live in time and place equidistant from us" (Isozaki, quoted in Reynolds 2002, 535).

## Endnotes

1 Today, the protection, conservation, and restoration of monuments constitute a discipline with its own discourse and history of varying theoretical approaches (see Jokilehto 1999).

2 Morris, founder of the Society for the Protection of Ancient Buildings (SPAB) in 1877, condemned restoration work or the reconstruction of a past.

3 Evans has been accused of interfering with the past he first brought to light (Papadopoulos 1997; MacGillivray 2000), even forging it and manipulating generations of scholars to believe what he had construed. Some of these accusations are exceptionally harsh and unjustified (Hitchcock and Koudounaris [2002, 43] even contest his epistemological competence and integrity).

4 Including the socialist notions of the Arts and Crafts Movement professed by Ruskin and Morris (Farnoux 2006, 362). See also Bammer 1990 and Blakolmer 1999.

5 Farnoux 2003, 37, fig. 3; Caloi 2010; Momigliano and Farnoux, eds., 2017.

6 Fyfe compared the Minoan triglyphs and half-rosettes to motives from the architecture of the Classical period (Fyfe 1903, 113, fig. 3).

7 Doll received his architectural training at the University of Cambridge and worked with his father, Charles Fitzroy Doll, an accomplished architect of the time (Kienzle 1998, 221–266). De Jong was an established conservation architect and draughtsman when he started working for Evans. He is largely responsible for the extensive use of concrete at Knossos (Kienzle 1998; Hood 1998; Papadopoulos 2007).

8 Unwin, in his book *Analysing Architecture*, has included the Royal Villa at Knossos among his 10 case studies, along with the works of Ventouri, Eisenman, and Scharoun, pointing out the diachronic aspects of architecture. He adds that, though speculation on "function" is important for archaeologists, for architects of all times there is much to understand in terms of the grammar of building and how it may be used (2009, 228–230).

# References

Abbreviations follow the conventions recommended in the *American Journal of Archaeology.*

Acar, E. 2001. "From Hut to Citadel: The Evolution of Housing and Settlement in Prehistoric Anatolia as Changing Patterns of Space and Time," in *From Huts to Houses: Transformations of Ancient Societies. Proceedings of an International Seminar Organized by the Norwegian and Swedish Institutes in Rome, 21–24 September 1997* (*ActaRom* 4°, 56; *ActaAArtHist* 13), J.R. Brandt and L. Karlsson, eds., Stockholm, pp. 11–21.

Adams, E. 2004. "Power and Ritual in Neopalatial Crete: A Regional Comparison," *WorldArch* 36, pp. 26–42.

Agrest, D., and M. Gandelsonas. 1996. "Semiotics and Architecture: Ideological Consumption or Theoretical Work (1973)," in Nesbitt, ed., 1996, pp. 110–120.

Alberti, L.B. (1755) 1955. *Ten Books on Architecture (De Re Aedificatoria)*, J. Leoni, trans. Reprint, London.

Alexopoulos, G. 2008. "Το ιερό και το μιαρό: Συμβολική και λειτουργική επιβεβαίωση μιας κοινότητας. 'Κέρατα καθοσιώσεως' και αγωγοί λυμάτων στο Ακρωτήρι Θήρας," in *Ακρωτήρι Θήρας: Τριάντα χρόνια έρευνας (1967–1997). Επιστημονική συνάντηση 19–20 Δεκεμβρίου 1997* (*Βιβλιοθήκη της εν Αθήναις Αρχαιολογικής Εταιρείας* 246), Ch. Doumas, ed., Athens, pp. 387–422.

Anderson, S. 1987. "The Fiction of Function," *Assemblage* 2, pp. 18–31.

Andreadaki-Vlazaki, M. 1988. "Υπόγειο άδυτο ή 'δεξαμενή καθαρμών' στα Χανιά," *AAA* 21, pp. 56–76.

Arnheim, R. 1971. *Entropy and Art: An Essay on Disorder and Order*, Berkeley.

———. 1983. "The Symbolism of Centric and Linear Composition," *Perspecta* 20, pp. 139–146.

Arnheim, R., W.M. Zucker, and J. Watterson. 1966. "Inside and Outside in Architecture: A Symposium," *The Journal of Aesthetics and Art Criticism* 25, pp. 3–15.

Athanasiou, K. 2011. *Συγκριτική μελέτη του πολεοδομικού ιστού της προϊστορικής πόλης του Ακρωτηρίου Θήρας, με τη συμβολή σύγχρονων τεχνολογιών*, Ph.D. diss., Aristotle University of Thessaloniki.

Atkinson, J. 2011. "A Small-Scale Reconstruction of the Settlement at Myrtos Phournou Koryphi," in Glowacki and Vogeikoff-Brogan, eds., 2011, pp. 27–38.

Aurenche, O. 1977. *Dictionnaire illustré multilingue de l'architecture du Proche-Orient ancien* (*Collection de la Maison de l'Orient méditerranéen ancien* 3; *Série archéologique* 2), Lyon.

Baines, J., and J. Málek. 1984. *Atlas of Ancient Egypt*, Oxford.

Bammer, A. 1990. "Wien und Kreta: Jugendstil und minoische Kunst," *ÖJh* 60, pp. 130–151.

Barthes, R. 1997a. "Semiology and the Urban," in Leach, ed., 1997, pp. 166–172.

———. 1997b. "The Eiffel Tower," in Leach, ed., 1997, pp. 172–180.

Begg, D.J.I. 1987. "Continuity in the West Wing at Knossos," in Hägg and Marinatos, eds., 1987, pp. 179–184.

———. 2004. "An Interpretation of Mason's Marks at Knossos," in Cadogan, Hatzaki, and Vasilakis, eds., 2004. pp. 219–223.

Betancourt, P.P., V. Karageorghis, R. Laffineur, and W.-D. Niemeier, eds. 1999. *Meletemata. Studies in Aegean Archaeology Presented to Malcolm H. Wiener as He Enters His 65th Year* (*Aegaeum* 20), Liège.

Betancourt, P.P., N. Marinatos, C. Palyvou, S. McPherron, S. German, N. Pouou-Papadimitriou, and T. Albani. 2000. "Το σπήλαιο τῆς Ἀμνισοῦ: Η ἔρευνα τοῦ 1992," *ArchEph* 139 [2001], pp. 179–236.

Betancourt, P.P., M.C. Nelson, and H. Williams, eds. 2007. *Krinoi kai Limenes. Studies in Honor of Joseph and Maria Shaw* (*Prehistory Monographs* 22), Philadelphia.

Bianco, G. 2003. "Two Different Building Modules of Measurement at Kommos—A Neopalatial Module in Building T and a Postpalatial Module in Building P," in *Metron: Measuring the Aegean Bronze Age. Proceedings of the 9th International Conference, New Haven, Yale University, 18–21 April 2002* (*Aegaeum* 24), K.P. Foster and R. Laffineur, eds., Liège, pp. 415–420.

Bintliff, J.L. 1984. "Structuralism and Myth in Minoan Studies," *Antiquity* 58, pp. 33–38.

Blakolmer, F. 1999. "Überlegungen zur Rezeption minoisch-mykenischer Kunst zur Zeit des Jugendstils," in *Akter der Tagung Antike Tradition in der mitteleuropäischen Architektur der zweiten Hälfte des 19. Jahrhunderts. Prag und Litomyŝl, 10.–15. November 1998* (*Studia hercynia* 3), J. Bouzek, ed., Prague, pp. 133–141.

Boullée, É.-L. 1953. *Architecture: Essai sur l'art*, H. Rosenau, trans. London.

Boulotis, Ch. 1985. "Μινωικοί αποθέτες θεμελίωσης," in *Πεπραγμένα του Ε' Διεθνούς Κρητολογικού Συνεδρίου* Α', Hagios Nikolaos, pp. 248–257.

Bradfer-Burdet, I., and M. Pomadère. 2011. "Δβ at Malia: Two Houses or One Large Complex?" in Glowacki and Vogeikoff-Brogan, eds., 2011, pp. 99–108.

Briault, C. 2007. "Making Mountains out of Molehills in the Bronze Age Aegean: Visibility, Ritual Kits, and the Idea of a Peak Sanctuary," *WorldArch* 39, pp. 122–141.

Broadbent, G. 1980. "The Deep Structures of Architecture" in *Signs, Symbols, and Architecture*, G. Broadbent, R. Bunt, and C. Jencks, eds., Chichester, pp. 119–168.

Brogan, T.M., and K.A. Barnard. 2011. "Household Archaeology at Mochlos: Statistical Recipes from the Late Minoan I Kitchen," in Glowacki and Vogeikoff-Brogan, eds., 2011, pp. 185–198.

Brown, A. 1989. *Arthur Evans and the Palace of Minos*, Oxford.

Burns, C.J., and A. Kahn, eds. 2005. *Site Matters: Design Concepts, Histories, and Strategies*, New York.

Cadogan, G. 1977–1978. "Pyrgos, Crete, 1970–7," *AR* 24, pp. 70–84.

———. 1992. "Knossos," in Myers, Myers, and Cadogan, eds., 1992, pp. 124–147.

———. 2004. "'The Minoan Distance': The Impact of Knossos upon the Twentieth Century," in Cadogan, Hatzaki, and Vasilakis, eds., 2004, pp. 537–545.

———. 2006. "Water Management in Minoan Crete, Greece: The Two Cisterns of One Middle Bronze Age Settlement," in *Proceedings of the 1st IWA International Symposium on Water and Wastewater Technologies in Ancient Civlizations: Atlantis Hotel in Iraklio, Greece, 28–30 October, 2006*, A.N. Angelakis and D. Koutsoyiannis, eds., Herakleion, pp. 447–456.

———. 2011. "Myrtos: From Phournou Koryphi to Pyrgos," in Glowacki and Vogeikoff-Brogan, eds., 2011, pp. 39–49.

Cadogan, G., E. Hatzaki, and A. Vasilakis, eds. 2004. *Knossos: Palace, City, State. Proceedings of the Conference in Herakleion Organised by the British School at Athens and the 23rd Ephoreia of Prehistoric and Classical Antiquities of Herakleion, in November 2000, for the Centenary of Sir Arthur Evans's Excavations at Knossos* (*BSA Studies* 12), London.

Caloi, I. 2010. "The Reception of the 'Minoans' in the Modern Art of Mariano Fortuny y Madrazo," *CretAnt* 11, pp. 279–299.

Calvino, I. 1972. *Le città invisibili*, Rome.

Campbell, I. 2004. *Ancient Roman Topography and Architecture* (*Paper Museum of Cassiano dal Pozzo, Antiquities and Architecture* A°, 9), London.

Carroll, L. 1917. *Through the Looking Glass and What Alice Found There*, Chicago.

Castro, R.L. 2007. "Forward," in *Chora* 5: *Intervals in the Philosophy of Architecture*, A. Pérez-Gómez and S. Parcell, eds., Montreal, pp. xi–xiii.

Chatzi-Vallianou, D. 1989. *Φαιστός*, Athens.

Chadwick, J. 1976. *The Mycenaean World*, Cambridge.

Chermayeff, S., and C. Alexander. 1963. *Community and Privacy: Toward a New Architecture of Humanism*, Garden City, NY.

Cherry, J.F. 1983. "Putting the Best Foot Forward," *Antiquity* 57, pp. 52–56.

———. 2003. "Archaeology Beyond the Site: Regional Survey and Its Future," in Papadopoulos and Leventhal, eds., 2003, pp. 137–159.

Chi, L.H. 1996. "On the Use of Architecture: The Destination of Buildings Revisited," in *Chora* 2: *Intervals in the Philosophy of Architecture*, A. Pérez-Gómez and S. Parcell, eds., Montreal, pp. 17–36.

Childe, V.G. 1964. *Piecing Together the Past: The Interpretation of Archaeological Data*, London.

Ching, F.D.K. 1996. *Architecture: Form, Space, and Order*, 2nd ed., New York.

Conrads, U. 1970. *Programs and Manifestoes on 20th-Century Architecture*, trans. M. Bullock, Cambridge, MA.

Cottrell, L. 1961. *The Bull of Minos: The Great Discoveries of Ancient Greece*, London.

Coulton, J.J. 1977. *Ancient Greek Architects at Work: Problems of Structure and Design*, Ithaca.

Croucher, K. 2005. "Queerying Near Eastern Archaeology," *WorldArch* 37, pp. 610–620.

Cummer, W.W. 1980. "Itinerant Aegean Builders," in *TUAS* 5, pp. 3–14.

Cunningham, T. 2007a. "Havoc: The Destruction of Power and the Power of Destruction in Minoan Crete," in *Power and Architecture: Monumental Public Architecture in the Bronze Age Near East and Aegean. Proceedings of the International Conference "Power and Architecture" Organized by the Katholieke Universiteit Leuven, the Université Catholique de Louvain and the Westfälische Wilhelms-Universität Münster on the 21st and 22nd of November 2002* (*Orientalia Lovaniensia Analecta* 156), J. Bretschneider, J. Driessen, and K. Van Lerberghe, eds., Leuven, pp. 23–43.

———. 2007b. "In the Shadows of Kastri: An Examination of Domestic and Civic Space at Palaikastro (Crete)," in *Building Communities: House, Settlement and Society in the Aegean and Beyond* (*BSA Studies* 15), R. Westgate, N. Fisher, and J. Whitley, eds., London, pp. 99–109.

D'Agata, A.L. 1992. "Late Minoan Crete and Horns of Consecration: A Symbol in Action," in *Eικων. Aegean Bronze Age Iconography: Shaping a Methodology. Proceedings of the 4th International Aegean Conference, University of Tasmania, Hobart, Australia, 6–9 April 1992* (*Aegaeum* 8), R. Laffineur and J.L. Crowley, eds., Liège, pp. 247–256.

Darcque, P. 2003. "Από το θησαυρό του Ατρέα στο παλάτι του Μενελάου: Ο τρόμος της ανωνυμίας στη μυκηναϊκή αρχαιολογία," *Αρχαιολογία* 86, pp. 24–30.

Darcque, P., and R. Treuil, eds. 1990. *L'Habitat égéen préhistorique. Actes de la Table Ronde internationale organisée par le Centre national de la recherché scientifique, l'Université de Paris I et l'École française d'Athènes (Athènes, 23–25 juin 1987)* (*BCH Suppl.* 19), Paris.

Davaras, C. 1972. "The Oval House at Chamaizi Reconsidered," *AAA* 5, pp. 283–288.

———. 1986. *Κνωσός και Μουσείο Ηρακλείου: Σύντομος εικονογραφημένος αρχαιολογικός οδηγός*, Athens.

———. 1989a. *Το ανάκτορο των Μαλίων*, Athens.

———. 1989b. *Γουρνιά*, Athens.

———. 1992. "Chamaizi," in Myers, Myers, and Cadogan, eds., 1992, pp. 78–81.

Davis, E.N. 1987. "The Knossos Miniature Frescoes and the Function of the Central Courts," in Hägg and Marinatos, eds., 1987, pp. 157–161.

Dawkins, R.M., C.H. Hawes, and R.C. Bosanquet. 1904–1905. "Excavations at Palaikastro. IV," *BSA* 11, pp. 258–308.

Day, P.M., and M. Relaki. 2002. "Past Factions and Present Fictions: *Palaces* in the Study of Minoan Crete," in Driessen, Schoep, and Laffineur, eds., 2002, pp. 217–234.

Day, P.M., and D.E. Wilson. 2002. "Landscapes of Memory, Craft and Power in Prepalatial and Protopalatial Knossos," in Hamilakis, ed., 2002, pp. 143–166.

De Craene, B. 2006–2007. "Cnossos: Haut lieu de l'architecture moderne?" *Revue des archéologues, historiens d'art et musicologues de l'UCL* 4, pp. 47–59.

de Sola-Morales, I. 1987. "The Origins of Modern Eclecticism: The Theories of Architecture in Early Nineteenth Century France," *Perspecta* 23, pp. 120–133.

Deshayes, J., and A. Dessenne. 1959. *Fouilles exécutées à Mallia: Exploration des maisons et quartiers d'habitation (1948–1954)* (*ÉtCrét* 11), vol. 2, Paris.

Derrida, J. 1997. "Architecture Where the Desire May Live (Interview)," in Leach, ed., 1997, pp. 319–323.

Devolder, M. 2005–2006. "From the Ground Up: Earth in Minoan Construction. The Case of Building 5 at Palaikastro," *Aegean Archaeology* 8, pp. 65–80.

———. 2013. *Construire en Crète minoene: Une approche énergétique de l'architecture néopalatiale* (*Aegaeum* 35), Liège.

Di Tonto, S. 2011. "Evidence for Domestic Activities in the Final Neolithic Period at Phaistos," in Glowacki and Vogeikoff-Brogan, eds., 2011, pp. 15–25.

Doumas, Ch. 1992. *The Wall-Paintings of Thera*, Athens.

Doxtater, D. 2009. "Rethinking the Sacred Landscape: Minoan Palaces in a Georitual Framework of Natural Features on Crete," *Landscape Journal* 28, pp. 1–21.

Driessen, J. 1982. "The Minoan Hall in Domestic Architecture on Crete: To Be in Vogue in Late Minoan IA?" *ActaArchLov* 21, pp. 27–92.

———. 1987. "Earthquake-Resistant Construction and the Wrath of the 'Earth-Shaker'," *JSAH* 46, pp. 171–178.

———. 1989–1990. "The Proliferation of Minoan Palatial Architectural Style: (I) Crete," *ActaArchLov* 28–29, pp. 3–23.

———. 1995a. "'Crisis Architecture'? Some Observations on Architectural Adaptations as Immediate Responses to Changing Socio-Cultural Conditions," *Topoi* 5, pp. 63–88.

———. 1995b. "Some Observations on the Modification of the Access Systems of Minoan Palaces," *Aegean Archaeology* 2 [1997], pp. 67–85.

———. 1999. "'The Archaeology of a Dream': The Reconstruction of Minoan Public Architecture," *JMA* 12, pp. 121–127.

———. 2002. "'The King Must Die': Some Observations on the Use of Minoan Court Compounds," in Driessen, Schoep, and Laffineur, eds., 2002, pp. 1–14.

———. 2007. "IIB or not IIB: On the Beginnings of Minoan Monument Building," in *Power and Architecture: Monumental Public Architecture in the Bronze Age Near East and Aegean. Proceedings of the International Conference "Power and Architecture" Organized by the Katholieke Universiteit Leuven, the Université Catholique de Louvain and the Westfälische Wilhelms-Universität Münster on the 21st and 22nd of November 2002* (*Orientalia Lovaniensia Analecta* 156), J. Bretschneider, J. Driessen, and K. Van Lerberghe, eds., Leuven, pp. 73–92.

———. 2009. "Daidalos' Designs and Ariadne's Threads: Minoan Towns as Places of Interaction," in *Inside the City in the Greek World: Studies of Urbanism from the Bronze Age to the Hellenistic Period*, S. Owen and L. Preston, eds., Oxford, pp. 41–54.

Driessen, J., and C.F. Macdonald. 1997. *The Troubled Island: Minoan Crete before and after the Santorini Eruption* (*Aegaeum* 17), Liège.

Driessen, J., and J. Sakellarakis. 1997. "The Vathypetro-Complex: Some Observations on Its Architectural History and Function," in Hägg, ed., 1997, pp. 63–77.

Driessen, J., and I. Schoep. 1995. "The Architect and the Scribe: Political Implications of Architectural and Administrative Changes on MM II–LM IIIA Crete," in *Politeia: Society and State in the Aegean Bronze Age. Proceedings of the 5th International Aegean Conference, University of Heidelberg, Archäologisches Institut, 10–13 April 1994* (*Aegaeum* 12), R. Laffineur and W.-D. Niemeier, eds., Liège, pp. 649–664.

Driessen, J., I. Schoep, and R. Laffineur, eds. 2002. *Monuments of Minos: Rethinking the Minoan Palaces. Proceedings of the International Workshop*

*"Crete of the Hundred Palaces?" Held at the Université Catholique de Louvain, Louvain-la-Neuve, 14–15 December 2001* (*Aegaeum* 23), Liège.

Eco, U. 1997. "Function and Sign: The Semiotics of Architecture," in Leach, ed., 1997, pp. 182–201.

Edlund, I.E.M. 1987. *The Gods and the Place: Location and Function of Sanctuaries in the Countryside of Etruria and Magna Graecia (700–400 B.C.)* (*ActaRom* 4°, 43), Stockholm.

Eisenman, P. 1984. "The End of the Classical: The End of the Beginning, the End of the End," *Perspecta* 21, pp. 154–173.

Eliade, M. 1961. *The Sacred and the Profane: The Nature of Religion* (*Harvest Book* 144), trans. W.R. Trask, New York.

Elytis, O. 1998. *Eros, Eros, Eros: Selected and Last Poems*, trans. O. Broumas, Port Townsend, WA.

Etienne, R., ed. 1996. *L'espace grec: 150 ans de fouilles de l'École française d'Athènes*, Paris.

Evans, A.J. 1899–1900. "Knossos: Summary Report of the Excavations in 1900. I: The Palace," *BSA* 6, pp. 3–70.

———. 1902–1903. "The Palace of Knossos: Provisional Report of the Year 1903," *BSA* 9, pp. 1–153.

———. 1927. "Work of Reconstitution in the Palace of Knossos," *AntJ* 7, pp. 258–267.

———. 1921–1935. *The Palace of Minos at Knossos* I–IV, London.

Farnoux, A. 1996. *Knossos: Unearthing a Legend*, London.

———. 2003. "Μινωίτες και Μυκηναίοι στον 20° αιώνα," *Αρχαιολογία* 86, pp. 36–41.

———. 2006. "Historie de l'archéologie et épistémologie," in *Mythos: La préhistoire égéenne de XIXe au XXIe siècle après J.-C. Actes de la table ronde internationale d'Athènes (21–23 novembre 2002)* (*BCH Suppl.* 46), P. Darcque, M. Fotiadis, and O. Polychronopoulou, eds., Athens, pp. 357–367.

Febvre, L. 1950. "De l'à peu près à la précision en passant par ouï-dire," *Annales. Historie, Sciences Sociales* 5, pp. 25–31.

Fenger, L. 1886. *Dorische Polychromie: Untersuchungen über die Anwendung der Farbe auf dem dorischen Tempel*, Berlin.

Fessa-Emmanouel, E. ed. 2009. *Αρχιτέκτονες του 20ού αιώνα: Μέλη της εταιρείας*, Athens.

Fisher, K.D. 2009. "Placing Social Interaction: An Integrative Approach to Analyzing Past Built Environments," *JAnthArch* 28, pp. 439–457.

Flannery, K.V. 1993. "Will the Real Model Please Stand Up: Comments on Saidel's 'Round House or Square?'" *JMA* 6, pp. 109–117.

———. 2002. "The Origins of the Village Revisited: From Nuclear to Extended Households," *AmerAnt* 67, pp. 417–434.

Forster, K.W. 1982. "Monument/Memory and the Mortality of Architecture," *Oppositions* 25, pp. 2–19.

Fotou, V. 1997. "Éléments d'analyse architecturale et la question des fonctions de trois bâtiments-'villas': La Royal Villa, le 'Mégaron' de Nirou, et le 'Mégaron' de Sklavokambos," in Hägg, ed., 1997, pp. 33–50.

Fotou, V., and A. Michailidou. 2006. "Problems of Interpretation in the Study of Neopalatial Architecture," in *Πεπραγμένα Θ' Διεθνοῦς Κρητολογικοῦ Συνεδρίου* A' (2), Herakleion, pp. 85–103.

Foxhall, L. 2000. "The Running Sands of Time: Archaeology and the Short-Term," *WorldArch* 31, pp. 484–498.

Frampton, K. 1996. "Rappel à l'ordre: The Case for the Tectonic (1990)," in Nesbitt, ed., 1996, pp. 516–528.

Frankfort, H. 1950. "Town Planning in Ancient Mesopotamia," *The Town Planning Review* 21, pp. 98–115.

———. 1970. *The Art and Architecture of the Ancient Orient* (*Pelican History of Art* 7), Harmondsworth.

Frederick, M. 2007. *101 Things I Learned in Architecture School*, Cambridge, MA.

Frontisi-Ducroux, F. 1975. *Dédale: Mythologie de l'artisan en Grèce ancienne*, Paris.

Fyfe, Th., 1903. "Painted Plaster Decoration at Knossos, with Special Reference to the Architectural Schemes," *Journal of the Royal Institute of British Architects* 10, pp. 107–131.

———. 1914. "Some Aspects of Greek Architecture," *Journal of the Royal Institute of British Architects* 21, pp. 489–496.

Giedion, S. 1967. *Space, Time and Architecture: The Growth of a New Tradition*, 5th ed., Cambridge.

———. 1971. *Architecture and the Phenomena of Transition: The Three Space Conceptions in Architecture*, Cambridge, MA.

Gkiasta, M. 2008. *The Historiography of Landscape Research on Crete* (*Archaeological Studies Leiden University* 16), Amsterdam.

Glowacki, K.T., and N. Vogeikoff-Brogan, eds. 2011. *Στεγα: The Archaeology of Houses and Households in Ancient Crete* (*Hesperia Suppl.* 44), Princeton.

Goodison, L. 2004. "From Tholos Tomb to Throne Room: Some Considerations of Dawn Light and Directionality in Minoan Buildings," in Cadogan, Hatzaki, and Vasilakis, eds., 2004, pp. 339–350.

Graham, J.W. 1959. "The Residential Quarter of the Minoan Palace," *AJA* 63, pp. 47–52.

———. 1960a. "The Minoan Unit of Length and Minoan Palace Planning," *AJA* 64, pp. 335–341.

———. 1960b. "Windows, Recesses, and the Piano Nobile in the Minoan Palaces," *AJA* 64, pp. 329–333.

———. 1968. "Further Notes on the Minoan Foot," in *Πεπραγμένα του Β' Διεθνοῦς Κρητολογικοῦ Συνεδρίου* A', Chania, pp. 157–165.

———. 1970. "Egyptian Features at Phaistos," *AJA* 74, pp. 231–239.

———. 1972. *The Palaces of Crete*, 2nd ed., Princeton.

———. 1979. "Further Notes on Minoan Palace Architecture: 1. West Magazines and Upper Halls at Knossos and Mallia: 2. Access to, and Use of, Minoan Palace Roofs," *AJA* 83, pp. 49–69.

Hägg, R. 1987. "On the Reconstruction of the West Facade of the Palace at Knossos," in Hägg and Marinatos, eds., 1987, pp. 129–134.

———. 1990. "The Cretan Hut Models," *OpAth* 18, pp. 95–107.

Hägg, R., ed. 1997. *The Function of the "Minoan Villa." Proceedings of the Eighth International Symposium at the Swedish Institute at Athens, 6–8 June 1992* (*ActaAth* 4°, 46), Stockholm.

Hägg, R., and N. Marinatos, eds. 1987. *The Function of the Minoan Palaces. Proceedings of the Fourth International Symposium at the Swedish Institute in Athens, 10–16 June, 1984* (*ActaAth* 4°, 35), Stockholm.

Hallager, E. 1985. *The Master Impression: A Clay Sealing from the Greek-Swedish Excavations at Kastelli, Khania* (*SIMA* 69), Göteborg.

———. 1990. "Upper Floors in LM I Houses," in Darcque and Treuil, eds., 1990, pp. 281–292.

Hamilakis, Y. 2002. "What Future for the 'Minoan' Past? Re-thinking Minoan Archaeology," in Hamilakis, ed., 2002, pp. 2–29.

Hamilakis, Y., ed. 2002. *Labyrinth Revisited: Rethinking 'Minoan' Archaeology*, Oxford.

Harries, K. 1985. "Modernity's Bad Conscience," *AA Files* 10, pp. 53–60.

———. 1993. "Thoughts on a Non-Arbitrary Architecture," in Seamon, ed., 1993, pp. 41–59.

———. 2000. *The Ethical Function of Architecture*, Cambridge, MA.

Hayden, B.J. 1982. "The Derivation and Architectural Context of Cretan Bronze Age Stoas," *ArchNews* 11, pp. 1–7.

Hawes, C.H., and H.B. Hawes. 1909. *Crete, the Forerunner of Greece*, London.

Heidegger, M. 1967. "Preface," in *Heidegger: Through Phenomenology to Thought* (*Phaenomenoloica* 13), 2nd ed., The Hague.

———. 1997a. "The Origin of the Work of Art (Extracts)," in Leach, ed., 1997, pp. 119–121.

———. 1997b. ". . . Poetically Man Dwells . . .," in Leach, ed., 1997, pp. 109–119.

Hellmann, M.-Ch. 2002. *L'architecture grecque: 1. Les principes de la construction*, Paris.

Herva, V.-P. 2006. "Flower Lovers, after All? Rethinking Religion and Human-Environment Relations in Minoan Crete," *WorldArch* 38, pp. 586–598.

Hiller, S. 1980. "The South Propylaeum of the Palace of Knossos," in *Πεπραγμένα του Δ' Διεθνούς Κρητολογικού Συνεδρίου* A' (1), Herakleion, pp. 216–232.

Hillier, B. 1996. *Space is the Machine: A Configurational Theory of Architecture*, Cambridge.

Hillier, B., and J. Hanson. 1984. *The Social Logic of Space*, Cambridge.

Hillier, B., A. Leamann, P. Stansall, and M. Bedford. 1978. "Reply to Professor Leach," in *Social Organisation and Settlement: Contributions from Anthropology, Archaeology and Geography* (*BAR-IS* 47), D. Green, C. Haselgrove, and M. Spriggs, eds., Oxford, pp. 403–406.

Hitchcock, L.A. 1997. "The Best Laid Plans Go Astray: Modular (Ir)regularities in the 'Residential Quarters' at Phaistos," in *Texnh: Craftsmen, Craftswomen and Craftsmanship in the Aegean Bronze Age. Proceedings of the 6th International Aegean Conference, Philadelphia, Temple University, 18–21 April 1996* (*Aegaeum* 16), R. Laffineur and P.P. Betancourt, eds., Liège, pp. 243–250.

Hitchcock, L.A., and D. Preziosi. 1997. "The Knossos Unexplored Mansion and the 'Villa-Annex Complex'," in Hägg, ed., 1997, pp. 51–62.

Hitchcock, L.A., and P. Koudounaris. 2002. "Virtual Discourse: Arthur Evans and the Reconstructions of the Minoan Palace at Knossos," in Hamilakis, ed., 2002, pp. 40–58.

Hoepfner, W. 2009. "Urban Planning in the Classical Period," in *A History of the Greek City* (*BAR-IS* 2050), A. Lagopoulos, ed., Oxford, pp. 169–183.

Hollein, H., and W. Pichler. 1963. "Forms and Designs," K. Rheinfurt, trans., *Arts and Architecture* 1963, p. 14.

Hood, S. 1971. *The Minoans: Crete in the Bronze Age*, London.

———. 1995. "Collingwood on the Minoan Civilisation of Crete," in *Collingwood Studies:* Vol. 2. *Perspectives*, D. Boucher and B. Haddock, eds., Swansea, pp. 175–179.

Hood, S., and W. Taylor. 1981. *The Bronze Age Palace at Knossos: Plan and Sections* (*BSA Suppl.* 13), London.

Hood, R. 1998. *Faces of Archaeology in Greece: Caricatures by Piet de Jong*, Oxford.

Iakovidis, Sp. 1989. *Γλας* I: *Η ανασκαφή 1955–1961* (*Βιβλιοθήκη της εν Αθήναις Αρχαιολογικής Εταιρείας* 107), Athens.

———. 1990. "Mycenean Roofs: Form and Construction," in Darcque and Treuil, eds., 1990, pp. 147–160.

Jokilehto, J. 1999. *A History of Architectural Conservation*, Oxford.

Judge, J. 1978. "Greece's Brilliant Bronze Age," *National Geographic* 153 (2), 142–185.

Kafka, F. 1983. *The Penguin Complete Short Stories of Franz Kafka*, N.N. Glatzer, ed., London.

Karadimas, N., and N. Momigliano. 2004. "On the Term 'Minoan' before Evans's Work in Crete (1894)," *SMEA* 46, pp. 243–258.

Karvouni, M. 1999. "Demas: The Human Body as a Tectonic Construct," in *Chora* 3: *Intervals in the Philosophy of Architecture,* A. Pérez-Gómez and S. Parcell, eds., Montreal, pp. 103–124.

Kern, H., 1982. "Image of the World and Sacred Realm: Labyrinth-Cities–City-Labyrinths," *Daidalos* 3, pp. 10–24.

Kienzle, P. 1998. *Conservation and Reconstruction at the Palace of Minos at Knossos*, Ph.D. diss., University of York.

Klynne, A. 1998. "Reconstructions of Knossos: Artists' Impressions, Archaeological Evidence and Wishful Thinking," *JMA* 11, pp. 206–229.

Konstantinidis, A. 1975. *Στοιχεία αυτογνωσίας: Για μια αληθινή αρχιτεκτονική*, Athens.

Kopaka, C. 1990. "Des pièces de repos dans l'habitat minoen du IIe millénaire avant J.-C.?" in Darcque and Treuil, eds., 1990, pp. 217–230.

Kostof, S. 1985. *A History of Architecture: Settings and Rituals*, New York.

Kotsiopoulos, A.M. 1985. *Κριτική της αρχιτεκτονικής θεωρίας*, Thessaloniki.

Koyré, A. 1948. "Du monde de l''à-peu-près' à l'univers de la précision," *Critique* 28, pp. 806–823.

Kruft, H.-W. 1994. *A History of Architectural Theory: From Vitruvius to the Present*, trans. R. Taylor, E. Callander, and A. Wood, London.

Krüger, M. 1982. "In the Labyrinth," *Daidalos* 15, p. 8.

Lao Tzu, 2002. *Tao Te Ching: The Way of Virtue*, trans. P.M. Byrne, Garden City Park, NY.

Laroche, D. 1996. "Σε αναζήτηση της προκλασικής αρχαιότητας," *Θέματα χώρου και τεχνών* 27, pp. 194–199.

La Rosa. 1992a. "Kamilari," in Myers, Myers, and Cadogan, eds., 1992, pp. 112–115.

———. 1992b. "Phaistos," in Myers, Myers, and Cadogan, eds., 1992, pp. 232–243.

———. 1997. "La 'Villa Royale' de Haghia Triada," in Hägg, ed., 1997, pp. 79–89.

Latour, B. 1993. *We Have Never Been Modern*, trans. C. Porter, Cambridge, MA.

Laugier, M.-A. 1775. *Essai sur l'architecture*, Paris.

Lavvas, G., and D. Philippidis, eds. 1983–1991. *Ελληνική παραδοσιακή αρχιτεκτονική* I–VIII, Athens.

Lawrence, D.H. 1964. "Middle of the World," in *The Complete Poems of D.H. Lawrence*, V. Pinto and W. Roberts, eds., New York, p. 688.

Leach, E. 1978. "Does Space Syntax Really 'Constitute the Social'?" in *Social Organisation and Settlement: Contributions from Anthropology,*

*Archaeology and Geography* (*BAR-IS* 47), D. Green, C. Haselgrove, and M. Spriggs, eds., Oxford, pp. 385–401.

Leach, N. 1997a. "Introduction," in Leach, ed., 1997, pp. xiii–xxi.

———. 1997b. "Phenomenology," in Leach, ed., 1997, pp. 83–84.

Leach, N., ed. 1997. *Rethinking Architecture: A Reader in Cultural Theory*, London.

Lebessi, A. 1976. "Ὁ οἰκισκος τῶν Ἀχαρνῶν," *ArchEph* 115 [1977], pp. 12–43.

Lebessi, A., and P. Muhly. 1990. "Aspects of Minoan Cult: Sacred Enclosures. The Evidence from the Syme Sanctuary (Crete)," *AA* 1990, pp. 315–336.

Le Corbusier. 1954. *The Modulor: A Harmonious Measure to the Human Scale Universally Applicable to Architecture and Mechanics*, trans. P. de Francia and A. Bostock, 2nd ed., London.

———. 1956. *Le Corbusier et Pierre Jeanneret: Œuvre complète de 1910–1929*, sixth ed., Zurich.

———. 1960. *Le Corbusier 1910–60*, Zurich.

———. 1986. *Towards a New Architecture*, trans. J. Rodker, reprint, New York.

Lefas, P. 1997. *Μετάφραση και σχολιασμός του Βιτρουβίου Περί Αρχιτεκτονικής Α′* (*Βιβλία* I–V), Athens.

Lenuzza, V. 2011. "'The Whole is a Freak': A Reassessment of the Spatial Organization of the Oval House at Chamaizi, Siteia," in Glowacki and Vogeikoff-Brogan, eds., 2011, pp. 59–70.

Letesson, Q. 2009. *Du phénotype au génotype: Analyse de la syntaxe spatiale en architecture minoenne (MM IIIB–MR IB)* (*Aegis* 2), Louvain-la-Neuve.

———. 2010. "From Building to Architecture: The Rise of Configurational Thinking in Bronze Age Crete," Paper Presented at the 16th Annual Conference of the European Association of Archaeologists, 1–5 September 2010, The Hague.

———. 2013. "Minoan Halls: A Syntactical Genealogy," *AJA* 117, pp. 303–351.

———. 2015. "Fire and the Holes: An Investigation of Low-level Meanings in the Minoan Built Environment," *Journal of Archaeological Method and Theory* 22, pp. 713–750.

Letesson, Q., and K. Vansteenhuyse. 2006. "Towards an Archaeology of Perception: 'Looking' at the Minoan Palaces," *JMA* 19, pp. 91–119.

Levy, M., and M. Salvadori. 1994. *Why Buildings Fall Down: How Structures Fail*, New York.

Lloyd, J.F. 2011. "The South House at Knossos: More than a House?" in Glowacki and Vogeikoff-Brogan, eds., 2011, pp. 163–175.

Loos, A. 1998. *Ornament and Crime: Selected Essays*, trans. M. Mitchell, Riverside, CA.

———. 2007. *On Architecture*, trans. M. Mitchell, Riverside, CA.

Lowenthal, D. 1985. *The Past is a Foreign Country*, Cambridge.

Macdonald, C.F. 2002. "The Neopalatial Palaces of Knossos," in Driessen, Schoep, and Laffineur, eds. 2002, pp. 35–54.

———. 2013. "Between Protopalatial Houses and Neopalatial Mansions: An '*Intermezzo*' Southwest of the Palace at Knossos," in *Intermezzo: Intermediacy and Regeneration in Middle Minoan III Palatial Crete* (*BSA Studies* 21), C.F. Macdonald and C. Knappett, eds., pp. 21–30.

MacGillivray, J.A. 2000. *Minotaur: Sir Arthur Evans and the Archaeology of the Minoan Myth*, New York.

———. 2004. "The Astral Labyrinth at Knossos," in Cadogan, Hatzaki, and Vasilakis, eds., 2004, pp. 329–338.

Mackenzie, D. 1907–1908. "Cretan Palaces and the Aegean Civilization IV," *BSA* 14, pp. 343–422.

Manning, S.W. 2014. *A Test of Time and A Test of Time Revisited: The Volcano of Thera and the Chronology and History of the Aegean and East Mediterranean in the Mid-second Millennium* B.C., Oxford.

Mantzourani, E., and G. Vavouranakis. 2005. "Achladia and Epano Zakros: A Re-examination of the Architecture and Topography of Two Possible Minoan Villas in East Crete," *OpAth* 30, 99–125.

Mantzourani, E., G. Vavouranakis, and Ch. Kanellopoulos. 2005. "The Klimataria-Manares Building Reconsidered," *AJA* 109, pp. 743–776.

Marinatos, N. 1987. "Public Festivals in the West Courts of the Palaces," in Hägg and Marinatos, eds., 1987, pp. 135–143.

———. 2010. *Minoan Kingship and the Solar Goddess: A Near Eastern Koine*, Urbana, IL.

Marinatos, N., and R. Hägg. 1986. "On the Ceremonial Function of the Minoan Polythyron," *OpAth* 16, pp. 57–73.

Marinatos, S. 1976. *Excavations at Thera* VII: *1973 Season*, Athens.

Marthari, M. 1990. "Σκάρκος: Ενας πρωτοκυκλαδικός οικισμός στην Ίο," in *Διαλέξεις 1986–1989 (Ίδρυμα Νικολάου Π. Γουλανδρή, Μουσείο Κυκλαδικής Τέχνης)*, R. Misdrachi-Kanon, ed., Athens, pp. 97–100.

———. 1997. "Από τον Σκάρκο στην Πολιόχνη: Παρατηρήσεις για την κοινωνικο-οικονομική ανάπτυξη των οικισμών της Πρώιμης Εποχής του Χαλκού στις Κυκλάδες και τα νησιά του βορειοανατολικού Αιγαίου," in *Η Πολιόχνη και η πρώιμη εποχή του χαλκού στο Βόρειο Αιγαίο. Διεθνές συνέδριο, Αθήνα, 22–25 Απριλίου 1996*, Ch. Doumas, and V. La Rosa, eds., Athens, pp. 362–382.

Martienssen, R.D. 1964. *The Idea of Space in Greek Architecture, with Special Reference to the Doric Temple and Its Settings*, Johannesburg.

McEnroe, J.C. 1982. "A Typology of Minoan Neopalatial Houses," *AJA* 86, pp. 3–19.

———. 1984. Review of *Minoan Architectural Design: Formation and Signification*, by D. Preziosi, *AJA* 88, pp. 600–601.

———. 2007. "Minoan Archaeology and the Quest for the Primitive Hut," in Betancourt, Nelson, and Williams, eds., 2007, pp. 1–8.

———. 2010. *Architecture of Minoan Crete: Constructing Identity in the Aegean Bronze Age*, Austin.

McNeal, R.A. 1975. "Helladic Prehistory through the Looking-Glass," *Historia* 24, pp. 385–401.

Mersereau, R. 1993. "Cretan Cylindrical Models," *AJA* 97, pp. 1–47.

Michailidou, A. 1981. *Knossos: A Complete Guide to the Palace of Minos*, Athens.

———. 1987. "Το δωμάτιο με τον κίονα στο Μινωϊκό σπίτι," in *ΑΜΗΤΟΣ: Τιμητικός τόμος για τον καθηγητή Μανόλη Ανδρόνικο*, Thessaloniki, pp. 509–526.

Michailidou, A., ed. 2001. *Manufacture and Measurement: Counting, Measuring and Recording Craft Items in Early Aegean Societies* (*Meletemata* 33), Athens.

Michelis, P.A. 1964. "Some Reflections on Architecture," *The Journal of Aesthetics and Art Criticism* 23, pp. 139–144.

Miller, N. 1982. "Editorial," *Daidalos* 3, p. 9.

Moholy-Nagy, S., D.F. Anstis, W.L. Creese, L.K. Eaton, A. Jackson, S. Kostof, F.D. Nichols, E.F. Sekler, and M. Whiffen. 1967. "Architectural History and the Student Architect: A Symposium," *JSAH* 26, pp. 178–199.

Momigliano, N. 2017. "From Russia with Love: Minoan Crete and the Russian Silver Age," in Momigliano and Farnoux, eds., 2017, pp. 84–110.

Momigliano, N., and A. Farnoux, eds. 2017. *Cretomania: Modern Desires for the Minoan Past* (*British School at Athens—Modern Greek and Byzantine Studies* 3), London.

Morgan, L. 2005. "New Discoveries and New Ideas in Aegean Wall Painting," in Morgan, ed., 2005, pp. 21–44.

Morgan, L., ed., 2005. *Aegean Wall Painting: A Tribute to Mark Cameron* (*BSA Studies* 13), London.

Moore, S.A. 2001. "Technology, Place, and the Nonmodern Thesis," *Journal of Architectural Education* 54, pp. 130–139.

Morris, S.P. 1992. *Daidalos and the Origins of Greek Art*, Princeton.

Mugerauer, R. 1993. "Toward an Architectural Vocabulary: The Porch as a Between," in Seamon, ed., 1993, pp. 103–128.

Muhly, J.D., and E. Sikla, eds. 2000. *Crete 2000: A Centennial Celebration of American Archaeological Work on Crete (1900–2000)*, Athens.

Muhly, P.M. 1984. "Minoan Hearths," *AJA* 88, pp. 107–122.

Mumford, L. 1938. *The Culture of Cities*, New York.

———. 1966. *The City in History: Its Origins, Its Transformations, and Its Prospects*, New York.

Müller, K. 1930. *Tiryns III: Die Architektur der Burg und des Palastes*, Augsburg.

Myers, J.W., E.E. Myers, and G. Cadogan. 1992. *The Aerial Atlas of Ancient Crete*, London.

Mylonas, G.E. 1983. *Πολύχρυσοι Μυκήναι*, Athens.

Nelson, M.C. 2007. "Minoan and Mycenaean Stone Revetment," in Betancourt, Nelson, and Williams, eds., 2007, pp. 17–22.

Nesbitt, K. 1996. "Introduction," in Nesbitt, ed., 1996, pp. 16–70.

Nesbitt, K., ed. 1996. *Theorizing a New Agenda for Architecture: An Anthology of Architectural Theory, 1965–1995*, New York.

Neufert, E. 2000. *Architects' Data*, 3rd ed., London.

Niemeier, W.-D. 1987. "On the Function of the 'Throne Room' in the Palace at Knossos," in Hägg and Marinatos, eds., 1987, pp. 163–168.

Nikolakopoulou, E. 2003. *"Ακρωτήρι Θήρας: Η πόλη σε κατάσταση έκτακτης ανάγκης," in Αργοναύτης: Τιμητικός Τόμος για τον καθηγητή Χρίστο Γ. Ντούμα από τους μαθητές του στο Πανεπιστήμιο Αθηνών (1980–2000)*, A. Vlachopoulos and K. Birtacha, eds., Athens, pp. 554–573.

Norberg-Schulz, C. 1980. *Genius Loci: Towards a Phenomenology of Architecture*, New York.

———1996. "The Phenomenon of Place (1976)," in Nesbitt, ed., 1996, pp. 412–428.

———. 1997. *Intentions in Architecture*, 10th printing, Cambridge, MA.

Nute, K. 1994. "Frank Lloyd Wright and Japanese Architecture: A Study in Inspiration," *Journal of Design History* 7, pp. 169–185.

Orlandos, A.K., and J.N. Travlos. 1986. *Λεξικόν αρχαίων αρχιτεκτονικών όρων (Βιβλιοθήκη της εν Αθήναις Αρχαιολογικής Εταιρείας* 94), Athens.

Osman, K.M., and M. Suliman. 1994. "The Space Syntax Methodology: Fits and Misfits," *Architecture and Behaviour* 10, pp. 189–204.

Paliou, E. 2011. "The Communicative Potential of Theran Murals in Late Bronze Age Akrotiri: Applying Viewshed Analysis in 3D Townscapes," *OJA* 30, pp. 247–272.

Paliou, E., D. Wheatley, and G. Earl. 2011. "Three-Dimensional Visibility Analysis of Architectural Spaces: Iconography and Visibility of the Wall Paintings of Xeste 3 (Late Bronze Age Akrotiri)," *JAS* 38, pp. 375–386.

Pallasmaa, J. 1996. "The Geometry of Feeling: A Look at the Phenomenology of Architecture," in Nesbitt, ed., 1996, pp. 447–453.

———. 2005a. *Encounters 1: Architectural Essays*, P. McKeith, ed., Helsinki.

———. 2005b. *The Eyes of the Skin: Architecture and the Senses*, Chichester.

Palyvou, C. 1984. "The Destruction of the Town at Akrotiri, Thera at the Beginning of LC I: Rebuilding Activities," in *The Prehistoric Cyclades.*

*Contributions to a Workshop on Cycladic Chronology*, J.A. MacGillivray and R.L.N. Barber, eds., Edinburgh, pp. 134–147.

———. 1986. "Notes on the Town Plan of Late Cycladic Akrotiri, Thera," *BSA* 81, pp. 179–194.

———. 1987. "Circulatory Patterns in Minoan Architecture," in Hägg and Marinatos, eds., 1987, pp. 195–203.

———. 1990. "Architectural Design at Late Cycladic Akrotiri," in *Thera and the Aegean World III. Proceedings of the Third International Congress, Santorini, Grece, 3–9 September 1989*, Vol. 1: *Archaeology*, D.A. Hardy, C.G. Doumas, J.A. Sakellarakis, and P.M. Warren, eds., London, pp. 44–56.

———. 1997. "Αποχετευτικά δίκτυα και εγκαταστάσεις υγιεινής της 2ης χιλιετίας π.Χ. στο Αιγαίο," in *Αρχαία Ελληνική Τεχνολογία: 1° Διεθνές Συνέδριο*, Thessaloniki, pp. 381–389.

———. 1999a. *Ακρωτήρι Θήρας: Η οικοδομική τέχνη (Βιβλιοθήκη της εν Αθήναις Αρχαιολογικής Εταιρείας* 183), Athens.

———.1999b. "Theran Architecture through the Minoan Looking Glass," in Betancourt et al., eds., 1999, pp. 609–615.

———. 2000. "Concepts of Space in Aegean Bronze Age Art and Architecture," in *The Wall Paintings of Thera. Proceedings of the First International Symposium, Petros M. Nomikos Conference Centre, Thera, Hellas, 30 August–4 September 1997*, S. Sherratt, ed., Athens, pp. 413–436.

———. 2002. "Central Courts: The Supremacy of the Void," in Driessen, Schoep, and Laffineur, eds. 2002, pp. 167–177.

———. 2003. "Architecture and Archaeology: The Minoan Palaces in the Twenty-first Century," in Papadopoulos and Leventhal, eds., 2003, pp. 205–233.

———. 2004. "Outdoor Space in Minoan Architecture: 'Community and Privacy,'" in Cadogan, Hatzaki, and Vasilakis, eds., 2004, pp. 207–217.

———. 2005a. *Akrotiri Thera: An Architecture of Affluence 3,500 Years Old* (*Prehistory Monographs* 15), Philadelphia.

———. 2005b. "Architecture in Aegean Bronze Age Art: Facades with No Interiors," in Morgan, ed., 2005, London, pp. 185–197.

———. 2006. "Οικοδομικές παρατηρήσεις μέσα από την τέχνη της Εποχής του Χαλκού: Τυποποιημένες, λυόμενες κατασκευές," in *Αρχαία Ελληνική Τεχνολογία: 2° Διεθνές Συνέδριο*, Athens, pp. 417–424.

———. 2007. "The Cosmopolitan Harbor Town of Ugarit and the 'Aegean' Aspects of Its Domestic Architecture," in Betancourt, Nelson, and Williams, eds., 2007, pp. 31–47.

———. 2009a. "The Comparative Analysis of Spatial Organization as a Tool for Understanding Aegean Bronze Age Architecture: Minoan and Mycenaean," in *Bronze Age Architectural Traditions in the Eastern Mediterranean: Diffusion and Diversity. Proceedings of the Symposium, 07.–08. 05. 2008 in Munich*, Weilheim, pp. 115–124.

———. 2009b. "Prehistoric Dome Architecture in the Aegean," in *Earthen Domes et Habitats: Villages of Northern Syria. An Architectural Tradition Shared by East and West*, S. Mecca and L. Dipasquale, eds., Pisa, pp. 39–49.

———. 2009c. "Πρόπυλα της Εποχής του Χαλκού στο Αιγαίο," in *ΔΩΡΟΝ: Τιμητικός Τόμος για τον καθηγητή Σπύρο Ιακωβίδη* (*Ακαδημία Αθηνών, Κέντρον Ερεύνης Αρχαιότητος, Σεριά Μονογραφιών* 6), D. Daneilidou, ed., Athens, pp. 537–563.

———. 2012. "Wall Painting and Architecture in the Aegean Bronze Age: Connections between Illusionary Space and Built Realities," in *Minoan Realities: Approaches to Images, Architecture, and Society in the Aegean Bronze Age* (*Aegis* 5), D. Panagiotopoulos and U. Günkel-Maschek, eds., Louvain-la-Neuve, pp. 9–26.

Papadopoulos, J.K. 1997. "Knossos," in *The Conservation of Archaeological Sites in the Mediterranean Region. Proceedings of an International Conference Organized by the Getty Conservation Institute and the J. Paul Getty Museum, 6–12 May 1995*, M. de la Torre, ed., Los Angeles, pp. 93–125.

———. 2005. "Inventing the Minoans: Archaeology, Modernity and the Quest for European Identity," *JMA* 18, pp. 87–149.

———. 2007. *The Art of Antiquity: Piet de Jong and the Athenian Agora*, Athens.

Papadopoulos, J.K., and R.M. Leventhal, eds., 2003. *Theory and Practice in Mediterranean Archaeology: Old World and New World Perspectives* (*Cotsen Advanced Seminars* 1), Los Angeles.

Papahatzi, N. 1999. *Παυσανίου Ελλάδος Περιήγησις* 2–3, Athens.

Pérez-Gómez, A. 1985. "The Myth of Daedalus," *AA Files* 10, pp. 49–52.

Petrakis, V.P. 2006. "Late Minoan III and Early Iron Age Cretan Cylindrical Terracotta Models: A Reconsideration," *BSA* 101, pp. 183–216.

Pevsner, N. 1948. *An Outline of European Architecture*, New York.

Platon, L. 1990. "L'urbanisme minoen: B. Espace intérieur et espace extérieur dans la ville minoenne," in Darcque and Treuil, eds., 1990, pp. 381–393.

———. 1997. "The Minoan 'Villa' in Eastern Crete: Riza, Akhladia, and Prophetes Elias, Praissos. Two Different Specimens of One Category?" in Hägg, ed., 1997, pp. 187–202.

———. 2010. "On the Dating and Character of the 'Zakros Pits Deposit'," in *Cretan Offerings. Studies in Honour of Peter Warren* (*BSA Studies* 18), O. Krzyszkowska, ed., London, pp. 243–257.

Platon, N. 1968. "Τα προβλήματα χρονολογήσεως των μινωικών ανακτόρων," *ArchEph* 107 [1969], pp. 1–58.

———. 1974. *Ζάκρος: Τὸ νέον μινωϊκόν ανάκτορον* (*Αρχαίοι τόποι και Μουσεία της Ελλάδος* 5), Athens.

Poursat, J.-C. 1996. *Fouilles exécutées à Malia: Le quartier Mu* III. *Artisans Minoens: Les maisons-ateliers du quartier Mu* (*ÉtCrét* 32), Paris.

Prelovšek, D. 1992. *Jože Plečnik 1872–1957: Architectura Perennis*, trans. D. Apovnik, Salzburg.

Preziosi, D. 1983. *Minoan Architectural Design: Formation and Signification* (*Approaches to Semiotics* 63), Berlin.

———. 2002. "Archaeology as Museology: Re-thinking the Minoan Past," in Hamilakis, ed., 2002, pp. 30–39.

Quatremère de Quincy, A.-C. 1832. *Dictionnaire historique d'architecture*, Paris.

Rackham, O., and J.A. Moody. 1992. "Terraces," in *Agriculture in Ancient Greece. Proceedings of the Seventh International Symposium at the Swedish Institute at Athens, 16–17 May, 1990* (*ActaAth* 4°, 42), B. Wells, ed., Stockholm, pp. 123–130.

———. 1996. *The Making of the Cretan Landscape*, Manchester.

Rapoport, A. 1969. *House Form and Culture*, Englewood Cliffs, NJ.

Rehak, P., and J.G. Younger. 1998. "Review of Aegean Prehistory VII: Neopalatial, Final Palatial, and Postpalatial Crete," *AJA* 102, pp. 91–173.

Relph, E. 1985. "Geographical Experiences and Being-in-the-world: The Phenomenological Origins of Geography," in *Dwelling, Place and Environment: Towards a Phenomenology of Person and World*, D. Seamon and R. Mugerauer, eds., Dordrecht, pp. 15–31.

Renfrew, C. 1972. *The Emergence of Civilisation: The Cyclades and the Aegean in the Third Millennium* B.C., London.

———. 1996. "Who Were the Minoans? Towards a Population History of Crete," *Cretan Studies* 5, pp. 1–27.

Rethemiotakis, G. 1992–1993. "Το Μινωικό 'Κεντρικό κτίριο' στο Καστέλλι Πεδιάδας," *ArchDelt* 47–48 (A') [1997], pp. 29–64.

———. 1998. *Ανθρωπομορφική Πηλοπλαστική στην Κρήτη: Από τη Νεοανακτορική έως την Υπομινωική περίοδο* (*Βιβλιοθήκη της εν Αθήναις Αρχαιολογικής Εταιρείας* 174), Athens.

———. 1999. "The Hearths of the Minoan Palace at Galatas," in Betancourt et al., eds., 1999, pp. 721–728.

Rethemiotakis, G., and N. Dimopoulou. 2003. "The 'Sacred Mansion' Ring from Poros, Heraklion," *AM* 118, pp. 1–22.

Reynolds, J.M. 2002. "Teaching Architectural History in Japan: Building a Context for Contemporary Practice," *JSAH* 61, pp. 530–536.

Riegl, A. 1982. "The Modern Cult of Monuments: Its Character and Its Origin," trans. K. Foster and D. Ghirardo, *Oppositions* 25, pp. 21–51.

Romano, D.G. 2003. "Minoan Surveyors and Town Planning at Gournia," in *Metron: Measuring the Aegean Bronze Age. Proceedings of the 9th International Conference, New Haven, Yale University, 18–21 April 2002* (*Aegaeum* 24), K.P. Foster and R. Laffineur, eds., pp. 247–256.

Roth, L.M. 2007. *Understanding Architecture: Its Elements, History, and Meaning*, 2nd ed., Boulder, CO.

Rowe, P.G. 1982. "A Priori Knowledge and Heuristic Reasoning in Architectural Design," *Journal of Architectural Education* 36, pp. 18–23.

Ruskin, J. 1849. *The Seven Lamps of Architecture*, New York.

Saidel, B.A. 1993. "Round House or Square? Architectural Form and Socio-economic Organization in the PPNB," *JMA* 6, pp. 65–108.

Sakellarakis, Y., and E. Sapouna-Sakellaraki. 1991. *Archanes*, Athens.

———. 1997. *Αρχάνες: Μια νέα ματιά στη Μινωική Κρήτη*, vol. 1, Athens.

Schmid, M. 1983. "Les portes multiples au 'Mégaron' du Palais de Malia," *BCH* 107, pp. 705–716.

———. 1985. "Esquisse du tracé d'un ensemble architectural de l'époque minoenne: Mallia, le Quartier Mu," in *Le dessin d'architecture dans les sociétés antiques. Actes du Colloque de Strasbourg 26–28 janvier 1984* (*Travaux du centre de recherche sur le Proche-Orient et la Grèce antiques* 8), Leiden, pp. 63–73.

———. 2011. "Spatial Analysis of House Δα at Malia," in Glowacki and Vogeikoff-Brogan, eds., 2011, pp. 109–117.

Schoep, I. 2004. "Assessing the Role of Architecture in Conspicuous Consumption in the Middle Minoan I–II periods," *OJA* 23, pp. 243–269.

Scranton, R. 1949. "Group Design in Greek Architecture," *ArtB* 31, pp. 247–268.

Scully, V.J. 1962. *The Earth, the Temple, and the Gods: Greek Sacred Architecture*, New Haven.

Seamon, D. 1993. "Dwelling, Seeing, and Designing: An Introduction," in Seamon, ed., 1993, pp. 1–21.

———. 1994. "The Life of the Place: A Phenomenological Commentary on Bill Hillier's Theory of Space Sytax," *Nordisk Arkitekturforskning*, 7, pp. 35–49.

Seamon, D. ed. 1993. *Dwelling, Seeing, and Designing: Toward a Phenomenological Ecology*, Albany.

Shaw, J.W. 1973. "The Orientation of the Minoan Palaces," in *Antichità cretesi: Studi in onore di Doro Levi* I (*CronCatania* 12), Catania, pp. 47–59.

———. 1978. "Evidence for the Minoan Tripartite Shrine," *AJA* 82, pp. 429–448.

———. 1987. "A 'Palatial' Stoa at Kommos," in Hägg and Marinatos, eds., 1987, pp. 101–110.

———. 2009. *Minoan Architecture: Materials and Techniques* (*Studi di archeologia cretese* 7), Padua.

———. 2010. "Setting in the Palaces of Minoan Crete: A Review of How and When," in *Cretan Offerings. Studies in Honour of Peter Warren* (*BSA Studies* 18), O. Krzyszkowska, ed., London, pp. 303–314.

Shaw, J.W., and A. Lowe. 2002. "The 'Lost' Portico at Knossos: The Central Court Revisited," *AJA* 106, pp. 513–523.

Shaw, J.W., and M.C. Shaw, eds. 2006. *Kommos V. The Monumental Minoan Buildings at Kommos*, Princeton.

Shaw, M.C. 1990. "Late Minoan Hearths and Ovens at Kommos, Crete," in Darcque and Treuil, eds., 1990, pp. 231–254.

———. 1993. "The Aegean Garden," *AJA* 97, pp. 661–685.

Simmel, G. 1997. "Bridge and Door," in Leach, ed., 1997, pp. 66–69.

Sullivan, L.H. 1956. *The Autobiography of an Idea,* reprint, New York.

Tafuri, M. 1980. *Theories and History of Architecture,* New York.

———. 1986. "There Is No Criticism, Only History: Richard Ingersoll Interviews Manfredo Tafuri," *Design Book Review* 9, pp. 8–11.

Tanoulas, T. 1991. "Greek Concepts of Space as Reflected in Ancient Greek Architecture," in *Concepts of Space: Ancient and Modern*, K. Vatsyayan, ed., New Delhi, pp. 157–172.

Thaler, U. 2002. "Open Door Policies? A Spatial Analysis of Neopalatial Domestic Architecture with Special Reference to the Minoan 'Villa'," in *SOMA 2001: Symposium on Mediterranean Archaeology. Proceedings of the Fifth Annual Meeting of Postgraduate Researchers, the University of Liverpool, 23–25 February 2001* (*BAR-IS* 1040), Oxford, pp. 112–122.

Thiis-Evensen, T. 1987. *Archetypes in Architecture*, Oxford.

Tilley, C. 1994. *A Phenomenology of Landscape: Places, Paths, and Monuments*, Oxford.

Tiré, C., and H. van Effenterre. 1983. *Guide des fouilles françaises en Crète*, 2nd ed., Paris.

Touliatos, P. 2000. "Timber in Shipbuilding in Prehistoric and Ancient Greece: The Early Influence on the Timber Structures," in *Restoration of Old and Modern Wooden Buildings*, A. Soikkeli, ed., Oulu, pp. 27–36.

Travlos, I. 1993. *Πολεοδομική εξέλιξις των Αθηνών: Από των προϊστορικών χρόνων μέχρι των αρχών του 19ου αιώνος*, 2nd ed., Athens.

Trigger, B.G. 1989. *A History of Archaeological Thought*, Cambridge.

———. 1990. "Monumental Architecture: A Thermodynamic Explanation of Symbolic Behaviour," *WorldArch* 22, pp. 119–132.

Tsakanika-Theochari, E. 2006. *Ο δομικός ρόλος του ξύλου στην τοιχοποιία των ανακτορικού τύπου κτηρίων της Μινωικής Κρήτης*, Ph.D. diss., National Technical University of Athens.

———. 2009. "The Constructional Analysis of Timber Load Bearing Systems as a Tool for Interpreting Aegean Bronze Age Architecture," in *Bronze Age Architectural Traditions in the Eastern Mediterranean: Diffusion and Diversity, Proceedings of the Symposium, 07.–08. 05. 2008 in Munich*, Weilheim, pp. 127–139.

Tsipopoulou, M. 1992. "Ayia Photia," in Myers, Myers, and Cadogan, eds., 1992, pp. 66–69.

———. 2002. "Petras, Siteia: The Palace, the Town, the Hinterland and the Protopalatial Background," in Driessen, Schoep, and Laffineur, eds. 2002, pp. 133–144.

Tzachili, I. 1997. *Υφαντική και Υφάντρες στο Προϊστορικό Αιγαίο: 2000–1000 π.Χ.*, Herakleion.

———. 2005. "*Anthodokoi Talaroi*: The Baskets of the Crocus-Gatherers from Xesté 3, Aktotiri, Thera," in Morgan, ed., 2005, London, pp. 113–117.

———. 2011. *Μινωικά εικαστικά τοπία: Τα αγγεία με τις επίθετες πλαστικές μορφές από το Ιερό Κορυφής του Βρύσινα και η αναζήτηση του βάθους* (*Βρύσινας* 1), Athens.

Tzedakis, Y., and S. Chrysoulaki. 1987. "Neopalatial Architectural Elements in the Area of Chania," in Hägg and Marinatos, eds., 1987, pp. 111–115.

Unwin, S. 2009. *Analysing Architecture*, 3rd ed., London.

Uys, J. 1980. *The Gods Must be Crazy*, directed by Jamie Uys, Los Angeles.

Valavanis, P., ed. 2007. *Μεγάλες Στιγμές της ελληνικής αρχαιολογίας*, Athens.

Vallianou, D., and S. Parchapidis. 1999. "The Acropolis of Smari (Crete): An Approach to the Planning and Construction of the External Walls (Enclosure)," in Betancourt et al., eds., 1999, pp. 873–881.

van Effenterre, H. 1987. "The Function of Monumentality in the Minoan Palaces," in Hägg and Marinatos, eds., 1987, pp. 85–87.

van Effenterre, H., and M. van Effenterre. 1969. *Fouilles exécutées à Mallia. Le centre politique* I: *L'agora (1960–1966)* (ÉtCrét 17), Paris.

Vasilakis, A. 1992. "Tylissos," in Myers, Myers, and Cadogan, eds., 1992, pp. 272–275.

Vassiliou, Th. 2009. *Ancient Lands*, Athens.

Ventouri, R. 1977. *Complexity and Contradiction in Architecture*, 2nd ed., New York.

Viollet-le-Duc, E.E. 1854. *Dictionnaire raisonné de l'architecture française du XIe au XVIe siècle*, vol. 8, Paris.

———. 1996. "Restoration," in *Historical and Philosophical Issues in the Conservation of Cultural Heritage* (*Readings in Conservation*), N. Stanley-Price, M. Kirby Talley Jr., and A.M. Vaccaro, eds., Los Angeles, pp. 314–318.

von Falkenhausen, L. 2003. "Architecture and Archaeology: A View from China," in Papadopoulos and Leventhal, eds., 2003, pp. 247–266.

von Reber, F. 1898. "Ueber das Verhältniss des mykenischen zum dorischen Baustil," *AbhMünch* 21, pp. 478–530.

Warren, P.M. 1984a. "Circular Platforms at Minoan Knossos," *BSA* 79, pp. 307–323.

———. 1984b. "Knossos: New Excavations and Discoveries," *Archaeology* 37(3), pp. 48–55.

———. 1994. "The Minoan Roads of Knossos," in *Knossos: A Labyrinth of History. Papers Presented in Honour of Sinclair Hood*, D. Evely, H. Hughes-Brock, and N. Momigliano, eds., Oxford, pp. 189–210.

———. 2000. "Sir Arthur Evans and His Achievement," *BICS* 44, pp. 199–211.

———. 2003. "Cretan Food through Five Millenia," in *Briciaka. A Tribute to W.C. Brice* (*Cretan Studies* 9), Y. Duhoux, ed., Amsterdam, pp. 271–284.

———. 2007. "The Roofing of Early Minoan Round Tombs: The Evidence of Lebena Tomb II (Gerokampos) and of Cretan Mitata," in Betancourt, Nelson, and Williams, eds., 2007, pp. 9–16.

———. 2008. "The Natural Setting," in *From the Land of the Labyrinth: Minoan Crete, 3000–1100 B.C.*, M. Andreadaki-Vlazaki, G. Rethemiotakis, and N. Dimopoulou-Rethemiotaki, eds., New York, pp. 13–18.

———. 2010. "The Absolute Chronology of the Aegean circa 2000 B.C.–1400 B.C. A Summary," in *Die Bedeutung der minoischen und mykenischen Glyptik. VI. Internationales Siegel-Symposium aus Anlass des 50-jährigen Bestehens des CMS Marburg, 9.–12. Oktober 2008* (*CMS Beiheft* 8), W. Müller, ed., Mainz am Rhein, pp. 383–394.

Watson, D. 1997. "Architecture, Technology, and Environment," *Journal of Architectural Education* 51, pp. 119–126.

Wenger, R. 1997. "Visual Art: Archaeology and Gestalt," *Leonardo* 30, pp. 35–46.

Wilde, O. 1909. "The Decay of Lying," in *The Complete Writings of Oscar Wilde* 7, New York, pp. 3–57.

Wilson, D. 1994. "Knossos before the Palaces: An Overview of the Early Bronze Age (EM I–III)," in *Knossos: A Labyrinth of History. Papers Presented in Honour of Sinclair Hood*, D. Evely, H. Hughes-Brock, and N. Momigliano, eds., Oxford, pp. 23–44.

Xanthoudidis, S.A. 1922. "Μινωικὸν μέγαρον Νίρου," *ArchEph* 61, pp. 1–25.

Yiannouli, E. 1992. *Reason in Architecture: The Component of Space. A Study of Domestic and Palatial Building of Bronze Age Greece*, Ph.D. diss., Cambridge University.

———. 2009. "The Emergence and Development of a Round Building Tradition in the Aegean and Crete," *Mediterranean Archaeology and Archaeometry* 9, pp. 89–113.

Zareifis, N.G. 2007. *Η αρχιτεκτονική του ιερού του Ερμή και της Αφροδίτης στην Κάτω Σύμη Βιάννου*, Ph.D. diss., Aristotle University of Thessaloniki.

Zois, A.A. 1992. "Vasiliki," in Myers, Myers, and Cadogan, eds., 1992, pp. 276–281.

———. 1996. *Κνωσός: Το εκστατικό όραμα. Σημειωτική και ψυχολογία μιας αρχαιολογικής περιπέτειας*, Herakleion.

# Index

Italicized page numbers indicate figures.